U.S. Intervention and Regime Change in Nicaragua

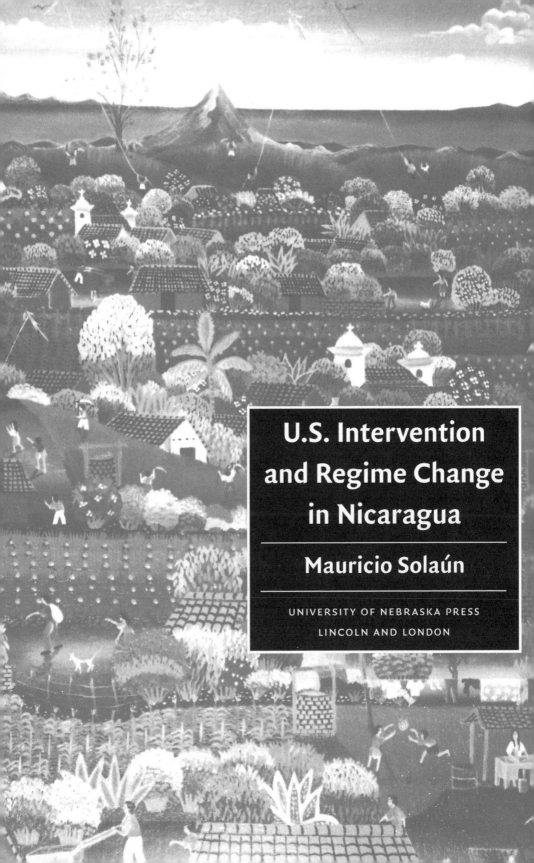

U.S. Intervention
and Regime Change
in Nicaragua

Mauricio Solaún

UNIVERSITY OF NEBRASKA PRESS
LINCOLN AND LONDON

Library of Congress
Cataloging-in-Publication
Data
Solaún, Mauricio.
U.S. intervention and regime change
in Nicaragua / Mauricio Solaún.
p. cm.
Includes bibliographical references and index.
ISBN 0-8032-4316-2 (cloth : alk. paper)
1. Nicaragua—Politics and government—1937–1979.
2. Nicaragua—History—Revolution, 1979.
3. United States—Foreign relations—Nicaragua.
4. Nicaragua—Foreign relations—United States.
5. Intervention (International law).   6. Solaún, Mauricio.
I. Title: United States intervention and
regime change in Nicaragua.   II. Title.
F1527.S55 2005   972.8525′2–dc22   2005041777

Set in Quadraat and Quadraat Sans by Kim Essman.
Designed by R. W. Boeche.
Printed by Thomson-Shore, Inc.

To the Americans who served with
me in Nicaragua: I learned from you.
To what could have been and was not.

Contents

Acknowledgments ix

Abbreviations xi

Prologue 1

1. Introduction 9

2. The Somoza García Legacy 33

3. The Golden Years 54

4. The Anastasio Somoza Debayle Period 79

5. Neutrality 92

6. Meditation 188

7. Partial Withdrawal 279

8. The Failure of U.S. Policy 285

Epilogue: Lessons 297

Notes 313

Bibliography 369

Index 381

Acknowledgments

I am indebted to many colleagues and friends who provided me with information and intellectual stimulation, and to the gracious support provided by members of the administrative staffs at the University of Illinois.

My views were clarified in exchanges with students and other audiences in the United States and abroad. My special recognition goes to Jennifer Rhodes, who accompanied me and helped me to research the post-1979 developments in Nicaragua during the summer of 1999.

The editorial work of Ed Henderson, Elizabeth Shaw Editorial and Publishing Services, proved indispensable in transforming my extensive detailed notes and materials into a compact, publishable text. And Teresa Finis converted my writing into a legible manuscript.

Finally, I am indebted to two reviewers of the manuscript whose constructive criticisms helped me to present in this book a better story of the Nicaraguan events.

Abbreviations

AMROCS	Association of Somocista Retired Servicemen, Workers and Peasants
ARA	Bureau of Inter-American Affairs
BAVINIC	Nicaraguan public housing bank
CEPAD	Council of Evangelical Churches of Nicaragua
CONDECA	Central American Defense Council
COSEP	Consejo Superior de la Empresa Privada
EEBI	Escuela de Entrenamiento Básico de Infantería
EE UU	United States
EFE	Agencia Efe S.A.
FAO	Frente Amplio Opositor (Broad Opposition Front)
FDN	Nicaraguan Democratic Force (Contras)
FDR	Front for the Defense of the Republic
FSLN	Frente Sandinista de Liberación Nacional
IAN	National Agrarian Institute
IDB	Inter-American Development Bank
IFI	international financial institution
IMF	International Monetary Fund
INDE	Instituto Nicaragüense de Desarrollo
INPRHU	Instituto de Promoción Humana
INVIERNO	Nicaraguan rural development program
MDN	Movimiento Democrático Nicaragüense
MILGROUP	Military Advisory Mission
MPU	Movimiento Pueblo Unido
NAFTA	North American Free Trade Agreement
NGO	nongovernment organization
OAS	Organization of American States
OPEC	Organization of Petroleum Exporting Countries
PLC	Partido Liberal Constitucionalista
PLI	Partido Liberal Independiente
PRC	Presidential Review Committee

SEDAC   Episcopal Secretariat of Central America and Panama
UDEL   Unión Democrática de Liberación
UNAN   Universidad Nacional Autónoma de Nicaragua, León
UNDP   United Nations Development Program
UNESCO   United Nations Educational, Scientific and
         Cultural Organization
UNO   National Opposition Union
UPI   United Press International
USAID   United States Agency for International Development
WMD   weapons of mass destruction
WOLA   Washington Office for Latin America

U.S. Intervention and Regime Change in Nicaragua

Prologue

In the spring of 1977 I was recruited from my academic post as a specialist in the political sociology of Latin America to become the U.S. ambassador to the Somoza regime. Washington had opted to implement a pro– human rights policy in the region that targeted several dictatorships. Anastasio Somoza Debayle was singled out in this humanitarian crusade because of the notoriety of his family's dynasty. Since 1974, under his leadership in his second term as president, the regime had experienced repressive retrogression and increased corruption. With the consolidation of his absolute rule, Somoza's personal life had decayed as well, which culminated in July 1977 in his serious illness and temporary absence from Nicaragua. Nevertheless, he had succeeded in keeping control of the military and civilian organs of the state in a society with minimal political participation outside government circles, ruled as it was under a strict state of siege. When I arrived in Nicaragua in September 1977, the strongman intended to remain president until the end of his current term (in 1981) and to retain the virtual political sovereignty by keeping control of the army. In the meantime the dynasty was supposed to continue through the meteoric military career of the dictator's son, Anastasio Somoza Portocarrero.

The plan seemed to be working—under some conditions repression can maintain regimes. The customary unarmed and armed opposition activity had been deflated into fragmented, very small groups; at the time of my arrival a truly national opposition movement did not exist. But neither did the regime count solid supporters among the broader society. There was also great expectation about the role that the United States was to play, with its new policy of distancing itself from the Nicaraguan government and encouraging opposition to it. Crucial social sectors were available to pursue a changed Nicaragua. Dynastic rule was increasingly anachronistic in the nation.

In this context convalescent Somoza decided to govern with a new face. Despite his premonitions that if he liberalized the regime he would be challenged by escalated, even tumultuous opposition, just before my presentation of credentials he ended state-of-siege rule and opened the door for the developing of opposition activities under the constitutional guarantees provided by his pseudo-democratic regime. The general had chosen to collaborate partially with the U.S. human rights policy, notwithstanding his misgivings about the administration's intentions. For instance, although he was unhappy with the interaction, he allowed me to establish very broad contacts with his adversaries. Somoza was self-possessed with a messianic sense of almost invincible personal power and irreplaceability.

The oppositions' reactions to a perceived weakened dictator were immediate. Both the unarmed and armed groups began to activate themselves. The now-allowed publicity campaigns took rancorous forms. Opponents held abhorrent philosophies and practiced very objectionable behavior, as if they were "heretics," real "criminals." The government participated as well in these manifestations of acute partisanship. As early as October 1977, Sandinista armed revolutionaries attempted to take over a few towns in conjunction with their call for a popular insurrection. Unarmed groups engaged in mass media campaigns and rallies to obtain and mobilize partisans. The opposition was still weak, however. Few people attended the rallies, the armed actions did not result in popular participation, and the uprising immediately collapsed. Any mass movement was still to be organized.

Significantly, from the outset the conflicts were centered on the regime or form of government itself. Led by the archbishop and some business leaders in response to the violence, a civic movement was initiated to negotiate the peaceable dismantling of the dynasty. In contrast to Somoza's plan, the "dialogue" movement sought an agreement between the parties for a democratic transition before the end of the president's current term in 1981. The parameters that ended in revolution had been established at the outset of my mission. Two steadfast strategies materialized: Somoza and his group would not leave power one day before the end of the term, whereas the various oppositions believed the term should be shortened.

In January 1978 Pedro Joaquín Chamorro, the principal leader of the opposition, was murdered—according to the government, a murder arranged by foreigners in business with the ruler. This martyrdom triggered an entirely new political situation. Abruptly the population that was previously resistant to calls to rebel went to the streets in protest. The political and civil elite got involved in the snowballing opposition. Almost immediately the movement for dialogue was replaced by demands that the president resign and by refusal to talk and negotiate with Somoza: he simply had to abdicate. Major business associations called a general, indefinite business stoppage until the president stepped down. The Roman Catholic hierarchy suggested the ruler's resignation to overcome the state of revulsion with the regime. Popular armed Sandinista rebellions were improvised. In short, a growing, relatively spontaneous and broad mutiny developed, combined with the formation of a national opposition movement, the Frente Amplio Opositor. With the FAO, a loose coalition of unarmed oppositionists and clandestine armed revolutionaries crystallized, although tensions remained in this marriage of convenience.

Most important were the strongman's reactions to these developments. Somoza had vast direct experience in quelling anti-regime disturbances. Because of chronic problems of legitimacy, the dynasty had a history of periodic re-equilibration through the use of rapid, repressive force. Yet on this occasion, despite the unprecedented levels of opposition facing the strongman, he decided to minimize the use of the National Guard against his adversaries, in order to maintain his partial collaboration with Washington's human rights policy. Although quite isolated, Somoza retained his grip on the state's military and civilian apparatus. The opposition still did not possess the resources to force his exit. For example, the penetration of Somocistas' interests in the economy made the stoppages only partially successful. The army's potential firepower still predominated. The general and his cadres were confident that they could remain on top. If chaotic destruction took place, others would be responsible for it.

Of course, the impasse was sustained by the undemocratic mindset of the ruler and his followers: they considered themselves to have an exclusive gift to govern the country. In the midst of the crisis, in late February 1978, Somoza's maximum "concession" was made: he would retire to private life in 1981. But the promise was unsatisfactory. The entire history of the dynasty had consisted of obtaining opposition acquiescence in exchange for a future democratic promise, always later reversed by pseudo-democratic manipulations supported by the Somocistas. (Somoza was aware that no one would believe his democratization promise.) Somoza and his family had always refused to build a nationally or internationally supervised impartial electoral system. He had very recently shown his colors, regressing to more extreme absolutism. Still, he maintained a strategic loyal following. Beyond careerism and the fear of reprisals if they defected, and an unawareness of the seriousness of the crisis, Somocista civilians had been socialized into subordination. There was a historically sustained conviction of powerlessness and inefficacy among them: the ruler would pay no attention; no dissidence would succeed. In many instances of ungovernability the military executes a coup d'état. In Nicaragua, however, long-term structural policies had resulted in the centralized control of the family in the army, deliberately assuring the unavailability of alternative potential leadership roles and command structures to rapidly replace the family. Ironically, this contributed to the total collapse of the National Guard when the general had to resign. Nicaragua's government exhibited both inflexibility

and resilient strength: it had lasted decades, and a major internationally supported revolution was needed to terminate it, because the army's continued
loyalty to the government kept it in control of the state, and the alternative of
negotiating a relatively peaceful regime transition was foreclosed.

In spite of the opposition's progress with the formation of the FAO umbrella
entity, serious organizational problems remained. It lacked a clear leadership
structure and was internally divided. Within the FAO some groups upheld
traditional authoritarian beliefs unsupportive of constitutional representative
rule—Nicaragua had never deviated from its history of a patrimonial state
without parliamentary institutions. There were also groups influenced by
Leninist authoritarian ideology. The FAO contained vocal, highly radicalized
members who demanded Somoza's total surrender, including the confiscation of his property and that of his friends and the entire reconstitution of
the state with a new army. The internal competitiveness for leadership in
the FAO radicalized it to prove one's anti-Somocismo. This resulted not only
from unprincipled personal ambition but mainly from a widespread fear of
Somoza's political and military resourceful, undemocratic machine and a fear
that a compromise with him, as in the past, would result in deflating the
suddenly growing opposition movement. Somoza kept saying that 1981 was a
reasonable target, that the opposition needed time to organize itself as a viable
democratic alternative capable of running the country. Indeed, the probability
of a successful democratic transition at this time was lowered not only by the
noted more or less endemic, predisposing factors but also by other situational
factors. Unfortunately, in his successful quest for total pseudo-democratic
power, Somoza himself had destroyed the viability of the most recent opposition electoral, democratic movement. Situational factors can change in
mixed authoritarian/democratic cultures. This was not a good conjuncture for
a democratic transition. It called especially for statesmanship and political
skills that the strongman lacked. Personality factors of powerful leaders play
a role in democratic transitions. Pseudo-democratic rulers voluntarily can and
have changed the nature of their regimes.

In the crisis the United States played a crucial role, raising expectations
with its human rights policy: its suspension of some economic and military
assistance programs and demands for regime liberalization had signaled a
new lack of support for the regime. Yet misunderstanding prevailed in the
Carter administration about the nature of international clientelism, the participation of foreign governments in the determination of a foreign government.
In search of a friendly international environment, client-state relations tend to
be established with countries with unstable, insufficiently supported regimes
on the local level. In maintaining "normal," friendly ties the principal power

allocates resources to the client government, resources that are seen by the regime's opponents as helping ("supporting") it, which is precisely what they wish to end in order to change the regime. Especially in polarized situations of regime crisis, pressures make it difficult for the United States to play a "neutral" role. Foreign intervention—the application of resources for regime maintenance or its termination—can be sought by insufficiently supported regimes and oppositions, seeking clientelistic alliances with the United States and other nations. This was precisely what happened during the entire Nicaraguan process: Somoza continuously demanded that the United States support his tenure, while the opposition demanded that we give him an ultimatum to remove him from power. President Carter did not come to terms with the reality that his policy had helped destabilize the Nicaraguan power structure. Because of his peculiar doctrine of "non-intervention," he refused to use U.S. power to break the impasse, at the cost of violent revolution and a major foreign policy defeat. American governments are held accountable by the U.S. citizenry for the transformation of friendly governments into hostile ones. The hymn of Nicaragua's new revolutionary government yelled, "Yankees, enemy of humanity." In the past, Americans have not opposed foreign interventions as an absolute principle. Nor were they supportive of costly stalemated foreign wars, nor of a "Policeman of the World" role with multiple, simultaneous costly interventions. Successful presidents had to find some balance in this dilemma.

Deficient domestic support and dependence on foreign backing to retain its government's tenure make client-states appear to be politically weak: a break with the United States, a word from the American ambassador, and the government will collapse, as the saying went in Nicaragua. Conversely, client-state mentalities can induce governments to depend excessively on U.S. patronage. This set of beliefs complicated the Nicaraguan situation. Based on its policy of non-intervention, the Carter administration initially adopted the pretense of neutrality. It formally claimed that it did not support Somoza but would not back the opposition changing the government; it was up to the Nicaraguans (who were killing themselves in the conflict) to resolve the deadlock, "a made in Nicaragua formula." But Nicaraguans expected and clientelistically acted to change the U.S. neutrality into an intervention. Somoza was hopeful that he could neutralize his enemies in the administration. For one, under pressure from a few members of the U.S. Congress, the administration reversed its policy and released loans that it had previously suspended on human rights grounds. This "supportive" retreat during the crisis reinforced the dictator's obduracy. Somoza felt that he could ultimately blackmail the United States. He reasoned that if the revolutionary forces grew, the United States would have to back him to avoid a Sandinista-led, Castroist revolution. The non-Marxists who prevailed in the FAO pursued a different blackmail: they would not compromise but instead joined forces with the revolutionaries, hoping that to avoid a Castroist, anti-American victory the United States would get rid of Somoza and give power to them.

Its professed claims notwithstanding, the U.S. human rights policy was confusingly ambiguous: the country would not intervene, but it had been interfering in Nicaragua's dynamics to determine its government. In late August and early September 1978 the bloodbath that all informed observers expected took place. The threat posed by chaos in the country, and the threat of the violence spreading into even greater convulsions in two of Nicaragua's northern neighbors, to an administration seeking reelection—indeed, clientelism has roots in the American political system—resulted in a change in U.S. policy. Reluctantly, Washington adopted the policy of mediating the Nicaraguan crisis. It chose the Organization of American States as its instrument. This slow-moving entity had had a history of ineffectiveness and substantial opposition to change Latin American governments. It was as late as October 6, 1978, that the OAS mediators arrived in Managua, and their mandate was for "friendly cooperation." The OAS could break the deadlock only if Somoza and the FAO agreed to accept its "good offices." The mediators sought, in fact, to obtain the strongman's resignation, organize the FAO into proposing a viable transitional coalition government of national reconciliation, and start negotiations between the parties. But the mediators faced insurmountable obstacles. First, Somoza refused to resign and form any government without his own participation in it, and Washington refused to employ the pressure necessary to change his mind. Second, the FAO refused to negotiate anything but the general's complete abdication and demanded that the mediation constitute a new government controlled by them. If the positions of the parties were not met, there would be war. It was not that moderate compromise plans were not proposed independently of the government and the FAO, but such plans did not carry sufficient political support, and the mediators did not have the authority and power to arbitrate a solution. Actually, to keep the FAO in the mediation, in the absence of Somoza's acceptance of not participating in a new government, the mediators felt forced to propose less than Solomonic formulas. But Somoza carried the maximum historical responsibility for the mediation's failure at the end of the year. Although the opposition's behavior provided attenuating conditions, more capable and reasonable political leaders shortened their tenure. Somoza had the option of adopting a preemptive strategy in conjunction with his recent illness. He always claimed that the majority backed him, but he also rejected the idea of an internationally supervised plebiscite on his tenure on grounds that he would lose it.

The mediation's failure had dramatic consequences. It proved to public opinion that the Somoza group would never peaceably leave power. The dictator listened to no one; not even the mighty United States had persuaded him to change course. Consequently, the Sandinistas' historically violent thesis became vindicated. The preference for a nonviolent solution collapsed, and by January 1979 the Sandinistas had displaced the FAO as the leaders of a reconstituted national movement to topple the government. Recent events had shown cumulative cycles of increased rebellion. In contrast to the rapid deflation of uprisings that characterized the regime's history, now each revolutionary wave had been bigger; the small National Guard did not control an already mobilized society at large; the revolutionaries counted on bases in Costa Rica, assisted also by Venezuela, Panama, and Cuba; and they had rehearsed and learned a repertoire of revolutionary techniques to be implemented in a coordinated push, by a critical mass at this final point of no return. Two conditions of some successful violent revolutions had been met: large numbers were dissatisfied with the regime and had hopes of succeeding in changing it; and the discontented felt that the extant impasse was the worst possible alternative, that the regime had to be changed regardless of costs and the sooner the better.

In interpreting why a revolution took place, I have been assisted by contemporary analytical frameworks that focus on the role of the state and its international relations that are conducive to successful regime overthrow.[1] I also focused on the material bases of the revolt: the chronic poverty and the socioeconomic changes that increasingly made the extant archaic form of government illegitimate. But in explaining successful revolutions it is necessary to translate economic changes into actual political changes. Prominent Marxists have argued that some political phenomena can exhibit an important autonomy of their own from socioeconomic matrices, that to explain revolution we cannot simply rest on the latter.[2] Successful revolutions consist of a culmination of political action, of the activation of resources by groups seeking to overthrow the government to construct a new form of government. They entail a fight between groups aspiring to staff and control the state. Naturally, the outcome will depend not only on the actions of the regime-changing oppositions but on the support and other resources, and the strategies as well, of the government. Fortunately, paradigms exist that help us to analyze the mobilization of resources into action by a regime and its allies, on the one hand, and by their opponents, on the other hand, exercising power in interaction with each other.[3] These political mobilization and control models are not incompatible with socioeconomic analyses; in fact, the political effects of economic processes can be effectively analyzed placing them within the concepts of such models.[4] In writing my Nicaraguan story I also was assisted by social-psychological explanations of revolution. Noteworthy are recently formalized, so-called rational choice approaches: the exploration of the changing incentives (perceived benefits) and disincentives (perceived costs) of the goal-directed behavior of participants.[5] The sentiments and expectations involved in cost-benefit behavioral equations are linked to various forms of alienation.[6] Contrary to Somocista propaganda, the uprisings served to further tarnish the government, not the rebels, with a general image of bestiality. A characteristic of the Nicaraguan process was its cyclical developments. Technically, all the uprisings were militarily failures. However, the subsequent uprisings proved to be much more potent and broad in scope. In this respect, they were not "defeats" but tactical "withdrawals," for the activists went into temporary military inactivity, while an increasing number of individuals had learned through observation more and more about the art of revolution and were willing to participate in the next bout as the alienation from the government intensified and spread. Throughout the entire process the expression of quasi-religious sentiments and visions was manifest.[7] Especially in cases such as Nicaragua, when a sudden, fairly spontaneous rebellion takes the form of a massive breakaway from customary social routines, our understanding is enhanced by paradigms of the sociology of collective behavior. They focus on the emergence of new symbols, collective moods and expectations, new collective definitions with new instructions and rules that preside over the rapid development of social movements to oust the government.[8]

This case study has a comparative focus. The historical analysis interprets the outcomes as conditioned by the past but not inexorably determined by it. Leaders have some degrees of freedom, which is why we can speculate about what could have happened if different options had been chosen. The principal sources for this book are my conversations with participants and the written materials that came to my attention. I did not tape any conversations. Each day I wrote a detailed journal on these sources. This book is an abridged version of that journal. It reflects my ideological preferences: the promotion of as peaceful as possible a democratization of Nicaragua. Although in some cases revolutions are justified, as in Nicaragua after the failure of our mission, given the described political realities, it was expected that a revolution would produce enormous human costs and material destruction—what a poor country does not need—coupled with a very improbable transition to democracy in the foreseeable future. This is why I did not favor a revolution, a position held virtually until my departure by many later prominent officials of the Sandinista revolutionary regime who had collaborated with the U.S. embassy. Nor did I favor General Somoza's anachronistic *continuismo* that closed the possibility of a more civilized solution than massive violence.

1. Introduction

This book is a detailed inside story of the role played by U.S. policy in impeding the institutionalization of democracy in Nicaragua and of its 1979 revolution. In the late 1970s, under the human rights banner, the United States launched a humanitarian, politically destabilizing crusade against a friendly dictator, a man who wished to remain a faithful American client but who refused to relinquish his personal political sovereignty. His rule was destabilized by the U.S. government and overthrown by a broad national and international coalition with which Washington was not fully comfortable. Washington's well-meaning, reformist policy sought democratization through moral suasion, minor economic sanctions, and peaceful instruments, yet there was violent revolution, and as the revolutionary regime groped to institutionalize a new form of authoritarian government and carve a new international role for itself, Nicaragua formed political alliances with self-professed adversaries of the United States. With their assistance Nicaragua militarized itself and even intervened in the affairs of some of its neighbors by backing revolutionary uprisings. The result was a dramatic escalation of violence in the region. The United States became involved yet again, attempting to overthrow the new government. This required a second war, this time in support of counter-revolution against the Sandinistas. To this day Washington remains involved in trying to influence who rules Nicaragua.

The real issue lies in the philosophical difference between the naked self-interest advocacy of "pragmatism" and moralistic "humanitarian intervention-ist crusades."[1] Realpolitik justifies policy by saying that although democracy is the best form of government for Americans, the objective of foreign policy is to further the national interest. It is not up to the United States to promote a form of government—to preach democracy or try to impose it on a foreign people. In contrast, democratic crusades make the promotion of such a regime a policy goal on ethical grounds, though the pursuit of other interests need not be repugnant to the pro-democratic rationalization.[2] Because in the twentieth century the principal adversaries of the United States were not democratic powers, it was not that difficult for the U.S. government to explain crude strategic interests, say the balance of power in realpolitik interests, as being pro-democratic ones—that is, to check the advance of authoritarianism.

There is a third rationalization: isolationism, the notion of a Fortress America that should not be involved in foreign adventures, that the United States does not have fundamental interests in given foreign regions, and so it should not or need not interfere or intervene in their domestic political affairs. This interpretation, however, has been less predominant in American governing circles involved in Latin American affairs.

Central to the ongoing debate is the issue of "international clientelism," the participation by a government (or combination of them) in determining a foreign government. Should the United States intervene or not (unilaterally or joined with others), supporting or opposing with various means foreign governments? Should the principle of non-intervention, of the absolute sovereignty of states to determine their own governments, be a sacred prohibition?

The facts are that foreign client patterns continue and that, as I document, U.S. policy toward Latin America has historically oscillated between realpolitik and democratic crusade rationalizations.[3] Why? The United States, a powerful democracy, operates in an international environment constituted by sovereign states; its citizens, whose interests must be ultimately reflected in policy, favor friendly, peaceful relations with other nations; and its government is compelled to have relations and exercise influence in the international community. But in the absence of a world government to adjudicate conflicts of interest, states project force in their relations. Furthermore, in the absence of consensus within nations to sustain democratic governments under the rule of law, more or less violent fights to determine their form of government tend to take place. In such settings there is no workable domestic, internal agreement on a form of government, but rather a tendency to participate in revolutionary processes, in government overthrows, and the repression of oppositions.

Regardless of the principal motive(s) for exercising international influence, whether it be, say, economic gain or in self-defense against others who could curtail U.S. sovereignty (i.e., its "liberty" or "welfare"), the United States seeks friendly, cooperative relations with other governments.[4] Such "normal" ties involve allocating public and private resources. These transfers can take multiple forms (e.g., economic or military links; income to the foreign government accruing from trade, investments, or assistance; symbolic manifestations of friendship, of "liking" the foreign government, etc.).

These conditions lead us into the intractable aspects of international clientelism and to the notion of the client-state. The United States decides to have friendly ties with a dictatorship of a less powerful state. That state does not have a consensual regime—its opponents classify it as abhorrent and wish to terminate it; in the absence of institutionalized elections, some force is thought necessary to change the government. Inherent in this situation is the interpretation that the powerful nation is supporting its friendly dictatorship, for the regime is not based on broad domestic support but rather on (various degrees of) repression or force. Intrinsic to these friendly cooperative ties are relations of dependency in which the United States engages in the business of supporting foreign governments, determining them, or carrying out foreign "intervention," because in fact it is providing resources to them. The historical zigzags between realpolitik and democratic crusades were fundamental to the problems that haunted us in Nicaragua.

A client-state, then, consists of a formal or informal alliance between technically independent states with different resources and power, in which the more important nation provides some services, giving resources to the foreign government and thus "supporting" it. In exchange, the client provides its patron with a political following and counter services. It is a mechanism to achieve political influence—support for objectives of the principal and for aspirations of client governments—in an international environment constituted by formally sovereign states. The client status is a variable, with some friendly governments not deserving the classification. Some nations are politically more dependent than others. At one extreme we can envision puppet governments, a simple mouthpiece; at the other extreme, truly interdependent allies. Client-states are placed somewhere in between, for their governments are supported by a foreign power that participates in the clientelistic game of determining a foreign government. Most significantly, this political dependency is related to the nature of the client's regime: it is not stable because of shortcomings in support by its own people. A tendency of client-state politics is for its citizens, for local factions, to look for international alliances, garnering political support from other nations in their pursuit of their own partisan interest to form a government. These processes tend to be exacerbated as domestic polarization increases in the absence of regime consensus. Clientelistic determination of foreign governments partly results, therefore, from the projection of power or influence by friendly governments in an unstable regime environment; it can also involve insufficiently supported democratic regimes and oppositions, which can seek clientelistic alliances. Clientelism tends to involve the United States in nasty processes of human rights violations.

Why the historical alternations between realpolitik and pro-democratic policies? U.S. support of a dictatorship need not result in its institutionalization. Client dictatorships—against Washington's wishes—can be destabilized even by rebellions of their nation's own democratic forces. Such crises place in relief the abhorrent nature of the authoritarian regime and the deficient character of its ruler. How can a self-respecting democracy continue to abet the dictator's gruesome repressive patterns? Within the United States, movements develop to withdraw support from the friendly autocracy and cause its demise. Why not support and contribute to local democratic forces?

But neither does U.S. support guarantee democratic institutionalization, though in some countries with mixed democratic-authoritarian cultures a pro-democratic American policy can make the difference. The more full-blown the U.S. intervention, the more costly it is. Obviously the United States does not possess the resources to impose democracies around the entire world; the need to have friendly international ties to preserve national interests always results in cooperating "realistically" with some authoritarian regimes, thus reducing the coherence of pro-democratic policies. In the absence of local democratic consensus, regime survival may require a degree and frequency of more or less costly foreign interventions that make a mockery of idealistic, do-gooder interference—democracy implies self-government. In the past the United States abandoned pro-democratic policies toward Latin America in the face of regional opposition against American "intervention" in the region. You can observe empirical factors that render both realpolitik and pro-democracy prescriptions untenable as a universal principle of foreign policy.

On the other hand, client-state dependency on a foreign power, combined with its common problems of legitimacy, contributes to the notion that the client government is very weak. Of course, the problem is compounded if the principal power has disproportionate resources, as in relations between the United States and the small countries near it. Such dictators tend to be fallaciously dismissed: a word from the American ambassador, and the strongman would resign and a new regime be created, as the saying went in Nicaragua. The history of U.S. interventions in Latin America has contributed to the thesis, even among some mainstream social scientists, that American foreign policy caused the region's absence of democratic institutionalization.[5] Nicaragua provides an uncomfortable example of lasting authoritarianism coupled with long-term U.S. clientelistic policies.

But there were domestic reasons to presume the inherent weakness of the Nicaraguan regime. Prior to the Somoza family, dynastic rule had no precedent in the country. Actually, although a few Latin American regimes seemed to have had a dynastic intent, the phenomenon was an anomaly.[6] The Nicaraguan regime's longevity was also exceptional. In the 1960s the most lasting regional regimes, other than Nicaragua's, were characterized by frequent changes in their rulers through elections, not by the continuation for decades of real power in the hands of a strongman or a ruling family. In fact, the then relatively frequent coups d'état were often triggered in response to the ruler's attempts to continue in power indefinitely.[7] In Nicaragua these manipulations were successful: they had always resulted in the continuity of the Somoza rule while maintaining the loyalty of the army. This paradox, mechanisms that precipitated regime breakdown in many countries versus the same mechanisms functioning to maintain the regime, deserves to be studied. The regime's endurance, with its recurrent cycles of unsuccessful uprisings followed by regime re-equilibration, is also of note.

In order to understand why, against U.S. government objectives, a large-scale popular revolution took place, this book explores how the regime remained in power in earlier periods, to establish comparative grounds to explain its rapid, subsequent collapse. This requires determining the regime's nature, its organization of power, its sources of support and opposition, and its modes of dealing with stress and recurrent crises.

Our attempts in Nicaragua to obtain a relatively peaceful democratic transition were stopped by the ruler's refusal to cooperate with our project and his retention of the loyalty of his civilian and military cadres, who reinforced the dictator's hubristic obduracy. We faced a dramatic paradox: the ruler and his group keeping control of the state's apparatus, amid their loss of control of the society at large that was in rebellion against them. In contradiction to the noted "theories" about Nicaragua's regime weakness, Somoza proved very difficult to unseat.

This issue of the retention of loyalty within the state's organs is significant: it shows limits to pro-democratic crusades. Widespread popular protests can be unsuccessful in changing an authoritarian regime unless foreign countries provide the military resources needed to defeat the regime's repression and overthrow it; such assistance was provided in Nicaragua by a coalition of Latin American nations, as opposed to the United States. In effect, so-called peaceful revolutions precipitated by unarmed citizen protests succeed if the dictator decides to abdicate, if the dictator is persuaded to step down and the regime is changed by actions involving the ruling cadres, or if the intransigent ruler is forced out by the state's cadres (often by a coup d'état).[8] Thus democratic crusades risk failure vis-à-vis a regime that maintains the loyalty of its own group, even if they consist of small organized numbers. In fact, U.S. pro-democratic policies even in Central America and the Caribbean have met several failures in changing targeted dictators unless Washington used its troops. Democratic crusades can prove costly. To succeed, one may have to be prepared to "intervene," which the Carter administration that I served was unwilling to do.

In sum, our failed campaign faced insufficient support for democracy. Not being authentic democrats, the Somocistas in power felt no moral compulsion to submit to the popular will. But authoritarian forces were strong within the opposition, and the moderate opposition was still poorly organized, reinforcing the Somoza group's self-perception as the best government. Miscalculations and excessive dependence on U.S. policy also blurred the stark alternatives. Foreign crusades can operate with naive assumptions about democratic readiness at particular times.

Finally, the unified inability of Nicaragua's ruling, decayed regime to meet the internal and external challenges that eventually destroyed it is interpreted focusing on its irreplaceable, although nontotalitarian and not truly charismatic, leader, who exercised unconditional control over his team and organizations. History accepts the essential role played by some special men.[9] General Anastasio Somoza Debayle's personality, political beliefs, and mentality—which included a traditionally based disbelief in Nicaragua's democratic viability and a belief in his own messianic invincibility and irreplaceability—blocked an opportune transition. We failed to persuade him to step down; nor were we able to break the absolute dependency of his cadres on him. Their seemingly irrational loyalty had grounds other than individual materialistic bases (e.g., careerism) and errors in judgment. There were deliberately created organizational or structural bases for dependency on the ruler, including formal and informal rules and roles worked out over the years among the followers and in the state's hierarchical organizations.[10]

The story of my experiences as U.S. ambassador to Nicaragua, from July 1977 to February 1979, seeks to clarify these issues of foreign policy, and the theories of revolution and democratic transition.

The Role of the United States

The vast topic of the role of the United States in Latin America is highly complex in its historical changes, the variety of international relations involved, and the multiplicity of government and private actors whose actions, not always coordinated, produced important results. Proper historical analysis would be an awesome task. Our scope is much narrower. Central America and the Caribbean, an area defined by many Americans as their country's backyard, has been a natural area of U.S. influence: it has experienced the most potent U.S. interventionism, including the overt use of American troops to determine governments.[11]

Early in its history the United States decided to check the exercise of European colonial power in the Americas—or the Western Hemisphere, as the region became known. To this effect, in 1823 President James Monroe proclaimed the doctrine that still bears his name. The United States at this time was an infant, weak country, threatened by European actions. The War of 1812, in which the British burned Washington DC, took place when Monroe was the secretary of state.

The young nation, however, grew in power and size—the latter partly at the expense of former Spanish colonies—and was soon a world power exercising its influence in Latin America. Indeed, soon after Monroe, in the 1840s, the doctrine of Manifest Destiny was developed, successfully claiming a quasi-religious right for the United States to territorially expand at the cost of weaker neighbors. It was finally President Woodrow Wilson (1913–21) who formally promised that the United States would "never again seek one additional foot of territory by conquest" from the Latin American countries.

Once the United States decided to project its power in Latin America, it was faced with two facts. First was the weakness of democratic rule. Political democracies even now still have not been firmly institutionalized in parts of Latin America. In the past no democratic regime had lasted half a century. Second, most of the region was characterized by political instability, with revolutions and coups. A lack of consensus on the form of government described local conflicts in which the local people struggled between authoritarianism and democracy and not uncommonly sought foreign alliances.

There is an additional significant fact: U.S. governments have been subjects to a resilient, long-term interpretation that what happens in Central America and the Caribbean, to narrow our focus, is ultimately of national interest. Further, U.S. administrations seek reelection and are themselves accountable for adverse international happenings, such as the emergence of hostile governments. At times in the early years of the Carter administration, for example, the position was adopted that these small countries were really not that important. This changed in the face of violent events and the internationalization of regional conflicts.[12] Another characteristic of local politics was the propensity in several countries to seek alliances with rival powers of the United States.

The historical dialectic of exercising influence in weaker nations with disorderly and perishable political institutions, in an environment with threatened and real international armed interventions, resulted in the noted rationalizations of U.S. foreign policy—democratic crusades and realpolitik—originally exemplified by the Monroe Doctrine and Manifest Destiny, respectively.

Consider the democratic cast in which the Monroe Doctrine was placed. The Monroe Doctrine, adolescents still are told in the United States, "practically guaranteed all the independent nations of the Western Hemisphere protection against European interference 'for the purpose of oppressing them, or controlling in any other manner their destiny.'" The Monroe Doctrine was construed as a promoter of self-determination and self-rule.

The years 1901–9 saw the beginning of the "big stick" policy, so-called gunboat and dollar diplomacy, with the frequent deployment of U.S. troops in Central America and the Caribbean.[13] Theodore Roosevelt, who had fought in Cuba's war of independence from Spain, posited his corollary to the Monroe Doctrine. Roosevelt "pointed out that weakness or brutal wrongdoing on the part of any of the smaller American nations might tempt European countries to intervene. It seemed to Roosevelt that European nations might well feel justified in trying to protect the lives and property of their citizens or to collect debts justly owed to them. Roosevelt asserted that the Monroe Doctrine required the United States to prevent such justified intervention by doing the intervening itself."[14]

Indeed, American governments felt that the problem of order—not only the weakness but the "brutal wrongdoing" of Latin American governments—affected U.S. interests. And what was the source of this alleged "indecency" of the southern neighbors? The absence of democracy! If these Latins would only learn the art of determining governments through election, as opposed to violence, and bind their polity to the rule of law, the problem would be solved. In a sense, it was only natural. Democracy is the method of government best known to American officials, one that has benefited and worked well for their nation. Governability would be the logical result of democracy if only it were adequately supported by the local people.

Beyond these problems of obtaining a stable environment for trade and investment, we must keep in mind the particular importance of rallying public support for foreign policy in the United States because of the highly decentralized nature of its regime and party system. To conduct policy, the executive needs congressional support; even if both branches of Congress are controlled by the same party, this does not guarantee support for policy. So there is a need to use simple, popular symbols such as a pro-democratic banner. More deeply, the puritanical sub-ethos in American culture identifies "democracy" with what is good in the "nation" and finds expression in a national propensity to moralize, to preach.

The period from 1907 through the beginning of Franklin Delano Roosevelt's administration in 1933 (with its new policy) was the time of maximum physical U.S. intervention in Central America and the Caribbean. These pre-1933 interventions found a legal basis in the international, pro-democratic Tobar Doctrine, named after Carlos R. Tobar.[15] In 1907 all the Central American countries signed international treaties incorporating the Tobar Doctrine of nonrecognition of governments that were the product of force. De facto authoritarian governments were condemned by treaty. Yet they materialized, and the United States considered it had the right to intervene to determine governments where democratic order had not been institutionalized.

In short, interventionist U.S. Latin American policies since the early twentieth century often took the form of—and were rationalized as—pro-democratic crusades. Latin Americans did not like this paternalistic interventionism, even though it had been justified because of the lack of democratic compliance by local groups.

When FDR changed policy, adopting (in principle) Genaro Estrada's doctrine of non-intervention and recognition of governments in control of their territory regardless of their origin and nature, the new U.S. policy was welcomed throughout Latin America.[16] However, American non-intervention was conditional: it did not mean an absolute prohibition, especially when governments seemed oriented to form clientelistic alliances with a foreign adversary. But very substantial American involvement in such processes became increasingly rare (e.g., as in Guatemala in 1954 and in Cuba seven years later). In the Dominican Republic in 1965, U.S. troops were again deployed to bring about a favorable government after a local uprising.

Latin America's welcome of FDR's Good Neighbor policy is easy to understand. U.S. territorial aggrandizement, the use of troops and prolonged occupation of some countries, and its self-designation of a forceful tutelage, especially in Central America and the Caribbean during the first third of the twentieth century, was inexcusable. Nonetheless, parallel to these occurrences, Pan Americanism appeared, the notion that common ideals among countries of the Western Hemisphere existed and called for inter-American economic and political cooperative ties. The modern Pan American movement, which dates from the First International Conference of American States held in Washington DC, in 1889, culminated in 1910, in the formation of the Pan American Union, the regional cooperative international body that was later transformed into the Organization of American States (OAS). Democracy had not become institutionalized.[17] Inter-American conferences that included the United States and the independent Latin American countries periodically took place under a cloud of fear and resentment because of unilateral U.S. armed interventions in a few countries. The United States wished to be responsive to Latin American aspirations to obtain legitimacy and cooperative friendly ties in the Americas. Thus with the Good Neighbor policy, a new Pan Americanism evolved that multilateralized the Monroe Doctrine. The OAS established its principles as non-intervention by American countries in each other's internal or external affairs; condemnation of any territorial conquest by forceful means; legal sovereignty or equality of all the American nations; and collective defense of the Americas from any attack.

A full cycle in inter-American relations had been completed. With the legal adoption of the principle of non-intervention, the earlier pro-democratic interventions under the Tobar-inspired treaties ended, and FDR adopted a realpolitik doctrine for Latin America as a whole. Ironically, however, this non-intervention was tied to the emergence of relatively lasting dictatorships in almost all of Central America, one of which was that of Anastasio Somoza García. The rise of Somoza family rule was linked to the newly adopted and acclaimed Estrada Doctrine, which led to the acceptance by Latin American governments and the United States of Somoza's coup d'état and dictatorship in 1936. As Roosevelt told his secretary of state, "Somoza is an s.o.b., but he's ours."

Thus we see that authoritarian regimes in Latin America have been maintained in part by their international acceptance. Cordial, "normal" U.S.-dictator ties have been objected to by many Latin American oppositionists because they serve to sustain dictators. Some regional leaders have opposed the principle of non-intervention by seeking alliances with foreigners to assist them in their quest to form governments of their own. Foreign intervention has not been the exclusive domain of American governments and citizens; some Latin Americans have also participated in it.

George Kennan, a senior American diplomat and advocate of realpolitik, has commented: "Democracy is a matter of tradition, of custom, of what people are used to. . . . It is not something that can be suddenly grafted onto an unprepared people, particularly not from the outside, and . . . by precept, preaching, and pressure rather than example."[18] Kennan would have us think that a pro-democratic foreign policy is ineffective, that such regimes cannot be successfully "imposed" from the outside. This conceptualization is faulty on two counts: it is too deterministic, as if tradition were paramount and innovation were not possible in history; and it obscures the fact that there are countries in which democratic and authoritarian forces coexist, and a resourceful foreign policy might make a difference as to which force wins. Consider, for example, what might have happened in the 1990s in Venezuela's turmoil with army and civilian unrest, if the U.S. government had actively supported a military coup d'état there, or if during that decade in Peru the United States had openly backed the civilian-elected president-turned-authoritarian-ruler to remain in power indefinitely. Kennan, however, is right: of all forms of government, institutionalized political democracy is the most consensual one; it ultimately must rest on broad domestic support.

Carlos Altamirano, the former secretary general of the Chilean Socialist Party during Salvador Allende's social revolutionary experiment, has stated: "In Latin America there is not a properly democratic culture, neither in the dominant classes nor the left. Therefore, it is difficult that democratic regimes with certain stability be established."[19] Altamirano's statement leads us to another important issue: the nature of foreign policy toward countries not only with insufficiently accepted or unstable governments but with uninstitution-alized regimes—that is, countries in which the citizens are in disagreement about their form of government. For such countries, democratic-authoritarian issues can exist locally and be highly divisive.

Not uncommonly, under such conditions of disagreement over regime the tendency is toward very polarized conflict: the counter-group is defined as if it were a collectivity of the Devil, heretics, criminals, murderers, and thieves, deserving repression. In short, an inclination exists toward highly partisan manichean politics, of *sectarismo* and *maniqueanismo*, to employ the commonly used vernacular. It is under conditions of democratic *institutionalization* that more peaceful and consensual forms of political conflict and competition develop, the converse being the case when a broad democratic consensus is considered by the participants to be absent.

Of course, democracy necessitates self-determination. Certainly a self-respecting democratic power should not seek to have a retinue of subservient client-states as its international environment. The determination of foreign governments for economic control is the least legitimate type of clientelism, as it undermines the autonomy of governments necessary to further national development. But the sociology of international clientelism should be better understood. For example, in 1984 David Lange was elected prime minister of New Zealand, and his new policy banning nuclear vessels broke the security pact involving New Zealand, Australia, and the United States. The alliance, the status of allies, was questioned, to the point that relationships with Washington became quite strained. No one in their right mind in the U.S. government, however, would have proposed that the CIA get involved in destabilizing the democratic Lange government, prepare to overthrow it, or commit some other provocative action. By contrast, the removal of dictator Ferdinand Marcos in the Philippines, two years later, was a scenario of client-state politics in which domestic conflict to determine a government is internationalized, and there is an obvious presence of foreign intervention in so-called domestic affairs, in which local factions participate in creating alliances with foreigners and demand that they actively assist in ending or sustaining the regime.

Although in post-1933 years not all Latin American countries were U.S. "client-states," the adoption of realpolitik non-intervention by FDR obviously did not end clientelism, nor the twin problem of democracy-revolution. The cited controversial intervention in Guatemala in 1954 notwithstanding, the fact that democracy progressively developed in Costa Rica after 1948, although not in any other part of Central America, and was accepted by the United States is significant.[20] It points to the importance of internal domestic factors. The United States has been willing and able to accommodate independent-minded democracies (e.g., Canada). The principal Latin American adversaries of the United States have not been democratic leaders.

The most dramatic example of the shortcomings in not promoting democracies in Latin America took place in Cuba in the late Truman through Eisenhower period. Fulgencio Batista's 1952 military authoritarian regime initially was readily recognized per the Estrada Doctrine. Illustrative of the clientelistic psychology of some dictators, Batista, who was weakly supported domestically, claimed that he was more "pro-American than the Americans." This symbolic subordination to a foreign power is propagandistic and does not necessarily mean that a puppet government has been constituted: it uses a foreign country to boost its own position. Indeed, the professed pro-American stance of some dictators can end when the U.S. government asks them to step down. Be that as it may, clientelism was part of the dynamics of the Batista years, produced local resentment, and ended in the 1959 Castro nationalistic revolution, though Cuba evolved rapidly to become part of the Soviet Bloc. But it became absolutely clear that American foreign policy had to change. A dictatorship could end in an anti-U.S. revolution and bring about the constitution of a "worse" dictatorship, one militarily allied with adversaries of the United States (remember the October 1962 Cuban Missile Crisis). Hence, after 1959 the United States revived the pro-democratic interventionism of the pre-FDR epoch.

Actually, in the 1940s the struggle between authoritarian and democratic rule was still alive, and in defiance of U.S. regional policy a group known as the Caribbean Legion (Legión del Caribe) operated. Its leaders in and out of power felt that their pro-democratic struggle required a special kind of subhemispheric integration. The legion's ideal was to constitute a regional axis supportive of social democracy. In this process democratic groups assisted each other crossing international borders, *intervening* in each other's domestic affairs, in contrast to the American policy that opposed the overthrow of authoritarian regimes friendly to U.S. interests.

The Pan–Latin Americanism of the legion (pre–Fidel Castro years), with its conception of interdependence and its search for greater regional integration, was ambitious. For example, it prompted Cuban involvement in support of democratic forces in the Caribbean proper (as in the Dominican Republic), in Central America (for instance, in Guatemala), and in northern Caribbean South America (such as in Venezuela).[21]

The legion died imperceptibly after the total collapse of democratic rule in Castro's Cuba. But it remained part of the collective memory. During the Nicaraguan Revolution it was present in the minds of General Somoza as well as Carlos Andrés Pérez—his Venezuelan nemesis—and, of course, in Costa Rica, both important interventionists in Somoza's overthrow.

It was up to John F. Kennedy to be the greatest exponent of a new, ambitious, hemisphere-wide democratic crusade, the Alliance for Progress. Initiated in 1961, Kennedy's first year in office, in response to the Cuban-Soviet challenge, the alliance consisted of an inter-American cooperative program of several billion dollars to aid the economic and social development of Latin American nations and consolidate democratic reform, in opposition to Marxist "Castroist" authoritarian revolution. Its democratic failures—notably in Brazil in 1964—cannot be principally traced to American policy objectives, however.[22] Latin America was not ready for, nor did it embrace, a continental democratic crusade; firmly established democracies were then very scarce. Richard Nixon's return to realpolitik (1969–74) was not helpful. When the next U.S. Democratic administration took office in 1977, only three democratic regimes operated among the twenty Latin American republics, and only one of them was in Central America and the Caribbean. It is fair to say, nonetheless, that the premises of the Kennedy-initiated democratic crusade—strong Social Democratic and Christian Democratic Latin American parties or movements—were not there in the furor of the increased nationalism and socioeconomic conflicts of those post–Cuban Revolution years, to enable American-promoted democratic institutionalization to take place (the exceptions—e.g., in Venezuela—notwithstanding).[23]

In a sense, the Nixon administration was party to and reflected the growing pessimism about democratic viability in the area. Thus another full cycle of a pro-democratic U.S. policy followed by realpolitik had taken place, fueled by other priorities in Washington and by Latin American realities. The Nixon period experienced a serious crisis of clientelism highlighted by the setback in Vietnam and developments in the strategically vital international petroleum business. The nasty overthrow of the Iranian government (1953) had not impeded the formation of the Organization of Petroleum Exporting Countries (OPEC) less than a decade later.[24] With it the industry experienced a realignment of ownership and power against the rich oil-importing nations, dramatized by the 1973 oil embargo on the United States by some OPEC members. It appeared that the international political and economic system was increasingly less susceptible to U.S. control—Secretary of State Henry Kissinger vocalized Spenglerian themes of decline.[25]

Vietnam was another watershed. The "clientelistic" war proved too costly. A national mood of pessimism developed against U.S. anti-revolutionary interventions abroad. The predicted "domino effect" had not worked to spread Marxist-Leninist regimes beyond Indochina. There was no guarantee that interventions would contribute to building decent, democratically ruled societies; there was no need to prop up friendly (even if anti-Communist) repressive dictators and be morally responsible for their gruesomeness. In addition, it was felt that Americans had had an "inordinate fear of communism," that there was no such thing as a cohesive Communist Bloc, and that there were serious weaknesses in the Soviet Bloc itself. A neo-isolationist spirit of Fortress America became quite strong, in an effort to avoid the ethical and practical costs of a clientelism not in opposition to all authoritarian forces. The Cold War goal of containing communism lost priority.

Actually, in this post-Vietnam mood, the U.S. Congress took the initiative in a return again to a pro-democratic crusade, a new one in its non-intervention component, by legislating the principles of what became the "human rights" policy just before the inauguration of Jimmy Carter in 1977. Statutes limited the authority of the president to deploy troops abroad and controlled the use of political covert action by the federal intelligence apparatus. Also prohibited were U.S. assistance to foreign police forces and military assistance to regimes that violated the human rights of their citizens. Economic assistance to said governments was to be suspended unless it directly benefited the poor.

The Carter administration adopted this human rights banner for its Latin American relations. It would not intervene overtly (with troops) nor covertly (e.g., organizing coups d'état, financing opposition groups) to change the region's dictatorships—this was considered foreign "intervention." But it distanced itself from the extant, mostly anti-Communist Latin authoritarian regimes, publicly attacking their human rights violations and manipulating assistance ties with them with the purpose of encouraging human rights reforms.[26]

The Carter team defined three types of human rights: the physical integrity of the individual, basic material well-being, and political rights. It claimed that its interest was greatest in stopping physical abuses, typically those associated with what might be called "police brutality"; then came fulfilling needs for food, shelter, education, and health; and last was the promotion of political rights associated with representative democratic government.

Yet the administration was faced with particular problems. Key instruments of policy were limited to the condemnation of human rights violators and the establishment of rewards and sanctions managing only relatively small assistance programs.[27] Second, by employing U.S. assistance instruments, it was biased against and tended to undermine friendly governments that truly wished to have close ties with the United States. Third, there was the incapacity to foresee that human rights policies can create political crises. The administration's doctrine against intervention limited its capacity to control outcomes.

There were reasons, however, for favoring the human rights campaign, especially in Central America. At that time, except in Costa Rica, the countries were ruled by authoritarian regimes. In Nicaragua, El Salvador, and Guatemala there were large U.S. military advisory missions supporting highly repressive rightist dictatorships. After decades of U.S. military assistance, including training, the military organizations were extremely brutal and involved with vigilante groups and death squads. Apparently U.S. assistance had not worked to produce civilized professional forces. Hence the rationale of pro-human rights actors to break the extant military relationships, withdraw regime support, and advocate the compliance of the local governments with civilized police norms. Both neoconservatives and neomarxists considered the regime's effects and foresaw the possible delegitimizing, violent revolutionary consequences of the human rights policy, with neoconservatives advocating the support of the friendly dictatorships, and neomarxists advocating support for social revolutions.[28] I differed from both in regards to Nicaragua: the United States was not to abet either the abusive status quo or a probable future unfriendly dictatorship. In any case, as later discussed, developments under Carter, Reagan-Bush, and Clinton showed the impossibility of sustaining the implementation of the human rights policy in its original conceptualization given the nature of the U.S. political system. But neither was it compatible with the implementation of a general policy supportive of authoritarian regimes nor, of course, of professed anti-American revolutions.

Despite such pluses as the Panama Canal Treaties signed under the president's leadership and the beginning of a democratization process in the Dominican Republic, Carter's foreign policy was considered ineffectual; the Soviet and other anti-American forces had expanded their influence, as in Afghanistan and Iran, respectively, and he was not reelected. Especially in Central America, the human rights cause had regressed: revolution, escalated violence, and more repression were the facts of life in Nicaragua, El Salvador, and Guatemala. Vietnam indicated the opposition of U.S. opinion to prolonged costly foreign interventions, but Americans do not like to see adversaries grow in influence and previously friendly countries turn hostile. They blame their government for such failures. Actually, a majority of Americans have supported brief surgical interventions that are few in number, limited in scope, not too costly, and that succeed in producing favorable changes in government, though the general public's aim is not the constitution of subservient clients.

The Carter team's peculiar "non-intervention" standard for Latin America had ignored these facts. Still, the administration did not entirely abandon attempts to determine the Nicaraguan government, even if ineffectively so, in response to pressures. In the United States there are officials, leaders, journalists, and organized interest groups that are pro-intervention, including those that favor intervention on humanitarian grounds.

The Setting

The United States had a long history of clientelistic policies in Nicaragua, principally guided by a geopolitical-commercial interest to build an interoceanic canal; after the canal was built in Panama, the United States sought to avoid the construction of an alternative canal in Nicaragua. Consequently, the twentieth century witnessed a series of U.S. interventions in Nicaragua that included occupations by its troops.[29] In 1909 a revolt broke out against dictator José Santos Zelaya, a nationalistic leader; upon delivery of a U.S. ultimatum, Zelaya left power.[30] This ultimatum became known as the Nota Knox, after Philander Chase Knox, the American secretary of state (1909–13). It came to symbolize one of Nicaragua's myths: that no government could sustain itself without the support of the United States. In 1912 U.S. Marines landed in Nicaragua to put down another rebellion—notice the relationship between U.S. interventions and local regime instability. The marines remained in Nicaragua almost continuously until 1933, when, with the inauguration of FDR, the new period of a less interventionist U.S. Latin American policy began.

The military interventions notwithstanding, the United States did not seek to establish a colony. Nicaraguans were to be in command of their state. Hence, before their departure U.S. troops had engaged in statecraft, forming a national constabulary—the National Guard—and supervising two presidential elections. But a democratic legacy did not take hold. In 1936 General Anastasio Somoza García, whom the Americans had left as the first head of the National Guard, executed a coup d'état against his uncle by marriage and successfully took over absolute control of the Nicaraguan state. This he left to his sons, who would be Nicaragua's rulers for forty-three years.[31]

With time the geopolitical interest in Nicaragua waned. In 1970, under Richard Nixon, the Bryan-Chamorro Treaty of 1916, which was signed during a U.S. intervention and which gave the United States exclusive rights to build a canal, was cancelled by agreement. There were occasional tensions between Washington and Managua tied to the Somozas' undemocratic patterns, but the Somozas were generally eager to cooperate with the United States (except for agreeing to relinquish their political sovereignty) and were supportive of American policy—they were proud to be known as U.S. "clients." Although the United States benefited from the friendship, with the adoption of the human rights policy by the U.S. Congress in 1976, my Republican predecessor as ambassador, James Theberge, initiated a process of distancing the two governments. This was escalated in the subsequent more liberal Democratic administration during my tenure.

When I received an impersonal and brief phone call in early spring 1977 from an unknown government official who asked me abruptly, almost cavalierly, if I would "accept going to Nicaragua as the president's envoy," I had an inkling that I would be faced with events of historical importance for the small nation. Nicaragua had recently been in the news as a debate unfolded in Washington between followers of the human rights policy, who wished to distance our government further from what they considered a highly corrupt and repressive regime, and those content with the status quo. Some felt that nothing of importance would take place in Central America.[32] Such opinions did not, however, reflect the debates being carried out in Washington and their destabilizing potential given regional political clientelistic traditions. Representative Nicaraguans had openly advocated in the U.S. Congress for the adoption of incompatible, polarized, American policies to stabilize or overthrow their government and predicted the dire role that the United States was to play in their nation's destiny.[33]

Different ethical and utilitarian themes also were used by Americans in the controversy. Among the sponsors of policy changes, a need was felt to give a renewed moral purpose to our foreign policy; this was believed to be out of the question if we retained close ties with dictatorships, especially those considered not vital to U.S. interests. Although for many of these reformers the United States was not to be too involved in determining and controlling foreign events, some felt that we should help end the Somoza regime. Regardless of the scope of their recommendations and their numbers, however, most of the sponsors of change within the U.S. government argued that our support for a repressive, socially unprogressive dictatorship was arresting progress in Nicaragua and would create strong enmity against us, which could eventually lead to the emergence of a government hostile to the United States if we did not change our course on time.

In contrast, the realpolitik advocates favored maintaining cordial supportive relations with the Nicaraguan government and not interfering in the internal politics of a friendly country. A few of those favorably disposed toward the government of Nicaragua claimed that it was a legitimate representative democracy. The majority considered the Somoza regime an acceptable form of government, especially because the alternative would most probably be more repressive and Communist-oriented or controlled. To them the Nicaraguan government deserved our support because it was a longtime friend and staunch ally that could become hostile if policy changes were implemented.

Nicaragua had been an unusually dependent client-state. The U.S. government had felt that the development of the Nicaraguan state by forming a strong centralized military force, to impede the recurrent "feudalistic" improvisation of armed groups in the nation, would increase the chances of a stable local political order, policed by the Nicaraguans.[34] This American attempt at modernization by strengthening the state was intended to reflect our own democratic institutions: the National Guard was supposed to be an apolitical, "professional," subordinated institution. Mirroring the U.S. democratic tradition, when the marines finally departed in 1933, a new president, Juan Bautista Sacasa, elected under U.S. supervised elections, was left in office.

However, this "democratic experience" was short-lived. Although the Guard successfully strengthened the state, in that political continuity was obtained and full-blown revolutionary war would not return until 1978–79, an unparalleled record of regime endurance for Nicaragua, Somoza García subverted the apolitical character of the Guard and under the banner of the Liberal Party founded his dynastic authoritarian regime. Essentially, state building resulted in establishing an old, pre-democratic form of government, notwithstanding the frequent claim of the rulers that it was a democratic republic. Nevertheless, this was not seen as a major problem by Washington, and Somoza García was then acceptable to a United States that had abandoned the interventionist, pro-democratic Tobar Doctrine for the Estrada Doctrine of recognizing governments capable of maintaining "law and order."

The U.S. government began a policy of friendship with the Somozas. Although it periodically took a few initiatives in favor of Nicaragua's democratization, the net balance was an acceptance of, and collaboration with, family rule in the light of broader priorities. In short, efforts at a direct grafting of democratic institutions failed. In Nicaragua a pseudo-democratic regime with a praetorian, essentially "patrimonial" National Guard and state resulted from a deliberate and clever policy on the part of the Somozas.[35]

Most Nicaraguans considered the United States (co)responsible for the dynasty because it had founded the National Guard and left Somoza in its control, and because of the locally much-publicized pro-American stance taken by the Somozas, who used their close relations with the United States as an instrument to elicit local support. We used the Somozas to maintain our influence in the region, and they used us by manipulating their pro-American stance.

In pursuing the political stability that would permit withdrawal of its forces, the United States did not seek to constitute a dictatorship nor a family dynasty.[36] Yet Americans were not in command of either the state or the opposition. Nicaraguans were not simply "puppets." Even under military occupation, the U.S. government did not legally hold the political sovereignty—laws had to be passed or decreed by Nicaraguans, not simply by American officials. Thus even under the increased leverage provided by the presence of the marines, American officials were dependent on Nicaraguan decisions to implement their program. It was precisely during the years of the American occupation that Nicaragua experienced very unstable politics.

The instability was not only traceable to a nationalist struggle against the U.S. presence, concretely seen in the rebellion of Augusto César Sandino, guided by his peculiar socialism.[37] Before Sandino, a chronic institutional crisis already had taken hold, and the problem of order was related by many Nicaraguans (and Americans) to the local "pathology of democracy." Revolution was considered a necessary and just tool by Nicaraguan oppositionists, who were largely friendly to the U.S. government, on the grounds that peaceful avenues to determine the government were inoperative, and the state was tyrannically, arbitrarily, or illegitimately used by the ruling leader or party.

American officials diagnosed the propensity toward civil war or revolution, blaming the local political culture for the problem. There was the weak support for representative institutions, specifically for fair or nonfraudulent elections. Nicaragua's was a history with continuismo, a number of techniques or illegalities used by government to remain in power. For example, a strongman might "reelect" himself through manipulated elections often characterized by the opposition's abstention from participating to protest against lack of guarantees. Alternatively, the oligarchic ruling party would change its leaders, but it was unwilling to rest power on the preference or consent of the people and refused to submit to authentic electoral results.[38] In short, elections were considered *not that important* by local elites who, although they claimed to believe in representative democracy, did not have a serious commitment to a democratic political formula. In the absence of free elections oppositions seeking power had to rebel.

Second, the insufficient support of or disregard for constitutionality, the rule of law and constitutional government, and the more civilized system of the dominion of the law as opposed to openly naked force produced fertile ground for rebellion. Noteworthy was the tendency to view law as a form rather than as rules binding upon the rulers. The weakness of the "formal legal integration" of the polity, that is, the huge disparity between constitutional provision, or the law on the books and in practice, was linked to a syndrome of partisanship and corruption of formal institutions of the state, elections included. And the constitution's inoperability was an integral component of the recurrent threat (or use) of force by rulers and oppositions. Constitutions, even formal, democratic ones, were treated as transitory texts. Support for constitutionality was considered the twin of a serious commitment to representative institutions, essential to arrest the spirit of domination and disregard for the people's will characteristic of local undemocratic practice.

Third was the prevalence of intolerance toward political opponents, the lack of mutual respect between Nicaragua's two traditional parties, the Conservative and Liberal. American officials wrote about the local inclination to extreme partisanship, *sectarismo*. The result of this political partisan intolerance was abuses of power and violent conflicts, a root cause of the unworkability of democracy and weakness of the institutions of the state. Partisanship undermined impartial vote counting; it eroded the rule of law; it impeded the establishment of modern, as opposed to patrimonial, bureaucracies in the state.[39] In effect, regardless of its sociological origin or basis, the practice consisted of state institutions partisanly appropriated by their incumbents being defined as if they were the "patrimony" of those leaders or parties who controlled them.

More extensively, the Americans found themselves in a polity where traditions of partisanship were so strong that there was no confidence that Nicaraguans were capable of "neutrally" managing public institutions. No state institution is "apolitical"—judges will apply a philosophy in deciding particular cases, for instance. But the problem resulting in insufficient confidence in, and support for, the state in Nicaragua consisted of a different kind of absence of "neutrality": for example, a Conservative municipal or county judge would not act as a "judge" but would act partisanly as a "Conservative judge," giving preference to a Conservative against a Liberal because of their common party identification. Judges were also corrupt in other ways, deciding in favor of their personal relations or those who materially bribed them.

American officials observed that this de facto reconstitution, transformation, or appropriation of state offices—an indication of the weakness or underdevelopment of formal legal political organization—impeded the impartiality to represent more general interests by government and the operation of a responsible, accountable government. Americans reported that elections were not carried out properly and that the local military (prior to the formation of the Nicaraguan National Guard) was corrupt and abusive. To a large extent the disorders were traced to the manner in which elites handled the state in relation to other elites who happened to be out of office, to an intra-elite political party, not class conflict; the destitute poor in general acquiesced to the social order or were manipulated by the elites.[40]

To solve the problem, the American occupation followed a two-pronged goal: American officials would (1) form a nonpartisan constabulary recruited equally from the two traditional parties (because it was considered impossible to find "neutral" or politically "uncontaminated" Nicaraguans); and (2) until this modern, professionally oriented police force was able to provide the impartiality to conduct real elections, count the votes, which they did in 1928 and 1932.

Our predecessors, however, encountered difficulties during the military occupation itself, beyond Sandino's rebellion. These problems were manifested *before Somoza García's ascendancy* and suggested the weaknesses in democratic culture existing among Nicaraguan elites. First, a lack of serious commitment to electoral institutions continued. For example, in U.S.-occupied Nicaragua, General José María Moncada, the elected president (1929–33) in the first U.S.-supervised elections to guarantee impartiality and an otherwise friendly leader to the United States, was involved in attempts at *continuismo*, trying to postpone elections and extend his term! An American official referred to Moncada's "treason." In the United States the general public would be "horrified" to learn that the first opposition leader peacefully elected to the presidency in Nicaraguan history subsequently did not wish to submit himself to elections.[41]

Movements against elections (or accusations of this) reportedly were found in other quarters as well, such as by Juan Bautista Sacasa, the civilian Liberal Party leader eventually ousted by Somoza García. There were initiatives to conduct a presidential election with only *one* candidate agreed upon by the two parties and accusations that the opposition would try to impose its candidate or mar the electoral process by organizing disturbances. About five decades later, I sympathetically identified with those who faced a family of problems similar to our own. I still recall President Somoza's challenge to me: "Tell Carter to come and get me."

Accounts also refer to the mania of constitution making—the attempts to convoke constituent assemblies or other mechanisms to change the constitution rather than implementing the existing one. There was an effort to create new institutions, especially those around the term in office, so as to legalize remaining in control of the state without public consultation. After 1936 this and other patterns of changing the political constitution were made a way of rulership by the Somoza family.

The earlier debate and problems around the National Guard were also telling. Prior to 1929 Conservative leaders opposed the formation of such a force. It seemed apparent to American observers that this was based on the desire to continue to use the state's armed forces or police as a key instrument to remain in office. An argument in favor of doing so was the belief that Nicaraguans were "incapable" of building an arm of the state not partisanly controlled by one political party. (I later became directly acquainted with this self-fulfilling prophecy that served the ruling elite by rationalizing their lack of zeal to build a modern democratic state.)

Actually, prior to 1926 the absence of enthusiasm for the National Guard seemed to have been wider. This led to the interpretation that members of the political opposition were also against its creation because they wished to keep open the traditional option of changing the government through revolution.[42] The stance vis-à-vis the Guard also was reported to depend not on principle but on the group's position in the political structure. Several observers of Latin American politics have emphasized the "non-ideological" or "opportunistic" character of regional politics, including their manifestations of violence, though no such valid general case can be made spatially or temporally.[43]

Furthermore, during the U.S. occupation, efforts by President Moncada to subvert and destroy the intended nonpartisan, apolitical nature of the National Guard were reported, as well as the supportive campaigns on this issue by organs of his Liberal Party press. My impression is that arguments in favor of constituting a partisan army were largely couched in emotional terms. At any rate, you can observe the difficulties found by the American officials stationed in Nicaragua to institutionalize a democracy—such was the resilience of traditional patterns with patrimonial rule without constitutional-parliamentary institutions. Whether the U.S. government had a right to "impose" democratic institutions on foreign elites is open to debate.

The story of Somoza García's rise to power is ironic indeed. Consonant with contemporary historical sociology, it consisted of a combination of innovation and reproduction of uses of the past. People make history both with freedom and under preexisting social conditions not autonomously chosen by them—inherited conditions serve both as constraints and facilitators of social action.[44] Many Nicaraguans blamed the United States for the Somoza family's rulership, partly to arouse our guilt and obtain support in their struggle to defeat the last Somoza dictator. This interpretation stretches the facts. There were predisposing characteristics in Nicaraguan society that facilitated Somoza García's political career. Against the original U.S. objectives, Somoza followed in the footsteps of several Nicaraguan predecessors, even as he provided his own personal mark on the disregard for elections and constitutional rule and on the intolerant partisan definition of the state as a fiefdom.

Historical accounts show that there were Nicaraguans sponsoring their caudillo's rise to power.[45] There were opponents as well as supporters, of course. In 1936 there was reportedly a petition to the United States from Nicaraguan notables to extend the practice of foreign supervision of elections to resist the threat of National Guard supremacy and assure future electoral fairness. International supervision was a recurrent, unfulfilled demand during the Somoza family years. Arthur Bliss Lane, the U.S. envoy, had tried to prevent a Somoza García coup d'état. Richard Millett writes:

> The departure of Lane removed the last possibility of open American opposition to Somoza's seizing the presidency. [His successor] was instructed to avoid taking any part in Nicaragua's domestic affairs, and was not even to engage in the efforts of mediation which occupied so much of his predecessor's attention. On April 30, 1936, the United States announced the official abandonment of . . . refusing recognition to . . . governments that came to power by revolution or extralegal means. (This meant that Somoza could now hope for eventual recognition no matter what means he used to gain power.) Within one month after the removal of this last American obstacle to his drive for power, Somoza resorted to violence against the incumbent administration.[46]

American efforts at statecraft during the 1920s and early 1930s can be criticized on various grounds: absence of a clear, coherent plan from the outset; excessive reliance on the National Guard as the key modern institution of the state; insufficient training of Guard cadres prior to U.S. troop withdrawal; and inattention to leaving in place operative electoral institutions with a provisional international supervisory component as needed. Such diagnoses place into question the intentions of the United States and the support at that time of Nicaraguans for democratic self-government. The undeniable fact is that it took until 1990 for the next election in which an opposition victory was recognized. It was also felt that the resilience of anti-democratic patterns had to be met still during the 1990s with an extremely large, "clientelistic" international presence, to develop organs of Nicaraguan civil society and state institutions, including continued foreign monitoring of elections, to sustain democracy's consolidation. After 1990 one still heard comments indicative of the remaining tentativeness of such a regime.

Ten years before Somoza García's coup d'état, U.S. envoy Charles Eberhardt wrote: "The time has not yet come, if it ever will, when a non-partisan constabulary or National Guard, organized under American ideas or ideals will be a success in Nicaragua. It is not wanted." The U.S. Mission in Managua accurately predicted that upon the withdrawal of the marines, the National Guard would become the key instrument used to prevail by force in the partisan political struggles. Indeed, in the face of the obvious failure at democratic institution building, in 1935, just months before Somoza's coup, Ambassador Lane concluded from Managua: "The people who created the [National Guard] had no adequate understanding of the psychology of the people here. . . . In my opinion [U.S. institution building] is one of the sorriest examples on our part of our inability to understand that we should not meddle in other people's affairs."[47] Notice the impact of local conditions on the advocacy of foreign policy changes. Perversely enough, the precise mechanism that the United States had tried to mold would serve as the instrument of enduring control for the new Somocista order.

2. The Somoza García Legacy

To understand the precipitous breakdown of order that ended in successful revolution, we must look more closely at the nature of the Somoza regime—how it developed, its sources of stress, how it had been able to successfully cope and survive. I mostly center attention on interpretations of these realities made by Nicaraguans before and during my involvement with their country. Of necessity we must be selective—the objective is not to review the interpretations but to establish a comparative basis for explaining the choosing by government and opposition of the strategies that resulted in a revolution.

There were three basic periods of Somoza family rule: Anastasio Somoza García's rulership, from his 1936 coup to his assassination in 1956; the ascendancy of elder son Luis Somoza Debayle, from 1956 to 1967, when he died of natural causes; and the period of dominance by brother Anastasio Somoza Debayle, from 1967 until his overthrow in 1979. Throughout those long years the form of ruling went through different subphases—we could even refer to several species of regime under the family's control—but our task is much more modest than an adequate historical survey of the dynasty.

In 1968 Mariano Fiallos Oyanguren wrote an exceptional monograph on Nicaragua's political system. His goal was to explain a decade before the Nicaraguan Revolution why and how the Somoza regime remained in place. At that time, the dynasty was the most enduring of all Latin American dictatorial regimes. Fiallos concentrated on the 1956–67 period and made a brief reference to the Somoza García years for background purposes. My reflections rely particularly on observations drawn from his essay, but I complement the analysis with my own materials and inferences.

The Context

Although leaders have options—especially those who for good or evil become "great" or very powerful—they are not completely protean figures. Somoza García's Nicaragua was still a backwater with a small proportion of educated, materially well-off citizens.[1] It was a small-scale rural society with an undeveloped money economy. This socioeconomic order is identified in the literature with personalism/familism, *amistad*, *compadrazgo* (friendship bonds, extended familistic orientations), patron-client ties of paternalism and protection, or personalistic dependency and loyalty. Under this system, businesses tend to be kept under the tight personal hold of a *patrón* assisted by his *hombres de confianza* (trusted, personal followers who are devoted to him), who in return get from him their dependent position in the business.

Such patrimonial organization is also common in premodern states: its origin is found in patriarchal authority centered around the household of the ruler *patrón*, the governance expanding beyond it, as people outside his household are involved in a still underdeveloped state. In this political system, restating Max Weber, the roots of the ruler's domination grow out of treating the state as his own personal household. The rules of such personal authority do not derive principally from a preexisting legal order but from moral and personal considerations. Hence, power is largely discretionary, and political support is rooted in filial piety and expected protection. A principal source of wealth of the patrimonial ruler and his officials is from appropriating the state, and the purchasing of their decisions, given the broad latitude for favoritism and arbitrariness; they enrich themselves from their control of the state.[2]

This classical textbook type is precisely what Somoza García—manipulating the favorable circumstances in his path—constructed and bequeathed to his sons. The "state is Somoza's personal farm" was a comment made by many Nicaraguans in those days to describe their political system. Using a democratic facade, in fact, even the "elected" Congress came to form a club of sorts of the loyal "friends" of El Jefe (the boss).[3]

Although dynastic rule was not in Nicaragua's tradition—this hurdle the Somozas had to overcome—the nation's undemocratic traditions did not help contain the ambitions of the founder and his heirs. Nicaragua's political heritage, in addition to the absence of a tradition with parliamentarism, consisted of still extant premodern bureaucracies with heavy doses of patrimoniality and weak attachment to the rule of law. Indeed, we must keep in mind that Nicaragua's great reformers—for example, Liberal general José Santos Zelaya, 1893–1909—had not chosen the development of democratic constitutional and electoral institutions as one of their reforms; Zelaya was a dictator.

In brief, in a gemeinschaft world of association based on bonds of kinship, affection, and so on, and with certain political traditions, General Somoza García established a regime that operated under this implicit political doctrine that linked it with its supporters. The ruler and state-owner is a father protector; his friends or followers are dependent on him. They behave well and are loyal, and their big brother or father keeps them well, gives them gifts. Such was the state that was re-created, one of the legacies of Somoza García to his children, who ruled from his death until the revolution. Notice the trap that may occur when romanticizing the restoration of a familistic social order, to terminate the alienation caused by modern impersonal social organization. In the past, *personalismo* was used to implement serious political injustices and was also associated with the underdevelopment or malfunctioning of large-scale (supposedly impersonal) economic organizations.[4]

To impose himself, General Somoza would use the strategic position that had been given to him by the U.S. government. The National Guard, his principal organizational basis of support, had been recently established by the U.S. Marine Corps, and he was its first Nicaraguan head; this opened opportunities for him to create new rules in a still unsettled developing institution.[5] Concentrating greater resources in a newly created constabulary psychologically enhanced its power in the eyes of many opposition leaders, accustomed to facing the far lesser developed state's physical force of the past.

Although not all groups held equally strong patrimonial values and attitudes—Nicaragua's political culture was not homogeneous, and there were groups that had republican, less patrimonial views—the general's founding coup d'état received important local support.[6] Thus in developing his strategies to alter the polity's configuration, Somoza used existing political organizations to modify them, one new, the other traditional: the National Guard and the Liberal Party, respectively. The first one—despite its small size—was an unusually strong force. The Liberal Party, by contrast, was relatively more progressive and populistic, more attuned to the social democratic discourse that had started to become popular in Latin America. Each of his two legitimate sons would be placed in each of these organizations to grow up in them and head them, to control the military and civilian bases of organized support for the regime.

Sociocultural configurations can be viewed as predisposing factors that serve as facilitators or obstacles for the materialization of political phenomenon. There are also situational factors influencing concrete historical conjunctures or processes. There even are instances in which chance plays a paramount role in the historical results. There are some cases in which the physical presence of a mortal but very powerful individual convincingly makes a significant difference in the outcome; on average the importance of "great men" is much greater in lesser-institutionalized polities and should not be forgotten. And Somoza García—not without opposition—gave a special and extreme discretionary patrimonial definition to the Nicaraguan state, as his household or property, and of his family as inheritors. His rule was not simply a carbon copy of the past.

At various points the founder could have given up ruling—some Latin American strongmen have peacefully stepped down and allowed democratization. Somoza García was urged to do so by Nicaraguans and (occasionally) by the U.S. government. But his insatiable lust to dominate, lead, and manage men prevailed until he finally left power *con las botas por delante* ("with a bullet on his chest and his boots still on").

At every turn Somoza García outmaneuvered his adversaries. Every crisis seemed to result in strengthening his power; one of them immediately reinforced the dynastic character of the regime. The General Somoza of my mission told me this story in 1977: "In the 1940s the U.S. government wished to see my father not reelect himself; the differences between the two governments produced a crisis in 1947, when my father backed by the Liberal Party organized the replacement of the president.[7] The United States broke relations with Nicaragua and withdrew the American officer supervising our Military Academy. My father immediately appointed me as the new director of the Academy, where I took charge of the education of the future officer cadres. And you see, Ambassador, the Somozas remained having the support of the people, and U.S.-Nicaraguan relations eventually became normalized."[8]

The story has historical significance. General Somoza, who had regard for very few men but identified strongly with his father, viewed the Somozas as charismatic and invincible partly through his father's successes in outwitting adversaries. Because of this legacy, Somoza was inclined to dismiss the human rights policy of the Ford and Carter years as simply another American unrealistic and temporary moralistic eccentricity; it was not until the very end that he realized more fully the consequences of our policy, that he had been defeated.

In short, although the "great man" theory of history has more limited applicability—especially in well-institutionalized, relatively depersonalized regimes (e.g., in the United States)—the role of a personality, of "charisma" (in Max Weber's technical sense, of the gift of the creator of a new normative order), cannot be dismissed in the establishment of the dynasty. The cult of founders of dynasties suggests their importance—their psychological predispositions, feelings and desires, personal goals attributed by their followers.

A new "regime"—a *new political order*, as the Somocista followers claimed—had been born.[9] It met with opposition until the assassination of the founder. For although facilitated by socioeconomic traits, dynastic rulership was not fully legitimized in Nicaragua's political culture; some groups sought a democratic regime, helping create a disjointed political culture with its pseudo-democratic rationalizations. Under these conditions a bifurcation took place: the patrimonial loyalty of followers tended to be translated into intense disloyalty by those not at the service of the ruler.

Main Regime Characteristics

In order for a ruling group to remain in control of the state, it requires support from the state's armed forces; if it holds elections, it must be able to rig them; and it must keep the population's protests or rebellions under control. During Somoza García's hegemony, basic successful principles to achieve these conditions were established, and in sharp contrast to some other caudillos, Somoza García left a more organized regime with lasting, relatively effective military and civilian organizations. [10]

Somoza followed personnel policies that resulted in only those loyal to him remaining in the National Guard. In every crisis of support, the founder moved very rapidly to purge from the institution the unfaithful (or those suspected to be so). His governance over the military was extremely patrimonial. He exercised wide discretion to appoint "his" men, those with his favor. For instance, in the 1940s, while still quite young, two of my contacts were appointed to very important senior positions "because of Somoza García's liking." They lacked any prior military training. Somoza's organizational legacy was a patriarchal centralized entity.

This did not mean total capriciousness in personnel policy. A natural way of being a "protector" of his men (patrimonially expected) is for the *jefe* (boss) to "know them," to take into consideration their personal and family needs, and to provide secure employment to the loyal; this is why soldiers faithful to the regime who misbehaved were usually at most reprimanded but not fired (a pattern abhorrent to the human rights activists in Washington).

However, the notion of building an independently minded officer corps with high levels of professional training was deliberately absent. This design remained beyond Somoza García. In 1977 I found out that Nicaraguan officers were not trained in the most prestigious foreign academies, such as West Point or its equivalent, for a simple reason: the need to impede the development of officers with the technical expertise and prestige to attract an independent following. Only a handful of individuals had been trained in such academies; the tradition was to promote them out of the National Guard (as well as officers with potential leadership status). During my mission, General Somoza Debayle was the only West Point graduate active in the army.

Centralization in the hands of Somoza García was eventually formalized by legal provisions, to avoid any possible misunderstanding as to who ruled the National Guard (especially during periods in which there were puppet presidents, while Somoza remained head of the army). The Guard placed itself beyond the control of any outsiders by legal privileges constitutionally afforded to it. Mariano Fiallos wrote: "Military crimes are to be judged solely by the army tribunals. . . . [P]olice activities . . . are a military function, and the excesses committed by officers or soldiers have been interpreted as falling under military courts of inquiry organized ad hoc. Thus, the possibility of sanctions against the military to enforce court or other civilian [government] orders is very limited."[11]

Indeed, the National Guard became a sovereign institution within the state, and its monopoly over organized military forces helped it become a sovereign power within the nation. Its formal powers were made very broad: all police functions, including intelligence; the administration of customs and control of the electoral process; immigration and emigration control; control of civil aviation; and control of various systems of communications. And at the top of the National Guard was Somoza García, overseeing an entity incapable of acting independently from him.

While in Nicaragua, I was very interested in learning about the possibilities of a military uprising. My informal contacts revealed strange attitudes among a few top officers with whom I had discrete exploratory contacts. They expressed inhibiting feelings that only President-General Somoza Debayle could maintain the Guard's cohesion; that they were incapable of acting on their own; that without the jefe none of them would be capable of running the organization, for it would be taken over by internal rivalries and disintegrate. These men were "echoes" of the Somoza son who now ruled the army. I saw the continuation of the pattern of deliberately creating an absolute dependence on the jefe for any serious decision.

The best internal statement on the National Guard during the 1970s is by Chester Y. Williams.[12] He noted the care taken by General Somoza Debayle in dealing with personnel matters, as he intended to maintain a paternalistic, protective image; he also reported the limited combat capabilities of the Guard—two years after his writing, the revolution triumphed. But his most important central theme is the low degree of expertise of the military leaders vis-à-vis General Somoza, and their obsequiousness toward him in technical decisions and routine daily events. For instance, he reports that the commander of the air force had no input into the buying of helicopters in a case that he studied. In addition to their primary duties in the military, many officers were involved in one or more private enterprises. In short, the National Guard was depicted as a low-pressure organization, making no major or excessive demands upon the skills and time of the officers, the highly energetic among them tending to opt for outside employment as well. The norm for promotion was obedience, patience, loyalty; the ultimate reward was a wealthy retirement.

This finding about the low levels of professionalism is of interest to comparative theories on the military. One school of thought views high levels of professionalism inhibiting the politicization of the military and hence their inclination to rebel and execute coups d'état. And yet we see how the Somozas used the maintenance of low levels of professionalization as a measure of control, with total success. However, such operational levels of professionalism are likely to result in the disintegration of the military when the established leadership is absent, as events in Nicaragua in 1979 eventually indicated.

The habit of subordination to Somoza in the daily operations, while (distrustfully) viewing their peers as their competitors for his favor, conditioned the military cadres to have the attitudes that I encountered. Comments made in early 1946 about the old Somoza by the U.S. ambassador in Managua show similar feelings of impotence:

> Somoza realizes that in the last analysis his strongest card is the Guardia Nacional. He has played, as only an expert can, on the loyalty, allegiance and feelings of the Guardia. Today there is confusion, due largely to Somoza, in the ranks of the Guardia. He wants both officers and men to look to him as the benevolent and beneficent father of the organization, to whom the organization owes everything. He is right in thinking that many hold this impression. He has managed to arouse feeling between [non-] and Academy trained officers. The impression left with them is, that only Somoza can manage that both groups continue in the Guardia. [13]

Ironically, both my General Somoza and his father claimed that their control of the Guard was indispensable to maintaining its discipline—the self-serving, self-fulfilling "I am irreplaceable; if I leave there will be chaos" notion—which consisted also of equating democratization or democracy with chaos. [14] And the founder, as early as he could, gave a dynastic dimension (a version of extreme patrimoniality) to the army: at age ten, Anastasio Somoza Debayle was enrolled in the National Guard as a noncommissioned officer; at sixteen, he was promoted to second lieutenant. The younger Somoza culminated his military training by graduating from West Point at twenty-one. [15] Throughout the years military rituals and symbolic acts involving the Somoza family, including the women, were developed—practices evocative of the homage to royalty of more formally and openly defined dynasties than the Nicaraguan pseudo-democratic regime.

The second pillar of organized support was the Liberal Party. Although the military can be and were used to rig elections, a government party is a very useful instrument to rally civilian participation for its cause and to neutralize opposition. Nicaragua was among the few Latin American nations in which the nineteenth-century tradition of parties labeled Conservative and Liberal survived both the Depression of the 1930s and World War II. Originally molded mainly around the church-state philosophical and constitutional cleavage (which helped to block the development of a national consensus on regime throughout much of Latin America), these original interparty distinctions had been blurred by the time of Somoza García.[16] The founder promoted a populistic, welfare state philosophical line within the Liberal Party, influenced by the New Deal and consonant with the ideological orientations that were in vogue in much of Latin America. The Liberal reformist platform was much more rhetoric than actual government policy. In social issues it was also influenced by the Mexican Constitution of 1917, which had considerable ideological impact in the region.

Under Somoza García, the Liberal Party became a nationwide political machine. Elder son Luis Somoza Debayle became his father's man in the party. There was nothing astonishing in the Nicaraguan machine—its context was a pseudo-democracy, with elections to be managed so that the government would win. The Somocista machine was cognate to the American experience with political machines—actually, my General Somoza liked to compare himself with Chicago Mayor Richard J. Daley. But Somoza's was a nationwide organization and was more powerful in that it obeyed the regime's *mentalidad* of partisan domination, ultimately threatening force (or employing it) in order not to lose control. We are talking of a well-lubricated—with bossism, clientelism, patronage, jobs, contracts—machine.

The machine's origins could be traced more to the political designs of control by a ruling group in office, facing an impoverished population available to receive benefits from it, than to any prior rapid social change, for Nicaragua was not developing rapidly.[17] Poverty and the virtual absence of social class–oriented organization of the populace facilitated the speed of developing the Nicaraguan machine. But it was also based on the traditional identification of local and regional leaders—landlords and merchants—with the Liberal Party. Professionals and intellectuals were co-opted into government service as well. The raison d'être of the machine was the existence of electoral politics, precisely to help manage elections.

The machine depended on local party notables, but as the state grew in size during the founder's tenure, the relative importance of the government bureaucracy increased. There was no organized civil service with tenure, and public employees were mostly Liberal Party members. In our principal source's terms,

> Because of patronage, it is assumed that [most] persons accepting public office belong to the majority (Liberal) party and all are assessed a contribution to the party treasury amounting to 5 percent of their salaries. This amount is deducted directly from their paychecks each month and delivered by the [government] to the party. Although this is not a principle contained in any statute, it is compulsory due

to the fact that refusal to pay (which is theoretically possible) would be practically interpreted as resignation from office. This gives the head of the party [Somoza] enormous financial power not enjoyed by any other political group in the country.[18]

Indeed, Somoza García developed a very powerful organ among civilians: the party was available to get out the vote and count it, to participate in public rallies and other demonstrations of support. The partisan transformation of the state extended from Somoza out into the nation, through not only the National Guard but the Liberal Party bureaucracy as well. And the legacy became a highly centralized apparatus:

In accordance with the party by-laws, the nomination of candidates for all offices is centralized so that all names are presented by the national party office. This includes candidates for municipal positions. There is no possibility of nominating local candidates outside of the officially [established system]. There can be no write-in campaigns. A single-ballot system exists in which one vote is counted for all national [and local] officials, all of whom are elected at the same time. Split ballots are not permitted.

By [Somoza] controlling the majority party, it is also possible to exercise direct control over Congress because of the fact that all candidates for congressional offices are nominated by the central authorit[y] of the party. The control of the Congress permits the exercise of considerable influence over the appointment of Supreme Court Justices.[19]

The study concludes:

It should be added that the Somoza[s] . . . inherited from their father the enormous fortune which the latter acquired . . . after he became an important factor in Nicaragua politics. This has enabled them to exercise added political pressure, by uniting the power given them by their great [private] investments in practically all important [economic sectors] to their power [in the] army and majority party.[20]

In short, the Somocista Nicaraguans allowed, and participated in, the construction of a highly centralized regime guided by a primary principle: the ruling group is composed of Somoza friends, a quasi-familistic club led by the anointed Somoza head, with the power to decide who is included in the club, and it is to be followed loyally. And this formula became traditionalized among them.

Institutionalization

Despite experiencing considerable stress, the regime survived for more than two decades after Somoza García's death. A way to interpret the problems about institutionalizing "old-fashioned, traditional" strongman rule is to focus on the personal nature of its authority and loyalty. Max Weber dealt with the problem of personalistic authority when discussing charisma, the belief in a leader perceived possessed with truly exceptional, extraordinary qualities. How can these qualities, the basis of the leader's following, and the legitimacy of his or her new rules be transferred to successors? How can charisma become "routinized"? Influential commentators have considered that personalistic rule is nontransferable.[21] Nevertheless, some forms of personalized authority have been legitimized (e.g., premodern monarchies, where the ruling family is widely viewed to possess a traditional, divine or sacred, right to govern).

Somoza García's rulership faced the problem of succession. Son Anastasio told me: "When my father was killed, I was the Director General of the Guardia Nacional. I called the officers in and told them, 'You have accepted and been loyal to me because I was my father's deputy. He is no longer with us. I want to know if you still want me to be in command.' They all answered yes, and this is why I have remained in charge of the institution." The problem of transferability of authority rested on the absence of an explicit, or legal, well-established rule about succession.

The sources of the regime's problematic institutionalization went beyond this, but you can see that calling our regime type "traditional" can be a misnomer. It was not based on traditional rules, customs, beliefs handed down for generations. Before the revolution, General Somoza was trying to obtain the retention of family control for a third generation, training his son to be his successor in the National Guard. But his succession was not formally established. In fact, Somoza's regime was not characterized by sufficiently broad-based (traditionally or otherwise) support to warrant being considered among the "legitimate" forms of government.

This leads directly into the pseudo-democratic nature of the regime: it formally claimed to be a republic and representative democracy. This is why though the regime's praxis was to obtain intergenerational continuation of family rule, there was an absence of openly defined rules about succession: the legal (constitutional) rule was succession through free elections. Although General Somoza was preparing the way to obtain succession by Anastasio Somoza III, the government never formally said so. For instance, President Somoza's position with me was that he could not truncate the military career of his son to please the U.S. government. At the same time, Somocista cadres considered that General Somoza intended to replicate his father's legacy, transferring power to the next generation. Needless to say, all of Nicaragua's opposition vehemently refused to accept any dynastic succession: its central rallying cry was to reestablish a "republic."

Constitutionality

Introductory textbooks tell us to view social problems as a result of conflict between values and norms or rules. This suggests the importance of the described tentativeness in fundamental constitutional matters. In Nicaragua the regime never formally adopted the norm that, in fact, operated after 1936—the ruler was a member of the Somoza family. There was a lack of normative crystallization, evocative (though with its own twist) of Emile Durkheim's anomie. Ambiguity was necessary to maintain a democratic pretense. The written constitution had to formally establish that the authorities were determined through free elections, otherwise we would not even be able to define the regime as pseudo-democratic—we might have called it a hereditary monarchy. The problem was not simply one of semantics, rather the pseudo-democratic pretense of constitutional rule and elections. The peculiar recognition and space given to the opposition in Nicaragua resulted in stressful political dynamics, which potentially threatened to get out of control and destroy the regime. Opposition had to be *repressed* to avoid a successful revolt.

Although family rule went through phases of more and less repression, within the pseudo-democratic dynastic genus it was on the average relatively mild—a *dictablanda* as opposed to *dictadura*, as Latins say—in that it allowed some (though variable) space to the opposition.[22] This resulted partly from the fact that Somoza García realized his innovation in a traditionalized two-party system, his Conservative opponents being drawn as well from the upper class. In the Nicaraguan system an opposition was legally recognized, and the representation in elections of some faction of it was sought by the government, though opposition strength experienced cyclic growth and shrinkage tied to repression.

Studies by Nicaraguans have dealt with the pseudo-democratic "principle of constitutionality." Although on the one hand constitutions were frequently changed or forcefully abrogated, on the other hand there was the feeling that "constitutionality" (rule in accordance with a formal constitution) should be restored soon. Two sources are attributed to this pattern: a legal tradition emphasizing form and the appearance of legality rather than substance or the spirit of the law; and the clientelistic subordination of local rulers, inclined to please the United States by rhetorically placing themselves within the democratic world.

Somoza García's constitutional abrogations and amendments resulted from his desire to remain in control. Presidents could be deposed by him (e.g., 1936, 1947), and with these acts the constitutions were broken by naked force, and new ones established, typically by a subsequent "election" of a constituent assembly to reestablish "democratic constitutional" rule. That is, the principle of constitutionality was manipulated in a Nicaragua supposed to be democratic because the rulers had no alternative claim to legitimacy.[23]

Also, although force was used by the National Guard, to maintain the two-party tradition ideally a political understanding would be reached with the opposition and a pact made with it on a new constitution. This pattern (e.g., the Conservative-Liberal pact of 1950) legalized the continuation of Somoza García in office in exchange for a constitutional prohibition of his reelection for the following presidential term and a guaranteed minority share of government offices for the opposition. Notice, once again, the founder's promise of being a democrat (that he would not reelect himself nor be dynastically succeeded).

Yet such hopes were dashed: Somoza García subsequently broke that pact and forced a "reform" of the 1950 Constitution to allow his reelection. (After the convention of the Liberal Party that nominated him, however, he was shot and died a few days later, on September 28, 1956.) In fact, constitutional changes also took place to expand or contract the presidential term, the former directly to benefit Somoza, the latter when someone else temporarily held the presidency. Thus, constitutional changes were made to obtain a momentary political advantage for the ruling group or to make some political action "legally" acceptable. Such treatment of the constitution not in the nature of the rule of law—the submission to a preestablished text by all, the government included—tended to result in political crises, unless a broad government-opposition constitutional understanding was reached, a *pacto*, as Nicaraguans called them.

The point is that the regime's nature, in and of itself, could lead to a political dynamic resulting in situations of normlessness, regardless of whether or not any socioeconomic changes posed additional problems to the regime. For example, as the regime was supposed to be democratic, there was a term in office—Somoza García was not a ruler for life. As time elapsed, the leader had to step down or run for reelection (which he could in some instances not legally do). But Somoza García did not wish to step down nor hold a free election. Obviously, the opposition considered unacceptable Somoza's illegal strategy to remain in control. Therefore, there always was a chronic potential constitutional crisis: Somoza needed to alter the constitution to remain in office for an extended period, or break it engineering some kind of electoral fraud.

This crisis dimension, the normlessness, of the regime type is precisely why many military coups d'état tend to occur in conjunction with the expansion of the presidential term or manipulated elections.[24] In Nicaragua, however, Somoza García was always able to prevail in the National Guard and rally its support to restore a repressive equilibrium. Notice that the mechanism that can trigger coups also can be used to remain in power, and that although not a consensual instrument, repression is a mechanism of the government to mobilize the support of its forces and crush its adversaries. In this respect the polity was re-equilibrated not by consensual mechanisms but rather through force, suppressing dissent; the regime's nature required it.

Elections

In an institutionalized democracy the regime does not tend to enter into crisis as the term in office lapses. A new lawful election takes place, thus reaffirming the democratic regime. In pseudo-democracies, though, their fraudulent character—the conflict over democratic/undemocratic patterns—can be exacerbated, as the issue of tenure and succession advances. In Nicaragua, elections were usually considered fraudulent by the opposition, yet the government felt that they had to take place for legitimacy. In simple words, "elections were contested by the opposition as being fraudulent, [with] government officials accused of exercising pressure, even of using violence to influence the nominations, to force people into voting, or to impede them from voting."[25] Again, in the Old Regime the hegemonía did not obey any explicit philosophical notion of a vanguard, as with the ideological and constitutional position that was formally given to the Communist Party in the Soviet Union; ideologically the idea was that free, competitive elections were the norm, but the praxis was of manipulating them.

My conversations in Nicaragua suggested that a sort of "collective unconscious" with the following themes was involved in the fraud. Ultimately there was a lack of confidence in the Nicaraguan people's ability to exercise sovereignty—the alleged incapacity for self-government of ignorant masses. Other themes were a spirit of domination based on the notion that we-rulers-know-best (reinforced by the conditionality in which the law was viewed); the acceptance of patrimonial patterns as tradition, "what works" or "the way we do things" here; domination tied to a Hobbesian conception of the polity—if we do not maintain ourselves aggressively on top, the others will crush us, and we are better than they; Nicaraguans need to be ruled by an iron hand lest chaos overtake the society; and a profound manichean partisanship against the opposition, even though when led as well by members of the upper class.

In any case, the result of this lack of confidence in elections was either "the abstention of the major opposition parties . . . because of charges of prepared fraud; or [elections] with the concurrence of the major opposition parties . . . but with their [eventual rebellion] because of the use of fraudulent practices and violent means to alter the results; or, finally, [elections] with a previous agreement as to what were to be [their] results . . . regardless of the voters, because this was the way in which the elections were planned in [a] pact signed by [the government and opposition]."[26] Indeed, democracy was not institutionalized, above all, because of the deficient commitment to it by the elites who prevailed.

As previously stated, prior to Somoza García, the country's politics had been dominated by two parties. In 1929 a period of Liberal ascendancy began, and Somoza capitalized on it by building an organization that became increasingly dependent on the bureaucracy. Splits within the Liberals were minor: the reliance of Somoza's Partido Liberal Nacionalista on the state and its centralized mode of operation made it the dominant, disciplined, nationwide party machine.

But in addition to this, Somoza García left another legacy affecting the opposition. During the American occupation Conservatives exhibited a tendency to factionalize around different leaders. However, the practice, as in some other traditional party systems (e.g., Colombia's), was for the factions to remain with the party label, the assumption being that reunification was an open possibility. The Somoza legacy in question was that only two parties became recognized by the law. "Only two parties can exist permanently. The party that obtains the third place in an election is automatically (legally) dissolved as is a party which decides not to take part in an election."[27]

We can interpret this characteristic in the light of the special Nicaraguan pseudo-democratic type. The ruler's wish to maintain the appearance of democracy meant that it was desirable to have some opposition participating in elections. To this effect, the legal personality of the opposition was given only to the faction that participated in elections. And since the 1950 Constitution, this faction was assured an automatic minority representation in the state (e.g., one-third of congressional seats, among other positions). In the context of the electoral manipulations, the regime sought to divide and create "pseudo-oppositions"—without the credibility of becoming the majority party in control of the state. The legacy was one of factionalizing and "buying off" oppositions, of enticing them into pacts with the government to subsequently "trick and use" them, opponents of the Somozas believed and remembered.

A consequence was the sporadic character of political activities. Public opinion surveys were not taken in the Old Regime, but a very small proportion of the population was involved in politics, and participation was subject to great fluctuations.

Large sectors of the opposition tended to abstain from contesting elections—highly competitive ones were the exception. Abstention served to denounce the illegalities of a regime that did not give change a fair chance. Demonstrations with overtones of violence were periodically staged by students, whose interest in politics is a tradition in Latin America. Interest groups occasionally engaged in public campaigns and demonstrations to lobby for, or oppose, government policy. However, "political action [was] of a sporadic and disorganized nature. The more enduring activities which require organization . . . and maintained and continuous [action] were absent, . . . save for the slightly more organized . . . activities of the [government] party."[28]

At the same time, oppositionists were allowed to own mass media organs. Political expression through the press was freer than the radio. Still, statutes gave wide powers to the government to censure, suppress, and control the media: "They are used, and abused (that is to say, even action beyond the authority given by the laws is taken) [especially] when violent demonstrations, revolts . . . take place or are about to take place and are viewed as dangerous. At this moment the use of decrees and police force suppresses from print or from the air those items defined as inciting further opposition action."[29]

Actually, the executive was given very wide constitutional powers. He could freely declare a state of siege or emergency and invoke martial law suspending civil liberties—and hence the legality of all opposition activity—and could submit the citizenry to controlled special military courts. The government had very substantial organizational capabilities to repress or facilitate opposition activity.[30]

The opposition became aware of this. During some periods there was a notion that there was not a good chance to defeat any Somoza, thus undermining the social psychological basis of protest and rebellion. There was a cyclic loss of interest in political activities, other than the limited mobilization to obtain favorable government policies for special interests. Political apathy (in addition to the effective government repression that negatively affected the sense of opportunity) resulted in an acquiescence supportive of regime maintenance. This is partly why one of the tendencies in the Old Regime was for powerless oppositions to make pacts with the government to share in a minority participation in the state. There was, however, a countertendency in the Somoza García years: periodic revolts against a ruler who thwarted democratic promises.

Rebellion and Repression

That rebellions did not progress into a successful overthrow of the government must first be understood in the light of the principle that, in general, the populace was normally committed to following habitual activities rather than employing violence to overthrow the authorities. Revolutions must go through the difficult process of breaking social inertia through innovation and learning.

Second, the discussed mechanisms of inducement and control implemented within the National Guard, which evolved into a psychology closely
identifying the interests of the institution with the Somoza family, resulted
in a military organization loyal to El Jefe. Thus any coup d'état to change
regime executed by the military alone or in coalition with civilians was not an
option. The organized civilian support provided by the Liberal Party was also
important and complementary, including its paramilitary functions.

Third, the swiftness with which Somoza García acted to repress any threatening, mobilized active opposition, quickly compressing it by invoking emergency measures (or simply in a de facto manner), impeded the growth in power
of revolutionary movements, thus blocking tendencies toward an "input over-
load" of demands and "output failure" of regime—that is, its breakdown.[31]

Notice that I have not been arguing in favor of the discredited "consensus
theory" of revolution. All large-scale contemporary societies show a lack of
consensus of values among the population, even when they do not experience
revolutions (e.g., the United States). More specifically, revolutions (visualize
Mexico in 1910, Russia in 1917, China in 1949, Cuba in 1959, Iran in 1979) consist of fights between groups seeking different forms of government. But this
dissent over regime is not sufficient. As indicated, governments can succeed
in mobilizing their own resources and repressing their opponents into defeat.

The historical record is clear: Sandino was killed to decapitate his movement; the National Guard was sent out to demonstrate its support for El Jefe,
imprison opponents, depose an unfriendly puppet president, or cow a lukewarm Congress; a state of siege and martial law was employed to impede and
dissolve opposition gatherings; the mass media was censored or banned to
control demand making and stop opposition mobilization from spiraling; the
strategy of "big lie" propaganda was used against opponents; and the university was closed to limit the opportunities for organization by those educated
youth most inclined to rebel. These measures were not taken constantly. But
there was no crisis involving public disorders or a direct threat to Somoza's
control in which the government did not show its total commitment to deflate
and conquer the opposition.

Consider an account of the ousting by Somoza García of the newly elected
president Leonardo Argüello, who wanted to retire Somoza to private life:

> At 2 a.m. on May 26, [1947] the Guardia struck. They seized . . . the Palacio
> Nacional (which housed the Congress and most government ministries) . . . and cut
> off all communications with the Presidential Palace. . . . Several Guardia officers
> loyal to Argüello were arrested, others took refuge in the Casa Presidencial.
> Somoza refrained from directly attacking the President, preferring to starve him

out if necessary. Meanwhile . . . Congress was informed that Argüello had tried to split the Guardia, murder Somoza, and dissolve Congress so that he could rule as a dictator. Coming from Somoza, the last charge sounded a bit strange, but surrounded by Guardia bayonets, the members of Congress were in no position to appreciate the irony. They did as they were told removing Argüello and installing Benjamín Lacayo Sacasa as provisional President.

Opposition political parties refused, despite repeated overtures, to cooperate with Somoza. In early September, led by [ex-President and Conservative patriarch] Emiliano Chamorro, they attempted to overthrow the government. As usual, the plans were discovered. . . . The Guardia was ready, and . . . put down the uprising with only a reported fifteen casualties. Chamorro, under the protection of the American Embassy, left for exile in Mexico, while hundreds of other opposition leaders were arrested in an impressive show of Somoza's strength. [32]

Notice that in successfully repressing the opposition, Somoza García was actually rallying support for his party. Repression can be a deterrent and de-flator of opposition activity or a source of reduced support for, and increased opposition to, the regime because of its perceived injustice. The point is well taken because in understanding why a revolution did succeed in 1979, we must look at these paradoxes and dilemmas.

The Nicaraguan system was not integrated by the rule of law. The *mandamás* and his *machos* carried out the use of naked force into the public arena to keep dominating the state. [33] It is precisely this phenomenon—the absence of constitutional rule supported by virtually all parties and the absence of a definition of the state as an institution not exclusively belonging to a ruling group—that critics alleging an absence of "national" institutions must have in mind. Nicaraguans supported their nation-state—the central issue was not secession.

Somoza García was able to rally enough domestic support from the struc-ture of power—the army, the party—to remain at the helm. A frustrated, powerless opposition became inclined to work out understandings with the caudillo. The 1947 crisis eventually culminated in the Liberal-Conservative pact and the new 1950 Constitution, which Somoza later changed to abrogate its prohibition against reelecting himself. By April 1948 the United States, which had opposed the strongman's reelection, recognized Somoza's new puppet government; several Latin American governments had already done so. [34] Subsequently the U.S. government had cordial ties with Somoza García, accommodating under the guise of "non-intervention" the style of politics repugnant to democrats that he bequeathed to his sons: to maintain power, use force; negotiate always from a position of strength; always remain on top; negotiate new "constitutions" and "elections" to continue in power; offer spoils to and pardon adversaries when you are secure.

Demands and Pacts

The dialectic between demands to end the regime and the desire to keep ruling resulted not only in rebellion but also in political pacts. A fundamental precedent was established in 1950 with the "Pacto de los Generales" of General Somoza García and General Emiliano Chamorro that produced the new constitution. It is pertinent to conclude by turning to the origins of the pact and of the constitution, for they reflect the core of Somoza García's political doctrine.

The Pacto's context was the desire of the government to stabilize its rule, while retaining the two-party tradition and avoiding the need to govern using sustained extreme force. Somoza García desired to increase the government's legitimacy after the internal turmoil and recent difficulties with the U.S. government. He also felt that he kept sufficient military force and capability to mobilize support to remain in power. There was also a perception of this situation as a reality by the principal opposition leader, General Chamorro. The opposition hoped that if it achieved an understanding with the ruler and cooperated with the government, the regime would evolve, and the opposition would be given a fair chance at winning the next election, in which neither General Somoza García nor any close relative could be a candidate.

The Pacto confirmed Somoza García as president for a new, expanded term, until 1957. An agreed upon "election" without opposition took place— notice the continued lack of institutionalization of (competitive) elections. The Congress was dissolved, and a constitutional assembly was "elected." Per the pact, it was automatically divided into a Liberal majority of forty and a Conservative minority of twenty, and it drew up the 1950 Constitution closely following the Generals' Agreement. The Assembly (presided over by senior son Luis Somoza) transformed itself into the regular Congress before ending its sessions. The principal provisions of the new constitution were a party system limited to two legal parties and a guaranteed, automatic representation for the minority party.[35] The two parties were expected to take part in the next election (February 1957) and subsequent ones; if one of the parties failed to participate in any election, it would lose its legal recognition and would be replaced by another party filing an appropriate application. The constitution barred the reelection of the president and the election of his close relatives to that post for the next election. Thus a cooperative opposition was exchanged for a chance to win the next election.

But the Pacto was broken by Somoza García, who subsequently amended the constitution in 1955 to permit his "reelection" for yet another term and to broaden the president's power to appoint substitutes to offices (such as in the Congress) in case oppositionists opted not to occupy them. Also, in conjunction with the dissolution of the pact and the subsequent campaign to "reelect" Somoza García, precedents were established to dispose of the opposition, which were implemented by both Luis and Anastasio Jr. and used after the assassination of the founder in 1956.

Awareness that the dictator intended to remain in power precipitated a crisis in interparty relations. A witness wrote:

> In April [1954,] a group of insurgents tried unsuccessfully to seize or kill President Somoza García. The group was disbanded by National Guard troops. Twenty-two of them were captured and sixteen were subsequently shot by the Guard. A state of siege was declared; President Somoza made the Conservative Party leadership responsible for the attempts; and several of the main Conservative leaders were jailed. [Emiliano] Chamorro and other members of the Congress were impeached [by the Liberal majority] and their legal immunities were taken away. They, and other Conservative leaders, were tried, deprived of their political rights and condemned to banishment in faraway villages.[36]

The government rapidly and violently controlled the opposition, both by declaring a state of siege and submitting the opposition leadership to physical control (prison, exile); such measures were a heavy blow to opposition organization and its capacity to mobilize itself against the regime. Yet the "macho politics" balance between retribution and deterrence was not genocidal—only a few were killed (supposedly directly related to the plot). Somoza García obtained the collaboration of a few Conservatives needed to reach a quorum for valid decisions in the legislature.

The 1950 Constitution had been changed to allow Somoza García freedom to remain in power. But it continued to encourage a subordinate, collaborative role among a traditional opposition led by socially "acceptable" leaders, offering them a minority share in the spoils of office. The notion of "constitutionality" was used to mean an understanding about a political order under a Somoza with the door open to "minority" representation in the state, but the Somozas were free to adhere to the constitution or change it to remain in power. These principles were deeply ingrained in the General Somoza I came to know.

Let us look at the electoral campaign, which was officially launched in 1956 and aborted with Somoza García's assassination later that year. Obviously, a guaranteed share of some public offices is insufficient for authentic, real oppositions—they seek to form the government. Neither is impending fraud acceptable to them.

The opposition formed a united umbrella organization, the Front for the Defense of the Republic (FDR).[37] It adopted a rancorous banner: Somoza was accused of being a "dictator" and a "criminal." It alleged that he was responsible for the murder of those killed in the 1954 plot. The government responded to the opposition by taking some Front leaders prisoner and deporting them without legal trial in spite of the constitutional prohibition.[38] A fair election was not going to take place.

The loosely united opposition organized a campaign to pressure Somoza García, without foreclosing the possibility of not participating in the election if he were the candidate. In June 1956 the Front issued unredeemable bonds to finance its activities and started a series of Sunday rallies. At first the meetings attracted small crowds, but by mid July they grew bigger and louder every week, until the last one in September, when the president was murdered, and opposition protest rallies ended. This was followed by emerging consternation and confusion.

The Somoza brothers' response was rapid and violent. A state of siege was declared, and there were massive arrests. The central park in Leon, where the murder had taken place, was converted into a concentration camp to hold prisoners, and about three thousand opposition politicians were arrested all over the country. Military tribunals were set up to dispose of oppositionists. Notice that these measures implemented by General Somoza Jr. were never introduced by him later, in the face of the 1978 crisis.

Until the president's shooting, opposition meetings took place; they were not entirely impeded nor dissolved by the National Guard. Yet the campaign was obstructed from progressing into full success. For example, organizers and individuals with campaign materials were periodically arrested. General Somoza Debayle mentioned to me an expression that serves to explain government strategy during his father's last campaign: "pruning." That is, you do not kill the entire tree (the opposition); you mold it so that it does not grow to overwhelm you; you limit its growth so that it remains a minority force.

In spite of the increased opposition, Somoza García did not back out of the campaign. In total defiance, and adding insult to injury, "in July he began transferring his military functions to his son Anastasio . . . by appointing him [first] Chief of the Air Force and [then Head] of the National Guard. . . . This was made necessary because the Constitution barred from the presidency those persons who were on active military duty six months before the election. Since the election was scheduled for February [1957], the appointment of Anastasio

Somoza, Jr., was made just in time to legalize his father's nomination."[39] The founder was further formalizing the dynastic-family nature of the regime at the very moment of increased opposition. General Somoza Debayle also did this at the end of my mission, promoting his son in the National Guard while rejecting a supervised electoral solution to the crisis that sealed his overthrow.

Thus Luis Somoza as head of the Congress assumed the presidency in 1956 amid a massive show of force to unambiguously constitute a *dinastía*. Neither was his hurried subsequent "election" (in February 1957) widely considered to have been free or fair. However, before this election, political prisoners had started to be released, and conversations were held with Conservatives to encourage them to participate. But Conservatives abstained on the grounds that a climate of terror still prevailed in the country. Parts of Nicaragua were still under martial law.

Illustrative of one of the patterns of opposition that remained until almost the end of the dynasty, a small sector of the Conservatives decided to make a pact with, and participate in, Luis Somoza's election for the spoils. Our source pertinently comments:

> The campaign was indeed very dull. All important opposition activities had prac-tically ceased. The Conservative [faction participating in the election] accepted beforehand the fact that it was to be a minority (with one-third representation insured). It was rumored that they received some money from the [government] to put up some posters and schedule a few meetings. The biggest one was staged . . . with no more than 300 persons in January. . . . Finally the election took place as scheduled. Very few people were seen at the polls, but the Electoral Tribunal declared Luis [Somoza] elected by a majority of [88.7 percent] of the votes . . . and a surprising 85.3 percent turnout.[40]

The "pseudo" oppositions alternated with "real" ones during the Somoza years. By the time of my mission, this history of "undignified" opposition had run its course, contributing to the obsession that I found among oppositionists against negotiating or making a pact with Somoza, lest they be perceived as selling out, in an unprincipled playing the game of the dictatorship— *hacerle el juego a la dictadura*. Nonetheless, in the mid 1950s, it had become apparent among most oppositionists that a democratic government required the retirement of the Somoza family from the political arena.

3. The Golden Years

The founder had left his own imprint on the country's political culture and structure. Not all was innovation—fraudulent elections antedated his tenure, for example. Yet Anastasio Somoza García had created a new dynastic order with new symbols and organizational patterns that survived his assassination. Power was transmitted to elder son Luis Somoza Debayle, already the president of Congress; he was backed by his brother Anastasio, the head of the National Guard. But a pure replication of the earlier Somoza García regime did not take place: now, although under the primacy of Luis, there were two Somozas, and Luis's temperament was more that of a politician than a military caudillo. Anastasio had attended West Point; Luis had graduated from Louisiana State University.

The assassination was followed by a wave of overreactive and retaliatory repression. Before the tragic murder of Pedro Joaquín Chamorro in January 1978, General Somoza Debayle still felt that the Chamorro family had been involved in a plot to kill his father—*una Chamorrada*, he called the event in our conversations. Though no proof was found, in 1956 Chamorro family members were mistreated, imprisoned, or exiled; many other Nicaraguans suffered as well.[1] General Somoza Debayle began his new career by showing how to deal with a presumed conspiracy, initiating massive repression against the opposition, including its leadership. Luis Somoza finished his father's term and was "reelected" for a second one. Power was handed over to brother Anastasio—who always retained command of the National Guard—in 1967, after elections that some observers thought were flawed.

However, the 1956–67 years (when Luis Somoza died and Anastasio II's hegemony began) were remembered by many in Nicaragua as the "golden" period of Somocista rule, because of its more "political" character when contrasted to the years of the other two Somozas, and because of its liberalizing dimensions. Starting with his inaugural address, Luis Somoza began to talk about a process of democratization:

In one of [Somoza's] press interviews he went as far as to say that his was to be a "transition government" from the strong system prevailing during his father's administrations to a future democracy. He [considered that] the conditions that had made necessary his father's "paternalistic method of government" had been slowly disappearing . . . and that, if such conditions continued . . . the Nicaraguan Government would progressively become a fully democratic one. He insisted that such process could not be carried out in a hurry . . . but that he felt confident that during his term the transition could be accomplished if only the Nicaraguan people, and particularly the opposition would cooperate. In several speeches, and at several of his bi-weekly press conferences, he continued to insist on the subject all during his administration. [2]

With Luis Somoza's ascendancy, the polity began a process of liberalization that included the development of a strong opposition movement committed to an electoral, democratic evolution. A generational change also took place in the Conservative Party, led by Fernando Agüero.

In 1963 Luis did not reelect himself. Although elected uncontested by the major opposition party, new president René Schick promised a "government by laws." His low-key administration included granting autonomy to the National University by constitutional amendment, even though it was a traditional center of opposition.

On Social Change

During these golden years a survey of socioeconomic indicators shows moderate social changes in the direction of modernization. [3] Nicaragua's population grew rapidly, thus increasing the potential demand for public services. It also became increasingly urban. Roads were improved, telephone service expanded, cheap portable transistor radios began to be seen everywhere, including in rural areas. Specialized publicity agencies proliferated as radio stations multiplied, and television service began. The per capita gross national product also grew (close to 3 percent per year), and the economy reflected relatively greater increases in the service and manufacturing sectors than agriculture—a trend of urbanization ongoing in most of Latin America. This, together with agricultural modernization, tended to increase demands in the expanded salaried working class. [4]

The polity was importantly affected by two changes in the international environment: the Cuban Revolution in 1959 and the U.S. response to it in 1961, the Alliance for Progress. With the initiation of the Fidel Castro regime, which was quite well received by many Nicaraguans, the country started to feel the pressures of the "export of revolution" from Cuba. Not only did social demands and protests occur, but there were also repeated violent uprisings to terminate the Somoza family's rule. With regard to the United States, the Somozas had to exercise caution because of the pro-democratic aspect of the alliance— notorious autocratic regimes were targeted, such as that of the Dominican leader Rafael L. Trujillo, whose 1961 demise was related to U.S. policy. The Somozas were also well known and could be placed in the category of old-fashioned strongmen, viewed in the early 1960s as dispensable by Washington. Not all U.S. initiatives to unseat "client" dictators were successful—at this time, François Duvalier in neighboring Haiti survived them, for example—but still the noted liberalizing trends of the golden years must have been reinforced by the American policy.

The Alliance for Progress undertook initiatives geared toward modernizing and strengthening the state. Nicaragua's government received guidance and aid in "institution building" in the socioeconomic sector: the formation of a planning office, the creation of a land reform institute to service the rural poor, a public housing agency, and educational reform, among others. The influence of international public agencies, both of governments (e.g., the U.S. Agency for International Development, USAID) and multinational agencies (e.g., the World Bank), in determining the policies of foreign governments has been criticized.[5] The pathetic state in which I found the educational sector suggests limited institutional modernization. But the combined economic growth and foreign financial and technical assistance resulted in a bigger, more interventionist state with a greater capacity to co-opt elements of the middle and lower class.

Both the Cuban Revolution and the Alliance for Progress contributed to the intense propaganda campaigns about the urgent need to "develop with social justice." The alliance added potency to the notion that a "revolution of rising expectations" was taking place, hence the urgent need to reform. In countries where regime breakdown materialized during those years, the United States was blamed by some for having contributed to unrealistically raised expectations and for escalating local political conflict.

The Somozas survived this "social change and mobilization,"[6] however. It could be argued ex post facto that the social changes were not large enough to result in conditions for revolution. Actually, during the Luis Somoza years there was a scarcity of popular organizations to articulate petitions on socioe-conomic matters and to pressure the regime for action—the proportion and numbers demanding policy from the authorities was quite small, though some protests took place. To explore this constraint, an exceptional opinion survey was conducted in one of Nicaragua's largest cities.[7]

What were the cultural bases of the low levels of socioeconomic demands? It was not an ideological disposition against government intervention in the economy—a very large majority did not support a laissez-faire philosophy. The "culture of poverty" (i.e., the awareness of poverty directly affecting the subject or his or her immediate environment) was associated with notions that the government should do something about it and side with the propertyless. Nor was public opinion happy with government social services. The majority did not feel that the government was benefiting them—the Somocista political machine did not touch everybody. The theoretical norms were not total passivity or acquiescence: the public felt that the media should broadcast complaints about the responsiveness and behavior of government officials, and most reported their willingness to initiate action to obtain better services.

Nonetheless, a radically different picture emerged with regard to actual demands: a large majority of those who had reported a readiness to act said they had not done so. Contacts with public agencies usually were not to complain about unfulfilled rights—rather most people appeared to be more "subject" members of the polity than active "participant" citizens; their most frequent contact with public offices was to receive widely publicized free services. Although class and education affected the individual's demand making, the conclusion for the low volume of collective action in the area of socioeconomic need was that most of the people dismissed it on customary grounds. There was a belief that they would not get any attention from the government, that there was no use in complaining because public officials would not respond to their petitions. That a few years later Nicaragua would experience a revolution with mass collective political participation in overthrowing a government is indicative of the limitations of cultural deterministic interpretations—crucial attitudes and people's expectations about the possibilities of achieving collective goals can change. However, it seems that given the conditions prevailing during the golden period, cultural and structural constraints inhibited demand making, and passivity—depoliticized inertia—was a mechanism of authoritarian regime maintenance.[8] Frustration vis-à-vis an inadequate government in the face of feelings of powerlessness can result in giving up demands rather than rebellion.

This low organizational condition notwithstanding, an incipient labor movement developed, and some urban and rural lower-class demands and protests occurred that involved the government on several counts. Above all, the chronic absence of a broad support for the regime was translated into a feeling by government that it had to be very careful of any escalation of conflict into public disorders, which could be capitalized on by an opposition seeking to replace the regime. Revolts attempting to overthrow the government periodically took place, including calls for a popular uprising and a general strike. The regime's nature per se made it susceptible to destabilization by protest-producing socioeconomic changes.

I should conclude that during the Luis Somoza period, the balance of the Alliance for Progress programs were positive for a regime promising evolutionary democratization. Real tangible accomplishments aside, the alliance contributed to a climate of "rhetorical reformism" in social matters, which gave élan to the ruling group. New socioeconomic government programs were initiated, and the governmental sector expanded with considerable increases in the national budget. Although the Somocista machine did not benefit everybody, the expansion of the public sector contributed to augment its dynamism. Not only did this contribute to increased regime morale, but occasionally Alliance for Progress projects could serve to defuse social class conflict issues.[9]

Economic Demands and Protests

The rural areas around Leon and Chinandega had experienced agricultural development with new cotton plantations. Their peasantry generally made only sporadic demands for better salaries and working conditions that might take the form of spontaneous protests and walkouts. However, in the late 1950s, members of the "Indian Community" of Subtiaba in Leon started to cut fences during the night; the idea was subsequently adopted by the Campuzano people of nearby Chinandega.

Subtiaba is a semi-rural borough of Leon, which is still referred to as an Indian community, although its inhabitants could be considered mestizos, individuals with the language and dress of the national community. In a not unusual pattern for Hispanic America, after independence a regime of "liberal reform" legally dissolved the community, transforming land ownership from communal into private individual property. The background leading to the protests involved issues of private property. After the liberal reform, "most of the land ceased to be in Subtiaba hands either because the [private] owners moved from [it] when they were successful or because they sold out when they were not. Besides, the progressive extension of the use of barbed wire fences in the farms had slowly been closing off to the inhabitants of Subtiaba, who are located about ten miles from the sea, access to the fishing places [and] mangrove wood."[10] The result: the Subtiabans began cutting fences, to the alarm of landowners and better-off sectors.

Let us look at the government's handling of these violations of property to illustrate the regime's mode of successfully handling disturbances caused by socioeconomic problems. The reaction was a combination of conciliation and firmness. First, the government stated that roads that had been recently closed by landlord fencing would be opened by the army, and the properties measured by experts to determine any illegal acquisition or expansion of properties; President Luis Somoza also promised to give the Subtiaba community farming and fishing equipment to assist its members. This was deemed insufficient, however, by local leaders who declared that what they really needed was land. Dramatizing their needs, about 250 community members entered a local hacienda and took possession of substantial land in it. The government's conciliation-firmness strategy was to have the army evict the land invasion, but the president promised that he would solve the land problem in time. The incipient labor movement joined the land tenure politics: the General Confederation of Labor expressed its support for the peasants through the media and included land reform as one of the petitions made to the president on Labor Day (May 1, 1959).[11] Again, Luis Somoza promised that land would be distributed.

On June 2 another occupation took place in a second hacienda. The government's reaction was not to immediately evict the land invaders, for it was involved in the priority problem of subduing an attempted armed uprising. Nonetheless, the following year, after the harvest had been collected, the army evicted the peasants. Several of them were arrested and later released after negotiations. At the same time, the government started to measure farms to determine property rights, and the president reiterated his intention to solve the landless problem. By May 1960, preventive measures were taken to impede the occupation of more farms, with the army patrolling the Subtiaba and Campuzano areas; yet the government also announced that it would buy land and distribute it to people in the region. During 1961 about three hundred titles were delivered to poor campesinos, including community leaders. In April 1963, the Agrarian Reform Law and its National Agrarian Institute were formally established, and by the end of the period under study, 604 area families had been given land titles. The forceful protests and demands for land stopped being a public issue. The government had used force and negotiations, and claimed that it had begun land reform measures (the need for which was widely held in Nicaragua during those years) to show that the Luis Somoza regime had a "reformist" identity.

An important area to understand specific economic grievances or aspirations and the government's handling of them is labor union activity. Although not well developed, labor unions were permanent working-class organizations, which could pose serious challenges.[12] During the golden years there were only a few active unions, largely in Managua and Corinto, the principal port. As is often the case in Latin America, labor was politicized. (There were three labor federations: one associated with the Somozas, the others Marxist and Social Christian.) General interpretations of these political links of labor are the relative oversupply of manpower and consequent low income and worker replaceability. The lack of a strong tradition with organization and lower-class education make it difficult to organize labor. Workers are highly dependent on better-off sectors to organize and successfully negotiate. Political parties, in and out of government, can have ideological (e.g., the commitment of Marxists to the working class) and pragmatic (e.g., the organization of grassroots support) reasons to be linked to labor unions.

These factors operated in Nicaragua. The links between a part of labor and the Somoza regime notwithstanding, labor was not purely a mouthpiece of the government. With the increased liberalization that took place during the golden years, the yearly Labor Day parades visibly grew with the attendance of opposition-linked unions as well. Since 1959, Luis Somoza had promised that he would try to meet some of the demands presented by the three major federations. However, as an indication of the government's class preference— its "populism" was quite limited—this attempt had stalled. Now, in the face of these pressures, the government adopted a strategy of measured concessions intended to show both flexibility and strength. On May 1, 1962, the president informed the public that a Labor Code reform bill was ready to be sent to the Congress. It was enacted in 1963. A minimum salary was established, and the Agrarian Reform Law was enacted. Although these reforms in practice were not that significant, they exemplify the reformist politics of the period.

Let us focus on the strikes or *paros* (work stoppages) of employees and workers. A clear tendency was for them to escalate into political events, to pressure the government into intervening and making direct concessions to the workers, or having the government force the private sector to accept demands. Of necessity, the government had to be compelled to make concessions when the issue was salaries and working conditions of its own employees.

Public school teachers had been organizing for some time, and in 1959 several groups had formed the Federation of Nicaraguan Teachers Unions; salaries were low, from $514 to $1,285 a year. In 1961 there were protests because salaries were not increased in the new budget. The following year, a broad movement (Operación Justicia) was organized to obtain salary increases. The operation successfully gained manifestations of solidarity from other unions, the mass media, student organizations, and even political parties. The issue became a national political problem involving partisan politics.

Faced with the potential disruption caused by the mobilization of protests and solidarity strikes (*paros*), marches, and demonstrations from various sectors—that is, its becoming a national political anti-government protest— the movement was declared illegal, and the mass media was ordered silenced.

To paraphrase Charles Tilly, costs were raised by declaring the stoppage illegal: threats now involved losing jobs; repressing the media was intended to reduce the opportunity to mobilize solidarity support, decreasing the movement's power.

On June 22, 1962, a test *paro* of twenty-four hours was declared by the teachers. Some rural schools did not join because they had not yet learned about it, given the censorship. However, the federation decided to indefinitely extend the stoppage. By June 24, the entire public school system was paralyzed, and the movement started to expand to the private school sector, whose teachers began supporting solidarity *paros*. The government yielded: the federation's leaders met with the president, and a minimum guaranteed salary of slightly over $1,000 was offered. The strike ended.

Not all strikes were that successful. In some cases no concessions were made to workers, who had not organized a nationwide mobilization scheme with broad political support along the teachers' lines. In 1962, the year of the teacher strikes, port workers went on strike. As before, the president intervened in the "illegal" strike, but this time the National Guard was sent to patrol the port, and after about a week, the workers returned to work with few gains.

After 1963, as threats of revolutionary political violence decreased, the government dealt more forcefully with strikes, more frequently using the military and jailing leaders temporarily without making concessions. But the tradition in the weakly legitimated regime was for the government to be involved in resolving events unsettling the daily routine of the people; collective protests were considered to be potentially far too threatening not to be quickly handled and resolved by government.

There were areas of tension between the government and the nation's traditionally established vested interests; the interests of the Catholic Church, for example, were not identical to the government's. "Liberal," anti-clerical ideology had resulted in the separation of church and state and a prohibition of religious instruction in public schools, which after a Catholic Church campaign was abrogated during this period. Despite the government's bias against labor union activism, the business elite did not perceive itself in perfect identity with the Somoza family. There were moneyed Conservative families, not only those identifying with the official Liberal Party.

There were protests and threats from business, as well as the middle class and other sectors that were also affected by new taxes. Typical arguments against them were the projected damage to the economy, including the adverse effects on employees and employment; and in the face of the regime's patrimoniality, there were allegations that the new resources would be mismanaged, and that adequate public services would not be forthcoming. Role theory predicts areas of conflict between the ruler and the moneyed. General Somoza often reminded me: "The rich here don't realize that there are other interests than theirs."

Despite the easy access of the "better sort" of people to the Presidential Palace—Nicaragua was a small-scale society with an interrelated network of family and friendship ties among its elite—there were economic issues that the business class felt it needed to address through collective public mobilization, including the use of direct action, such as marches, ad hoc assemblies, and threats of general stoppages. Similarly, there were occasions when the government felt that it had to deal with the protests of business by silencing media news, declaring demonstrations illegal, and so forth. The business class not only mobilized itself to obtain changes in policies altering the preexisting economic balance with the government but also to obtain benefits such as subsidies and payment moratoriums in the face of sectorial economic crises.

In short, the expected symbiotic relationship between the rulers and the nation's vested interests was subject to disequilibrium. The government resorted to strategies of negotiation, compromise, and coercion, which also tended to involve the president himself and were subject to variation according to circumstances. The regime's objective was to pacify the elites into continued acceptance of its rulership, which could entail reversing policy or compromising. In some instances, for example, the establishment of a new tax was abandoned, whereas in others a revised compromise rate resulted from negotiations.

In sum, during this period, although there was not a high density of social class interests groups, and especially lower-class organizations were weak, there still was lively input making in areas of economic demands that the government had to address. However, an important central tendency was to transform economic demands into protests against the rulers. As such, the regime faced truly political processes that could become quite sensitive. This inclination to politicize demands was manifested in the tendency to rally support from other sectors, and to employ direct action. Formal petitions could be reinforced by propaganda campaigns in the media involving a variety of groups, political parties included, even if the issue was an increase in salaries. Demands were also strengthened by the collection of signatures; assemblies, marches, demonstrations; solidarity strikes; and more violent acts. These tactics sought to show the broad support that one had and to impress upon the authorities the likely dangers in terms of both loss in support and in increased opposition. If favorable outputs from government were not forthcoming, a potential scenario was that a disorderly nationwide protest movement against the regime itself might progress.

A corollary government strategy resulting from the more or less explicit assumption that the regime was not adequately or broadly supported was to employ control mechanisms to suppress or reduce the flow of demands so that they would not escalate into major disorders. Throughout these processes there was an underlying notion of a worst possible scenario for the rulers, that an armed rebellion would be linked to protests and strikes. Although the army never overthrew the Somozas, there was a deliberate policy to assure its loyalty, and occasionally personnel purges took place—indeed, the possibility of losing National Guard support was a real worry for the rulers, upon which they continued to act during this period.

The government used a carrot-and-stick approach. Its methods included warnings to those involved in certain demands; injunctions to the mass media prohibiting the coverage of news related to demands in order to avoid the continuation and extension of unrest and opposition mobilization in other areas; the declaration of the illegality of strikes, paros, and other forms of direct action; the arrest and prosecution of individuals involved in demands; the use of pro-regime agitprop or paramilitary organizations to fight, intimidate, and suppress meetings or demonstrations of opponents; the employment of the National Guard to forcefully break up demonstrations and meetings and to control outbursts of violence.

Yet, at the same time, the government did not close the door to negotiation and compromise, meeting some demands (even if partially so) to show "reasonableness" and "fairness" and thus maintain support. Usually the authorities held talks with representatives of the groups; repressive measures were adopted, but the president often sought to show flexibility or responsiveness. This could take the form of promising to take certain measures such as enacting new legislation to meet demands, postponing the undesirable government acts being opposed, or accepting the demands in various degrees.

The government tended to satisfy economic demands more when they appeared to have broad national support and when they seemed sustained by well-established organizations. The government showed flexibility as well when it was confronted with more pressing problems for regime maintenance, as in the face of invasion by an émigré revolutionary force. Conversely, when the government was less fearful of an additional loss of support, the rulers were inclined to more freely use their political space—a pattern of suppressing demands, especially those of working-class entities, thus demonstrating ideological preferences and the "principle of authority." At the same time, the government wished to project another side, that although being "the boss," it was nevertheless willing ("paternalistically") to discuss issues with the affected interests. Finally, the government resisted and *never accepted* some demands that it deemed to be of paramount direct political importance to regime maintenance, such as relinquishing family control over the National Guard and allowing the international supervision of elections or the development of an adequate, nationally run administrative apparatus so that elections would be free.

Although General Somoza Debayle was familiar firsthand with these outlined measures of control, after September 1977 he would not adequately draw from this repertoire, which proved most damaging to his survival. Also, after January 1978 all the key actors generally *refused* to directly negotiate with the president.

Violent Inputs to Overthrow the Regime

We are left with a vital area: demands—that is, collective action, both armed and unarmed, violent and peaceful—to replace the regime. From its inception, the Somoza rulership was subject to considerable recurrent stress because it was not legitimized by tradition or by widespread adherence to a constitution. The Somozas periodically had to prove their leadership, and this often entailed the use of force against those seeking to replace them in office; conversely, the unwillingness of the rulers to be replaced resulted in a tendency within the opposition to employ illegalities and violence to terminate Somoza governance.

Technically, low regime differentiation resulted in a tendency to equate changes in the authorities—the incumbents—with the need to change the regime itself, that is, change the form of government, the basic operating political constitution.[13] In contrast to an institutionalized and stable democracy, where changes in the authorities or the ruling party do not entail a change in the form of government (e.g., usually the change from Democratic to Republican administrations in the United States), this differentiation was absent in Nicaragua. For one, the basic unwritten but operative de facto constitutional rule that National Guard control remain with the Somoza family would have to be changed if a new party came into office. Thus the change in authorities entailed basic normative constitutional change. This is not an idle incursion into the sociology of law: it shows crucial adjustments that had to be worked out to end Somoza rule or for the peaceful evolution of the regime into a democracy. But such changes can be made if the rulers have the political will to accept the opposition's election by the people.

In Nicaragua, "real" oppositions—unarmed or armed groups credibly pursuing control of the state or to form their own government—sought to change the regime, which escalated the conflict. It tended to ideologize into a struggle between "dictatorship" and "democracy" and undermined the constitutional integration of the polity necessary for peaceful, relatively orderly, competitive politics.[14] In the absence of a broad support for the basic constitutional rules, the tendency was toward recurrent states of normlessness and crisis.

Oppositions had not found environmental conditions to organize and mobilize into powerful movements, either electoral or revolutionary. It took some time for the opposition to "awake" from the consequences of Somoza García's shooting, and it only gradually reactivated actions. It is not surprising that as the opposition started to move into the open under Luis Somoza, demands initially centered on obtaining freedom for political prisoners and the return of exiles. The mass media was first to criticize with the gradual increased "normalization" or liberalization after the February 1957 elections; relatively greater freedom of written and oral expression than of other political activities was a trait of the Old Regime.

Armed Actions

Before the initiation of Fidel Castro's regime, some subversive activities took place in Nicaragua, as well as invasions of émigrés from Costa Rica and Honduras. But the success of the Cuban Revolution added impetus to the spirit of rebellion, both as an example and because of its support. Immediately after Castro's triumph, in May 1959, 114 rebels disembarked in Olama and in Mollejones (in the departments of Matagalpa and Chontales) by plane from a well-known training camp in Costa Rica; a general strike was planned to trigger a revolutionary uprising. Among the revolutionaries were Pedro Joaquín Chamorro; Tomás Borge, later one of the nine Sandinista Comandantes to rule Nicaragua; and Carlos Fonseca Amador, the founder and spiritual leader of the Frente Sandinista de Liberación Nacional (FSLN), who was killed in November 1976. Illustrative of the different background of the rebels, although some came from prominent families with an anti-Somoza tradition, Fonseca was an illegitimate son whose father worked for Somoza.[15] In his case you can observe the possible impact of "inconsistencies" in social standing or status—an early fashionable hypothesis of American sociologists—in the rebellion.

These operations ended in failure. The rebels were apprehended, a few killed, and their units disbanded by the Nicaraguan National Guard. Civil strife continued, including sporadic terrorist acts, student demonstrations, and a university strike to protest government repression and killings. Other smaller-scale, foreign-based incursions into Nicaragua were planned or carried out. But once again the groups were captured, disbanded, and dissolved by the National Guard or the police forces of the host countries.

Nicaragua's borders were never totally secure, which helps explain later developments during my tenure. Even when cooperative, Nicaragua's neighbors adhered to a policy of providing political asylum and did not generally hold their Nicaraguan revolutionary visitors under tight control. Thus, again in November 1960 two armed groups from Honduras and Costa Rica planned to enter Nicaragua in coordination with a national uprising. The National Guard units of Diriamba and Jinotepe were attacked. However, because of the collaboration of the Honduran Army and the Costa Rican Civil Guard, the émigré groups were unsuccessful in their invasion plans, and the Nicaraguan government quickly reestablished full control.

This was the last important uprising to take place until 1967, closing the period under inspection in this chapter. Although the Sandinista movement was founded in 1961, for a long time its activities did not go beyond low-level, sporadic acts of violence. Until 1977, the FSLN subsisted in the relative isolation of the rural *foco* strategy and the low urban profile of its activities; only exceptionally did it engage in spectacular events such as hostage taking. [16]

The Cuban Revolution (Cuba was then socioeconomically much more developed than Nicaragua) and internal regime contradictions, more prominently than any conspicuous disruptions caused by very rapid socioeconomic change, had helped to escalate political action against a weakly legitimated government. An increasing number of politically deprived citizens, including young members of the social elite not belonging to government circles, had felt that revolution was possible: this model and a perceived increased chance of success was an engine of revolutionary action. [17] But the revolutionaries were incapable of mobilizing large numbers of people into armed revolt or of sustaining a rebellion by generating recurrent, increasingly large-scale collective action.

Government Control of Violent Opposition

Regardless of the map of expectations held by the population from the late 1950s, crucial to the avoidance of regime breakdown before the late 1970s were the responses by government to violent revolutionary inputs. The nature of the demands of the revolutionaries was such that to survive the regime simply could not satisfy them by dismantling itself; the government had to respond by suppressing these demands, reducing their flow, controlling them. If they could not be preempted entirely, revolutionary collective outbursts had to be isolated, reduced, minimized. To keep risks tolerable, the optimal objective was to apprehend and control the actors and to dissolve their organization in order to impede any possible sustained mobilization of large numbers of participants, actively demanding regime termination. Indeed, to survive, in principle, the regime must place itself between a point of optimal equilibrium in which collective action to terminate it is totally absent (or nearly so) and a point in which the insurgency has developed a critical mass, the crossing of which would dramatically increase the probability of, or result in, regime collapse. I should note that unstable regimes having the compliance of their armed forces need not experience revolutionary collapse or breakdown, even in the face of serious crises and substantial violence—illustrative is the post-1958 period of civilian rule in Colombia beyond the twentieth century. Revolutionary movements must not be capable of developing substantial popular support and mobilization to defeat the regime.

The Somoza brothers successfully impeded the growth of revolutionary actions beyond the Olama and Mollejones and the Diriamba and Jinotepe events; after the latter the opposition's violent strategy dramatically contracted and became relatively unimportant.

What were the government's policies that resulted in the control of armed opposition by the early 1960s? Their axes were the absence of a broad agreement on regime and also the lack of a totalitarian intent by government that would preclude the existence of any politically independent, intermediary groups between the individual and the state. [18]

At the outset we introduced the notion that during these "golden years" the Somozas followed a strategy of promising liberalization-democratization combined with responses to quell the escalation of demands. Tools were also used to bolster support for the rulers in the international arena. The challenge posed by John F. Kennedy's (1961–63) pro-democratic Alliance for Progress was met by Nicaraguan participation in the Bay of Pigs invasion. Nicaragua also collaborated with Lyndon B. Johnson's military action in the Dominican Republic in 1965. During this time Nicaragua also followed policies to neutralize the export of revolution from its neighbors. Luis Somoza settled the border dispute with Honduras, accepting the 1960 International Court of Justice decision against Nicaragua. Similarly, with the backing of the United States during these years, more cooperative ties developed with Costa Rica, especially after the 1959 Olama and Mollejones events.

These political-diplomatic initiatives did not suffice. The rulers were clear that they needed a military component to their strategy. Top priority was given to quickly quell the rebellions through the marshaling and application of military force, while implementing personnel policies to maintain a loyal National Guard. Among other post-1956 practices: limiting the level of foreign military training to avoid potential rivals within the Guard; sending abroad military officers on diplomatic missions; providing employment in Somoza family private enterprise to individuals deemed "better" in nonmilitary occupations; implementation of mandatory retirement of officers; and court-martial of officers on charges of conspiring against regime.

Of particular importance are the ways that were used to control the violent opposition, which principally consisted of armed invasions by exiles, the formation of armed groups to attack military *cuarteles* and take over cities and towns, calls for general strikes and stoppages, disruptive demonstrations of protest in cities, terrorist acts, and attempts to develop National Guard conspiracies.[19]

I report only government-opposition tactical interaction around the two principal rebellions, Olama and Mollejones (1959) and Diriamba and Jinotepe (1960).[20] I faithfully, though freely, edit Mariano Fiallos's descriptions made public a decade before my mission, when the Somozas still successfully maintained themselves in power and controlled the polity, and no one foresaw the 1979 regime collapse.

Immediately after the fall of Batista, the Nicaraguan government began to take precautions in view of the increasing rumors of invasions. Two days after the victory in Cuba, scattered protest demonstrations took place and were dissolved by the Nicaraguan National Guard. The president sought to intimidate the opposition, warning that in case of a revolt drastic repressive measures would be taken. Several preventive detentions, interrogations, and searches for arms were carried out. By mid March 1959, the physical pressures on the opposition intensified, and to escape from possible arrest or other physical harm measures, several oppositionists took asylum in foreign embassies.

To unmistakenly show that the government would fight opposition direct action, the Frente Populares Somocistas, the regime's paramilitary groups, were activated to intimidate and contract opposition activity. (These actions were stopped following protests in the media, at this time not under total government control.) During the following month, government repressive actions continued: the president restated his threats, and several more people were arrested, individuals interrogated, and homes searched.

The opposition continued, however, its plans of coordinating an invasion with a general strike. In May 1959 the president held meetings with the General Confederation of Labor and reportedly promised that the government would take pro-labor measures if the workers did not participate in a general strike. On May 31 a state of siege was declared, and martial law was imposed. The right of assembly was suspended, the media fell under tight government control, and all political prisoners were subsequently tried by military courts.

On June 1 the Olama and Mollejones invasion and work stoppage were in effect. Prominent upper-class business leaders who defiantly met in Managua's Chamber of Commerce building to support the stoppage were arrested; those who did not open their stores had their licenses canceled. In addition to severe censorship, three opposition newspapers, including P.J. Chamorro's *La Prensa*, were closed. On the rural invasion front, the National Guard was mobilized to locate, surround, and capture the rebels who had landed in the Olama and

Mollejones areas. In a few days practically all the rebels were captured (two were killed). They were convicted by a military court in December. With the cooperation of the Honduran Army, the rebels were dispersed.

In addition, the military were kept busy in the principal cities and towns, patrolling the streets, dissolving demonstrations, enforcing media censorship, and implementing the travel restrictions and curfews that had been imposed. Luis Somoza wanted to negotiate.[21] However, the data show a consistent government policy to impede the spiraling physical acts by the opposition. In sharp contrast to my period, in 1959 the government captured the nucleus of armed oppositionists—the acting revolutionary leaders—and those defiantly engaged in the stoppage, including prominent businessmen; thus the government obtained physical control of its principal challengers. Also, state-of-siege measures were maintained until the plan and activities to overthrow the government were under control.

Nevertheless, by mid-1960 there were violent demonstrations once again, and terrorist explosions and rumors of conspiracies to terminate the regime were spreading. In November the large towns of Diriamba and Jinotepe were captured by rebels who overran their *cuarteles*. Martial law was reinstated, and the National Guard was mobilized: some five hundred men with heavy artillery and tanks recaptured the cities. Also, with international cooperation invasions of émigré groups were stopped, and most importantly, the rebels who took over the two towns eventually surrendered and were placed under military jurisdiction. In contrast, during my mission, there was a very substantial international support for the revolt, and General Somoza Debayle followed a different policy.

For a start, in 1978 the government was suddenly faced with a much greater number of individuals demonstrating against it in the streets. Second, the government (partially receptive to American pressures) did not invoke martial law for quite some time and allowed the mass media to maintain a climate of agitation for insurrection, which contributed to recruiting more and more rebels. The National Guard was deliberately ordered not to dissolve many demonstrations, allowing training in street protests for many new activists who would play a crucial supportive role in the spiraling rebellion.

In short, the same General Somoza who as head of the army had acquired vast experience in conquering opposition action explicitly allowed the development of various insurgent activities under the premise of avoiding a break with Washington and the belief that the opposition would have to come to terms with him. Whereas during the Luis Somoza years not only were revolutionaries dispersed, but leaders were captured as well; this did not take place during my time, when few leaders were captured, few rebel entities were destroyed by the government, and many groups involved in physical opposition self-dispersed to regroup again later, rather than being captured and dissolved by the government. And then, in 1978–79, the dynasty also faced much greater domestic opposition and a different international situation—the moderate opposition of the U.S. administration, and the Venezuela-Panama-Costa Rica plus Cuba axis supportive of Somoza's overthrow.

It should not come as a surprise that the successful revolution can be partly traced to the inadequate methods of control followed by the government. This must also be included in any explanation, not only the more widely reported tragic and cruel human events that were substantially the historical responsibility of General Somoza Debayle. It is nonetheless sadly ironic that a man who viewed himself as a realistic fighter—he once told me that Luis wanted to give up power in one of these crises because he thought everything was lost—would in the end be the victim of his psychological inclinations, political mentality, and misjudgments, despite his early and long successful experience with political-military control.

The Electoral Route

By the end of 1960 the regime's success in overcoming revolutionary uprisings, combined with its promises of democratization, resulted in a change in the definition of the situation: the opposition elite, concretely the Conservative Party, was willing to act as a legal opposition and organize itself to explore the electoral route for the 1963 elections. A token miniscule "official" opposition—a pseudo one—had collaborated with the government for a small share of patronage. But a larger Conservative Party, potentially capable of mobilizing under its traditional label a mass following by an energetic leadership, especially some caudillo, was basically dormant, "disorganized." A few new groups had materialized, led by men without a proven capability to develop a substantial following and lacking the traditional party labels with broad recognition, but mostly these were coteries that did not seem to do much more than meet in the leader's living room—thus Luis Somoza's expression "sofa parties," still used during my time.

The adoption of the electoral route by a real opposition—one credibly seeking to end the dynasty—was not easy. The memory of the breaking of the 1950 interparty pact to reelect Somoza García was recent enough. Luis Somoza's promise to establish a "fully democratic" regime might be a ploy to obtain broader support and contract opposition violence. We are dealing with a politics with a heavy dose of ambiguity and deceit, but not without hope.

Despite the uncertainties a new, younger, perhaps more credible generation was in charge of the Liberal Party. In mid-1960 the Conservative Party began reorganizing, with the selection of Fernando Agüero as its new president. Years later, the vigorous and charismatic Dr. Agüero would explain to me that the Conservative change to his younger group took place without any major crisis or conflict, as the natural process of the aging of the old guard, leaders who had ruled Nicaragua before 1930. Dr. Agüero added that violence was proving unsuccessful: the Somoza brothers should be given a chance to be democrats.

The reinvigorization of the Conservative Party as a legal, electoral alternative until the end of this period contributed to the isolation of the remaining violent groups. (Remember, although the Sandinista [FSLN] movement was formed in 1961, at the beginning of my mission it still had few activists and was dismissed as an unviable alternative by many influential observers.) Thus, during the golden years the regime's survival resulted not only from its noted successful repressive component but also from the channeling of political energy into peaceful means, encouraged by a liberalization related to a democratization promise. This expanded the basis for a consensual, legal, competitive politics with increased political pluralism.

The final abortion of this process in 1967 and subsequent events served to virtually close the doors to an electoral solution during my tenure. Although history is not entirely predetermined, it is affected and limited by precedents (José Ortega y Gasset's "man's circumstance"). It is in this light that many Nicaraguans told me it was tragic that our peaceful reformist diplomacy had not taken place earlier, during Luis Somoza's period of democratic promise and the opposition's commitment to elections.

The preparation for the 1963 election faced problems. First was the concern that fair elections would take place; there were also divisions within the unarmed opposition. From the outset Agüero started to demand that the coming elections be held with a (not precisely specified) presence of the Organization of American States as a way of securing impartiality. Nicaragua still had not developed authentic electoral institutions.

Truly remarkable was the poverty of the intellectual debate. The central conflicting issue expressed by the key political elites was not in the nature of different ideologies of modernization. The case was not that the ruling group conservatively opposed extending the vote to the working people on grounds that it would endanger the system of property or would result in the tyranny of the majority, as when European social democracy was developing.[22] Rather the cleavage was because a principal political sector of the upper class (not manning the state) felt that the Liberals were pseudo-democrats. The government did not take elections seriously.

Consider that our conceptualization of international "clientelistic" politics is applicable to this case with its continuing psychological *dependencia*
on foreigners: unarmed oppositionists were seeking the involvement of international actors to assist in solving the otherwise "domestic" or "internal"
political issue of counting votes. (This issue of OAS involvement in supervising
an election was a stumbling block in peacefully solving the crisis in late 1978
to abort the costly revolution. Later events, however, showed that rulers can
engage in electoral fraud in the presence of international observers—for example, Ferdinand Marcos, Philippines, 1986; General Manuel Antonio Noriega,
Panama, 1989; Alberto Fujimori, Peru, 2000.)

Inextricably linked to the lack of confidence that the government would
comply with the legality of competitive politics, the process of mobilizing
support by Fernando Agüero became increasingly conflictive, thus pointing
to the difficulties of institutionalizing "loyal" real oppositions in pseudo-
democracies. An observer wrote:

> [The opposition meetings] were resumed in May 1961 and became more and more
> violent in their demands. Agüero said that if the OAS presence was not requested by
> the government his party would not take part in the elections. He said that he was
> convinced that this would result in national tragedy of unforeseeable consequences.
> On June 14, the situation had become so tense that the [Catholic] Church hierarchy,
> through the Archbishop of Managua made public its preoccupation that if the
> electoral problem was not solved with an understanding a Cuban-type Communist
> takeover could take place. . . . Such an understanding would have been a resort
> to the [past] formula of bipartisan agreement. . . . The Archbishop offered his
> mediation to put Agüero and [Luis] Somoza in contact. The mediation was accepted
> by both parties and a meeting was arranged in the Vatican [ambassador's] residence.
> During the meeting Agüero demanded the technical assistance of the [OAS] and
> Somoza refused. No agreement was reached.[23]

Nonetheless, Agüero continued the tactic of organizing weekly demonstrations throughout the country to gain and show the opposition's popular
support and to pressure the government to conduct real elections "supervised"
by the OAS. By 1962 the youthful Conservative movement had gained momentum with truly huge rallies in the largest cities, and in April Agüero went to
Washington to explore the possibility of OAS assistance for the 1963 contest.
His return on July 15 was a great success; a gigantic demonstration received
him.

Not all was favorable. Other opposition factions activated themselves behind a platform that excluded international supervision or observation. However, the meetings of factions other than Agüero's Conservatives were small;

they never reached the same popularity, and Agüero was left as the leader of the "real" opposition.

More important were the actions of the government—was it really an "enlightened" administration committed to constituting a democratic republic? The ruling Liberals started their reactivation at the end of 1961. The party launched a campaign to inscribe new partisans, the process culminating in the 1962 convention that proclaimed René Schick Gutiérrez their presidential candidate.

My understanding of Schick is of a loyal, reliable administrator for the Somozas. But consider the 1962 constitutional reforms adopted by the Congress, which were billed as the mechanism to implement Luis Somoza's promises of democratization, the electoral process included. Among the reforms were the following: (1) Now that a Somoza would not be president, there was a reduction of the term to four years, thus undercutting Schick, who could not be reelected. (2) The legal recognition of only the two largest parties after the election was retained, but the number of signatures needed to be recognized as a party prior to the election was reduced. This meant that it was easier for smaller dissidences to form, be recognized as a party, and participate in the 1963 elections. Thus opposition factionalism was deliberately encouraged to increase the chances of electoral participation by weak groups more susceptible to manipulation. (3) Several parties were allowed to participate in the election. The allocation of seats in the Congress and pertinent bodies was through proportional representation, and a minimum representation of one-third was guaranteed to all opposition groups taken together. Thus, opposition factionalism was again encouraged by providing posts to smaller groups. (4) Vitally, the ruling party retained control of the Electoral Tribunal, and the opposition's minority share was divided between the party second in the previous election and the one that obtained the most signatures in the current application for legal recognition.

In sum, the Somozas retained majority control of the electoral machinery (and total control of the army) and deliberately acted to divide the opposition. The government was unwilling to accept an international presence in the election, to implement the changes in the registration and system of balloting sought by oppositionists, to purify the lists of voters, and to obtain more reliable elections than in the past. The government was unshakable in the points that counted for continued family rule. Unwilling to dismantle the pseudo-democracy, it would not compromise and, for instance, seek international technical assistance to "modernize" elections. Such assistance was welcomed only in areas of "development" that could strengthen the regime's machine. Thus the Somozas' "nationalism" in refusing only foreign electoral inputs was suspect. It was another case of the unwillingness to surrender power to the "out" elite, while rewarding collaborationists willing to participate in the regime's "democratic" charade—the old Somoza doctrine of hegemonic, patrimonial rule without really a new wrapping.

For the opposition, 1963 was not their finest hour. The government's support and machine were alive. The Somocistas might not have won a majority in a free election, but they were certainly a force to contend with—consider the large demonstrations that they organized in January 1963. The government's campaign strategy was to promise concessions, such as reforms granting autonomy to the university and religious education in public schools to please influential publics in selected areas, but to make no concessions in areas immediately linked to retaining control over the state. The bulk of the opposition behind Dr. Agüero abstained from participating in an election deemed rigged beforehand. But there was a small Conservative group willing to participate in them—Diego Manuel Chamorro ran against Schick, pretending that "authentic" elections had taken place. He obtained 9.5 percent of the vote and was subsequently appointed to the Supreme Court for his services. Through its abstention, the real opposition, unarmed and unprepared to revolt, lost momentum. Protests were minuscule on election day.

Agüero did not abandon the search for peaceful evolution. However, what had been only a rumor—that General Somoza, who remained the head of the National Guard, would be the next candidate of the Liberals—now was much closer to reality. Already in 1963 campaign signs began to appear in support of General Somoza. He acted like a candidate, visiting towns throughout the nation. In late 1965 Luis, the party's senior statesman, formally asked brother "Tacho" (General Somoza's nickname) to accept the candidacy; ominously, the conversations between Luis Somoza and Fernando Agüero on electoral reform broke down.

In early 1966 the Liberal national convention met to "modernize" the party. With the osmosis characteristic of the Somocistas for American political ideals (other than implementing substantive political democracy), the party's new Declaration of Principles agreed with Alliance for Progress concepts about technocratic economic planning and agrarian and social reforms, while emphasizing the role of private enterprise in development that was so dear to General Somoza. Yet the strategy of not relinquishing power had been maintained: another constitutional reform was passed in 1966, making concessions in the field of education, including concessions to the Catholic Church, but not in electoral matters. And the next presidential term was expanded to five years.

After the constitutional reform was promulgated, the opposition began its electoral campaign. Again weekly meetings and demonstrations were organized throughout the country. But now Agüero dropped the notion of any international assistance, supervision, or observation of the election. His demand was that the opposition be given immediate representation in the state's electoral organization to participate in the supervision of the scheduled registration of voters. However, the government refused to do so on legal technicalities.

Conservative crowds got involved in a campaign of protests, and in October 1966 virtually all opposition groups united in a front—the National Opposition Union (UNO). But realities were far from the spirit of democratic politics. An observation:

> There were several incidents during the four registration Sundays. Members of the Association of Somocista Retired Servicemen, Workers and Peasants (AMROCS) exercised pressure to impede registering. Fights resulted and UNO member[s] were killed [in two towns]. It was charged that the AMROCS [were armed and] had the support of both the National Guard and the electorate directorates in several parts of the country. The [opposition] also charged that because of the lack of their representatives on the electoral boards the [Liberals] had registered nonexisting persons, and also registered Somoza supporters several times in fraudulent preparation for the elections. [Every week] the annulment of registrations was asked for by the opposition and each time the plea was rejected.

> By early December, the opposition had "definitely become convinced that the February [1967] elections would [result in the] victory of [General Somoza]. After Christmas, . . . [oppositionists] started to schedule daily sit-in-protests in [large cities]. After a few days the sit-ins grew bigger and the AMROCS began to harass those who were taking part in them. Several fights resulted until the sit-ins were stopped by army intervention."[24]

Fernando Agüero's flexibility, being willing to compete electorally without a prior guaranteed purity of suffrage, was not paying off. Nicaragua had lived through a refreshing period of hope for "transition" and "democratization," now aborted by techniques to "elect" General Somoza Debayle. This was precisely the opposition's interpretation, manifested in its laudatory remarks about President René Schick upon his death (August 1966): he had represented a "transition" that was being retrogressed, rather than evolving further democratically.

Nonetheless, although the crowds at Agüero's rallies and demonstrations were larger than those mounted for General Somoza, this did not mean that Somoza had no support. The Somozas had large resources. The Liberal Party was the only truly national organization with agents in all population units, because local government functionaries were part of the machine. Local officials could be used to staff the rural electoral boards. Given the partisanship and lack of state neutrality, the Liberal Party was the only organization that operated without being harassed by government agencies and state-protected groups. The party used state vehicles to transport people to their demonstrations and rallies. It also benefited from the "voluntary" financial contributions of public employees, as well as the well-informed, inside advice from government technicians. General Somoza Debayle's platform had appeal among better-off sectors: a technocratic-oriented public administration that would rapidly develop Nicaragua economically and promote a well-functioning private enterprise system, all within the U.S. international sphere of influence.

Prominent businessmen who years later wished to extricate the country from the general's rule contributed as well to his presidential campaign. The still more conservative Catholic Church had benefited through the educational component of the last constitutional reform. Hence, although the government's political machine probably would not have carried a free election, General Somoza had measurable support among the *clases* or *fuerzas vivas*, the basic traditional societal interests, concretely business and religion. And as later discussed, there are reasons to believe that despite the formal rhetoric about democratic values among Nicaraguan elites and public, simultaneously there were currents of opinion with reservations about the true local relevance of real political democracy, which facilitated accommodating electoral irregularities by many, though not all, among the politically interested.

The last opposition mass rally took place on January 22, 1967. Indicative of Agüero's capacity to mobilize the people, perhaps as many as sixty thousand gathered in Managua. The occasion served to manifest the weakness of the polity's formal legal integration: by noon, the crowd began to call for a military coup d'état to overthrow the regime and reorganize the state's constitution, so that free elections could be carried out. But the National Guard did not rebel. It dissolved the demonstrators, inflicting heavy casualties. About a thousand—including Dr. Agüero—took over Managua's Gran Hotel, where they held hostage some eighty foreigners, mostly Americans. The hotel's occupation was ended through the mediation of the Catholic Church and the diplomatic corps. But once again, in crisis the facade of a government bounded by law evaporated: during the evening and the following days, opposition leaders were jailed, and some were tortured.[25] With the potential protest organizers controlled, the February 1967 elections took place without disturbance. A few weeks after the "election" of his brother, Luis Somoza died of heart illness. Thus, again Somoza rule would fall in the centralizing hands of only one caudillo controlling both the army and party.

Mariano Fiallos's scholarship permits us to observe another manifestation of the Somoza doctrine during these elections: "The opposition charged the Electoral Tribunal and the government with fraud and the widespread use of the army and paramilitary organizations under its protection, to impede free access to the polls, not only to the voters, but also to [opposition] representatives in the local electoral boards [throughout the country]. Evidence in support of the charges was presented . . . but the Tribunal took no action." He concluded: "Although it is impossible to determine from a strictly scientific point of view the exact results . . . the above facts, added to the [traditional patterns] . . . in electoral matters, and to the comparison of the size of the anti-Somoza and pro-Somoza demonstrations scheduled during the campaign, would seem to lead to the conclusion that the great majority of the votes [70.9 percent of the total] reported for the Liberal Party was exaggerated by the Electoral Tribunal."[26] It was another case of shameless official numerical tampering.

There was another aspect to the Somoza doctrine: the allocation of a minority share of offices to the opposition to achieve a semblance of pluralism under the family's hegemony. A Senate seat was offered to Agüero as part of the 33 percent opposition share of offices. The opposition was not prepared for, nor really committed to, a violent challenge to the Somoza regime. General Somoza was inaugurated without further complications.

The historical patterns surveyed describe cycles in which the alienation produced by the regime breaking promises and formal legal rules—the normlessness—resulted in rebellions. Yet the government's effective mobilization of its resources to control and repress the opposition resulted as well in feelings of inefficacy or powerlessness—another social-psychological form of alienation. The democratic promise was once again aborted, and another precedent had been established for the opposition's fear and resistance to using the electoral route during my tenure.

Why, in contrast to cases in which electoral fraud leads to a prolonged period of escalated violence (e.g., Colombia after the late 1940s elections, El Salvador after the 1972 election), was the brief civilian revolt followed by General Somoza's consolidation? First, the core leadership around Dr. Agüero chose not to follow nor return to the armed route—the Sandinistas were operating with a radical ideology and were a minor fringe grouping. The

Conservative leader was not inclined to armed action, a position he maintained through the fall of General Somoza some twelve years later.

Second, at the time, General Somoza had an important amount of support. He maintained National Guard loyalty and the backing of a unified Liberal Party machine. Somoza had support as well among business groups. The Catholic Church had benefited from the Somozas and also acquiesced to the "election." Based on my early contacts in Nicaragua, the country's elites still had to develop a strong democratic culture.

Third, a closer look at the election indicates the tight control maintained all along by the Somozas over the military-electoral process: the government had obtained opposition electoral campaigning without making any significant administrative concessions for suffrage purity. The bloody protest days before the election, inciting the National Guard to rebel, precisely demonstrated the opposition's impotence. The opposition was practically begging the military to overthrow the regime. The January event was a desperate act on the part of the opposition that resulted in the physical control of leaders by the Nicaraguan government and deflated popular expectations. Indeed, a unique survey taken around that time suggested so—over 70 percent of the respondents said that they would not vote in February. It was worthless to do so; the citizenry had given up.[27] Once again the population's dissatisfactions and protests were kept under control.

In sum, a series of factors had resulted in a period of liberalization. The shock of the founder's murder, Luis Somoza's personality interacting with the problems produced by the chronic weakness in legitimacy, the threat of the Cuban Revolution, the challenge of the American democratic crusade with the Alliance for Progress, and the tradition with two upper-class-led parties with formal democratic ideology, all seemingly contributed to the democratization that we have reported. Yet the changes were more in style of governance than substance. In the case of Nicaragua in 1967, the responsibility for the arrested democratization predominantly laid with the Somoza brothers—their unwillingness to establish a system to count the votes honestly. You have seen the political energy wasted because of an atavistic incapacity of a ruling group to seriously commit to democracy.

4. The Anastasio Somoza Debayle Period

From 1967 until the Sandinista victory twelve years later, General Somoza Debayle was the master of the Nicaraguan state. With Luis Somoza's death, the polity had returned to the more classic pseudo-democratic form of rule by a strongman. I concentrate here on describing developments that led Nicaraguans to interpret the situation facing them at the beginning of my mission in late 1977. These were transmitted by our contacts and were part of the more immediate understandings that contributed to choosing the strategies that subsequently resulted in the revolution. Remarkably, I found quite broad consensus among my contacts—a few members of the Somoza family inclusive—that the devastating Managua earthquake of 1972 was a critical turning point ushering in a ludicrous period of exacerbated kleptocracy, wanton National Guard repression, debauchery of the ruler, corrupt expansion of his personal business empire and mismanagement scandals in it, and a syndrome of normlessness further delegitimizing the Somocista state.

From 1967 to 1972 General Somoza served the term to which he had been "elected." In 1972, a new Liberal-Conservative pact resulted in another political constitutional change: the National Junta of Government was constituted, a triumvirate executive with two representatives of the ruling Liberal Party and one from the Conservative Party. Fernando Agüero had finally given up and accepted a minority status for the Conservatives in exchange for his participation as a "quasi-president" in the triumvirate and a change from the previous one third to a 40 percent minority party share in the spoils of the state.

That same year, however, Managua suffered a devastating earthquake that virtually destroyed the entire city. Somoza, who had remained the head of the National Guard, acquired emergency powers to cope with the disaster. Somoza-Agüero relations deteriorated and resulted in the 1973 crisis with the reorganization of the triumvirate: Conservative Edmundo Paguaga replaced Agüero with party acquiescence. In 1974 another constitutional change led to the dissolution of the triumvirate and the "election" again of General Somoza as president to serve now for what would be a very long (1974–81) period of heavy-handed rule, interrupted in 1979 by the revolution. Somoza's reelection for such an extended period proved to be the last straw or, in the terms of one of my regular contacts, Frank Matus Lugo, "the drink one should not have prior to driving home from a party."

The Pristine Somoza Doctrine

During his hegemony General Somoza ruled under his father's doctrine. The new absolute ruler was hidebound. There were the old constitutional changes tied to the continuation of regime—constitutions remained transitory political pacts expediently negotiated or adopted to retain and "legalize" holding power. Also, presidential terms continued to be manipulated to minimize the tenure of non-Somozas in the executive and to expand it when the general was to be the president. (One of these manipulations was the triumvirate. According to one story, when asked by an ambassador why he had created a plural executive, Somoza replied: "The presidency is like a beautiful girlfriend—you don't leave her with only one of your male friends to take care of her in your years of absence lest they fall in love with each other.") And there was the willingness to accommodate an opposition, now giving it a slightly enlarged share in the state, in exchange for its acceptance of Somoza rule, which continued to be nonnegotiable. Real elections were not the determinant of the authorities; the interparty pacts served to divide offices, thus predetermining outcomes and postponing elections.

Good governance was considered by the doctrine as stabilized in the two-party tradition: the ruling party is the permanent majority and ideally obtains the cooperation of a loyal opposition through a "symbiotic" relationship assigning to it a minority, subordinate position in the state. But the overriding principle was to retain power ultimately by dominance, not consent. In the face of an uncooperative real opposition, the strategy was to activate one's support and find and legalize a collaborative group relatively docile to the regime, willing to accept payoffs to divide and weaken the opposition.

In short, a *estado prebendario*—a "prebend" granting state, allocating sinecures, status, or monetary rewards to those who cooperated—was at the core of the doctrine. Pacts were altered to favor the rulers. The historical balance by the time of my arrival was the widespread belief that the Somozas could not be trusted; that they tricked those who collaborated with them to impose their will; that they divided the opposition, and they used and *desprestigian* (corrupted and forced a total loss of prestige upon) those groups that made pacts with them. The weight of these factors, inherited and continued by the ruler, became one of the basic impediments for Nicaraguans negotiating among themselves a political solution to the acute crisis precipitated in January 1978. Not any democratic promises, not one more "pact," became the motto.

Oppositions

The main opposition, on the other hand, had also reproduced earlier accommodating patterns. Rather than transform itself from a civic electoral movement to an armed movement, the Conservatives waited for and used a very limited opening—the possibility of negotiating an enlarged subordinate minority share—to collaborate with Somoza. A conspicuous precedent was the 1950 pact between Somoza García and General Emiliano Chamorro; then, as in 1972, Somoza Sr. successfully sought to maneuver his "election" for another expanded term. In our conversations the general of my mission repeatedly insisted that he had taken absolute control because of the devastation of the earthquake (following which the National Guard had engaged in riotous patterns). Somoza saw himself as the messianic man to reconstruct the country after the disaster.

Years later, I asked Dr. Agüero why he had made a pact in 1972 with Somoza and participated in the triumvirate. His answer was that his followers had lost confidence in Somoza holding a fair election, the route that had failed in 1967, so he wanted to explore the avenue of democratization through collaboration. But one could not trust and compromise with Somoza; he had betrayed Agüero, "illegally" purging him from the triumvirate. The result was General Somoza's consolidation of power through a not seriously contested election in 1974, in which again a Conservative pseudo-opposition played the old trick of participating for the spoils, even though the election's outcome was predetermined. By then Agüero had become a political cadaver.

Not all oppositionists had given up: Pedro Joaquín Chamorro formed a coalition of unarmed factions constituting the Unión Democrática de Liberación (UDEL). This miscellany of groups, ranging from Conservatives and ex-Somoza Liberals, Social Christians and Social Democrats, to Marxists-Leninists, abstained in protest from participating in the 1974 election. And the armed opposition, the Sandinistas, continued. But the fact is that General Somoza had consolidated his rulership, for these real oppositions had no strength to block his election and continued power. Another cycle of opposition growth followed by contraction and decline into powerlessness had taken place.

Significantly, and coinciding with his return to the presidency, General Somoza imposed a prolonged state of siege, the result of his overreaction to the December 1974 house kidnapping of a group of prominent Nicaraguans by a few Sandinistas.[1] This act had an immediate propaganda impact, demonstrating that the FSLN was alive. After this, the Nicaraguan government followed an aggressive anti-Sandinista policy that kept the movement off balance. A few government contacts told me that the state of siege had been maintained deliberately so that its media censorship facilitated the increased kleptocracy.

Although the December terrorist act initially served to boost Sandinista morale, its consequences were negative for the movement. First, it was followed by the fragmentation of the FSLN with the formation of a new group, the Proletarian Tendency, which sought the adoption of a more Leninist strategy, the organization of the proletariat as the basis for the eventual revolution, as opposed to short-term terroristic acts. Second, Somoza successfully met the December shift in Sandinista tactics by adopting a more dynamic offensive with extensive repression.

Here is an appraisal of Somoza's new policy by Sandinista Omar Cabezas:

> All our structures, our safe houses, the whole network of collaborators had been destroyed, the people terrorized. Get one person out of this town [without being killed or captured] and you've accomplished something major, really major! The trouble was that our networks were so fragile that all the houses had been evacuated; the collaborators were all being arrested. There was only one house left that we hadn't used before. . . . [I]t was necessary to clear out [the city], which had become one gigantic rat trap. "Look brother we're in deep shit. The problem is, you can't stay here. We don't have safe houses. . . ." Brother, let me tell you, that poor guy just about died when we told him [we're in the FSLN] because the Guard had just been murdering people in the mountains, and the repression in the [area] and the battles were all very recent; so our presence there spelled disaster for them.[2]

Repression can make the life of revolutionaries most difficult, one of fleeing, distrust, and increased isolation. Governments can create politically hopeless conditions, when imprisonment can become for some a welcome relief to escape from the underground. That small numbers of activists remained in the movement has been attributed to their quasi-religious vision and faith, sacrificing for the cause. There was also comradeship: loyalty to those who have died and become martyrs, fidelity to companions who remain.[3]

My contacts explained that support for the Somozas had gone through cycles: at times public opinion was quite unsupportive, to be followed by a resurgence of support. This proved quite frustrating to persistent oppositionists.[4] In the case at hand, the largest sector of the Conservatives, with their most effective leader, Dr. Agüero, simply tired of making an uncompromising opposition. They were socialized into subordination by the strength of the Somoza military-political machine.

Second, the confusing events around the earthquake and the desirability of strong and proven leadership to overcome the devastation played into

Somoza's hand. He concentrated power on himself and subsequently moved to politically destroy Agüero—potentially his greatest rival, he told me. The earthquake reinforced the strongman's absolutist, messianic self-conception.

And with the beginning of the Richard Nixon administration in 1969, extremely friendly, supportive American-Nicaraguan ties developed, until the initiation of the human rights policy during Gerald Ford's administration carried out by my predecessor, James Theberge (1975–77). Under Nixon, the embassy notoriously sided with Somoza and encouraged opposition accommodation to his rule. Given American influence among resourceful Nicaraguan sectors, this contributed to regime maintenance. Symptomatically, Dr. Agüero reported to me that the U.S. ambassador encouraged him to make a pact with Somoza. Controversially, our envoy maintained very close personal ties with Somoza, "as if a member of the family." Illustrative of the American role, with the subsequent withdrawal of support with the implementation of the human rights policy, processes for destabilizing the regime were initiated.

Once the state of siege was established in December 1974, the unarmed opposition also suffered a severe blow: the right to assemble, freedom of the press, and other rights were suspended (until my arrival, September 1977). Thus, after General Somoza's accession Nicaragua did not live the democratizing promise of the golden years—the government never allowed an equivalent growth in opposition opportunity, mobilization, and influence.

Regime Decay

In sum, at the time of my recruitment to go to Nicaragua the nation had recently experienced a period of authoritarian retrogression.[5] Illustrative of the role attributed to precipitating events by elites, many viewed the earthquake as a triggering factor resulting in changes in political values and organization or structure.[6]

First, indicative of Somoza's regal attitude, to cope with the crisis he inducted his son, Anastasio Somoza Portocarrero, into the National Guard. In spite of Somoza's lack of any previous military training, in contrast with other recruits, he immediately became a captain and then a major. Somoza Portocarrero's meteoric military career subsequently included heading the newly formed academy and elite corps, the Escuela de Entrenamiento Básico de Infantería (EEBI); such moves indicated General Somoza's desire to continue the dynasty. When I arrived in Nicaragua, friends of the president personally informed me that he planned to remain in control of the state beyond 1981, and that his intention was to consolidate his son's position as the heir. Thus the country had not moved to republicanize its political culture but had gone in the opposite direction.

Further, in contrast to his earlier more cautious behavior, Somoza had been ruling under the state of siege for an unusually long period. Under its protection, patrimonial values became exacerbated and extended throughout the state, the court system included.

It was also reported that the president was following a life of debauchery, that his dissolute ways would impair his health. His heavy drinking and offensive behavior were no secret. An extramarital alliance, which he chose not to legalize, isolated him from the social life expected of a president: after the earthquake, a "White House"—a proper executive residence—had not been immediately rebuilt, to the detriment of sociability between the president and the nation's elites. Thus, in comparison to bygone more pluralistic years, evolutionary hopes had diminished. Many of my contacts emphasized that in contrast to his brother Luis's ability and flexibility to defuse crises, Anastasio was a macho mandamás who was incapable of compromise and who had to be met by force.[7] The scenario was classic: a verification of Lord Acton's assertion that power tends to corrupt, and absolute power corrupts absolutely, that the ruler understands only force (hence the crucial role the United States had to play).

Beyond these developments, some directly related to General Somoza's personality, and factors conducive to distancing him from the business community in this post-earthquake period, business leaders had noticed the competitive entrance of the president's interests in areas of economic activity that the Somozas had not sought to penetrate in the past; given the prevailing corruption, this posed problems of disloyal competition to vested interests.

I recall my first visits with General Somoza: based on his visitors and telephone conversations that he received, he seemed more of a businessman (in association with foreigners—some with a moral reputation that was locally questioned) than a full-time ruler.[8] There was latent dissatisfaction among the business community, a natural strategic pillar of a conservative regime.[9] Given the weakness at the time of the Nicaraguan left (especially of the Sandinistas), in sharp contrast to conditions in some other countries (e.g., the Latin American Southern Cone in the 1970s, where Marxist revolutionary strength had contributed to precipitate "reactionary" authoritarian regimes to crush the left), Nicaraguan businessmen did not feel immediately threatened and in dire need to support a government decaying in image but still relatively friendly. Closer to home, in contrast to neighboring El Salvador and Guatemala, where by 1977 interclass political conflict had taken the form of the kidnapping and murder of prominent local and foreign businessmen and vigilantes sponsored by proprietorial classes, these rancorous patterns were absent in Nicaragua.

Indeed many businessmen, especially among the young, were available to actively oppose the government, particularly if they saw U.S. participation in the process. This they did during my mission.

In addition to the resentment that an expansion in power and absolutism can cause in the outer circles of elite power, predisposing some of the wealthy against the ruler and his inner circle, during the general's years in power, the economy had continued to progress moderately and become much more urban. [10] There is disagreement among observers whether prior to the initiation of the revolution Nicaragua experienced an economic crisis. Certainly, it did not suffer a financial-economic meltdown (as in the collapse of the Argentine government in 2001) nor a retrogression in the population's standard of living evidenced by a continuing decrease in national per head income (as in the final breakdown of the Uruguayan regime in 1973). In Carlos M. Vilas's words: "Examination of the actual evolution of the Nicaraguan economy and the way it was tied into the world capitalist economy at different periods, shows it to be insufficient in itself to produce a crisis. Rather, the fall of the Somocista dictatorship was the product of a revolutionary political crisis, which at a certain point in its evolution activated [subsequently] an economic crisis." "If economic crisis is understood to mean stagnation or recession, it would seem hard to argue that there was an economic crisis in Nicaragua." "If economic crisis is understood to mean a strong movement of decapitalization, . . . one cannot properly speak of an economic crisis in pre-Revolutionary Nicaragua in this sense." "The most that one can say, based on facts, is that there was a tendency toward a deceleration of economic growth." [11]

No one is presenting a rosy picture of satisfaction with the socioeconomic conditions. In the decade of the general's domination agricultural capitalist development with concentration of land and rural proletarianization continued, and the movement of large proportions of the population away from the land accelerated. This rapid urbanization was not absorbed by rapid industrialization, as its pace was slow. While the urban service sector grew rapidly, there was a lag in the creation of high-payment employment. As throughout Latin America the urban areas experienced concentration of wealth, poverty, unemployment, and squatters. A more complex society with movable populations brought into circulation (social mobilization in academic jargon) had taken hold. It was to be expected that these developments, combined with the poverty, had increasingly made the archaic dynastic form of government illegitimate—yet the general gave all signs of wishing to continue and reproduce it again. As we saw in the previous chapter, the regime's nature made it susceptible to destabilization with socioeconomic changes. During the state-of-siege years their effect had only been suppressed from open expression.

With the economic changes taking place, a more differentiated society with a growing middle class was developing, yet this class still lacked the organized numbers for an important autonomous role of its own. Middle-class interest groups were very scarce. In my contacts with organized groups, the presence of individuals of patrician background was conspicuous—people of middle-class extraction blended with those of a higher-status background, thus suggesting their relatively low operational independence. At the same time, the traditional political parties, which were in a lull of activity, were mostly led by notables. The Sandinista top leadership was of relatively less privileged extraction, but there were extensive ties between the traditional "good families" and the social revolutionaries. Hence, the reported middle-class "dependency" posited by various essayists seemed strongly manifested in Nicaragua, but with its own twist—the upper and middle class would actively mingle in the revolution to come.

At all events, in 1977 there were aspiring sectors of the middle class that, similar to the business elite, felt politically underrepresented and did not perceive themselves as threatened by prospective or actual political change; undoubtedly, among them there were desires for change if it implied their self-development and progress.[12] The Somoza family had been ruling for over forty years. The general's rule was perceived as increasingly corrupt and repressive. There was no overriding interest on the part of the bulk of the Nicaraguan middle sectors to back the continuation of Somoza rule.

Another conventional interpretation is that poverty is the "father of revolution." There remained a very extensive, forsaken sector of the population with very low access to social services, in some segments below the Latin American experience. Although the Nicaraguan Revolution was not a lower "class" uprising—the factories and commercial enterprises were closed by the owners, not by rebellious workers taking them over; there were not widespread signs of the lower class vindicating violence, such as executions of landlords by peasants, peasant refusals to pay rents, or the like—even if the middle class was not personally affected by the socioeconomic deficiencies, conditions were not propitious among the literate, internationally aware middle class to have pride in the poor conditions associated with their political system.[13] Thus middle-class sectors other than local traditionally rebellious students were available to mobilize against Somoza, especially if they saw American initiatives raising expectations and undermining the Nicaraguan government. Conditions existed for the forming of a broad coalition against the ruler, and coalitions are essential to the success of large-scale revolts.[14]

In contrast to this potential for active organized opposition against the government, winds of change actually had already prevailed in an important entity—the Catholic Church. Following international modernizing currents, the Nicaraguan Church had become more active and increasingly involved in the community, and it had started to carry out the ecumenical message of Vatican II and the social activism on behalf of, and "preference" for, the poor of the Latin American Episcopal conferences. Within the Nicaraguan Church, a sentiment prevailed that was very critical of both the government and local social conditions.

At the beginning of 1977 the bishops, in a pastoral letter censored by General Somoza, had openly protested the government's authoritarianism, its violation of human rights ("terror, tortures, rapes"), and its unresponsiveness to the poor, while demanding an increased democratization and political and religious freedom.[15] Prior to my arrival, the denunciations by some members of the clergy of violations of the human rights of the poor by the National Guard were picked up by Nicaraguan oppositionists, American and Nicaraguan human rights activists, and our embassy, and had become central in the opposition's campaign. By the beginning of the Carter administration, the violations already had resulted in the suspension of part of the U.S. military assistance and were a key source of information for the congressional debates on Nicaragua prior to my confirmation by the U.S. Senate in the summer of 1977.

The Nicaraguan Church wrote a prelude for the implementation of the American human rights policy. Although during my tenure the local bishops did not formally support a violent revolutionary solution, but rather repeatedly voiced their concern for peace, several members of the clergy were publicly involved in the revolution, without ever being admonished or disciplined by the hierarchy. The church's role went beyond the traditional ones of regime support, the sponsorship of general public policies in pursuit of what it considers to be the "common good," or acting as a specific interest group in search of its special spiritual and material interests, to escalate demand for regime change. This was evidenced very early, before the end of 1977. Not only were the more radical clergy who espoused the so-called liberation theology actively against the regime, but generally the Catholic establishment sought a change in it.

Indeed, just a few days after my arrival, on a trip to northern Nicaragua I met with the region's bishop. He played for me tapes of peasants complaining about the horrors committed against them by the National Guard in their counterinsurgency campaigns. To my surprise he volunteered the need for Somoza, through a U.S. initiative, to resign "to overcome the unjust political impasse." The bishop reported his dialogue with village priests and local members of religious orders involved in the Christian *comunidades de base* (base or grassroots communities). These clergy were participating in organizing the common poor people into religious communities or groups. The groups went beyond religious purposes and addressed basic community needs. Naturally, the absence and inadequacies of public social services resulted in community anti-government attitudes and activities repressed by Somoza's military. As I learned about this time from three American missionaries threatened with deportation by the Nicaraguan government—one of them hurt by the police—*comunidades de base* activities could be coordinated with Sandinista revolutionaries. Actually, some members of the clergy identified themselves as FSLN Sandinistas. In any case, the *comunidades* would play an important role in mobilizing the masses and in articulating a Christian, not Marxist-Leninist, leftist input into the heterogeneous coalition of forces that made the revolution.[16]

It was in this context of erosion of support for the government that the president suffered a heart attack in July 1977. Somoza's sickness had an important psychological impact. He was out of the country for several weeks, yet the nation survived without him. After his return from hospitalization in Miami, virtually no one saw him for months; when I first met him on September 23, only a few key officials and business partners had seen him since his return, including members of the cabinet. The president moved his residence away from Managua and dramatically curtailed his social activities. There were frequent and recurrent rumors that he had another setback, that his death was imminent. The president's image of the physically huge, omnipresent, omniscient, ruthless leader began to evaporate. Oppositionists wanted a new government to be constituted in the face of the president's visible absence. Readers will readily understand that in the small-scale society that was Nicaragua, part of the power accruing to Somoza was related to the fear carried by his ubiquitous physical presence. His intransigence and violent reactions in the months to come would consolidate him as an evil figure.

These were the unsettling, destabilizing local conditions that coincided with the implementation of U.S. policy. When Pedro Joaquín Chamorro was assassinated in January 1978, from all strata of society the processes of mobilization against the government and of organizing to replace it exploded and acquired momentum against Somoza, who was perceived to have been weakened or crippled by the new, unsupportive U.S. government in response to which he finally had stopped ruling under a state of siege. That militant oppositionist Chamorro's assassination precipitated such a spontaneous, intensive, and extensive outburst of antagonism against the regime, in which suddenly the people's protests in urban settings outpaced their organization by armed and unarmed preexisting opposition cadres, suggests the background of alienation or estrangement of the people that existed in the country: the Chamorro tragedy served as the catalyst for a widespread revolt because of the extant smoldering discontent.

Mirage?

It is not exceptional, however, to attribute permanence to repressive regimes, especially to those that experience little opposition activity, until there is an abrupt uprising that develops into a relatively rapid collapse of the regime.[17] This was the assessment provided by the CIA when briefing me just a few weeks before my departure to the field. Somoza, unless he died from his illness, which was doubted on the basis of U.S. extant intelligence, would remain controlling the country. Before lifting the state of siege by the Nicaraguan government a month later, the regime appeared firmly in place, measured by the scarcity of opposition activity both unarmed and armed against it. And the government's structure was quite strong in terms of men, money, and arms vis-à-vis those of the fragmented contenders. It took a very broad national coalition, militarily supported internationally—it took a war to end the regime.

However, with the consolidation of the last Somoza's absolute power, political life began to freeze: the parties' activism was gone, and a relative de-activation also took place in the ruling party. When we arrived in September, the masses were not receiving much input from Liberals and Conservatives, and few among the young were being recruited into the traditional parties. The regime had become "militarized," giving priority to its armed action and control over "politics." In less than a year, it would become absolutely clear that political grassroots activity had shifted into new (armed and unarmed) groups, precisely those Marxist and Christian groups that had experienced the brunt of the government's repression, thus being kept from growing.

The situation was conducive to a mirage of stability, which overestimated the regime's strength. The government had left a politically vacant, wide, idle space. Under existing terms, regime repression was working, despite its political sclerosis, with its military campaigns. But the regime's dynastic, patrimonial profile was anachronistic in the light of the social and economic changes that had taken place. Given the chronic weakness of legitimacy and history of periodic crises, it was to be expected that the country experience an escalation of conflict in the face of situational changes—Nicaragua faced an unstable, turbulent system. General Somoza expected this when he finally lifted the state of siege. In our first meeting, with tragic premonition Somoza said: "I just lifted the state of siege so that you did not have to share in the historical responsibility of the consequences of this decision. I knew that your government had instructed you to ask me this; we are going to have to face difficult times with my adversaries." The general was trying to win me over with his paternalistic show of friendship, but he was the only one responsible. Somoza always held a very positive view of himself and a very pessimistic view of his countrymen and the prospects of democracy in the country.[18]

The stage was set for political change. The U.S. human rights policy was actively encouraging change, as was the militant position of the Catholic Church. Much discontent prevailed among the business, middle-class, and popular sectors; and there was an eagerness for action on the part of oppositionists and revolutionaries. What remained to be settled were the timing and results. Just days before P.J. Chamorro's assassination, Horacio Aguirre of *Diario Las Américas* warned me: "You have to be very careful. Nicaragua is a gunpowder keg. All that it will take is for you, the Archbishop, or Chamorro to be killed for an uprising to start."

In the following chapters I tell a story with its illusions or mirages of a somewhat loony, messianic strongman who had become increasingly despotic, who was perceived wounded by sudden illness, who confirmed the power of the United States by acceding on its behalf to suspend the repressive control under the state of siege that had been working for him. The story is of his fed-up adversaries, who cornered him, unwilling to give him a chance to enact again the well-known legerdemains of the dynasty, who steadfastly demanded that he shorten his tenure, and who cleverly formed a very broad social class coalition involving both the plutocracy and the masses in a revolutionary movement.[19] And it is the story of an American administration that claimed not to support an extremely isolated dictator but that was incapable of firmly opposing his eccentricity and *obcecación* (blind obstinacy) to remain ruling at all costs.[20]

The revolution was a rebellion against a man who claimed that he was the only person capable of ruling—including politicians and soldiers of his following, whom he privately dismissed as inept—a man who could not good-naturedly face the reality that times had changed, and that his nation considered his rule obsolete. In contrast to the actions taken by the Sandinista regime a decade later, at no point was Somoza willing to contemplate shortening his rule after the January 1978 crisis, not even to test public support for his tenure through a U.S.-suggested referendum. He insisted he remain ruling in the midst of very broad rebellion for three more years.

But before the revolution's success, not one of the opposition's conditions was agreed upon. The impasse was sustained by the patrimonial complete subordination of the state's military and civilian cadres to Somoza, which impeded his being persuaded to compromise or his being replaced by his people rather than continue fighting for him. The impasse was also sustained by Somoza's unrealistic strategy. In order to continue collaborating partially with the American human rights policy, in contrast to the past, in early 1978 he did not move swiftly to repressively dominate and control the opposition, especially its leadership. The task would have been formidable: the Somozas had not faced such a level of internal and external opposition before. Therefore he progressively lost control of the entire society except his small civilian-military machine. It was an impasse that had to be overcome to normalize social life; the belief that only violence, the sooner the better, could reequilibrate and liberate the society from a worse possible situation spread, capturing public opinion.[21]

5. Neutrality

Thus the military and economic intervention of the United States in Central America from 1898 onward typically weakened independence and popular governments and strengthened military dictatorships.

Robert A. Dahl, Democracy and Its Critics

In retrospect, the policy debates in Washington [about Nicaraguan policy] seem unreal. They appear now as desperate efforts to find a way to influence a flood of events that surged far ahead of Washington's real power or understanding.

Anthony Lake,
Somoza Falling: A Case Study of Washington at Work

The enactment of the human rights legislation by the U.S. Congress during the Gerald Ford administration initiated a process of distancing ourselves from the Nicaraguan government. The Carter administration further reassessed United States–Nicaragua relations. This more liberal group vigorously sought to publicly condemn the Somoza government for its abuses and was less concerned about maintaining the niceties prescribed by good manners in its dealings with the president of Nicaragua. Virtually all the instruments available within the constraints self-imposed by the advocates of the human rights policy were used against General Somoza.[1]

The human rights policy not only targeted Nicaragua: the cases of Chile, Paraguay, and Uruguay come to mind for the intensity of the campaigns implemented by the respective U.S. ambassadors. That successful revolution took place within Latin America only in Nicaragua is a reminder of the importance of local factors in the outcome—which can be forgotten by critics of the role of the United States in the events.

The policy that we applied was unplanned. It has been noted that much of American foreign policymaking follows a fragmented process often referred to as "bureaucratic politics." The Nicaraguan policy developed in the context of never-ending heated discussions in Washington involving transient political functionaries and permanent bureaucrats, as well as some members of the Congress and other interested parties. The nature of the policymaking makes it imperative to interpret it in terms of the resulting decisions; only in this respect can we talk about an administration policy, seeking peaceful democratization in a friendly U.S. client.

The idealistic but also unrealistic policy went through four stages up to the success of the revolution: neutrality, mediation, partial withdrawal, and counterrevolutionary initiatives and mediation.

A Misnomer

In spite of the differences of opinion that I encountered in my preparatory briefings in Washington, it was absolutely clear that my mission was to implement the human rights policy. I had understood in my conversations with various officials that the prevailing idea was to emphasize to the government of Nicaragua the need to respect the physical integrity of its citizens, that is, those rights associated with due process. I had been told in the key State Department unit regularly linking embassy operations with Washington (the assistant secretary for Latin America) and in the National Security Council that the administration's immediate priority was not to promote democracy abroad but rather to end reported brutal, repressive patterns.[2]

Nevertheless, as I started my mission I knew that the sense of the policy was peaceful democratization. This was implied by the total consensus I had found that we would not use forceful means against Somoza to change his government and in the "goals and objectives" that Washington cabled to me upon my arrival in the field. I was explicitly instructed to pursue the country's "peaceful democratization," including human rights and the orderly movement toward free national elections.

That these differences in opinion existed only confirmed my belief that Washington still lacked a clear idea of what to do.[3] The absence of political clarity was discomfiting, but I embarked on what I personally considered an exploratory mission, hoping that with time a coherent policy would develop in Washington. I knew that in political terms the current policy could only mean that the United States wished to see Nicaragua's democratization.

First, the protection of oppositionists was largely the target of the human rights campaign. Prior to my appointment, Washington had been privately and publicly asking General Somoza to lift the state of siege and restore constitutional guarantees. Such measures tended to redistribute local political resources. The hitherto severe limitation or suspension of opposition rights would be lifted, as well as the censorship of the mass media, which, given the regime's noted "limited pluralism," was partly in opposition hands. (For example, the largest newspaper, La Prensa, was owned by the opposition.) Thus the administration had gone beyond the defense of individual physical-integrity rights to include liberalizing measures affecting the polity at large.

Given the regime's nature, I expected trouble. As we saw, its fraudulent character had tended to result in periodic physical fights between the government and oppositions, in which the key issue was the regime's termination—its democratization. The Nicaraguans would make this a crucial issue, as debates carried out in 1977 in the U.S. Congress already showed by the public testimony given by Nicaraguans.

Beyond this, prior to my recruitment the United States had contributed, as classical sociology says, to altering the local "definition" of the situation. The administration had publicly been critical of Somoza, suspending the disbursement of the bulk of its military assistance. Such actions do not go unnoticed in countries in which American troops have been used. From the beginning, I was instructed to maintain a certain distance from Somoza—be "correct" with the government—while developing close widespread personal contacts with "legitimate" opposition forces.

The still widely misunderstood policy became known among some of its supporters by the misleading term of "neutrality." It was "neutral" in that, following the interventionist constraints of the general human rights policy against direct involvement in changing foreign governments, we were not to place ourselves entirely within either the camp of the government or the opposition. We had signaled a new alienation from Somoza, but the embassy was not to side with the opposition to the extent of organizing the overthrow of the government, nor was it to help organize the opposition or finance any of its factions. This was too interventionist a policy for the human rights philosophy.

The policy was to avoid a decisive action in favor of either side. But it was not a policy of evenhandedness or indifference; hardly so, as Washington was openly critical of the status quo and favored changes. We were, in fact, not being neutral but were encouraging opposition and undercutting support for Somoza. Operationally, then, the objective was political evolution, the policy stressing that these changes had to be "made in Nicaragua." The solution had to be worked out by the Nicaraguans on their own, not by a formula arrived at with direct participation of the United States in local statecraft. The latter smacked too much of our interventionist "imperial" past that had led to the Vietnam problems.

As the formal goal was not the forceful overthrow of the government, the embassy was restricted from direct contact with the still small Sandinista factions (intelligence links were maintained, however, and during my tenure the information gathered was adequate). But we kept direct relations with virtually all groups, including with unarmed oppositionists who were spokespeople for the FSLN insurgents. The breadth of our contacts is indicated by the fact that during this first phase I was personally in touch with three of the five members of the first Sandinista-dominated junta that replaced Somoza—Violeta Barrios de Chamorro, Sergio Ramírez Mercado, and Alfonso Robelo Callejas. It has been argued that a major defect of the policy was the lack of direct relations with the violent revolutionary groups. Clearly this would not have led to a peaceful solution. Their strategy was precisely to overthrow the government violently. In sharp contrast with some theaters, in Nicaragua the U.S. ambassador had very frequent and close contacts with oppositionists, and although this did not please the dictator, he did allow it.

The management of this so-called neutrality was not easy. Given Washington's unwillingness to help organize the internal political dynamics, its success was contingent upon Nicaraguan decisions. I had found a working consensus against "intervention" between "conservatives" (mostly career Foreign Service officers) and "liberals." The conservatives—basically opposed to an activist human rights policy and led by Assistant Secretary Terence Todman—did not wish to destabilize Latin American governments; destabilization might be dangerous and costly. The liberals, by contrast, philosophically were against "intervention" because it was considered imperialistic and unnecessary to defend U.S. interests in Latin America under extant conditions. This group was guided by the belief that U.S. interventions had harmed Latin America. There also was a lingering sense of American powerlessness in foreign affairs among the group. Yet these liberals were not against the "interference" in domestic affairs entailed by the public human rights campaigns that undermined the foreign governments.

Although the task seemed formidable, I proceeded to carry out my initial instructions, lured by the excitement of my new position. From the outset I sympathized with key goals of the policy. The restoration of a moral purpose to our foreign policy was timely. I thought it unjustified to maintain close supportive ties with brutal dictatorships simply because they claimed friendship with the United States. The conservative argument that these regimes were more benign than the "totalitarian" ones aligned with our adversaries was not entirely satisfactory. U.S. military missions in Central America were far too large and prone to be entangled in the ongoing repression. A more ethical policy might reduce the anti-American attitudes of local anti-regime groups and the inclination of some of them to engage in terrorism against Americans. The United States should not be involved in empire building or in interventions to maintain subservient client-states; it should not and could not take responsibility for ruling Latin America.

But I was uncomfortable with some assumptions and aspects of the policy. I did not agree that the Soviet Bloc would not pose a threat to legitimate U.S. interests in Central America (nor did I feel that the armed victory of Marxist-Leninist-influenced revolutionaries would create satisfactory societies).[4] What was truly revolutionary in the region was to build democracies, not new dictatorships. Further, with the human rights policy the U.S. government had constituted itself in a "tribunal" that publicly judged unilaterally the performance in this regard of other countries. Foreign governments were openly accused of horrendous crimes. This could only create international conflicts for the United States. (As a reaction to the human rights policy, in 1977 several Latin American countries refused to accept U.S. military aid; instead they would purchase arms elsewhere or manufacture them to reduce dependence on the United States).

More than the complicated issue of the new net balance of opinion about the United States abroad created by the new policy, I was concerned with the way the policy was being implemented. Purists claimed that Washington was not to intervene to determine foreign governments. This was not exactly so. Before my arrival in Nicaragua the administration had taken measures that could only be interpreted locally that the United States wished to see others rule the country. Indeed, Washington was not seeking to determine who exactly should be the country's new rulers, but it had to be interpreted that the United States did not wish Somoza to remain in office. Hence, in Nicaragua the U.S. claim of "non-intervention" was widely considered disingenuous.

In sum, the human rights activists defined non-intervention to mean no U.S. involvement or assistance in the process to plan a change in government (although it was legitimate to undercut it) on grounds of not wanting to determine who ruled Nicaragua.[5] What if U.S. policy helped to promote rising conflict and human rights violations? What if the policy helped to increase the power and likelihood of success of professed anti-U.S. revolutionaries? The policy lacked a political plan and adequate consideration of the aspirations and intended behavior of its foreign recipients. Contrary to their idealistic objectives, the human rights sponsors would not be able to end the U.S. government's clientelism in Central America nor disassociate it from the consequences.

Normlessness
Unarmed Opposition

The immediate effect of lifting the state of siege on September 19, 1977, was to initiate a state of normlessness at the core of polity: an explicit—at first not as intense but ultimately enduring—constitutional crisis took hold. Liberalization resulted in a crisis of regime, with demands that Somoza family rule end. Oppositionists sought to terminate the regime as soon as possible. Lifting of the state of siege "legalized" opposition activity to gain power. It combined with the absence of a democratic tradition, little confidence in elections, the lack of a traditional constitution, the frustrations created by the recent authoritarian retrogression, and the fact that the date to legally gain power and even to participate in minor elections was four years in the future.[6] This gave a generalized feeling that a pre-1981 strategy should be explored and followed. Somoza could not be trusted. Many oppositionists told me that they wished a democratic solution before the U.S. president's term ended (also in 1981) because they feared that Carter might not serve a second term and that his successor might not be as friendly to their cause. Oppositionists started to use their new freedoms to demand negotiations: they were tired of playing a pseudo-democratic game, to see if in 1981 Somoza would finally change his mind and hold free, fair elections. Peaceful democratization required Somoza's willingness to retire to private life and a National Guard free from family control.

The opposition immediately launched a public campaign defining the rulers as illegitimate, lawbreakers, criminals. At a minimum, the authorities were publicly accused of systematically engaging in embezzlement, electoral fraud, and human rights abuses. The Somocistas implicitly projected that their goal was the continuation of the dynasty through the eventual timely promotion of Anastasio Somoza Portocarrero, then a major. They proclaimed the "legality" of the regime and of the last elections, adducing that any opposition demand to change the regime prior to 1981 was anti-constitutional and hence illegal. Government spokespeople did not lose the opportunity to accuse the opposition of encouraging terroristic crimes: they were the real criminals, the rhetoric went. The polarization was compounded by the ideologization of conflict. Opponents were labeled as representing totally unacceptable, diametrically opposed, abhorrent ideas and values (e.g., Communists, tyrants, totalitarians, etc.).[7]

Peaceful democratization called for working out new, commonly binding rules to channel the open political competition that followed the lifting of the state of siege. In the face of the verbal exuberance and polarization, as many visitors observed to me, the embassy found itself on a tight rope. From the very outset my personal decision was to minimize public statements, which could only alienate and irritate at least one of the parties, while maximizing private contacts with unarmed leaders and groups to gain acceptability and support for my mission.

Armed Opposition

Dissent over the regime acquired another particular virulence. Among the Sandinistas, a third faction had rapidly formed: the Tercerista Insurrectionalist Tendency (i.e., third position). They felt that the situation had changed against Somoza, so their objective was not long-term success through the organization and indoctrination of cadres and developing a following, nor the tactic of a war of attrition from relatively secure, remote rural bases. (It is noteworthy that one of the Sandinista factions still called itself Guerra Popular Prolongada [Prolonged Popular War]; the other faction was the Proletarian Tendency.) The objective now was to change the regime as soon as possible through a nationwide violent insurrection.[8]

As early as October 1977 the Sandinistas launched minor military offensives to occupy several towns. The pattern was not new. The Terceristas were pursuing a strategy similar to one of those followed earlier in Nicaragua. They were combining attacks against military units to take over population centers and incursions from bordering countries with calls to a mass rebellion. The events, however, proved to be simply small, armed actions, as a popular uprising triggered by the attacks did not take place. Importantly, in sharp contrast to the then-prevailing patterns of violence in other Central American nations, acts of terrorism against the integrity of well-known *private* citizens, elements of the plutocracy included, still were avoided. This facilitated acceptance of the movement by the establishment.

Also of great significance, a group of prominent citizens—including members of patrician families and the *haute bourgeoisie*—constituted a political front, the Group of Twelve. The Twelve, as they became known, issued a manifesto seeking Somoza's unilateral resignation, the confiscation of the property of his family and friends, the abolition of the National Guard, and a role for the Sandinistas in the envisioned process of pluralistic participation that would follow democratization. The seed for a broad opposition alliance including Marxist-Leninist-oriented violent revolutionaries had been planted. The Twelve had become the "civic" (i.e., unarmed) bridge and front for the Sandinistas. Naturally, the Twelve's intransigent platform could not be peacefully implemented and was of doubtful success at that time. Successful *peaceful* democratization is more likely with the development of *mutual guarantees* among the parties: the Twelve's extreme anarchic position demanded Somoza's surrender.[9]

The majority of the unarmed (the "moderate") oppositionists and elements of the private sector, on the other hand, took the occasion of the October revolutionary actions to recruit the Catholic archbishop, Miguel Obando y Bravo, to pressure Somoza for negotiations to peacefully democratize the country and terminate the dynasty. A month after my arrival, the pattern by unarmed and non-Marxist groups of using Sandinista violence to dismantle the regime had begun.

Somoza brusquely refused to negotiate, stating that he would be willing to sit down and talk after the municipal elections scheduled for February, a position he took only after my remarking that I thought Washington would be unhappy if he refused to dialogue. Somoza's strategy was to gain time and not dismantle the regime, at least until his term expired; he knew that the opposition was trying to disrupt this constitutional schedule and terminate his rule earlier. For Somoza, the extant constitution had been enacted in good faith with the Conservatives and could not be changed until it ran its course in 1981. He never willingly changed this initial position.

The general was also moved in his stalling by the prevailing organizational weakness of the opposition. Sandinista groups, in the process of building a mass basis, were still small. (Under Fidel Castro's sponsorship, unification of the Sandinista factions was finally achieved in early 1979.) The unarmed opposition was also divided: most party "factions" remained not much more than small coteries with sociability functions. Ironically, this was partly the result of Somoza's success after the earthquake in engineering his enhanced control and reelection. The unarmed opposition's main resource was the daily La Prensa, and as its owner informed me, the long period under the state of siege had not helped opposition organization.

Thus, in the eyes of the Somocistas there was little urgency to negotiate with what was a still weak opposition with apparently little capability or, given its fragmentation, authority to negotiate any binding agreement. The Somocistas' unwillingness to recognize opposition validity was sustained by their sense of superiority and intense manichean partisanship against all other political groupings. This operated during my entire stay and was a major impediment to working out a civilized solution to the developing impasse.

A Popular Embassy

I was extremely busy during my first three months in Nicaragua. I wished to reach privately as many groups as possible to explain our policy and our desire to see peaceful change and eventual democratic evolution, while refraining from actively supporting the government or organizing the opposition. This I explained to my multiple contacts to minimize miscalculations, build up a reservoir of confidence and goodwill, and have support when the tough problems that I feared would present themselves came along.

Although I was concerned with the implications of the verbal and written intense partisanship (i.e., *sectarismo*) and the still minor acts of violence, I was comfortable advocating the country's peaceful democratization. Somoza's model of dynastic authoritarian *continuismo* was worn out; sooner or later it could no longer be maintained. The violent route, given the apparent unshakable subordination to Somoza of the National Guard, would be full of uncertainty and very costly. As revealed by the propaganda of the October armed actions, the *violentos* held messianic and apocalyptic misperceptions of their own about an almost immediate victory. There was no guarantee that they could win (especially with reasonable costs), and I understood the strong authoritarianism within Sandinismo.

As the policy evolved, I told the Nicaraguan government of the desirability of giving liberal, democratic guarantees for opposition activities and encouraged conversations and a political compromise between the government and the opposition. But, according to my instructions, when the opportunity arose, I conveyed to all that the desired peaceful changes would have to result from Nicaraguan decisions, as opposed to any U.S. plan.

As the American ambassador, I was warmly welcomed by many groups. Early access was difficult only to a few of the more radicalized sectors, such as a few pockets within the National University and armed revolutionary activists. I was particularly interested in reaching private business, professional, religious, and civic organizations and leaders to inform them about policy, seek their friendship, and show an active concern on the part of my government.[10] I felt that some form of participation on their part would be necessary for any peaceful or moderate solution, and I wanted to lay the groundwork for such an eventuality.

The response was quite favorable. Increasingly I received invitations from throughout the country to visit many organizations and less formalized groups. Because of Somoza's unshakable control of the National Guard and over the bulk of the arms, and the perceived power, credibility, and liking of the United States by the upper-, middle-, and popular-class *fuerzas* or *clases vivas*, I noticed a predisposition on the part of my contacts to encourage our taking an active role in the process. I discovered very scarce support for the local government; despite reservations about the extent to which Nicaragua could be ruled democratically, there was an inclination to seek political change and a widespread feeling that only through decisive U.S. pressure would peaceful evolution be feasible.[11] The local equation was very simple. Nicaraguans believed that General Somoza would not voluntarily relinquish his control. To achieve this without a war, the United States had to pressure him, delivering some "offer that he could not refuse." Note the clientelistic psychological dependency. The equation made sense, however.

In spite of my repeated statements that we would not "intervene" in Nicaragua, still many of our friends ultimately expected a successful U.S.

initiative in their country. This and Somoza's unwillingness to shorten his term by a single day constituted the core dilemma that Washington chose not to resolve.

Nicaraguan officials were aware of my government's desire for change. I remember having early conversations with a few individuals close to the president, including members of his family, who privately said that they understood the need for improvement. Two or three told me that the Somozas had been in power far too long, that there had been too much corruption, and that what was needed was an easy, gradual transition. Many exhibited toward me the interpersonal warmth and generosity of which Nicaraguans are proud, and that I still hold dear. But there were some of the president's friends who told me about their concern that the United States was really trying to depose Somoza, to score a human rights success. It was rare not to hear Somocistas proclaim their allegiance to the United States—"*somos americanistas, amamos a su país*" (we are pro-American, we love your country), expressions delivered with the almost palpable, sincere, strong emotion so common to Nicaragua's ethos of fealty. I often heard this expression of loyalty and of alleged betrayal: "When you have needed us we have given you our support; we are your true friends. Why do you betray us withholding your support? You are leaving us alone to face the hatred of our common enemies." The Somocistas had converted the grand cultural ethos of personalism, familism, and *amistad* (intense friendship) into political doctrine: friends (*amigos*) should stay together; enemies (*enemigos*) should be discarded.

There were also those, reflecting the local potential for escalating conflict, who told me that the opposition was a bunch of Communists, criminals, worthless, despicable nonentities, that oppositionists were the true human rights violators. It was indeed ironic that our policy also sought protection for those armed revolutionaries whom our government was never ultimately happy to see attain power, and whose victory was vehemently defined by them as a U.S. defeat.

Opposition politicians had a different perspective. They said they understood that a "made in Nicaragua" formula to solve the problems was in principle desirable, that there was no need for the United States to employ the forceful, gunboat methods of the past to change governments. But they rarely resisted the opportunity to make me aware of the U.S. government's responsibility for Somoza's rule because of our founding of the National Guard, conferring its leadership to Somoza García, and the continued historical ties with the Somozas. Many expressed their belief in our alleged quasi-magical powers to accomplish, at a minimum cost, any monumental political change. Many believed that all that was needed was my will to use our "magic wand":

simply ask the president to resign. The underlying assumption was clear: Somoza remained in power merely because we did not do enough and thus supported him. This position was held until the very end.

In the last analysis, opposition strategy sought a total estrangement between the two governments as the test of our "neutrality"; more precisely, the test was our contribution to change the regime. Although such psychological reliance on us at times frustrated me because it ran counter to Washington's policy, given Somoza's control of the National Guard and perceived inflexibility, it was only natural that these individuals unwilling to risk their lives in combat and desirous to avoid war would in their powerlessness be so dependent on us. Obviously, the safe way to "persuade" a General Somoza with a proved history of authoritarian recalcitrance to stop ruling was the deliverance of some American ultimatum. This did not mean that Somoza would have given up power short of an imminent U.S. deployment of troops against him. But the opposition believed that Somoza would never voluntarily stop ruling. The United States had the capability of pressuring him out, and there were *no ethical grounds* for Washington not to deliver an ultimatum to Somoza. Washington supporters of so-called neutrality encouraged anti-Somoza forces while refusing to accept the consequences for the local real actors.

As I was repeatedly told, we had brought a breath of fresh air. Suddenly there was hope; we were leavening the polity. As a sign of our high symbolic status, I was frequently treated as a "proconsul" of sorts. I recall being militarily saluted by some members of the National Guard in my tours throughout the country, and the embassy's hand was seen behind many government decisions. We had created, trained, and armed the National Guard. Many felt that the Guard would respond to us, if we only tried.

When Washington suspended a few developmental loans in 1977, much hope materialized that the end for Somoza was in sight. When, against my strong opposition, Washington approved two loans the following spring (claiming publicly now that they were not intended to support the regime but to assist the poor), our government, including the embassy, became defined in the local media as co-responsible for the "human rights abuses" attributed to the rulers. "Human rights" became a fundamental slogan in the contest to control the state. This new propaganda piece became incorporated into the highly conflictive matrix of mutual accusation of collective criminality. In these post-siege days, one could not escape being exposed to the vitriolic, incendiary, anti-government (and anti-opposition) messages in the press and radio, campaigns that continued in spite of the periodic fines and temporary suspension of some programs by an uneasy government. (The press was uncensored, and although periodically some radio programs were fined or temporarily suspended, at no point was the entire opposition radio silenced.) Virtually all of my contacts on all sides perceived our "neutrality" as avoiding a definite commitment and our historical responsibility.

The Detonator

The assassination on January 10, 1977, of La Prensa's publisher, Pedro Joaquín Chamorro—"P.J.," as we affectionately called him in the embassy—proved to be the turning point. I was in the embassy's aid section trying to make sense of the assistance policy when I heard the news. My immediate reaction was to think that if this news was true, my agenda for the new year of trying to influence the most powerful oppositionist and Somoza to work out a mutually guaranteed process of democratization had collapsed.

I had been about to develop a real relationship with Chamorro. I had felt apprehensive about the kind of relationship I would be able to establish with someone who had been portrayed as a vehement, difficult man. I was also intrigued by the fact that Chamorro had not become a unifying leader of the opposition. Yet I had met a serious intellectual who showed modesty and a sense of humor about himself. I could comfortably and openly exchange views with him.

La Prensa had not always treated me wisely. One day, for example, it had published sections of my book on military coups d'état, with the implication that according to my theories, a coup was possible in Nicaragua. This kind of "unguided missile" could only make my task more difficult. I always received apologies for such erratic behavior and never maintained any grudge. My political purpose had priority, and La Prensa was to play a role in it. From the outset, my relationship with P.J. was honest and frank. In our last meeting we had agreed for our families to spend a long weekend together.

Yet I was not overly sanguine about the success of my project. Surely there was need to tone down the ongoing debate—including La Prensa's style of highlighting accusations of collective criminality against the Somocistas—if the agreed-upon dialogue between the parties involving Archbishop Obando y Bravo was to succeed. In my second conversation with Somoza, when I was formally presenting credentials, he was crude, arrogant, and rude. He told me that he knew everything that happened, that if I wished to be informed I should ask him. He criticized two members of the embassy's staff and suggested that I seek to replace them, and in the presence of the Vatican's ambassador he jokingly referred to putting his son in charge of the military, as if to continue the dynasty. But after Washington suspended two assistance projects and after a long social visit arranged so that we could get to know each other better, Somoza had become less lordly and distant and accepted dialogue with the opposition. We still had time, I thought—the opposition had to grow and become better organized and coherent. Chamorro had started public rallies, which were still very small. Democratization was worth trying. Surely other individuals could also rule the country. These were the thoughts that sustained my efforts.

Immediately after Chamorro's death, Somoza implicated a few American citizens of Cuban origin in the crime. The government media carried the accusation against them in riotous Managua; mobs attacked Plasmaféresis, their business. Fearing for their lives, these citizens sought refuge in the U.S. Embassy. After consultation with and instructions from Washington, they were soon asked to leave the chancellery when the crowds and imminent physical danger vanished. They wished to leave Nicaragua, but the Nicaraguan government would not permit them to on grounds of their involvement in the crime. Thus they again returned to the chancellery, once again fearing for their lives.

The issue was straightforward. The United States could not ask that culprits be left free. But we could and did ask that if the Americans were suspects (and consequently not allowed to depart the country), they be brought under the protective control of the government, and speedy legal procedures be carried out. Symptomatic of the atrophy of the regime, these American citizens were neither indicted nor allowed to leave Nicaragua, nor put under the local government's protection and custody.

As we had not progressed, I solicited a meeting with Somoza himself. Per my talking points as drafted with embassy officer Jay Freres, it was to be absolutely clear that I was not asking the Nicaraguan president to let the men go free and leave the country.

"*Presidente*," I said, "I am sorry to bother you, but I have four American citizens who fear for their lives."

"Fear," he said, raising his voice, "yes they should fear. We Nicaraguans have different customs. But Chamorro abused the Cubans and he did not realize that they are not the Somozas."

Somoza, elaborating on a personal vendetta, expressed that although he could have killed Chamorro several times, he did not wish to do so—having him alive proved that the Somozas were not the tyrants the allegations implied.

"The problem of the U.S. citizens has to be solved," I said. Somoza answered that it was solved; they could leave the country.

"They can leave?" I answered in disbelief.

"Yes. I am giving instructions to that effect."

My private reaction was that this arbitrariness—first publicly accuse the men, then let them go scot-free—would harm him. Yet for reasons of his own Somoza dealt negligently with the problem at this crucial time. He might have feared the adverse publicity of a long trial, which would have been internationally reported as well. The accused knew too much about Nicaraguan government illegalities, two of the accused had told me. They would not remain silent.

It is noteworthy, in spite of the well-known presence in our chancellery of Chamorro's accused assassins in Managua, where law and order had broken down, that not a single demonstration or protest was geared against the embassy. Our pro-democratic message had created a positive local image prior to P.J.'s murder. Oppositionists had other plans for us. Within a matter of days, these plans became known.

In any case, we were very sensitive to maintain the embassy's independence from the departure of the U.S. citizens from Nicaragua. They left the airport on their own, in transportation privately arranged by themselves—no U.S. government vehicle was ever used on their behalf.

Naturally, public opinion involved the president himself in the plot to assassinate Chamorro. A populace that the opposition had not been able to mobilize in years in any substantial way responded with riotous protests in the streets. In reaction to the tragedy and its cover-up, a broadly based movement started to materialize, asking Somoza to resign.[12]

In short, the assassination shattered pending plans for an early 1978 diálogo mediated by the archbishop; it resulted in a broad refusal to talk and negotiate at all with the president, intensified the regime crisis, and dramatically shrank the acceptability of continuing Somoza's rule. The assassination of Benigno Aquino five years later in the Philippines showed similarities in energizing the opposition, but the bulk of the opposing populace accepted the electoral route that he had advocated to change the regime. Chamorro's legacy was different—he had not been sponsoring electoral participation but abstention.

The president refused to step down. Despite the disturbances that signaled, in *New York Times* correspondent Alan Riding's words, the beginnings of a "national mutiny," Somoza, with the loyalty of his group and desirous of American support, did not reestablish the state of siege. In the past, in order to survive, the Somozas had swiftly moved repressively, impeding the growth of public disturbances and revolutionary organizations. The situation was now more serious. The government had less support: a lot of people were out on the streets protesting in various parts of Nicaragua, and a fairly generalized strike would take hold. The opposition mass media was allowed to continue to report on the protests and incite the people to rebel.

Yet in spite of his threats, Somoza did not move to decapitate the opposition at this early time in which he had relatively more resources. In fact, many oppositionists continued to meet with me on a regular basis. Through the coming months, very few opposition leaders were murdered; the harassment and imprisonment of a few of these leaders was exceptional and brief. You should not think that I am not aware of the brutality of the process—I would be officially involved in several cases of rape, murder, and disappearances of both American and Nicaraguan citizens in which the National Guard was directly implicated. But a paradox of successful revolutions is that the government does not employ *effective* repression because it cannot or because it lacks the will. Somoza started to allow the organization of a critical mass, a broad movement to forcefully unseat him. In his memoirs he regretfully observes that his concern about a further deterioration of relations with the United States induced him to follow such tactics—which he had told me he was doing so that I would inform Washington. Naturally, this reaction to our "protective umbrella" for the opposition further undercut his position as the opposition, vengeful of his past repression, learned tactics, recruited, grew, and was emboldened. "Because of you I am not feared now," a frustrated Somoza told me. "Oppositionists are very stupid; they don't realize I want to give a chance to democracy."

Somoza had only reluctantly been willing to dialogue or negotiate with his adversaries. Now, after Chamorro, he earnestly wanted to do so, but the opposition refused: he had become a "devil incarnate," an "untouchable" to be avoided. Throughout this new period Somoza and I were in frequent contact. But from now on, neither the opposition nor Somoza would budge from the political deadlock. In mid-1978, Karen DeYoung of the *Washington Post* reported Somoza's position: "I'm a hard nut . . . . They elected me for a term [until 1981], and they've got to stand me." With greater local flavor Somoza was quoted earlier in his newspaper: "*Como dijo mi padre, ni me voy ni me van*" (As my father said, I will not leave nor will they make me leave).[13]

The Stoppage

Throughout the second period of our mission, from January to the major uprising of September 1978, the embassy was under strong pressure to abandon "neutrality." Before Chamorro's untimely death I had started visiting business associations, assuming that a peaceful evolution would be more likely if a political center gained strength. In fact, Chamorro had encouraged my involvement to create a favorable climate for progressive change among the initially not very politically active business leaders. He also wished to use me to establish links with the National Guard. Much propaganda had been made of my visits.

One of the entities to which I had become close was a civic association of businessmen headed by Alfonso Robelo Callejas, the Instituto Nicaragüense de Desarrollo (INDE). The old chambers, such as Cámara de Comercio, Cámara de Industrias, and so on, continued in existence, but there had been an initiative to form an umbrella organization to encompass the entire private sector, soon activated as Consejo Superior de la Empresa Privada (COSEP), and to involve it in socioeconomic development projects. INDE was a nongovernment organization, not a business interest group proper, that implemented the development projects.

Around its banner a group of young, largely foreign-trained businessmen and professionals with civic and political interests had started to participate in efforts to democratize the country. Many of them viewed the established politicians as inadequate, corrupt, or ineffectual, and aspired to play a role in transforming the political arena. Robelo had become involved as an unofficial spokesman of the business community in organizing the *diálogo* with the archbishop, Monsignor Obando.

Robelo, who eventually became one of the members of the first Sandinista junta, came to my office to inform me of the rapidly developing climate within several business chambers to end Somoza's rule and their plan to organize a general strike. His hope was that the U.S. government, the archbishop, or "someone" else of importance would approach Somoza and persuade him to resign.[14] Following the spirit of my instructions, I did not tell Robelo that we backed Somoza, nor that I opposed the stoppage.

In the intensified visits that I received during these days of abrupt alienation from the president, it was not unusual that I express sympathy for the opposition, however. For example, I received a group of women who brought me two tear gas canisters marked "Made in the U.S.A." They blamed the U.S. government for the "repression" against them. I finally told them, "I am not and can not be a party in this crisis. I do know that in Chile women protested against Allende by banging their *cacerolas*" (cooking pans). And so the practice was initiated in Nicaragua. We had quite a frank, open mission, and perhaps to many eager oppositionists the embassy appeared to countenance their goals. Unfortunately, no envoy—and there were several—was given the authority to apply American power to resolve the crisis. But my staff and I were always successful in patching up differences with virtually all of the civic, unarmed leaders.

I maintained regular contact with the archbishop. He inquired about the possibility that my government could obtain Somoza's resignation. Monsignor Obando knew that the bishops could not persuade him to resign. With the strike on, the bishops officially made a statement advocating a "civilized route" to resolve the crisis. The following day (January 29) the religious orders and communities of Managua asked that the president resign, in a communiqué backing the stoppage and blaming the government for the consequences of not accepting "civic change."[15]

The stoppage had been organized by the principal urban business groups and involved the two largest non-Somoza financial groups. However, it had not entirely paralyzed the nation's economic activity; in no city was it claimed to be over 80 percent effective, because the Somoza family owned a substantial portion of the economy. Strategic economic activities tied to the government, in addition to the bureaucracy proper that remained loyal, kept some businesses functioning. Transportation services, such as city buses with ownership ties to the Guardia Nacional, also continued operating.

On February 6, 1978, the strike was formally ended. I had kept in touch with the "stoppage movement" with regular visits by William Baez Sacasa, a key actor on the Robelo team. I was worried that the non-Somoza business sector would suffer a political defeat; postdynastic Nicaragua needed its active participation. Their formal communiqué adequately saved face. The strike was defined as a peaceful, civic, renewable instrument to democratize the nation, and it could be called again at the appropriate moment.

Toward a United Opposition

During the next months, until September 1978, opposition activity snowballed, encouraged by a virtually uncensored, incendiary mass media. Somoza could not govern without at least reimposing the state of siege, but he would not do so, perhaps also led by his pride. Somoza repeatedly stated that if others wanted to lose money and destroy the country, it was up to them.

By April several of the basic components of the model of insurrection that would finally succeed the following year had been rehearsed, although on a small scale and insufficiently coordinated:

1. Armed action encircling Guardia Nacional military compounds (*cuarteles*) in towns and cities to capture and disable them—none had yet been captured—as in Masaya, first in October 1977.
2. Armed and unarmed people in the streets building barricades, stopping traffic, and so briefly liberating for some time towns or sections of cities from government control, as in February 1978 in Monimbo.
3. Incursions into Nicaragua of small groups of armed men from neighboring countries (mainly from Costa Rica). The first armed border crossings had taken place in October 1977 from the south (San Carlos) and the north (Ocotal).
4. A general stoppage.

Although Somoza had never before faced such widespread resistance, the opposition still had to overcome its fragmentation. Mobilization and collective action had gotten ahead of any tight organization. The opposition demanded the strongman's resignation, but it lacked a structure to articulate policy beyond this rudimentary position.[16]

On April 1, the formation of a broad opposition front, the Frente Amplio Opositor (FAO), was announced to include the various opposition factions. The Sandinista commandants, who were clandestine, were not directly present in the FAO but were represented in it by the Group of Twelve. The emerging alliance of Sandinistas, unarmed opposition, and interest groups was not a firm one, nor did the Sandinista historic leaders yet have the upper hand. Umbrella opposition organizations had precedent in Nicaragua, the most recent one being Chamorro's UDEL. Peculiar to the FAO, however, was its tie to the armed opposition and its refusal to repudiate violence. After the October events there had been public condemnation of violence, leading to the formation of the *diálogo* movement. Now the situation was different: the unarmed opposition, although privately holding reservations about the armed route and the Marxist-Leninist orientations among core Sandinista leaders, would not publicly condemn violence unless the president resigned. The unarmed opposition felt that without a U.S. commitment, it could not alone terminate Somoza's rule and so must rely on popular protests and violence.

Technically those in the FAO were only "politicians." But although formally outside the FAO, the Catholic Church, with its formidable organization down to parish and *comunidades de base* levels, and the main urban business chambers were also in opposition. The majority of prominent families had turned to opposition, including two of the three top financial groups (the third was Somoza's).

Also in opposition without governmental control were key organs of the media, including the main newspaper and several popular radio stations. Foreign governments could also be counted. Cuba did not hold a pro-revolution monopoly. The Venezuelan and Panamanian governments were committed to "defend Costa Rica against government of Nicaragua aggression," while Costa Rica increasingly was becoming a base to export revolution to Nicaragua. Venezuela and Panama were assisting the Nicaraguan opposition and prodding the United States to kick Somoza out.

At the same time the Sandinistas' following was rapidly increasing, and their cadres were organizing fights and street actions—although not all of these activists were "ideologically" Sandinistas, in the original sense of the term of membership in the Frente Sandinista de Liberación Nacional (FSLN).[17] Even sons and daughters of very prominent families were "Sandinistas," and with time their numbers increased. The point is that a fairly spontaneous, growing rebellion had taken hold, with participants in the disturbances with different political self-identities, whom the population sympathetically called *los muchachos* (the kids) and considered to be Sandinistas.

In the FAO, then, there was broad ideological heterogeneity: the common denominator was "Somoza should have left yesterday." Was it a democratic movement? Certainly not in any united sense. I found oppositionists who held reservations about the desirability or viability of a representative democratic regime in the country. The total collapse of the U.S. policy at the end of the year brought about the FAO's replacement by a Sandinista-dominated, more strongly authoritarian coalition.

Yet the FAO's heterogeneity contributed to its radicalization. In search of leadership roles, many members vocally competed to show their anti-Somoza stance to gain credentials. No one would talk to the dictator. The alternative left seemed to be that either the United States would obtain Somoza's resignation (and somehow help organize a new government), or there would be war. This only reinforced the general's most intransigent contempt for men "who are not men enough to meet with me," and his conviction that the opposition was not a desirable, even viable, alternative to rule.

Somoza's Unshakeable Public Commitment

My relationship with Somoza and his group had not been good. In fact, in my first month in the country I had brought to the attention of Luis Pallais Debayle, the president's first cousin and spokesman with whom I always maintained a frank and cordial relationship, that I had close links with the opposition only because Somocistas had deliberately kept distant from me. Luis's initiative to link me with the Somocista clique took the form of a large dinner party given for my family, where I discovered an incredible pattern. Only the wives of the functionaries present were available to be photographed with me except for members of Somoza's family. For example, I was engaged in a conversation with a cabinet minister and three women when a photographer from *Novedades*—the government's newspaper, run by Pallais—approached us. The minister literally ran away from our group so as not to be photographed with me.

The antecedent was that Cornelio Hueck, until recently president of the Congress, had been suddenly purged by Somoza soon after my arrival in the country. It was alleged that this was the result of inviting us to his house, making contact with me prior to my presentation of credentials while convalescent Somoza was still secluded in his hacienda. In fact, Don Cornelio had been the first of a handful of Somocista officials who during my tenure talked to me of the need to replace Somoza. I should note, however, that Hueck was unable to create dissidence: he was totally socially *ostracized* by the Somocistas. More than one of them told me that Hueck was too ambitious and thus deserved his ousting. From the very outset we had reasons to believe that no viable initiative would materialize from the ruling group to persuade the president to compromise: they were totally subordinated to the irreplaceable leader. This was the old Somoza doctrine accepted by his team: chaos is the alternative to family rule. What if the general suddenly died?[18]

Somoza was still a distant figure. Faced with the post-Chamorro crisis, the president changed tactics: he made an effort to become close to me and started calling me to see him on a one-to-one basis at least once a week. I think he believed he could win me over, that I would realize that he was the only leader with an organized following capable of ruling. In his view what he needed was only the backing of the U.S. government to stop the rebellion of all but the die-hard Sandinista *violentos*.

During this phase I perceived a man who combined a sharp natural intelligence with an unaffected frank disposition and projected warmth and *simpatía* toward me, though he retained the messianic self-image and tough defense of what he thought was his self-interest, extended to his group and nation. This is an immature opposition, Somoza was telling me: "You see, I have not reimposed the state of siege, I have not repressed the opposition. They need time to organize themselves. Why don't they come to negotiate a solution?" Somoza's message in a sense was diabolic: "These people are unreasonable. I am trying to be democratic." As the opposition did not meet his terms, he could only come to one conclusion: "I really tried. There is no alternative for me. This country is incapable of democracy, so I must be supported."

Somoza tried to have me trust him, have me recognize that he was "a man of his word." He repeatedly told me that now he was eager to negotiate with the opposition, that I should convince them to speak to him. His position seemed reasonable. How could the dynasty be dismantled in a relatively peaceful manner without negotiations with him? Somoza's uncle and family patriarch, Luis Manuel Debayle, whom I personally liked and enjoyed, kept in close contact with me. Very early he had given me a diagnosis: "What is needed here is a slide"—he gesticulated—"an easy stepping down of the family from running the state, to live peacefully in a country not controlled by Marxist-Leninist dictators."

In the face of the deadlock, I concentrated my efforts with Somoza. Unfortunately, when I explored the general's position, he refused to step down before 1981. In fact, he had never denied that he intended to stop being president at that time but still retain command of the National Guard. Although I had no instructions to do so, I persuaded him to say publicly that he would relinquish political power, leaving both the presidency and the National Guard at the end of his term.

I had in mind eliciting a policy initiative from Washington to induce government-opposition negotiations, as no sector of the opposition was willing to negotiate without a U.S.-led mediation. Subsequent points of discussion became the role of his son and half-brother, José R. Somoza, in the military. Somoza repeatedly told me that if he replaced them—a sign of moving away from hereditary rule—he could not maintain the loyalty of his army. At one point, spokesman Luis Pallais Debayle informed me that it was easier for the president to resign than to replace members of his family and retain his office. This was undignified. In the issues that counted, the dynasty never made concessions.

Terence Todman's Initiative

Except for the small Somocista circle, virtually all my contacts prescribed Somoza's resignation as the solution: the archbishop, top financiers, the collaborationist oppositionists who shared a minority of the state's offices (the Conservative, locally called Zancudo, i.e., "parasitic," faction), and so on. The Twelve agreed on this, for the alternative of a war was too costly and its outcome still uncertain.

I knew that Washington refused to ask Somoza to resign. While in Caracas, the president of the United States responded to an initiative of Venezuelan president Carlos Andrés Pérez to obtain Somoza's resignation. He agreed with Pérez about the promotion of human rights but was not willing to go as far as to try to do anything about Somoza's resignation.[19] Again, the United States could "interfere" in the domestic human rights performance of Nicaragua but not "intervene" to change its government.

On February 7, I met with Somoza at his base of operations, the Bunker, for lunch. We talked for about two hours. The conversation was based on the instructions that I had received: the U.S. government felt that its national interests were being threatened by the crisis and violence, and by the potential for destabilization in Central America; our objective was a nonviolent solution to the crisis, which we did not see happening. We observed a continued polarization. Although our highest priority was to see an orderly process of change in Nicaragua, we were not seeking to remove Somoza from power extralegally.[20]

Todman had gone over the points with Guillermo Sevilla Sacasa, Somoza's brother-in-law and ambassador to the United States, but during our conversation I handed Somoza a sheet of paper with the following items contained in Washington's cable:

The Nicaraguan government, including the National Guard, should show maximum restraint in dealing with strikers and demonstrators.

The Nicaraguan government should take no vengeance or reprisals against individuals or firms that peacefully participated in the strike.

The president should identify changes that can be made in advance of any formal dialogue, and announce and implement them.

The president should continue to seek conversations with responsible opposition leaders.

The president should inform opposition leaders that he is willing to accomplish changes in the electoral process that will permit additional parties to obtain official status and express their views building up to fair and open elections.

Control of the Guard should be institutionalized outside the family.

It would be advisable for the president to appoint a broadly based national investigatory commission with full legal powers to investigate the assassination of Dr. Chamorro.

It would be helpful for the president to announce that the Inter-American Human Rights Commission was being invited to Nicaragua, to hear any complaints anyone might wish to make regarding human rights violations and to conduct appropriate investigations.

The State Department had moved in the right direction: Somoza had to take the initiative. Notice, however, that in fact Washington suggested tying Somoza's hand. He was advised not to repress the opposition, while still formally not taking the leadership to mediate the conflict.

Somoza opened the conversation by indicating that he agreed in principle but needed time to implement the reforms, and conveyed his pleasure that the Sandinistas had been defeated in their recent attacks, the strike had ended, and the municipal election had taken place without any major violence. Actually, the municipal election had taken place without any popular participation—it was generally interpreted as an example of the fraudulent electoral charades, an indication that Somoza would not change and relinquish power voluntarily. Nor had the protests and violence on the streets ended; in a few days the important strategic uprising of Monimbo would take place.

Somoza was worried that if he unilaterally undertook some of these reforms he would be left with less to bargain with. I nevertheless wished to sound as positive as possible in carrying out the démarche. "We are trying to help you as a friend, not take advantage of you. It is essential that you decide what you want to do: go out as a leader who transferred power as a democrat or leave office as a dictator. I am sure that the United States would be willing to help in the first case."

Somoza said, "I have gone through a lot, from the experiences that I learned from my father who was a great politician 'who did not allow anyone to sit on his chair,' to the many years that I waited to become president. No one is going to believe that my intentions are democratic; I know the opposition, they will not permit the success." His country was as democratic as it could be, and Americans simply did not understand.

I returned to the basic problem, the increased potential for violence. In the past during periods of liberalized rule, the Somozas had taken advantage of the opposition's tendency to become radicalized, using this as an excuse for repression. What was needed in Nicaragua was true reform to allow for democratic participation without the escalation of conflict.

Somoza referred to the new respectability that was being given to the Sandinistas through their new linkages with oppositionists and their operations in Costa Rica. Indeed, I commented, previously the FSLN was essentially an isolated movement, but with the new militancy of the political opposition and the private sector they were gaining respectability.

Why did Somoza not reject Washington's points outright? His strategy was to gain time. His reaction may also have reflected an interest in exploring if he could use us to influence the opposition into a more accommodating position of dialogue. I was unconvinced that he had accepted the message. Perhaps more than ever he believed that the opposition would not allow any honorable exit for him and his family to remain in Nicaragua as influential "private" citizens, given the refusal of all his opponents to discuss any issue with him. Curiously, the embassy's report to Washington ended with this comment, which I paraphrase: Somoza may feel that if conditions become acute enough the United States would prefer to back him rather than let the Sandinistas or chaos prevail. Somoza's strategy ultimately led to the "Somoza or the FSLN" alternative. Washington really did not back either.

February ended with a mass rally of government forces. The official estimate was two hundred thousand participants, a very inflated figure, even considering that the apparatus of the state was forced to participate. At the rally, Somoza made a speech with the following points:

thanks to the National Guard for its peace efforts;
that Conservative forces and businessmen had caused the work stoppage;
his openness to dialogue with all of the nation's sectors, and willingness to revise the terms of a new national pact;

his willingness to leave the presidency and the directorship of the National Guard in 1981, "so that Nicaragua has a democratic evolution,
and our armed institution evolve for the benefit and well-being of all
Nicaraguans";

his support to form a commission of "illustrious and impartial citizens"
to examine the criminal case of Chamorro's murder [the case was
plagued with irregularities and lack of credibility, however, and no
prominent Nicaraguan was willing to participate in any government-
organized commission]; an attack against the United States—those
who talk about human rights but "historically beat the blacks," who
keep their Indians as second-class citizens, and have riots and looting
in their cities;

a series of promised social reforms to be paid by the business community, i.e., the strikers [a symptom of the lack of élan of the isolated
government none were implemented];

the meeting's slogans: "no te vas . . . te quedás" [Somoza stays], "Viva la
Guardia Nacional," "Viva el Partido Liberal."[21]

What was to be done in the face of the local reality of the government's total
isolation and escalating opposition by all the rest of the society? I thought that
Washington should try to mediate the impasse with involvement of the highest
administration level. It was a risky involvement for there was no guarantee
that the strongman would comply with the obvious need to shorten his term.
The need to deliver an ultimatum and even to use force against recalcitrant
dictatorships to avoid diplomatic defeat was part of the historical record. (It
remained being so in the future; to wit, the invasion of Panama in 1989 by Bush
Sr. and Haiti in 1994 by Clinton). But a top-level mediation was worth trying
in order to avoid the impending war. President Carter mediated the Egypt-
Israel conflict and would be involved in several other international efforts
after leaving office, including mediating in the 1990 mutual "guarantees" for
Nicaragua's democratic transition.

The Embassy Unable to Mediate

My hopes that at least the embassy would play an active role in working a
compromise were soon dashed. On February 17 we received a cable from the
deputy secretary of state with new instructions on the role that the embassy
was to play "until further notice." Deputy Secretary Warren Christopher was
the highest official with whom I had transacted business. Because of his role
in implementing the human rights policy, a committee to administer U.S.
assistance had been named after him; he had become known in Washington
as "Mr. Human Rights."

My new instructions were to avoid getting involved in "internal political maneuvering" in Nicaragua, avoid being seen as "propping up" the government or backing the opposition's attempts to "unseat" Somoza, and, at the same time, maintain the public and private campaign for human rights and for an "open" political process (which, in fact, had become one of convulsive and violent conflict). The embassy's role was simply to preach to the parties not to engage in violence and repression and to express support for negotiations between them.

In addition, the embassy could not serve to "guarantee" the behavior of the government nor the opposition. We could not become a "middleman" between the parties in conflict or advise them on how they should resolve their differences. It was for the contending parties—the Nicaraguans themselves— to get in contact with each other. The embassy could not carry "messages, proposals, or assurances of any kind."

According to the cable, some opposition groups wished to persuade the embassy that the U.S. government should organize Somoza's removal from power. The embassy was to make clear to these groups that this had a "purely Nicaraguan internal political character," and that the United States would play no role in it. Finally, we were advised that in order to implement the new instructions we should reduce our contacts with both the government and opposition for the "immediate future."

I was most upset with these new instructions. It abdicated any U.S. leadership, in spite of the desires that all Nicaraguans manifested to the embassy. Its "neutrality, not total indifference" was doctrinaire. To begin with, to the extent that the Nicaraguans were capable of peacefully evolving their system into one respectful of human rights, they would have not "needed" the American human rights policy. An activist U.S. policy already had been implemented, explicitly signaling withdrawal of support from Somoza. A "chance" event had precipitated a crisis that resulted in the growth of opposition to a man who had given indications that he had not wished to give up power but rather intended to perpetuate family rule. The strongman had the command of the bulk of the military force. What was the opposition to do? Demobilize, not fight to change the government, obey Washington's desires to peacefully negotiate with a distrusted dictator?

In my view the U.S. formula was irrelevant and irresponsible. When the chips were down, Washington was refusing any responsibility in helping to work out the solution. To preach, to play with the politics of a small foreign country (e.g., suspending loans), apparently was not considered an "intervention" in it; mediating a conflict was. A bloodbath was coming. Unfortunately, though gentlemanly and very well meaning, Warren Christopher did not seem fully aware of local realities. There was rigidity, a combination of moral arrogance and cowardice in the policy of "neutrality." It confused the Nicaraguans.[22]

Consultations

Assistant Secretary Todman had organized a meeting of chiefs of mission in Washington for February 27; all U.S. Latin American ambassadors were to attend. Thus rather than protest my new instructions, I sought clarification of them. On March 2 I met with Assistant Secretary Todman to express my concern: we had been making some progress, but with Chamorro's assassination a chaotic situation had developed. I felt that I could not accept Christopher's new instructions restricting my contacts with all groups—why have an ambassador in Managua? Either the U.S. government had confidence in me or not. I had not been imprudent in my contacts.

Todman agreed. There was a double standard; we were willing to negotiate and mediate in other theaters, but not Nicaragua. The mood that prevailed in the administration was that instructions would never be given to ask Somoza to step down because of the hold of the "non-interventionist" principle; but no more military assistance would be forthcoming. No more USAID programs would be approved until public order was reestablished.

At the end of our meeting, Todman drafted new instructions for me to present to Christopher. I agreed with the draft's diagnosis of the risks facing our policy, the possibility that it would result in a total fiasco. Todman was advocating the maximum feasible at the time:

Instructions to the Ambassador:

As a result of our consultations during your recent visit to Washington and the opportunity that visit afforded us to review the present situation in Nicaragua, we offer the following comments and instructions.

It is our joint conclusion that the current situation is a serious one, presenting enormous potential for increasing polarization, violence and chaos. There is the possibility of civil war, increased repression by the current government, the emergence of a repressive retrogressive right-wing dictatorship or a Castro-style regime emerging out of the present impasse. Any of the aforementioned would constitute a major setback to our human rights policy and our interest in the democratic evolution of Nicaragua.

While we must continue to maintain a posture of non-intervention in Nicaragua we believe that the United States cannot abdicate its role of leadership and moral responsibility.

Without imposing any solution the U.S. must assist the concerned parties in working out a peaceful solution to the present difficulty. A U.S. position of inactivity could well lead to a continued deterioration in the already critical situation possibly involving neighboring countries. Such developments would be detrimental to our national interests. As Nicaragua is a test for our human rights policy it would also be inappropriate to completely wash our hands of the present crisis and merely sit by, watching events take their course at the probable cost of considerable death and suffering.

In accordance with the aforementioned conclusions the following instructions are offered to guide you during the immediate future:

1. Avoid identification with any faction.
2. Encourage all to work for a democratic solution to the present crisis.
3. Continue your normal contacts with all legitimate forces in the society.
4. As you deem appropriate, assist in clarifying and encouraging compromise between opposing factions and positions. This should not, however, include negotiating on behalf of any groups nor guaranteeing any agreements.

The dynamics of the situation since my initial contacts had led to a change in position by Todman's unit: it had explicitly adopted the goal of democratic evolution. Initially Todman had sought to maintain friendly ties with the Nicaraguan government, limiting the scope of the human rights campaign to private representations to General Somoza. At this stage, he wished to see U.S. support for a political plan to end the crisis and avoid the predictable escalated war involving several countries. All my contacts had come to believe that the optimal solution—which I shared—was to obtain Somoza's resignation.

Observing the struggle over decisions and the convoluted language used to hide political positions, I did not feel proud of, nor confident in, the administration. But in the subsequently slightly modified final version of the new instructions, I was allowed to maintain my contacts and explore possibilities for a negotiated settlement. Thus I felt that I did not have to resign. I could live better with the new instructions to try to prepare the groundwork for what I hoped would eventually be an arbitrated solution by the United States. This I actively did in the following months, until we organized in Managua the petition by local groups to bring the international mediation by the Organization of American States that the U.S. government finally was willing to initiate.

That for some people "neutrality" was a label to disguise a policy of confrontation with and destabilization of the Nicaraguan government became perfectly clear the following day in my meeting with Mark Schneider, the deputy assistant secretary of state for human rights. He wanted to terminate all of our assistance programs to show that we did not support Somoza. My reply was that our withdrawal from Nicaragua might be unsuccessful, as it was in François Duvalier's Haiti; P.J. Chamorro had thought we had to maintain some assistance ties in order to impose conditions on Somoza.

Schneider stated that the opposition lacked any real organization and sophistication, but what we should not do was support the 1981 electoral solution. "I would like to see a coalition between the opposition and the National Guard that would make a coup d'état before 1981, and then hold an election."

I disagreed that a coup was a possibility. A couple of days later, I visited Robert Pastor at his National Security Council office. Pastor understood my frustrations. "I am an activist like you, but we must not make the error of [President] Kennedy—we should neither change the government nor structure the solution."

Unfortunately, we were left with propaganda and the manipulation of our very small assistance programs, dependent on the moral rebirth of dictators who would see the light in response to preaching and would ultimately follow our wishes. What simplemindedness. Others would be the ones to ask dictators to step down or overthrow governments.

Return to Managua

The solution had been left to the Nicaraguans despite the concentration of physical force in the hands of Somoza. This was a human rights campaign in a country considered unimportant; with the withdrawal of American power, more violence was a real option.

On March 8, 1978, I returned to Managua. That same evening, political officer John Martin was giving a small reception, attended mainly by oppositionists. Although it had been a long day, I decided to attend. Oppositionists were especially eager to find out about developments in Washington, and I could not offer them what they wished: an ultimatum to Somoza. I challenged Ramiro Sacasa, Emilio Alvarez Montalván, and Pedro Quintanilla to negotiate with Somoza.[23] One of them commented that only if the United States organized and guaranteed negotiations might unarmed oppositionists be willing to participate. Of course, this was precisely what I was prohibited from doing. At this stage we always found substantial numbers willing to negotiate the regime's termination, provided that the United States participate in this effort—this is why we were able in a very short time to obtain broad support in the country for an international mediation, when Washington decided to participate. The continuation of the "Nicaraguan crisis" resulted from Washington's decision.

I was very frustrated. How could I pressure Somoza to make concessions and to democratize when the opposition was unwilling to take the risk to discuss with him or representatives of his government any terms of such a process? This was precisely one of Somoza's excuses. I understood that of singular importance was the suddenness of the popular revolt: oppositionists were fearful of calming the people and thus losing momentum against Somoza, who ultimately could not be trusted unless the United States controlled him. It was only because of the human rights policy that Somoza had liberalized the situation and the opposition gained strength to begin with—this was a well-understood fact. Oppositions had been defeated so many times by the Somozas. For them it was *basta* (enough). Yet negotiations seemed a necessary first step that had to be taken. If Somoza did not compromise, then a destructive revolution would be more legitimate.

All the cards had not yet been played. On the one hand, Somoza was hopeful that he could still prevail in Washington. On the other, the unarmed oppositionists hoped that in the face of the chaos that was being created, Washington would come to their rescue and decide to get Somoza out. In a sense the two forces were blackmailing us. Somoza said that he would be ousted only by the Sandinistas, a worse "Communist" alternative. The moderate opposition replied that only if Somoza resigned immediately would a Sandinista revolution not take place. Despite the reduced anti-communism that prevailed in Washington at the time, both sides hoped that the United States would impede a Sandinista victory.

The embassy had entered a period in which we had lost popularity. Mariano Fiallos Oyanguren, then the rector of Universidad Nacional Autónoma de Nicaragua (UNAN), the principal public university based in Leon, said the problem was that everybody thought that the United States was behind the strike and was going to oust Somoza. Nicaraguans, prone to wishful thinking, wanted us to solve the problem. There was going to be more violence. In Leon the street actions to overthrow the government were largely spontaneous but were also organized by the Marxist students and Christian activists. To restore American prestige, we had to persuade Somoza to make immediate concessions, Fiallos said.

Meanwhile, Somoza sought to influence the U.S. government. Rather than take actions against my mission, he repeatedly asked me to inform my contacts that we backed him. In his proverbial contempt for others, he insisted: "These people are very stupid, Ambassador. They are creating all these problems thinking that the U.S. is ultimately going to rescue them. Your government's policy is irresponsible. Poor little Nicaragua." He had told me that he would cooperate with me more than other Latin American presidents would with U.S. envoys. In Somoza's opinion the equation of the impasse was simple enough: under the impression that we sympathized with them, the unarmed groups maintained the pressure on us to get him to quit. So we had to back him, the faithful client, the general insisted.

He was playing the role of the man committed to democratizing the country and collaborating with Washington. Time was on his side. In a press conference he said that "The national situation was developing, slowly but surely toward normality." The state of political agitation could not be erased from one day to the next, and the government had to deal with the maintenance of the *orden público* without impairing public freedoms (e.g., not reestablishing the state of siege). The government was doing all that was possible to show the citizenry its great patience and leniency (being very tolerant even of punishable illegal acts). Always optimistic about his ability and luck, Somoza said that the majority backed him, and that the same citizenry was going to get tired of the senseless acts, the seditious protests and violence of youth being pushed by agitators.

And his maintaining the international image of his government had succeeded, he said. In five instances Somoza referred to the public stance taken by the president of the United States in Caracas against the Venezuelan government's desire to obtain Somoza's resignation. He was very pleased. He was going to continue to cooperate with Washington's human rights objective. He admonished the opposition: "What I do not wish is that this country continue in violence based [on the notion] that someone is going to come to overthrow the government. No one is going to come to topple this government."

The general wished to build the basis for a new "*convivencia nacional*" (peaceful living together) through dialogue or negotiations. The opposition could talk to him or to representatives of the Liberal Party, whichever they preferred. Somoza proceeded to enumerate issues that had been raised by the opposition; he was willing to negotiate practically all of them, except shortening his term. In any case, if the opposition chose not to collaborate, his government would proceed unilaterally to make democratizing reforms. But he would remain in office for three more years.

On April 15, I went to see Somoza because of instructions to urge an invitation to the Inter-American Commission on Human Rights of the OAS. Apparently, although the U.S. president had refused in Venezuela to participate in asking Somoza to resign, there had been agreement in supporting the visit—the Venezuelans had been trying to use the commission to pressure and discredit the Nicaraguan government.[24] Somoza would not be placed in a position of appearing to have invited the commission under international (i.e., United States and Venezuelan) pressure, he said; but his government had remained in contact with the commission and had responded to petitions from it. He was contemplating an invitation at the opportune time: the recent public statements in Caracas indicating the ongoing, limited cooperation between the presidents of the United States and Venezuela against Nicaragua made it impossible now.

Somoza said, "I remain a friend of the United States, but you must understand that to protect myself I have had to make new friends among the Latin American dictators; to invite the Commission might disappoint them; I may need them some day." Remember, at this time most Latin American countries were under authoritarian rule, which reduced the likelihood of anti-Somoza policies being supported in the OAS. Somoza wished to communicate to Washington that he would not be pushed around, and that he could try to rally support from the hemisphere's authoritarian regimes. It was only about a year later, in the face of the carnage brought by the final popular uprising, that the OAS chose to condemn Nicaragua.

Somoza agreed that the visit might diminish the "international campaign" to discredit him, yet he remained unyielding.[25] What guarantees were there that the United States would not continue to harass him even after the commission had come and gone? Becoming more agitated, Somoza said that during his recent visit to El Salvador its president had told him that the Inter-American Commission's visit there had not served to quiet down the convulsive situation that El Salvador was experiencing. He had tried to follow our suggestions, but we had not transformed this into support for him. Our human rights policy had encouraged insurrection in Nicaragua, and we were not helping to find a solution. "I am a man of principle," he said. "When [CIA director] Allen Dulles asked me what I wanted in payment for the use of Nicaragua to launch the Bay of Pigs invasion [against Castro], I told him that I wanted nothing, that we were friends. But now I want to know what is in it for me if I invite the commission? I am not being a rebel just to be one. I have accepted your suggestions to move toward a democratic evolution because this is the best for Nicaragua, but what we are seeing is an increase in violence. Brazil and the group of Latin American dictators will not vote in the OAS for a commission visit. You should tell Washington not to try to force the visit because they will lose."

As for his stance on human rights, Somoza referred to the ongoing student strike: "Their leaders hoped that I would force them physically out of the schools. I am only pressuring their administrations with closing them if classes are not restored," he said. He also reminded me that he had invited the International Red Cross to inspect the conditions of all prisoners in the local jails to end the ongoing hunger strikes by protesters. He would remain faithful to his principles and political ideology: "I could do as some dictators, arming the poor people, but I won't. Neither will I run away from Nicaragua." This was the *new* Somoza doctrine that proved fatal to him: coexist with the opposition not negotiating with him and seeking to overthrow him, claiming that he was on the path of democratizing the country while planning to continue at the helm for three more years.

The following Saturday, Somoza opened our meeting by complaining about the U.S. "economic boycott." He said that to obtain a bank loan, a Nicaraguan agent had had to visit sixty-three banks, and alleged that the U.S. director of the Inter-American Development Bank (IDB) was not only voting against loans to his government but actively "boycotting" all the projects. If such practices continued, Somoza threatened, a confrontation between our two governments might be unavoidable, for he would have to prevent the "financial suffocation" of Nicaragua.

"An obstacle to the approval of loans by banks," I said, "might be the feeling that your government has overextended itself. In my conversations with American bankers I've learned also about a concern about some practices, such as Nicaraguan officials skimming off large portions of new loans, which go to their pockets."

Somoza said that he was aware of such problems. However, his raising of the financial issue seemed to serve to let me know that he knew that the State Department still resisted true cooperation with him but was about to release some loans to him. Indeed, he said, "I am disappointed that decisions easing the economic boycott of my government have come only through pressures of the U.S. Congress, and friends such as Congressman Charlie Wilson [Democrat, Texas]."

I am not sure if Congressman Wilson single-handedly persuaded Warren Christopher to reverse himself and approve the loans, though he played a role. I was told that the decision in process was based on pressure because the administration was approving loans to countries with worse human rights records than Nicaragua's (according to the ranking of human rights organizations); that this showed a bias against Nicaragua, and if the loans were not approved, the administration's Foreign Assistance Bill would be jeopardized in House of Representatives committees. Perhaps the parties involved in this decision were unaware of its dangerous consequences within Nicaragua.[26] Naturally Somoza perceived that he had triumphed over Washington, which could only strengthen his confidence that he could "lick" his "liberal" adversaries.

Somoza told me that the political situation was no longer directed by the unarmed opposition; the Marxist revolutionaries were seeking to destroy the traditional political forces and looking for a pretext to start a bloodbath. The

United States would be responsible if this happened, he claimed. The Venezuelans were giving money to the Sandinistas to acquire arms.

He then recalled my raising the possibility of his resigning the post of chief director of the National Guard and promulgating electoral reforms more acceptable to the opposition. "If I appoint a new chief director, not from my family, the opposition will simply say that he is a figurehead, that he has no real influence in the National Guard, that I am making a meaningless gesture," he concluded. Unfortunately, the tradition of Somoza absolutism was so firm in the collective conscience that I believed he was correct.

Somoza repeated his concern over the possibility of a "bloodbath" as a result of Venezuelan financial "intervention." The Mutual Defense Pact (the Rio de Janeiro Treaty) might have to be invoked to control the spread of violence in Central America if the United States did not back his reforms so that negotiations crystallize, he said. "I urge you to tell the opposition that you are not going to overthrow me, that you believe in my democratic intentions and plan to back me until 1981."

Thus, not only many oppositionists but Somoza as well felt that negotiations would materialize if the U.S. government participated in organizing them. I continued expressing to my contacts my concern about the possibility of violence and specifying my instructions that I could not sponsor or guarantee any specific political solution.

Powerful Yet Impotent Somocistas

The general's demand was not sensible in the context of recent history. How could the United States vouch for his intentions? According to his plan to enact the democratic reforms for 1981, he would go through the motion of sending them to his rubber-stamp Congress to approve them twice, which was locally interpreted as maintaining the constitutional "democratic farce." He had already been in office in this term about four years, yet he would not give up power a day early.

This is why various sensible Nicaraguans favored a constitutional solution without Somoza. In early May, New York Times writer Alan Riding reported on the formulas: the president resigns; then a coalition government is formed including the National Guard and the ruling Liberals; the president's successor would be constitutionally appointed by the Congress—even a Liberal could be acceptable; all political sectors subsequently could participate in a dialogue to negotiate reforms for a truly democratic electoral solution with a new, elected president taking office at a prudent time; the moderates were seeking to obtain the withdrawal of support for Somoza from his army and party.[27] Riding believed that the deadlock was shifting the political spectrum leftward, because

Marxist-oriented activists were the ones actually operating at the grassroots organizing students, workers, and slum dwellers to rebel. To abort the trend, Somoza had to go, and the sooner the better.

Although unhappy with our policy, a few government supporters remained in regular contact with me. I sought to know the Somocista camp better and to express my genuine personal interest in Nicaraguans, and I wanted to keep options open. My longest and most sustained contact was with Luis Pallais Debayle, the president's first cousin and spokesman. Periodically we met with our families and a small entourage of his Somocista friends, usually with Ricardo and Leda Parrales. Midyear in 1978 Pallais explained the government's 1981 strategy, focusing on the electoral reform. The Somoza camp, he said, did not wish to revise their bill of constitutional changes because they felt that "anything that Somoza proposed would be automatically rejected." What the Liberals would do was withdraw the electoral proposals that the opposition had objected to and ask the small Conservative Zancudo faction still in the Congress to work out with the rest of the opposition an acceptable electoral package. But this device to achieve negotiations did not work. Representatives René Sandino and Julio Ycasa Tigerino had been speaking of the need to first form a more neutral government of national unity without Somoza that would take the country to general, free elections.

Pallais found comfort in what he considered Alfonso Robelo's failure to rally the business community into a second general strike and felt that after the "failure" of the next Sandinista violent offensive the unarmed opposition would come to its senses and want to dialogue. As had been the case in Cuba, the ongoing revolutionary process was not locally ignored. And although it was cumulative (its waves experienced increases in power), it also experienced failures, which served to maintain the government's optimism. Indeed, Somocistas kept a distorted perception of their power. Pallais said that Liberals were still the majority: they would win any election, and after the sacrosanct 1981, a Liberal administration, with Somoza exercising the natural influence of a retired leader, would take charge.

Pallais informed me that he had taken the initiative with El Jefe for the Twelve to be allowed to return to Nicaragua. Initially Somoza had angrily reacted to the Twelve's demand that he resign and their pro-Sandinista statements ("how much do you want me to give to these people, mis nalgas?" [literally, "my buttocks"]), but he had "recapacitado" (a change of mind). Now they would be allowed to return.

About two weeks later we met again at my official residence. It was a Saturday, and Pallais was happy. His government had accepted the items that he had been told it should implement at the Washington office of the assistant secretary for Latin America: except for the solution to Chamorro's assassination, Somoza had complied with the conditions for improving our relationship, Pallais opined. The Inter-American Commission on Human Rights had been invited; Somoza would receive a delegation from Amnesty International, the private human rights group. The Twelve were free to return to Nicaragua (to participate in a revolution, I must add). The Liberal congressional majority had decided to favorably study a bill from a Conservative deputy for a political amnesty. Notice that the inhibitions in Washington to address the issues that were real in Nicaragua fed into Somocista illusions about their position vis-à-vis the United States and Somoza's erroneous belief that to succeed he only had to neutralize us.[28]

The government's party still was unable to generate autonomy from the monarch. On the one hand Somocistas generally claimed a distorted view of party-army power—the majority, the invincible military force; on the other they exuded a sense of impotence to act independently of the general's instructions. No one from his ranks would tell him that there was need for a pre-1981 compromise to safeguard party-army interests.

An interpretation for party discipline that privately more "independent" Somocistas at this time volunteered was that it was based on the fear of being purged: Somoza would not listen; they would not be able to carry an independent following of their own and hence would fail. Recent events showed this—recall that the president of the Congress had been purged and become a political cadaver. Compared to Somoza, these men seemed impotent. The ruling family had acquired a mystique of charismatic institutionalization that was reinforced by its success. The general himself partook in this charismatic self-assurance and had the intelligence and concentrated political, military, and economic resources to act and be above all others, an "untouchable." A vicious circle had been created: the "leaders" in contact with him were where they were only because of Somoza's will and their loyalty to him. Most just could not view their own interests as threatened by his continued leadership. The embassy was left with the task of getting rid of Somoza and catapulting my visitors into power.[29] Despite my efforts, I could not find men who were not "disloyal" but at the same time were independent from Somoza to face him and tell him anything he did not want to hear.

A Major Defeat by Washington

In spite of statements from the White House that ambassadors were the true heads of mission, the embassy's USAID section sought an independence of its own under the philosophy that aid programs were "apolitical." The claims were not credible. In Nicaragua, suspending loans to Somoza meant the administration already had given the aid a political definition: it symbolized approval-disapproval for the Nicaraguan government's human rights performance.

I felt that the agency had positive effects. Some social services for the poor might not have existed at all if the United States were not involved in promoting them. The agency also had a role in spreading a modernizing philosophy of social democratic progress, and it sponsored some local technocratic cadres whose leadership would help develop more modern public entities, increasingly responsive to their constituencies.[30] But the overwhelming predominance of a patrimonial officialdom in Nicaragua's public sector hid whatever progress was being made by such "modernizing" individuals. There was the problem of a deliberate secretiveness with me by the embassy USAID on the operations of local corrupt government entities in partnership with the United States.

USAID had recently come under criticism in Washington on two counts. First, the bulk of the money loaned remained in the United States. The *Washington Post* had this to say: "In fiscal 1977, about three dollars out of four earmarked for bilateral economic assistance were spent for technical knowhow, services, products and commodities in [the United States]. Companies and consultants at home, rather than poor people abroad, receive most of AID's economic development funds." Second, the agency's auditing practices had come under fire, the top USAID administrator having replaced the auditor general, claiming "general incompetence" in this unit.[31] Nicaraguans and prominent American businessmen in Managua resented the secretiveness of USAID operations and its seemingly inappropriate auditing of Nicaraguan government operations, which resulted in inadequate handling of corruption. There were also complaints that our assistance strengthened the government's political machine.

Upon arrival I had been faced with USAID-Nicaragua's ludicrous doctrine that U.S. resources not be misappropriated (e.g., if U.S. funds used to build a new school were properly budgeted, it did not matter that the local government never staffed and operated it; there was nothing wrong using U.S. money to build other new schools that would remain nonoperational). Amid a public scandal, USAID officials had come to tell me the Nicaraguan public housing bank (BAVINIC) was bankrupt, partly as a consequence of a corrupt administration. Now my staff wished to "save the bank" with new assistance, offering a consultantship and a new $10 million loan. I did not agree: BAVINIC should show its commitment to reform by footing the bill. The staff's reply was that it could not afford it. Certainly we had not been doing enough to help reform the Nicaraguan public sector.

Another area of continued concern was Managua's reconstruction following the 1972 earthquake. Despite the repeated statements of my local functionaries that it would be promptly terminated, the pipeline remained unspent—the program just did not progress, as the infrastructure was not there to implement it. This was another area of "surprises." Local USAID ultimately had to recognize that it had been misrepresenting the situation to me. On February 10, 1978, I wrote in my journal that I had been told that the program could at the earliest be terminated in two more years. I had been kept informed by some of the embassy State Department officials about reconstruction problems. The construction sector was especially susceptible to irregularities. The human rights policy of maintaining a distance from Somoza required a low profile with the government.

Abelardo Valdez, USAID's assistant administrator for Latin America, was aware of the embassy's concern and had been responsive. He had sent me a letter: a representative of his would be coming to assess the reconstruction program and cut it back so expenditures be consonant with U.S. policy in Nicaragua. During my recent visit to Washington he had agreed to reduce the USAID mission to about nineteen Americans. I said that I had been lied to all along that the reconstruction program would be completed on schedule. I also expressed anger to the Central American USAID director, who claimed ignorance about these problems and the reduction of personnel. I wanted to set the record straight and not be responsible for reconstruction failures and scandals.

However, the report, which involved USAID functionaries who had historical ties to the program and, hence, were not entirely "impartial," consisted of a typical, "bureaucratic response," to spend available money by June 1979, ironically the time of the total collapse of the Somoza regime.

I did not foresee any progress in the Reconstruction Program for the next few months, and the deputy secretary of state told us in Washington that he had decided no new loans would be approved. But less than a month after my return to Managua, Nicaraguan desk officer Daniel Welter informed me (March 23, 1978) that they were contemplating new loans! Given the change in mood at this higher level of the State Department, Todman and Central American desk officer Wade Matthews had also started to contemplate resuming military assistance shipments, probably nonlethal goods. Another bout of conflictive bureaucratic politics had started.

There were those within the State Department who felt that it was not time to rock the boat, disturbing the embassy's relationships with the Nicaraguan parties in conflict and making it difficult for us to remain working with them. But the initiative to resume military shipments suggested that there were those wishing to "normalize" relations with Somoza and prop up his government in the face of the rising unrest.

Notice that a signal of approving the loans was to give up pressuring Somoza. Was Washington abandoning its so-called policy of neutrality? I had reason to believe not. The decision demonstrated a lack of consistency in implementing policy. A small group of American legislators had temporarily prevailed.[32] Indeed, the American press reported the amazing public rationalization of administration officials: the loans were not intended to support Somoza; the aid met "congressional and administration guidelines about providing direct benefits for Nicaragua's poor and needy." After all, the decision was not that bad, because "the ban imposed by the administration . . . on transfers of military equipment to Nicaragua remain[ed] in force."[33]

This explanation was, of course, absurd. The *same* loans had *publicly* been suspended earlier by the administration on human rights grounds. That they were approved now implied improvement in that situation. We were damaged politically by this reversal. First, Somoza was unhappy with Washington's management of the decision. He wished that the administration would reverse itself and publicly back his regime and plans. Second, the opposition was dissatisfied with Washington for not taking a firm position against Somoza. Third, Somoza knew that his friends had been able to reverse the administration's position; he had reason to believe that he could defeat it again. How could we obtain from him the political concessions needed to avoid the impending war?

I felt that I had to move quickly to save U.S. options in Nicaragua against the nonsense that still prevailed. As soon as I learned about the decision, the embassy's opposition was immediately reported. On March 25 we addressed a cable to Warren Christopher, Assistant Secretary Todman, and Assistant US-AID Administrator Valdez. Realizing that I had been defeated, we subsequently reiterated that the general assistance levels be maintained.[34] We sought a compromise: that the larger Education Loan ($7.5 million) not be approved, but that the loan for nutrition ($3.5 million) be authorized. Even then we did not want it approved immediately. "We should avoid the appearance of siding with the government or the opposition . . . at this time." If this were not possible, we suggested that "it would be most desirable that announcement of the nutrition loan's approval be coupled with announcement of grants or other assistance to non-government groups to be in line with my instructions to project an image that [the] U.S. Government does not side with any specific group in the current polarized situation." Note that we were trying to obtain an aid policy coherent with my instructions to avoid confusion in Nicaragua.

On April 20 we were informed that Warren Christopher was going to approve the entire package and that there was no intention to give a formal, official press release on the loans. As the representative in the field, I wanted to avoid flip-flops that would make the U.S. government totally irrelevant, if not an object of contempt.

The embassy had to explain to Nicaraguans the change in policy. On April 21 we cabled Washington suggesting the press release that we intended to make to counter the predicted use of the new assistance as "support for Somoza." The gist of the proposed press release was a simultaneous description of assistance both to the private sector and the government, stressing the nature of the programs and their target groups. On the 24th, I talked with John Bushnell, Todman's deputy, who was acting as assistant secretary. He said that the congressional backers of the loans would accept postponement only on technical, not political, grounds.

In sum, USAID–Nicaragua, showing its lack of political sense and questionable priorities, dissented from my analysis. The final cable said that the education project had a reasonable probability of success. It did not matter that a revolution was in the making, nor that the Nicaraguan government was under severe budgetary problems. Even in better-administered U.S.-Nicaragua projects, as in the rural sector, U.S. disbursements were being held up because Nicaraguans had already been unable to meet their financial obligations. The final absurdity was that neither of the two loans was actually implemented. Moreover, Somoza's congressional friends' success in Washington proved unhelpful to him, misindicating that he could play the human rights "game" with the administration—that his partial collaboration with us rather than the decapitation of the opposition could keep him going.

We had to cross the Rubicon without any press guidance from Washington. We decided to issue our own communiqué, enumerating both private sector and government projects being funded. I could not assist the notion that the administration had changed course and was "backing" Somoza now. This was irresponsible; it could reduce the political space allowed to eventually pursue a more activist "mediation" role, a widespread local desire and demand. It was obvious that the loans per se would not stabilize the regime.

On May 16 the worst-case scenario crystallized: a UPI cable reported $12 million in loans to the government. There was no mention of the private sector projects being funded, including one for oppositionist INDE, the institute linked to stoppage leader Alfonso Robelo. The cable concluded: "The assistance program to Nicaragua in the current fiscal year is for $20 million, of which only $2.9 million is for military purposes."

The UPI statement could only create confusion, and the $20 million figure was inaccurate, as was the amount for military aid. The embassy had not yet been notified that the education loan had been technically completed or that there had been any approval of military assistance. Thus we issued the communiqué we had written that included the private sector grants and only the nutrition loan. Our press release referred to these projects and concluded: "According to the mandate of the Congress of the United States, these contributions of the American people are to benefit Nicaraguans with the most scarce resources. In addition to these approved projects a program of educational development is under consideration."

The La Prensa–Novedades competition to demonstrate that the U.S. government condemned/supported Somoza, respectively, had continued. For instance, on May 12 the elimination of military assistance to Nicaragua in a congressional committee was construed by La Prensa as follows: "The Violation of Human Rights Continues, The United States Eliminates the Last Military Assistance." The following day Novedades replied using a letter of protocol from the president to Somoza: "Carter to Somoza: I Appreciate Your Message and Support."

We had activated our personal contacts with both sides. Considering the extant polarization and the strategic role attributed to us, the local response was moderate. On May 17 Novedades published our communiqué, as well as a Washington Post article describing the background of the decision.

That same evening La Prensa featured a long article: "Blackmail and Duality of U.S. Loans." It was based on an Associated Press story of the congressional pressures and reported the continuation of anti-Somoza attitudes in the State Department (e.g., the loans were intended to benefit the poor, not prop up the government; the United States would do nothing to counteract Nicaraguan demands that Somoza resign, La Prensa said). It dismissed the "humanitarian" nature of the loans, based on the opposition's article of faith that no assistance channeled through the Nicaraguan government ever reached the poor. It characterized U.S. policy as "ambiguous."

The following day's editorial was more comprehensive. Although the United States would continue to implement a human rights policy, the Nicaraguan people must be indignant in the face of any support, even if minimal, that provided respite to the dictatorship. The loans are a form of intervention against the people's struggle to end the tyranny, and they have come at a time when the government's "collective criminality" had increased. The struggle would not end. In the following days La Prensa published a few letters from concerned citizens deploring the decision, but they were more anti-Somoza than anti-American.[35]

An exception to the generally discrete way that the embassy was treated was the statement of Rafael Córdova Rivas, the good man who headed the Chamorro-founded UDEL.[36] According to him, because the loans were approved, the government had "brutally repressed" students on strike. He concluded: "In other words, the people of the State Department and the American Ambassador to Nicaragua, Mr. Mauricio Solaun, are responsible directly of whatever student massacre might be committed in the country, because with that decision to give new credits to Somoza [they] drugged the human rights policy." We were part of the heroic/sacrificial campaign heavy on symbols, which involved imputing guilt by association by all sides.

Novedades was still unhappy with the insufficient support given to the Somoza government by Washington and spoke of the U.S. government "duality." Nicaragua was a "friend" of the United States that "had always served the highest interests of democracy, but because of a bad interpretation of the human rights doctrine has been treated with singular injustice." Washington's foreign policy was so bad, it argued, that it had resulted in the president's loss of support by the American people, below the levels of Nixon during the Watergate crisis, and that the United States was losing its sphere of influence in the world, especially in Latin America.[37]

Catholic Church Declines Role

The Catholic Church was a natural channel to mediate the conflict. In early June, Jack Martin, the head of the political section, and I visited Archbishop Obando, who said that very few were willing to talk; in his opinion the bulk of the oppositionists were already committed with the FSLN to support violence. It would not be fruitful for him to come out in favor of negotiations. It was also evident that no single opposition group had the numbers or the prestige to carry by itself the opposition to dialogue.

Nonetheless, the monsignor asked what Somoza would be willing to give. Clearly nothing short of advancing an election, a supervised one as was taking place at that time in the Dominican Republic, and eliminating family control of the National Guard might work, I said.

Unfortunately, there were reasons to be very skeptical of Somoza's willingness to make any concessions. Public military ceremonies and Somoza's statements about his son's military interests were interpreted by even some of his followers to indicate that he would never abandon control but would exercise it through Somoza Jr. Novedades publicized the family's military role with a huge front page photograph of the two Somoza officers—son and half brother—welcoming the Somoza president on his return from the United States.[38] The Novedades editor was aware of the dynastic Somoza Jr. propaganda. That same day he commented to me that it was probably scaring people about Somoza's intentions.

I got the impression that the archbishop believed that the opposition was planning to carry out a major coordinated violent uprising, to then bring the

Catholic Church and the United States into the picture. The hierarchy would feel compelled under these conditions to ask Somoza to resign so that peace would prevail. The scenario was not an idle speculation.

We continued approaching the top Catholic hierarchy. On June 7, 1978, I visited the pope's ambassador, Monsignor Gabriel Montalvo, a Colombian whose father had played an important role in that country's Conservative Party politics at the time of the traditional *violencia*. Somoza viewed the nuncio as friendly toward him; because of this I always felt that he would be more receptive to Montalvo's initiatives, certainly more so than to those coming from the archbishop, whom he personally disliked.

Monsignor Montalvo conveyed positive news. The pope was sending a message to the bishops, which he had helped write, asking them to mediate the conflict at the opportune time. What was needed, I said, was to encourage something other than "pact or revolution": the first consisted of agreements helping to consolidate the Somozas in exchange for a minority share of offices; the second had never succeeded since the creation of the National Guard, and its triumph would imply a slaughter that might not result in a democratic order with social justice. Perhaps because of his awareness of my desire to see him play a role in working out a negotiated solution, the nuncio subsequently became increasingly distant toward me. I was disappointed by his irrelevant role, especially in the months to come.

The refusal of Washington to mediate prompted the Colombian ambassador, Oswaldo Rengifo, to ask me if Somoza had thought about using a group of ambassadors to mediate the conflict. For Somoza, however, there were only two real ambassadors—the American and the Vatican. I also approached a few European Union ambassadors to assist a local settlement, although I had no high expectations of any positive result from these conversations. During the Somoza years it was expected that the United States exercise the leadership of democratic nations. As the ambassador of the Netherlands (who did not permanently reside in Nicaragua but periodically visited me to obtain information) told me in June, "You should not abandon Nicaraguans to their fate. They deserve a better deal."

Opportunity for the National Guard?

My contacts with the army had been very limited. Our defense attaché, Colonel James McCoy, a recent arrival in the country, had considered it inappropriate to organize a large reception at my official residence for the officers. He had felt that it would be a source of embarrassment, that few would wish to attend, that there were "implications of disloyalty" because of our policy. But McCoy took the initiative in July to offer a luncheon at his house for a handful of the very top command. The senior officers were Somoza's half-brother, General José

R. Somoza, the acting director of the Guard, and General Armando Fernández, the new chief of staff.

To my surprise, General Iván Alegrett came to speak to me alone in the patio when the opportunity arose. Alegrett was a soldier known for his impetuous personality, and he was feared as prone to violence. Forcefully and directly he told me, "You are the only one responsible for the current violence and chaos." I replied that he was wrong. The country had been ruled for too long under the state of siege. After years with no freedom of expression, people started expressing themselves vehemently, and with Chamorro's assassination the situation exploded.

Chamorro was not loved, Alegrett answered. He was the pretext. The problem was that the United States was not backing their friends any longer, and this was encouraging the opposition. Then General Alegrett delivered his message. It was not the usual complaint of many Latin American officers who felt abandoned by their former ally, the United States, now turned unreliable because of the human rights and arms transfer policies. He was very worried. He understood that an amnesty was a good political move to place the opposition on the defensive, but, he said, when Juan Domingo Perón offered one recently in Argentina, the result was greater violence from terrorism.[39] He was very concerned about the future of the National Guard. "We are internally divided; Somoza is the only unifying force among us. What if he dies?" he said.

General Alegrett elaborated another scenario. "In a crisis there will have to be a pact between the Guardia Nacional and the private sector in opposition, lest chaos overcome Nicaragua. Ambassador, you are the only one who can help us: never before has there been such a prolonged period of unrest and opposition strength. Rebellions have always been short-lived and narrower in scope. You know that the Guardia will be the ultimate victim—we will be shot as in Cuba. Politicians can escape, but we will be destroyed; probably this is what keeps us under discipline."

He added that Somoza maintained control of the Guardia by "cutting throats." Those who showed some independence and who appeared to have a potential following were purged. "I know," he continued, "that change is needed and inevitable. I know that I am not acceptable to the opposition. I am encouraging the few officers who speak out internally. I personally like Fernández. I am willing to back him, but what we need is a 'man with balls.' "

This was the first "constructive" conversation that I ever had with an army officer. Many oppositionists hoped for a coup d'état. I showed interest without elaborating much, but I was surprised with the content of the conversation. Washington was adamant about not helping organize a coup against Somoza. A few weeks later Alegrett mysteriously died in an airplane accident. Had he engaged in this kind of conversation with others, who blew the whistle (the *soplo* much practiced within the Guardia) about the possibility of his being disloyal? Somoza had "gotten rid of" the two most outspoken critics of his *continuismo* with me, first Cornelio Hueck, now Alegrett. Such events confirmed the belief among Somoza's team of the hopeless risks of showing independence from the boss.

I subsequently spoke with Generals Somoza and Fernández. The latter complained about the Communists agitating in the schools and cities. I played it safe, backing their president's policy of minimizing physical confrontation. What was needed was patience, I remarked. "The unarmed opposition is hopeful that the Sandinistas can mount another armed offensive that with their assistance can break the Armed Forces; if this fails, I hope that the opposition will accept reality and be reasonable, willing to negotiate a political solution." Both agreed, José R. Somoza adding that patience was needed.

I met with the minister of defense, General Guillermo Noguera, who was the only army officer who periodically sought me out. General Noguera informed me about his plans: he was going to retire from the Guardia and wanted to enter politics; as an army officer he could not be involved in politics because Nicaraguan tradition was like West Point's doctrine that active officers are "apolitical" and loyal to constituted authority. This was no hidden contact. He informed me that he wished to set a date for a large testimonial dinner honoring me, with invitations sent not only to government officials but to other sectors as well. We set August 18, 1978, as the date. General Noguera's aspirations did not generate the following required for viability, unfortunately. In assessing him, I understood that the headship of the Ministry of Defense was a bureaucratic position without a command of its own forces.

Somoza's Political Opening

In the meantime, the president's plans remained intact: an opening (*apertura política*) to legalize activities of multiple opposition groups (rather than the extant restrictive system); permission for the Group of Twelve to return to Nicaragua; renew calls to negotiate a free election for 1981.[40] Yet there was no concession concerning the fundamental issue, the possibility of an earlier termination of the dynasty through legal means. No negotiations were taking place. It was as if the ruler's objective was to show the United States that he had tried to democratize, but it did not work because of the opposition.

On June 24, 1978, the Twelve returned to Nicaragua to engage in the conclusive fight to overthrow the government. At the same time some members of the group lobbied for the United States to get the Somoza family out of the country. Indicative of the contradictions inherent in a schizophrenic or disjointed government policy, the official propaganda virulently dealt with their return: "The Twelve and the Blood," *Novedades* accused.[41]

I do not recall the size of the turnout to receive the Twelve in Managua; their own sources referred to some one hundred thousand people. But the huge crowds brandished Sandinista symbols, refuting any doubts as to what forces they represented. The Twelve were nothing without FSLN support. La Prensa reported that these Sandinista agents would work within the Broad Opposition Front (FAO). Its headline read: "The People Voted Again: Somoza Out! The Broad [Opposition] Front Confirmed with Facts. Dictatorship Is Cadaver." The next day it editorialized on the need to strengthen the FAO because no opposition group by itself could achieve the democratization of the country.

That same day I met with Foreign Minister Julio Quintana, who had been incorporated into the cabinet late in the previous year as part of Somoza's image building in the post–state of siege period. Several of my Somocista contacts considered him a leader; some oppositionists viewed him acceptable to head a transition government. He was concerned. The United States had better information than he did, but he had been told the Venezuelan government was financing the Twelve—it had paid for the costs of organizing their reception in Nicaragua. An international movement to unseat the government was underway. He added that it was noteworthy that no banners or signs of the Conservative Party or (Chamorro's) UDEL were waved in the welcoming manifestation—they were all for the FSLN, Cuba, the Communists, he said.

I tried to build up his self-confidence to see him play a role in negotiations. "People are attributing to you the decision to allow the Twelve to return," I said. "I have been encouraging the opposition to negotiate a civic-electoral solution, arguing that the alternative will result in an unsuccessful, costly bloodbath. Some of them show interest, but they don't know how to work it out, and you are an acceptable man to some of my contacts."

Quintana answered, "The Chamorros do not view me as an unacceptable compromise. I want to go and see Doña Violeta [P.J. Chamorros's widow]; I am going to clear it with the president." He asked whether I backed him. "I am a conciliator," he said, adding, "I think that you want Eduardo Montealegre [the financier] to be president."

My reply: "I have never hinted to *el Presidente* any name because it might be counter-productive." Quintana's professed interest in negotiating a compromise was mere promise.

La Prensa's Interest in a Compromise

The day after the Twelve's return, I talked with Xavier Chamorro, P.J.'s brother and now director of La Prensa, and Danilo Aguirre, one of its top editors. I had discussed with Aguirre the advantages of elaborating demands as a basis to negotiate regime termination and had been encouraged by the newspaper's publishing an article by Alberto Saborío—a legislator friend of Aguirre—in support of negotiations; in the highly polarized climate it took courage to do so. Aguirre opened our meeting by introducing this notion, and I elaborated: "In my opinion, if there is going to be a peaceful solution, the opposition will have to participate in a compromise. Somoza commands the army; one has to give a 'reasonable' exit to one's enemy."

Aguirre agreed, feeling that the insurrection would not succeed at this time. Indeed, the revolution succeeded only when Somoza rejected a final compromise the next December. Aguirre added, "It is going to be very bloody, and it is an anarchic process that the unarmed opposition does not control."

Xavier interjected that the sooner Somoza left, the better to democratize and pacify the country. I argued that a position between Somoza "today" and Somoza "forever" was logical: it did not entail a "pact" with him. Yet for my visitors 1981 was so far away. Above all, Somoza had to compromise.

Personally, I was convinced that despite all the wrong signals, the administration would not be supportive of "Somoza 1981," especially in the face of the ongoing revolt. It would not back the regime militarily. Thus I stated, "I cannot assure you that Washington will make firm representations for an earlier settlement, but the elaboration of a packet of opposition demands to culminate in a guaranteed election would be a move in the right direction for the opposition's and Nicaragua's advantage."

My objective was to get my visitors to understand my genuine desire to have the opposition allow the United States to be more helpful to their cause. I talked about our assistance to the government and emphasized that retaining a small amount did not encourage Somoza to break the military relationship with us and call in larger missions, perhaps from the Chilean or Argentine dictatorships. It would be the easiest course for me to suggest, but I think we must keep a foot in the government.[42]

I feel Chamorro and Aguirre realized that I was trying to help. They were mostly upset that Somoza used these ties as evidence of U.S. support for him— such symbols were very important in the emotional country that Nicaragua was, they said. We also touched on the importance that Washington had given to a thorough investigation of P.J. Chamorro's case. Their consensus was that without having some foreign agency, such as the FBI or Scotland Yard, take charge of it, it would not progress.[43]

We also talked about my past problems with the opposition, my "Cuban connection," which became an unpleasant personal factor for me, as a few Cuban-born individuals were very close to Somoza, which lent itself to imputing pro-Somoza influences on me. The key to a solution rested both on Somoza and La Prensa, supporting an electoral solution, in which all groups not committed to violence could participate. If the opposition was the majority, it had no reason to oppose this route as the least costly and truly democratic one.

The conversation ended with a reference to substance: the United States government would not overthrow Somoza because of its "liberal" ideology and lack of congressional support. It was important that the opposition develop a strategy of compromise that the United States could back, pressuring Somoza to do so. Chamorro summarized that the opposition preferred a peaceful democratic solution, and my visitors speculated on the possibility of organizing an internationally supervised election, perhaps with a candidate of national union. The embassy was establishing on its own the groundwork to facilitate a mediation.

In addition to its human and economic costs, the links between the violence and a future democracy were not that clear. Reynaldo Antonio Téfel, later a member of the Twelve, wrote in La Prensa about the FSLN's "new democratic position" and the need to overthrow the government to avoid a "Somocismo Without Somoza."[44] I personally liked Téfel and enjoyed his company, but the kind of government that the Sandinistas conducted after their violent victory proved his democratic prediction wrong. Téfel's catchy phrase was an oxymoron.

Carter's Letter to Somoza

In early July I received another surprise. I was informed that the president of the United States had written a letter to Somoza. I did not like its message. In the first place, it revealed a misunderstanding of the processes that we were going through: no reference was made to the developing revolutionary situation. President Carter was misinformed. For instance, he praised Somoza for allowing the Group of Twelve to return to lead "peaceful lives in Nicaragua," but their commitment to the violent route was no secret; they themselves openly declared it.

Most importantly, the letter could be construed by Somoza as support for his apertura política, which the FAO had rejected. Specifically, it appeared to endorse his 1981 electoral solution, for it praised Somoza's intended electoral reforms. I thought it fine that Washington show evenhandedness. But no opposition group supported a three-year waiting period to test electoral strength. We had been encouraging a compromise; some Nicaraguans had been speaking of a solution through phases culminating in a free election. Did the letter mean that the U.S. government would now back Somoza's 1981 formula? I believed that the letter was another indication of good intentions with little clarity on actual local conditions and a lack of any viable political plan. I was sure that contrary to the apparent message of the letter, Washington was not supporting Somoza's electoral plan.

What I felt was needed was for the U.S. president to get involved in mediating the local conflict. He should at least back his agents in a high-level mediation. What we did not need was to again confuse the situation. Indeed, if Washington was not going to back Somoza until 1981, the letter could only be counterproductive. But apparently the letter did confuse Somoza. These were his words, later written from exile:

> The letter . . . came at a time when I needed encouragement, and particularly from the United States. I accepted this letter in good faith and presumed it had been written on a good-faith basis. Long ago I should have learned that when dealing with Mr. Carter, good faith, logic, and reasoning had no meaning at all.
>
> I thought so much of the letter and its significance that I had sent my Foreign Minister to arrange a meeting with Carlos Andrés Pérez [the Venezuelan President who was leading the Latin American coalition to replace Somoza]. I thought so much of the letter that in a time of strife and mounting problems, I went back to Venezuela to see Pérez.
>
> After reading the letter for the first time, my immediate impression was one of satisfaction. I thought 'at least, Mr. Carter is going to get off my back.' That presumption was totally erroneous. As I flew back to my troubled country, the real meaning of the letter hit me. I recalled that President Pérez showed no emotion at all when I told him I had received a friendly letter. . . .
>
> In retrospect, I could now see that Pérez probably knew the contents of the letter: he evidenced no interest in [it] and quickly advised me that his position had not changed—I "had to go." Again, my hindsight vision was excellent. I could now see that Pérez and, most likely, all of the other conspiratorial countries had knowledge of Mr. Carter's letter before I ever received it.[45]

Somoza continued:

> In reality, this White House letter was a ruse and ploy. When the letter was written, it was anticipated that, as a result of the friendly tone, I would cooperate with those forces which were determined to destroy me and the government of Nicaragua. This is not an opinion or a prejudiced conclusion, it's a fact.
>
> The deceit . . . is unbelievable. He wrote me a nice letter on June 30, 1978 which in essence, outlined the favorable conditions in Nicaragua and, to his way of thinking the good work I was doing. Then on July 23, 1978, the Washington Post quoted the Carter Administration as saying: "We told Somoza that if he reimposes the state of siege, closes opposition papers, or arrests opposition political leaders, the U.S. Ambassador will be recalled and we might break relations. We

are not intriguing against any opposition faction. The fact is, we're against Somoza."

I found myself once again in disagreement with "policy"; I was sure that the letter would be leaked and create difficulties for the administration. This did occur in the United States, but not in Nicaragua, where it was disregarded, and the opposition did not wish to raise a new problem in its relations with the embassy.

Thus on July 11, once I heard about Carter's letter, I requested a meeting with Somoza to inform him about its message. I did not tell him that a signed letter was being sent; the embassy decided to make only an oral presentation of the message to Somoza, while explaining to Washington the advantages of not delivering the document.

Somoza was very pleased with the message. He said that he was encouraged that the president was able to see through the propaganda against him. "My philosophy is the same as Carter's" he said, "but as you can see, Ambassador, Nicaraguans are not Americans. It is difficult to rule the tumultuous Latins. I want you to know that I'm in favor of human rights because I will need mine protected when I am out of power." What Somoza wanted still was quite simple: a public statement from the United States government that it supported him until the end of his term. The president's letter would be suitable for this.

Somoza was definitely counting on the growth of Sandinista strength to benefit his cause. "I had misgivings about allowing the Twelve to return," he said, "but by letting them freely demonstrate, people can see the Communist infiltration in them." He couldn't realize how illegitimate his rule had turned, how fed up the people were with him.

At the end of the meeting he expressed hope that some political understanding would be worked out. He felt there was no need for a political pact, just an agreement on an electoral mechanism that would deliver the decision of the voters. He was willing to accept a reasonable number of OAS supervisors to monitor the election.

And to show that his political organization was a reality, the government provided large enough crowds of captive members. July 11 was the "Day of the Nationalist Liberal Party," a yearly ceremony that commemorated the successful Liberal revolt of 1893. Large groups of people drawn from the bureaucracy participated in a series of public acts, whose symbolic center was the "general-president" trying to convey a "Caesarist" imagery of populist rulership.[46] His message was *machista:* the party (of *machos*) would not be intimidated by Communist terrorists nor by the Americans. The *machopolitik* of the ruler was acclaimed by those present with the usual shouts of "*no te vas, te quedás*" (don't leave, stay in power). The capacity to convoke several thousand government employees had a feared meaning for oppositionists. Somoza still had a machine more organized than any other group, which increased the risks of accepting responsibility for following an electoral strategy.

I could not tell him in the light of my instructions that the situation was untenable: he should reimpose the state of siege and take historical responsibility for bestial, genocide repression, or he should prepare his early exit. The first option was unacceptable and unviable.

On July 15 Somoza repeated his pleasure about the president's letter. He asked me how the president had obtained the information. My quick reply: "The very same embassy reporting that you have often told me that is biased against you, and, of course, the press." He raised the issue of U.S. military assistance, which per public reports the administration did not wish to include in its proposals to the Congress. He was actively lobbying to obtain it and wanted the administration to show its willingness to cooperate with him. This was one of the signals from Washington that he felt would stabilize his rule.[47]

Once again I was defeated: Washington decided that the president's letter should be delivered. On the same day that we received the instructions, I made an appointment with Somoza. However, the meeting was postponed by him to the following morning (July 21) because a rocket had been fired from the Intercontinental Hotel against the headquarters of the National Guard (probably it was intended for Somoza's personal compound).

Washington opted to have me make the following statement when delivering the document: "I am under strict instructions to observe that the letter is a confidential communication between President Carter and you, and neither the text or the existence of the correspondence should be disclosed. If you have any response which you would like to transmit to President Carter in a confidential channel, I am at your disposal. Since he signed the letter, President Carter has become aware of recent incidents and violence, and has instructed me to express his deep concern over these incidents and his continued strong hope that there will be no reversal of the positive direction which you indicated you would take."

He said he understood the letter was "personal" in nature and that he would inform me when his reply was ready. The general was not pleased. He asked me what the embassy had to do with the new instructions. There was a lack of chivalry, an unwillingness to try to work out with Somoza an elegant, realistic, pre-1981 solution, while at the same time we would not "overthrow" him.

August proved to be eventful as the confrontation took more dramatic and violent forms. As an indication of the crisis-management mission in which I was increasingly embarked, my vacation in the United States was interrupted.

On August 1, as expected, the letter was finally leaked in the Washington press. The letter presented a mixed message. On the one hand the president of the United States had praised Somoza's promise to hold a free election in 1981; on the other his government was still accused of human rights abuses and told that we wished to see greater democratization.

The *Washington Post* addressed the real problem:

> But we have a . . . complaint on the substance of American policy. The letter and the leak are premised on a view of Nicaragua that may be fundamentally wrong: that what the United States is dealing with in Nicaragua is a human-rights problem. . . . But what the United States is really dealing with in Nicaragua, or so we increasingly suspect, is a revolution. It is comforting to think that the aging Dictator Somoza will somehow fade away and be replaced in the scheduled 1981 elections by moderate democrats friendly to the United States. Such is the polarization and violence now building, however, that President Somoza may be forced out in an explosion well before 1981 and replaced not by centrist democrats but by elements politically and ideologically beholden to the guerillas of the Sandinista National Liberation Front. A "second Cuba" in Central America? It is not out of the question.
>
> For Mr. Carter to write Gen. Somoza as though the question were how to manage a process of gradual and peaceable change seems beside the point. He would do better to figure that the imminence of a major upheaval requires an urgent diplomatic initiative, one meant to help bring representative popular government to Nicaragua before that possibility is preempted by escalating violence. An argument over American policy toward Nicaragua is essential, but it ought to be on the right question.[48]

Somoza's daily published these headlines: "Carter Congratulates Somoza; Security Council of the United States Stimulates the Government of Nicaragua; Acknowledgment of Respect for Human Rights."[49] Otherwise the issue went basically unnoticed in Nicaragua.

About this time *New York Times* correspondent Alan Riding had increased his visits and had longer meetings with me. He wrote critically on U.S. policy.[50] His report on the so-called neutrality read: "Not press General Somoza to resign and . . . not go out of its way to keep him in power. . . . Reassure the President that it will not organize his enemies against him but would strongly disapprove if he reimposed the state of siege in order to smother the opposition." The policy was failing: (1) there were no negotiations nor compromise in sight; (2)

a united offensive involving all key groups in an all-out violent insurrection was coming—"the longer Somoza hangs on to power but fails to assert his authority," Riding wrote, "the more extreme his opposition will become"; (3) there was widespread dissatisfaction in Nicaragua with the U.S. policy.

Why the policy failure? The U.S. government would be pleased to see Somoza resign in order to defuse the crisis. But "to help Somoza's opposition in order to insure that the 'right kind' of regime succeeds him would be to practice just the sort of intervention . . . [detrimental to] Latin America in the past. . . . General Somoza's associates warn that he is not about to flee. . . . That vow seems certain to condemn Nicaragua to violence and anarchy." The final message: Washington would not act decisively even to impede the triumph of an adversarial Communist-inspired government.[51]

Trip to the United States

A few hours before my departure for the United States (July 26–August 8), I met with Somoza to get his response to Carter's letter. He told me that the notion that his son was creating an army within the army was a lie from the opposition. He also asked me to intervene in Washington about stopping revolutionary activities in Nicaragua planned from Costa Rica. If nothing was done, he would have to go into Costa Rica in "hot pursuit" of the activists. He wanted to see the anti-terrorist agreement (i.e., the Rio Treaty) binding the United States to assist him in such cases.

There had been two FSLN attacks on small border posts. The Costa Rican government claimed that it was not trying to assist in Somoza's overthrow, simply that it did not have the capabilities to stop the cross-border activities. "When a Sandinista crosses our border he also crosses the Nicaraguan border—why don't the Nicaraguans stop them?" But Costa Ricans were not really candid. They would not go, for example, to the OAS, raise the border issue, and insist on the necessary international control to stop the activities against Somoza. The fact is that the Somoza government was very unpopular in Costa Rica; hence anti-Sandinista actions on the part of the local government had political costs that it would not incur.

I sought to clarify my situation in Washington. I had been in the field about a year, a new assistant secretary was taking over Latin American operations, and Nicaragua had become a vital spot. I was ready to leave the post. I had worked hard to overcome prejudice and maintain options for the administration. This I had achieved. I had working relations with the local government and cordial ones with the core of the opposition. The embassy had not pleased the key forces: in the field we had not vocalized support for "Somoza 1981," nor had the "ultimatum to Somoza" been delivered. The latter was not my fault. I felt, as did Nicaraguans whom I respected, that as events had developed, an early departure by Somoza (some resignation and election formula) was in the best interest of Nicaragua, Central America, and the United States. I knew that Fulgencio Batista should have left power in Cuba much earlier, rather than seek to end his term of office.

One thing was obvious: the phase in which U.S. policy found itself was exhausted. It needed to be changed lest it result in total irrelevance. The United States had to act to break the impasse, as all Nicaraguans demanded. If the government opted to support Somoza until 1981, I would resign. I was willing to stay for a few more months only if Washington decided to change course and help work out the resolution of the crisis. It is true that in the late 1970s the post-Vietnam syndrome against interventionist adventurism was strong—the American political system would not have accommodated sending the marines to Nicaragua. But this was not the only option available. If the administration was to avoid being involved in a fiasco—with the negative domestic political consequences that this could have for it—the current policy of no assistance or involvement in the process of changing Nicaragua's government prior to 1981 had to be changed. Why not a top-level mediation? I did not wish to be associated with a debacle. I was at peace with myself, and I had done all I could.

The New Assistant Secretary for Latin America

Assistant Secretary Todman's exit had been elegant. The career diplomat was leaving to serve in "a major ambassadorial post in Europe," the first black American to hold such a post.[52] Although Todman supported the president's human rights policy, he had been in disagreement as to the way to implement it—allegedly he "had not been pushing the rights cause strongly enough." From the outset Todman had been against the "carrot-and-stick" component of the human rights policy in favor of a "private diplomacy." "The poor living in authoritarian regimes should not be doubly punished" was his conservative, realpolitik preference. He was also inclined to maintain military assistance ties to support U.S. influence and security goals in addition to human rights. He felt that Latin America was important for U.S. security. From the beginning he had been opposed to linking policy to the democratization of Nicaragua, on the grounds that this was interventionist.

Todman had been defeated. Loans and military disbursements had been suspended before my recruitment. Nonetheless, he had courageously articulated his position, so much so that in my informal contacts in Washington a couple of the more neutral Foreign Service officers had expressed the opinion that only because he was black had the liberals not dared fire him.

I had been troubled by Todman's stance. First, I thought that he would not succeed in obtaining support for normal relations and assistance ties with Somoza. This lack of coordination affected the embassy's USAID section, exacerbating confused "bureaucratic" politics. Second, given Nicaraguan attitudes, a successful policy required a clear political objective: the country's democratic evolution. The opposition had publicly stated that it would fight to change the regime. The success of our mission was also contingent upon their behavior; hence the advisability of devising a political plan in support of the nation's democratization. Todman had opposed such "interventionism."

As events moved rapidly in the post-Chamorro period, Todman had interpreted the administration's opposition to overthrowing Somoza into support for a democratic evolution, with space given to the embassy to assist in the implementation of the policy. Todman did not oppose a U.S. mediation, which made me feel politically closer to him. If we did not support a 1981 solution, we were, in fact, encouraging a pre-1981 solution. This required an active American role in the field to help overcome the local deadlock.

Todman's exit was well received by the Nicaraguan opposition, attentive as it was of news from Washington. He became a scapegoat for why the United States had not done what the opposition really wanted, as if Nicaraguans had forgotten the public position of the president of the United States against "intervention." In this view Todman had "very good relations with the dictators"; his "ambiguity had emboldened Somoza." According to local publications, either the human rights policy had to end, or Todman had to go.[53]

Before his transfer, Todman went to Costa Rica for the inauguration of the newly elected president. The embassy was informed that he had taken the opportunity to talk to the Nicaraguan foreign minister, Julio Quintana, who was also in Costa Rica. Todman raised a new issue, suggesting that like the outgoing Costa Rican president, Daniel Oduber, Somoza should resign so that an interim government acceptable to him could be formed to lead to free elections in 1981. Washington had started to communicate the idea of Somoza's early departure. The widespread "apolitical" stance that I had encountered and considered unrealistic during my recruitment before the Chamorro crisis had been dropped by knowledgeable officials.

On the morning of July 27, I met with the new assistant secretary, Viron P. Vaky, and the group directly involved in Nicaragua. I thought it symptomatic that Wade Matthews, director of the Central American Desk, was absent. All these months Matthews had maintained opposition to withholding assistance from the Somoza government on realpolitik grounds. I respected and trusted him, but his sending signals to Managua that were out of line with the unfolding policy was confusing to operations. Matthews soon moved to another position within the bureaucracy.

The assistant secretary went straight to the problem. He was fearful that "another Cuba" would occur, that Somoza would not want to give up power to defuse the situation. Vaky was considering that vital U.S. interests were at stake but felt he had to act within the notion that Washington would not be willing to employ force to change the government. Recently the ambassador to Venezuela, he was well aware of the initiatives in progress of the international anti-Somoza coalition to overthrow Somoza. But given the administration's philosophy, he would have to rely on a measure of bluff to succeed; this was a serious concern for Vaky.

I commented that revolution had triumphed in Cuba because Batista had been unwilling to retire from power, which meant imposing a puppet president at a very late hour. We had to exercise all our influence to avoid this and even be willing to threaten to cut all ties with Somoza. The problem up to now was that there had been a lack of credibility in, and unwillingness to work out, a compromise. The embassy's encouragement had only resulted in some interest in making counterproposals to Somoza; we had to help work out a compromise.

An operational problem remained in the tougher line that we were intended to adopt. I later raised with both Vaky and Sally Shelton, one of his deputy assistant secretaries, my reservations about terminating the military training for the coming year. This meant that we would be signaling to Somoza before any negotiations started that our military relations with his government would end, thus dropping this bargaining chip to obtain his collaboration. The nature of the assistance process and timing was problematic, though. The administration would have to go to the Congress now and defend the assistance to Somoza before any mediation had been announced. You can see the difficulties of implementing a "carrot-and-stick" policy, given extant legal procedural constraints.

The day ended with a visit by Vaky and myself to the deputy secretary to discuss the situation. A memo with an embassy statement of two days earlier had been sent to him: "There have been steps during the past year toward improved respect for human rights and democratic change while, at the same time, there have been heightened political polarization, revolutionary activism, and militance on the part of oppositionists, which at times have resulted in physical confrontations and some acts of Government of Nicaragua heavy-handedness and human rights abuses." Among other incidents reported: a one-day general strike, a rocket attack on Somoza's office, two Sandinista attacks on small southern military posts, several confrontations between demonstrators and the National Guard, and at least a dozen deaths during the month. Somoza had asked me several times for a supportive U.S. government statement to calm opposition violence, but he felt no need to reestablish the state of siege at this time.

The problem was how to work out a solution accepted in Nicaragua. I knew that a U.S. mediation would be broadly welcomed, the main stumbling block at the time being Somoza's 1981 obsession. Vaky was fully aware of the danger of the Nicaraguan situation and was committed to influence the higher level to change policy. During our visit the highest official monitoring Nicaragua was bluntly told by Vaky about the political risks involved: "another Cuba". Warren Christopher agreed that we should follow a more active role, provided that we acted cautiously. The United States could not intervene in Nicaragua, he said. He saw the need to give guarantees to Somoza in working out a peaceful settlement.

The possibility of an American diplomatic fiasco was not simply that the reproduction of another Cuba with the model of Communist Party rule would take place. It was understood that the core top FSLN military leaders were not ideologically trained strictly in Marxism-Leninism but rather were attracted to and influenced by it. Moreover, as "Sandinismo" grew, it had increasingly become a heterogeneous multiclass movement (that even included some distinguished members of the plutocracy) with various ideological currents within it (that involved prominent and grassroots clergy and social democrats). A central problem was that regardless of the new regime to be formed, a revolution would bring devastation to Nicaragua with very serious disruptive repercussions to its neighbors. And the U.S. government would partake in the responsibility for these events.

I left Washington persuaded that there would be a change in policy. I did not know what dose of cajoling or pressure would be required to change Somoza's 1981 axiom. I had the same opinion held by my predecessor, Kennedy Crockett (1967–70), who had remained living in Nicaragua and with whom I kept in contact, that it might take a very prominent American army general, or the president of the United States, to persuade Somoza that he would have to abdicate. Somoza knows, Crockett had told me, that you can always appeal decisions within the U.S. government, that what an envoy says may not be what the secretary of state or the president thinks; he will play games with you. And he did.

In August there was also awareness in other Latin American capitals of the need to defuse the crisis. For example, in Costa Rica, Daniel Oduber again discussed with American diplomats the Venezuelan, Panamanian, and

Cuban workings to replace Somoza; the succession of Tachito (Somoza Jr.) was considered a regime absurdity, a virtual atrocity, especially in the late 1970s. The Nicaraguan foreign minister and Alfonso Lovo Cordero, a member of the 1972–74 junta, could represent Somoza's party. The Mexican foreign minister said Washington should obtain Somoza's replacement before it was too late and a victory of the radicalized Sandinistas took place. Yet Washington still hesitated to use any of its substantial power and was asking other Latin American governments to mediate the conflict.[54]

The Catholic Church's Call for Peace and Democracy

While I was in the United States, the Catholic hierarchy specified its formula for peace: the Episcopal Conference issued a pastoral letter on August 2 calling for a Christian social democratic order and an end to the violence. The following day the Presbyterial Council of the Archdiocese of Managua, headed by the archbishop, further specified the formula. The statements reflected the known preparations for a mass uprising and the spreading strength of an apocalyptic current of opinion to violently resolve the crisis. There was danger that within the government small groups with an independence of their own would engage in wanton violence of revenge (Somoza was aware of the problem of controlling his men). The anarchization of the society had not yet achieved the costly levels of the near future, though any engagement of the National Guard tended to result in its proverbial brutality, especially toward the common people.

The Presbyterial Council issued a document on August 3, 1978, stating that although the sides were preparing themselves for mutual destruction, the majority—public opinion, ordinary Nicaraguans—opposed the escalation of government repression and of revolutionary insurrection. There were bases for a political understanding as all sectors "coincide in accepting Democracy as the solution to the national problem."[55] What were the impediments to a solution?

> Large sectors do not believe that there can be Democracy if those who guarantee it are those who currently hold the [state's] power; and those who hold the power distrust any solution that is not theirs, with which the solution . . . is immeasurably moved away. It is not our job to judge the causes that have produced this distrust or lack of credibility. We see the obstacle and we observe that that obstacle instead of diminishing has grown, producing a situation of rejection and of impossibility of dialogue, with the catastrophic consequences indicated. [Somoza ought to resign]: the government could, as an option within this policy of mutual concessions, promote with its retirement the formation of that national government, which upon obtaining the support of all, would impede the fall of Nicaragua into a vacuum

of power and anarchy which is always a threat in the processes of change. . . .
We invite our leaders and all the active social forces [fuerzas vivas] of our people
to reflect on the suitability, feasibility, and urgency of a transitory and national
solution, based on the agreement and mutual concessions of everyone.

The archbishop, a future cardinal and a prudent, thoughtful man, had
decided to make public his assessment that the optimum viable solution was
for the president to resign.

I kept ready for the call for mediation from Washington that I hoped for. Thus
on August 11 I visited Archbishop Obando y Bravo.[56] On the assumption of
Vatican preference that the hierarchy not become too tied to any political party,
Monsignor Obando noted that he had been forced to take a stance because
the politicians had proved incapable of going beyond asking Somoza to leave.
He had suggested that Somoza resign; he had called for concessions from all,
reconciliation, and the formation of a national government. The statement
had been sufficiently general to provide a basis for the politicians to make it
more precise. Obando would be willing to mediate the conflict later on.

I felt that he had taken the stance partly in response to pressures from
inside and outside the church that he take on the leadership in helping to solve
the problem; surely he wanted a popular, morally attractive, vigorous Catholic
Church. Hence I commented that the need remained to negotiate a solution
with Somoza before his resignation, and that a timetable (or steps) had to be
worked out. Congressman Alberto Saborío's approach was an example of a
sensible plan to find a solution, I added. Although Monsignor Obando agreed
that ultimately there would be a need to negotiate a solution, he had taken
"his" position: only if Somoza was willing to resign might it be feasible for
him to participate in negotiations.

Somocistas

Somoza himself took care of publicly denying the possibility of shortening
his term: "Nothing nor no one will break the Constitution; neither [I] nor
the [Liberal] party will leave power; the struggle for the 1981 elections starts
today," were the *Novedades* headlines. There was nothing illegal, of course,
in the president resigning and the formation of a government of national
unity. The general used the term *prebendas sociales* in reference to the system
of "social welfare with liberty" that his party had supposedly delivered to
the people. This suggested the patriarchal, patrimonial premises of regime,
for currently *prebenda* most commonly means "sinecure" rather than the old
historical meaning of "charitable gift."[57]

The party was the majority, Somoza continued to repeat. He referred to the number of votes delivered by the party, as well as the numbers gathered in the last three Liberal rallies: 150,000 on February 26; 60,000 on May 1; 40,000 on July 11, he claimed. It irked me that the Somozas had always refused to accept neutral, international electoral supervision, if they were such a majority.

Somoza's was an act of "magical realism": the Orwellian capacity for doublethink with its fantasies and impossibility to have a meeting of the minds to solve the crisis.[58] His course had been established. In explicitly repudiating a government of national unity, Somoza asked how power could be distributed to opposition groups that even lacked the tapestry of being political parties and had not obtained any votes to measure their support. It was because of his own support that he did not resign, he said. In conjunction with the speech, Luis Pallais Debayle informed me that the government had given up trying to search for a dialogue and would mobilize the party for the 1981 solution.

Three days after my return to Managua, I met with Pallais at the deputy chief of mission's residence. Always optimistic and pleasant, Luis's reaction to the archbishop's statement was not that negative. "At least it is a document that can be negotiated," he said.

I was as direct as I could be: "as a hypothesis," would Somoza be willing to retire earlier? I also suggested that some solutions did not need any prior constitutional change—specifically, that the president could implement the archbishop's formula. If he resigned, a new Liberal president could form a cabinet of national unity. What I wanted to see was a national *abrazo* (reconciliation).

Luis commented that he wanted to visit the archbishop to find out his plan; he had told Somoza not to take the archbishop's position personally. It would be impossible for Somoza to implement the reorganization of the Guard, retiring the family, as a single issue, for it would be interpreted badly by the army that he was sacrificing his family, not himself. Somoza would only be willing to shorten his tenure if he thought it would solve the problem. At the same time, Luis suggested that the foreign minister, who constitutionally could not succeed Somoza until the 1981 election, was the only Liberal really with presidential caliber. The Liberal Party had become a stale organization, he commented.

I had suggested to individuals close to the president that a pre-1981 compromise might be the only solution. On August 24 I received a cable from Washington: Somoza was pressuring the U.S. government to replace me, and so was the Cuban Miami lobby. I was not surprised. I had been appointed on the initiative of friends in Miami, especially Maurice A. Ferré, the city's mayor. From the outset he was very upset that Nicaragua was the destination chosen for me, for in Miami there was a strong pro-Somoza sentiment among Cuban Americans. If I needed to be reminded, I had just received a letter from my mother, who resided in Florida, stating that "every single Cuban wants Somoza to remain in power," feeling that they had been "useful fools in allowing [dictator] Batista to leave" to be replaced by Communist Castro. What political underdevelopment.

In any case, I had decided to close my Nicaraguan adventure and not serve beyond the new phase of mediation being devised in Washington. I did not wish to share responsibility any longer. Going back to my permanent university job simply required notifying them before the semester began. I had not yet done this, but I was not hiding my intentions to a few close friends.

The fact that the Somocistas thought a new ambassador might mean their troubles would be mitigated or solved was indicative that they were not in step with the new verities facing them and intended to put up a fight to remain in power. However, the frustrations caused by my "missionary without force" or "interference without intervention" mission were real. There were rumors that I was going to be replaced—a local radio station announced it on the grounds that political officer Jack Martin and Patricia Haigh of the Economic Section really ran the embassy; in a theater a woman asked my wife, Joan, "When are you going to leave?" I was vulnerable to being made scapegoat of our inability to replace Somoza.

Although there had been a scandal in the Ministry of Health, and we had learned that the Ministry of Education was in arrears in projects with the World Bank and the Inter-American Development Bank, as if following Parkinson's law that bureaucracy grows most when it accomplishes the least, USAID refused to postpone its two new loans. The presentation of credentials of the new Costa Rican ambassador on August 16 allowed me to see Somoza in a most unfavorable light. I had been talking with a member of his cabinet about USAID. He suggested that we speak to the president, so we approached him. Somoza abruptly dismissed his minister. "You don't know anything," he said loudly, pushing him aside. The general started talking to me as if the silenced minister did not exist. The humiliation did not alter the loyalty of the minister, but it did show Somoza's contempt for his people. It was dramatically clear why Somoza's cadres were totally subordinated to him: it was futile to do anything other than what was expected to please him. They feared his confrontational reaction, and no one could change his mind.[59]

I wished to see Roberto Incer Barquero, the president of the Central Bank. A graduate from the same program that I had attended at Yale University, he was respected by the business community. He might be more independent, a Liberal presidential aspirant. Another business stoppage was being planned for the following week; there were also efforts being carried out by oppositionists to organize labor in several sectors, and a few labor strikes had developed. Incer dismissed the stoppage. It would take place, but the government maintained intact its (predominant) military and financial resources. The opposition was wrong thinking that it could overthrow Somoza through some "apotheosic" act, he stated.

Incer felt a need to justify his participation in the government. Being an honest official, he had wanted to resign, he said, but he had been persuaded by Somoza the previous November that there would be administrative reforms with new personnel, and the only route to democracy was by uplifting the government (i.e., the common rationalization that things would be worse if I did not collaborate with the government).

Then Incer elaborated on what he thought was Somoza's plan, a modified version of the René Schick experiment, who was the president between the two Somoza brothers' presidencies. The general would not be president nor the titular head of the National Guard, but from his hacienda he would keep control of the situation. His son would remain in the Guard as its de facto head, and given his status, Somoza himself would continue overseeing the party. Party control would permit him to depose through its congressional majority any president who became *díscolo* (wayward). This was precisely the opposition's great fear and source of intransigence. Incer was concerned with U.S. policy. In his opinion, only the United States or an act of God could terminate what he called the "Somocismo sickness." So much depended on the leader's will. What if the United States deposed him—couldn't he return as Napoleon had once done?

Contact with *La Prensa*

I had persisted in trying to keep working relations with what I considered the center of gravity of the unarmed opposition. *La Prensa*'s role in a peaceful resolution was crucial. Our relations had not been easy. However, I had always treated *La Prensa* ethically, with as much candor as permitted and with consideration. I had told P.J. Chamorro: "I expect that you defend your interests but wish that Washington coincides as much as possible with them."

Controversial issues remained that were summarized by Chamorro's widow, Violeta Barrios, in a letter to the president of the United States published August 21. Doña Violeta used the lack of progress in the investigation of her husband's assassination and the embassy's public commitment that we would be as helpful as possible in assisting with the investigation to ask President Carter to uncover some answers. The government of Nicaragua continued accusing Pedro Ramos, a Cuban American residing in Florida, of contracting the assassination. But the initiatives that it might have taken to obtain extradition still left much to be desired. I must assume the government continued to fear the embarrassment of a public trial involving foreigners who had been its partners. Doña Violeta praised the progress made toward clarifying the assassination in Washington of the Chilean ex-foreign minister Orlando Letelier (in which some Cuban exiles were also implicated).[60]

In her letter Mrs. Chamorro also praised the human rights policy, "the hope that the incorporation of [its] dimension in the foreign policy of the United States has awakened." However, she observed problems: "We Nicaraguans expect and wish a greater and permanent consistency in the American foreign policy with the human rights ideals. In this perspective we lament the recent offering of loans to Somoza's government because rather than encourage democracy and justice, they strengthen the repressive positions of the dictatorship." But, "on the other hand, we are encouraged and at the same time observe with hope . . . the distancing that under diverse forms has been established between American foreign policy and Somoza's interests."

This "positive" aspect, which no attentive oppositionist could deny, had allowed our efforts toward La Prensa to progress. On August 17 I had lunch for the first time with P.J. Chamorro's eldest son, Pedro Joaquín Chamorro Barrios. He made exceedingly clear the dilemma facing La Prensa. He agreed that my scenario of a peaceful compromise while democratizing Nicaragua was the rational solution. But there were problems: (1) there was the spilled blood;[61] (2) the Sandinistas would not accept negotiations, and all oppositionists were fearful that they would lose prestige if they deescalated the demands; (3) the distrust of Somoza combined with fear that toning down the debate would result in a loss of momentum—people might forget and give up, especially if 1981 became the accepted term. "Before my father's death," Pedro Joaquín said, "We weren't able to get more than 4,000 people to attend a rally." La Prensa was also to some extent a prisoner of history.

Danilo Aguirre

The practical problem of managing the news coverage of the signing of the USAID loans was pending. I expected a U.S. mediation at any time. It was thus vital that the loan ceremonies not lead to another cycle of estrangement between the embassy and the opposition, fueled by a negative propaganda reaction to the loan's publicity.

I met again with Danilo Aguirre, then La Prensa's deputy director, frankly explaining the loans' origins and purposes and stressing that Washington's objective was not to "support" the Nicaraguan government, though Somoza

would encourage such an interpretation. I concluded with a respectful statement: "You must treat the loans in the light of your interpretation of the best
interests of Nicaragua, but I hope that your paper's coverage will not distort
their politically neutral objectives."

I was pleased. Aguirre observed the extreme unpopularity of the loans, but
he agreed. La Prensa was very important in forming public opinion, he said;
hostile coverage of the loans could play into Somoza's hands, creating the
impression that the United States stood against the opposition; this could
only disconcert the public. Aguirre hoped that Novedades and the American
press would not provoke a controversy, so that La Prensa could use the low-key
approach they had used in covering Carter's letter to Somoza.

Aguirre saw three critical areas: the Guardia Nacional, electoral reform,
and an amnesty. He said he would consult with Xavier Chamorro, "but I am
prepared to meet with a representative of the government if there is a possibility
of working out a solution. A full-blown war would be a disaster." (In fact, it
later left Danilo's son dead and a country in ruin.)

On August 18 I received both Luis Pallais and Alberto Saborío to explore
the possibility of negotiations between the government and La Prensa. I was
stepping beyond the boundaries of my formal instructions. However, I thought
only these contacts could break the impasse, and that the new climate in
Washington was for greater involvement in solving the crisis. Events such as
this one could only help establish grounds for the inexorable need to mediate,
I rationalized.

Luis addressed Saborío's statement on reorganizing the National Guard.
Somoza, he said, was interested in extending the rule prohibiting members of
the president's family from being in the National Guard, but he wanted any
changes to be made following constitutional (i.e., congressional) procedures,
and for them to be part of a package agreed upon by the opposition. The
president feared that if he made concessions, he would be asked again the
following day to resign. Luis's tone was conciliatory.[62] He wanted to meet
with representatives of La Prensa, Xavier Chamorro and Danilo Aguirre. The
United States had to provide the umbrella here as currently in the Dominican
Republic, he added. In short, rather than propose a serious plan of regime
termination, the government was using dilatory strategy, proposing the discredited congressional rubber stamp and demanding the impossibility that
the entire opposition commit itself to back any formula.

Saborío told us that what La Prensa wished was a peaceful democratic change
because of the uncertainty and costs of a tactic to obtain an opposition military
victory over the National Guard and the danger that undemocratic elements
would prevail if chaos spread. Luis Pallais then commented that the govern-

ment did not oppose the archbishop's doctrine, only Somoza's resignation. Although I noted the limitations of my formal instructions, it was agreed that the two of them would meet with La Prensa at my official residence, and that someone from the embassy would be present. Obviously it was better that I be there, so I decided to participate in the next meeting, on August 21.

Pallais was given a document establishing the basis for negotiating a compromise. Crucial to it was a two-step process to work out a solution *constitutionally*. Constitutional changes required approval in two legislatures; thus speed was essential so that the changes could be in place and fully approved when the second legislature opened in May 1979. The date was a good target: the revolutionary wave that finally ousted Somoza was initiated at that month's end. The crux was that the structure of the executive would be changed, and it was recommended that a triumvirate be formed with one representative each from the government, the political opposition, and the private sector.[63] This government would preside over general elections in 1981. Indeed, as we have been arguing, compromise options can remain alive during a substantial part of a revolutionary process—revolutions can be aborted with the proper strategic choices. Years later, in long exile, Luis Pallais, perhaps remembering one of these initiatives, told me, "Somoza was given the opportunity."

There were other reasonable voices. On August 21 La Prensa published an article by Humberto Belli Pereira, the young social scientist who participated in a meditation group related to the archbishop.[64] The article was remarkable in its empathy with all groups. All parties had to make concessions so that the common good would prevail. No party was being asked to surrender; rather, mutual guarantees had to be worked out.

Belli observed both the strengths and anxieties of the parties. Somoza's military-civil machine could not be dismissed; the general feared that the legacy of family rule might end in chaotic revenge against him and his followers. The opposition, on the other hand, could not be dismissed as a nonviable force without broad national support, and it feared that once again a negotiated understanding would result in them being tricked into Somoza's *continuismo*.

Alberto Chamorro (brother-in-law of Alfredo Pellas, scion of the most traditional, wealthiest family, and both reputed kingmakers within the Conservative Party) asked for an appointment "due to his concern over the situation." He criticized the "emotionalism" of the opposition and the increased strength of the FSLN. "You have the opportunity to solve the crisis. What is needed," he said, "is for you to meet with the two heads of the largest non-Somoza financial groups to line up the large business sector to finance the democratic opposition." This would be followed by meetings with all Conservative factions, as well as Ramiro Sacasa's Liberal group and Alfonso Robelo's newly formed Movimiento Democrático Nicaragüense (MDN).

I wondered why the embassy had to be directly involved in the meetings. Chamorro said that "the United States can not abdicate its leadership role here. There is so much distrust that without guarantees or active mediation by your government and, possibly, the archbishop it is impossible to create the conditions to begin negotiations." I asked if there was any person who could become a true leader of a unified opposition in negotiations. No, Chamorro answered, not without outside support. It was clear, and as customary Washington was informed, that the basis for a quick welcoming of U.S. mediation endured. The regime had little support outside the state's structures.

Increased Sandinista Pressure

I was on the phone with Luis Pallais Debayle, who was in the National Palace presiding over the session of the Chamber of Deputies that August 22, when he told me that he had to hang up because there was some sort of disturbance near him. The armed Sandinista operation had begun.[65]

This type of action—physically occupying a public building and holding hostages to gain publicity and ransom and to win the liberation of revolutionaries in prison—had been planned for some time. We had obtained intelligence on a similar operation intended for a foreign ballet; to spare the risks and costs to the innocent public, the embassy had privately divulged the information, and the performances were canceled. The palace's capture served other functions. It showed the revolutionary capability and the government's weakness in controlling the population. It was designed to influence the people and rally support for the cause. Its contribution to the process of converting people into "Sandinistas" was suggested by the masses who turned out to cheer the revolutionaries on their way to the airport after the operation successfully ended.

The seizure brought international attention to the cause. It also obtained the release of a few dozen Sandinistas who were in prison (including Tomás Borge, subsequently one of the Nine Comandantes of the Revolution, the sovereign power of the eventual revolutionary government) and a $500,000 ransom payment from the government.[66] Edén Pastora, the commander of the operation—"Comandante Zero"—became a romantic hero of the struggle to oust the dictatorship.

As soon as she learned that her husband had been captured, Nadia Pallais visited me in my office. In December 1974 Somoza had once paid ransom to liberate hostages. He had stated that it would be the first and last time that he would compromise. Fearing her husband's death if a military rescue operation was carried out, Nadia simply told me that I could not abandon Luis; the American government had the greatest influence with Somoza.

At 7 p.m. Nadia called my wife, Joan. She had just talked to Luis, who had a gun pointed at his head and had said that there was not much time left. He would be executed if Somoza did not make the concessions. Twenty minutes later, I talked to Somoza. Above all, the personal esteem in which I held Luis and Nadia (and my desire to maintain a working relation with Luis) made me decide to override my preference not to be a mediator. Somoza asked me to come and visit him that evening at 9 p.m.

I recall the state of expectation and anxiety that had overcome Managua: all media stations were placed under National Guard control. We canceled a public concert that was going to take place at the residence and the flights of two U.S. Air Force planes scheduled to arrive; we did not wish to give the impression that the U.S. government was militarily involved in the event, whatever its outcome. I also remember that as my official automobile was stopped for identification before entering the military compound where Somoza's office was, a soldier on duty asked for two cigarettes. The professionalism of the little National Guard seemed hopeless.

As usual, Somoza received me promptly. We talked for only about twenty minutes. He reported that the bishops had informed him that ten people were dead, and he referred to the demands made by the Sandinistas. He said that he had contemplated military action but had decided to negotiate because "lives cannot be regained, but money is ultimately negotiable." Somoza then told me that two weeks earlier he had gone to Venezuela to speak with President Carlos Andrés Pérez: "Pérez and I talked for several hours. He proposed that I resign in favor of a government of national unity in return for guarantees of my life and property. But once I leave power, no one can guarantee me anything."

Somoza assured me of his flexibility. He did not want me to misinterpret his criticism of the archbishop's initiative in favor of a new government. He then gave me the FSLN "war communiqués." "Everyone is criticized in the document—your embassy, private business, the opposition," he commented. The Sandinistas would not stop using violence until a Communist revolution took place. (His resignation would not pacify the country.) Somoza added that he had spoken to the papal nuncio to explore the possibility that the Conservative Party—members of which were being kept hostage in the palace as well—get parliaments of different nations to condemn the attack, and he hoped that the U.S. government would also condemn the "criminal acts against noncombatants." He had made contact with Venezuela to see if they would receive the Sandinistas; Panama had already accepted them.

I had found him tired and slightly depressed, somewhat on the defensive in the face of the spectacular action, to the point of verbally expressing acceptance of the need for a compromise. I returned to see him the following day, August 23. Instructions from the State Department provided the reason to visit. He complied with my request, providing us with the details: the following morning at 9 a.m. the estimated forty terrorists and around fifty released jailed revolutionaries would leave for Panama and Caracas; Venezuela was providing the transportation.[67] There were seven confirmed dead—all Guardia Nacional—and possibly one civilian.

Somoza handed me copies of the documents, including handwritten notes from the revolutionaries, as well as communications from both sides of the negotiations. He was doing what he liked best: the friend of the United States collaborating with us to keep us informed. The general said, "This terrorist act is the most serious mistake the Sandinistas have made. Their imprisonment of so many Nicaraguans of all social classes will serve to dash their public support, and it will frighten the business sector because of their clear statements about the Communist type of government they seek to establish." He thought this would encourage businessmen to start talking with him. He then thanked me for Washington's statement condemning the palace's occupation.

Somoza appeared much more relaxed than the previous night. He had regained his confidence and projected the belief that he had triumphed over the Sandinistas. I saw him as a combative, resilient man guided by wishful thinking that support would come again his way. He could not believe in defeat. His mind was not totally disconnected from reality, but it was clouded by unrealistic messianic hopes and egotism.

Marxist-Leninist Influence

The operation's popularity in the streets was obvious, Somoza's interpretation notwithstanding. As earlier noted, Sandinismo consisted of a broad coalition to overthrow Somoza.[68] Nonetheless, the FSLN at this time could be conceptualized as a set of concentric circles composed of different types of activists and followers in which the innermost armed circle was inspired by Marxist-Leninist thought.

The Sandinista group involved in the operation showed such an influence. In the first place, their published documents advocated the constitution of a "popular democracy" with a "popular army"; no primacy was given to free elections. The objective was to establish a system in which the participation of peasants and workers "would occupy the directorship which corresponds [to the working class] as the determinant force that it is in the production of the wealth from our country."

Calling for the unity of all the FSLN factions, in Leninist fashion, the group viewed itself as the *vanguard* "of the oppressed, the exploited, the working class, of the great working masses of our country." And in a document in which practically all political groups were condemned, the Sandinista military vanguard defined the organized working class in the unions and in the Nicaraguan Communist Party (Partido Socialista Nicaragüense) as pillars of the construction of the future society.[69]

In contrast to statements typical of Latin American democratic oppositions, the documents made no mention of constitutional democracy. There was reference to democratic freedoms, including freedom of religion, but as if indicating the weight of an "anti-bourgeois" ideological tradition, no usage was made of the "natural rights" lexicon of area democratic oppositions.

The low probability that a political democracy would be established following a Sandinista victory was suggested as well by the intense partisanship, the documents' *sectarismo* intolerance. The language was full of quasi-religious references; of all the opposition groups, the Sandinista idiom maximized "nonsecularity," thus more intensely manifesting these items drawn from the general culture.

The "War Communiqué," for example, stated that no compromise was possible: the "armed popular Sandinista insurrection" would not end until the National Guard and the civilian Somocista coteries were "*destroyed.*" The other documents opposed *any negotiations* with Somoza or his party: they restated that since October 1977 they had opposed any form of dialogue (including, explicitly, the early initiative organized by the archbishop and the private sector); they also condemned the general post-Chamorro stoppage, in that it had sought Somoza's resignation and the constitution of a new government without destroying the National Guard.

The "Minimum Program" to end the violence was the confiscation of all properties of the Somoza family and the formation of a new army. Obviously, under such terms nothing was possible other than a Sandinista military victory. The dead would be the responsibility of the Somocistas, who would not accept this solution; compromise formulas were a "Somocismo without Somoza."

A caveat is pertinent. Marxist-Leninist-inspired revolutionaries throughout Latin America believed intensely at this time that the establishment of a "popular democracy" required the constitution of a new army. The recent dramatic collapse of Salvador Allende's "electoral route to socialism" indicated—especially when contrasted to Cuba—the need to dissolve the old army.[70] The Sandinistas made a call for military defections that went basically unheeded.

In August 1978 Colonel Bernardino Larios, who did not command troops, went into exile to join the revolution. We did not give much importance to this isolated act as a plausible crack in the Guardia Nacional. Actually, Colonel Larios became the Sandinista minister of defense, but soon after the revolution he was purged and jailed.

The quasi-religious inspiration of the revolution was manifest. In their struggle the Sandinistas were in quest of personal salvation, immortality. They were noble men and women—their search for the heroic was extremely intense. They "swore loyalty to [their] dead and [were willing] to die standing up," thus also activating traditional personalistic macho themes.

They were continuing to fight "so that the[se] heroes and martyrs remain in the heart of the people"; if they died they would be saved, would become immortal in time and space. It was as if the revolutionary action was both real suffering and protest against it, a way of self-realization to achieve freedom, power, complete fulfillment. The quest for immortality intersected with a messianic, apocalyptic vision of the inexorable personal and collective triumph. Not only were their dead triumphant; all their military actions were triumphs!

The relatively small-scale military combats that they previously had been able to conduct, which many outsiders had viewed as tragic, misguided attempts, were now proclaimed victories and steps to hasten the inexorable final triumph. The utopian fight was so that "for the first time the children and youth be happy." Any compromise was a "crime of high treason," and "enemies are all those who wish to *mediatizar* [dull and deviate, i.e., mediate] the struggle which we have headed." Why? "Those who try to further a change without dissolving the National Guard are accomplices . . . betray the blood of the martyrs of the people." And the moderates, those who sought to compromise precisely to avoid the war's cost, were threatened with a call to the Sandinista "popular militias" and "combat units" to be alert against their treason. Indeed, violent revolutionaries exercise coercion.

In sum, the proclamations suggested that a new Sandinista *hegemonía* was sought, in which the Somocistas and National Guard would be completely excluded from participation in the state. Typically, those who counted were "Sandinist": the *pueblo* (people) "*sandinista*," the *masas* (masses) "*sandinistas*," and so on.[71] The undemocratic language singled out *not* "national" entities (e.g., *el ejército*), but partisan entities (e.g., the army *sandinista*), a discourse cognate to the hegemonies that with different coloring permeated much of Latin American history. Judging from its publicity, the FSLN was not inclined to constitute the highly differentiated state required for an institutionalized democracy. At best, it might constitute a Sandinista pseudo-democracy with a more intensive and extensive socialist dimension than the earlier Nicaraguan ones, I thought when reading these documents. It was ironic that the local weakness of the democratic ethos would have to expect such outcomes from revolutionaries who claimed to represent the radical transformation of their country.

The documents also outlined the plan to organize a general insurrection (a classic *levée en masse*) to crack the National Guard. The idea was a national uprising that would culminate in an apocalyptic "great insurrectionist combat." (This "final offensive" was launched a few days later; the government did not fall, however.) To prepare for that event, it was stated, more units would be created in places of work—workers were to participate both in the unions and the guerrilla forces; people would form fronts in the barrios and towns. The revolution had to become a day-to-day activity, a new, emergent, parallel social organization or routine: "The working people must convert into a weapon everything on hand, to kill the 'ears,' *orejas*, to execute the National Guards . . . to build barricades, throw bombs at Guardia patrols, in sum, harass Somoza's criminal forces at every moment and hour."[72] The people were to be organized in popular militias and combat units. This organization was to culminate in the creation of armed revolutionary fronts and military columns for larger-scale armed combat operations, a militarily organized nation-in-arms for "the daily and generalized combat in cities, fields and mountains, making of the Sandinista war a reality."

Somoza was mistaken in interpreting a popular repudiation of the palace operation. My wife, Joan, commented on the attractive symbolism of a photographed female teenager who had chosen the road of sacrifice, going into exile with the departing group because she wished to construct a better Nicaragua. Despite my ideological differences with the FSLN because of the indications of its lack of firm commitment to representative democracy, I admired Sandinista idealistic heroism to construct a better Nicaragua. Since its origins the country had been in search of a more solid national identity and sovereignty. Ruling group predatory intransigence might have to be broken through force. The developing popular mobilization and opening of the elite were needed for the nation's modernization and more just welfare. In any case, large numbers of Nicaraguans had vicariously enjoyed the coup perpetrated against the stuffy strongman. Many wondered why the Somoza family did not leave them alone, resigning and departing from the country with their millions.

By now conditions of public order were such that even if the conflict were successfully mediated, the FSLN, with its stated uncompromising revolutionary objectives, could pose serious problems for stabilizing a new government.

Not everyone was optimistic in the embassy. One of our politically more acute State Department officers sent me a memo addressing government and Sandinista intransigence. "There is no alternative to Somoza that would not be quickly swept away by the extreme left were it to assume power—let's be damn sure of the assumption before we go any further!" It was not evident that in Somoza's absence a coherent, strong government could be formed that would be backed by the National Guard. Nicaragua was in a mess because the democratic forces and the nation's army were organizationally weak. Somoza had not allowed the former to institutionally stabilize and grow, and he had been organizing the succession of his son in the Guard only to guarantee the perpetration of Somoza rule.

But it was too late to retreat. The key forces had clearly stated that they would not support the president's tenure for his term. The only alternative was some U.S. mediation to work out as elegant and peaceful a solution as possible. The internal memo also viewed this option as problematic. If Somoza did not cooperate, the U.S. presence in Nicaragua would be drastically reduced, and our relations with his government would be terminated.

The memo was quite disturbing in its sense of powerlessness. My mode of operation was direct and unassuming; some opposition leaders had become sufficiently close that they informally visited me to talk. One of them told me in my office: "It is lamentable that your government is not any longer using the CIA to organize oppositions as a mechanism to strengthen the political center, nor is Washington in the business of organizing coups." I interjected: nor do we deliver ultimatums to change governments. He laughed and said, "You just don't have enough instruments to work with." He was right.

Another Work Stoppage

On August 22 Reynaldo Antonio Téfel, the very active Social Christian in UDEL, and hence the FAO, who later joined the Twelve and was a prominent Sandinista official, came to visit me. His rhetoric was truly "liberationist," revolutionary: "*estamos en la recta final*" (we are in the final lap), he said. "The planned strike will oust him [Somoza]." "Use your military mission to support a coup d'état," he asked me.

The FAO had called for a revolutionary strike starting August 25, a general, indefinite stoppage until the government fell. "Firm and united, it corresponds to us in these moments, to give the decisive battle that will place us on the road to obtain the liquidation of the Somocista system, and the establishment of a true democracy . . . the stoppage will not cease until the fall of the Somocista regime." The FAO complemented the National Palace event. The final communiqué that was made public contrasted the strategy of the unarmed opposition to that of the Sandinistas: the opposition strategy did not advocate employing physical violence, but it shared the desire to terminate the government. The indefinite strike sought to "overthrow the Somocista dictatorship and the democratization of Nicaragua [but] through civic actions"; the "great National Stoppage, in addition to a citizen's right, is an instrument of the civism in which we have framed our struggle." The immediate objective was the removal of the three Somozas from all public offices and the constitution of a "Gobierno Nacional," the archbishop's government of national unity.[73] Despite some resistance to participating in another strike and tensions in the business community, obviously the more radical sentiment had prevailed. The statements underlined the competition of unarmed oppositionists with armed ones to prove their anti-Somocismo. In fact, as the archbishop commented, contacts existed for coordinating a major uprising involving both sectors.

I was sure that the government would not be overthrown. Things had changed, however. Revolutionary activities at my arrival had been concentrated in small groups sustained by their ideological and emotional frame of mind through their incapacity of success because they were unable to achieve popular participation. Now the circles of revolutionary actions had dramatically expanded.

The government intended to divide the private sector and obtain its compliance by threatening reprisals. On August 29 the Central Bank president went public, saying that the business sector, in its adherence to the strike, indicated that it was incapable of defining its interests. The stoppage would not significantly weaken the government, which would remain in place, but would seriously weaken the private sector. In the face of this lack of judgment and political independence and given that foreign financial sources were drying out at an accelerated rate, the result was going to be that neither the government, the Central Bank, nor private banks and firms would be able to obtain the foreign credit required to avoid the virtual paralysis of the nation's economy. Consequently, drastic measures had to be taken: finance only those businesses that remain open; guarantee external loans only to those businesses; intervene in the closed firms; prohibit the foreign and local refinancing of such firms; prepare a massive plan of public works in Managua to compensate for the ensuing increase in unemployment. On that same day the government suspended the legal personality of the nation's Chamber of Commerce.

Private-sector response was immediate through the Instituto Nicaragüense de Desarrollo (INDE), the organization that Alfonso Robelo had headed. The stoppage was a patriotic and determined component of the struggle to establish the proposed transitional Gobierno Nacional, a legitimate means of civic pressure to obtain its constitution. The private sector had shown its independence vis-à-vis all groups, including the government. It had been searching for civil formulas of national unity to resolve the crisis, in alliance with the Catholic Church. "That before history the two positions be clearly defined, those of us who search for a peaceful solution supporting eminently civic protests, and those who fasten themselves to an absolute and corrupted power, which is repudiated by all the nation's sectors and which propitiates the spouting of [Marxist-Leninist] doctrines, creeds, and groups which do not count with the support of the majority of the country." This was the Somocista message turned on its head: the longer Somoza remained in power, the greater the likelihood of a Communist solution.

Meanwhile, Somoza publicly recognized that he was facing a new phenomenon. He stated: "One can say that the Frente [Sandinista] was practically liquidated [then] and that the new people who came to make this [National Palace] assault mostly are new [individuals] whom they have [recently] collected." The Sandinistas were recruiting in the schools, and the Group of Twelve had broken their previous isolation. "[The Twelve] have made the Front politically open," Somoza said.

Yet he dismissed the combined challenge of the Sandinistas and unarmed opposition. In apparent conflict, he also defined the Sandinista simply as a chronic, manageable problem. The National Guard "would be ready to face an escalation of these activities"; there will be "an orderly development of our institutional government." Somoza also dismissed the FAO's general stoppage—he seemed almost bored by it. With the contempt characteristic of an extraordinary ego, he said, "I wish them good luck to those of the strike." In the "fight," the Liberal Party was winning because the people were realizing that the government was trying to provide services and the others were trying to interrupt them. The ideological ferment also occurred in other countries, Somoza commented, more blasé than arrogant. The state seemed to suffer from *abulia* (lack of energy), and the Central Bank's proposal to meet the stoppage was not implemented.

What were the government's plans? "From now on Nicaragua will continue with its normal life." Somoza would remain governing "democratically." The state of siege would not be reestablished, and the temporarily suspended media news programs would return to normality (i.e., to conduct their fiery, alarmist opposition and call to revolt that fostered the extant climate of dissatisfaction, excitement, and revolutionary expectations beyond interpersonal networks). As a "statesman and president," Somoza could not have sacrificed the lives of thousands of Nicaraguans by militarily intervening at the National Palace.[74] He praised the professional discipline of the military. In short, the government would continue to allow open opposition with a restrained army that would guarantee "peace and national order." Somoza's goals remained unchanged.

Somoza added this statement in *Novedades* on August 26:

Regimes are democratic or not, according with the cultural level of the people, thus I confess that Nicaragua is not absolutely democratic because we do not have the education so that the laws function correctly, and whoever does not recognize this in Nicaragua today, is not talking—let us say—realities, but yes, we have determined for ourselves that the children of the men who live in this country be more educated, so that they be more democratic. The Nicaragua that Somoza García, my father, lived is not a shadow of the Nicaragua in which I am living. . . . Yet it must be recognized that I, like the other politicians who live here now, recognize that we have a country that has evolved, and that has developed in the last ten years, and that we have a youth which demands new opportunities.

He had to realize that he was playing a different international and domestic game, one that was demanding that he resign, but his platform remained "*yo o el caos*" (rule under my terms is the only alternative to chaos).

The U.S. Press Looks at Nicaragua

Nicaragua was not at peace. On August 25 the *Miami Herald* editorialized: "Somoza's Regime Is Doomed—And U.S. Course Is Clear." The *Herald* noted the incapacity of the Nicaraguan government to cope with the situation: "now there is a lack of strength to repress"; the regime was immobile, decayed, incapable of generating the energy to triumph. The paper also suggested policy: "The United States has had too much to do with maintaining the antidemocracy in Nicaragua. This country's attention and efforts should be directed to the other side. The Nicaraguan people's side."

On August 31 the *Washington Star* published an article by Jeremiah O'Leary, the well-connected journalist, titled "U.S. Begins Review of Nicaraguan Policy." According to O'Leary, in the light of the growing violence, threat of civil war, and possibility that a Central American nation might fall under Marxist rule, administration spokespeople felt that an American activist policy was needed.

There were several alternatives, none of them "easy," O'Leary wrote. The principal scenarios: (1) provide increased support to Somoza to enable him to survive until 1981; (2) urge Somoza to step down so that a non-Marxist government of national unity, including the official Liberal Party and the National Guard, could be formed; (3) some variation of the status quo urging Somoza to exercise restraint; or (4) United States intervention.

The first alternative was not discussed: an administration that had been disassociating itself from Latin dictatorships on human rights grounds did not have the stomach to support a discredited regime into trying to brutally restore order. Nor was the third option elaborated—it was the policy that was failing.

The second option was preferred. The ideal was to have a moderate, democratic government with sufficient support to survive without harsh police measures and without any major U.S. involvement in terms of money, arms, and troops. This required that any government would obtain fairly broad local support. Yet there were problems. Foremost was the prediction that the general would say no to U.S. advice, that he would not step down but would stay in power and fight. Officials thought if Washington publicly called on Somoza to resign "for the good of his homeland and the Western Hemisphere," it might be the kiss of death for his regime. It was argued that "the Somozas have stayed too long and any government that replaces them might be too weak to resist the far left or the hard right." The disorganized state of the unarmed opposition made it difficult to run a government challenged on both sides, officials believed.

As for the fourth alternative, officials reported the opinion that in the face of Somoza's intransigence, the only solution might be U.S. intervention to change and assist in constituting a government of national unity to avert war. The lingering sense of impotence manifested throughout the article was related to the fact that the administration "would never dream of sending troops to Nicaragua for any reason except invasion by a foreign power." The administration's explicit parameters had never changed.

The internal debate publicized in Washington was covered in Nicaragua. For instance, La Prensa on August 30 addressed an Associated Press cable about a Washington Post editorial: policy was paralyzed because of internal contradictions within the administration. Some officials favored asking Somoza to resign, but these officials had been stopped by functionaries who argued: (1) that the United States needed to avoid an act that would appear to be an intervention, even if this is to get rid of a discredited ruler; or (2) that it was unwise to allow the fall of a proven friend when the alternatives were anarchy or a leftist dictatorship.

The first defense encouraged continuing the extant power vacuum and chaos, an ineffectual policy: we do not ask Somoza to leave, but neither do we help him to remain in power, undermining him instead with human rights representations. The second, "conservative" reason had lost thrust.[75] It already had taken form in the internal advocacy of an activist policy to mediate a change in the government and avoid a political disaster, for the Nicaraguans and Latin Americans were incapable of providing a satisfactory resolution.

In the face of the administration's indecision, the Washington Post suggested a purely Nicaraguan solution: that those close to Somoza urge him to place the national interest above other considerations and promptly create a transitional government before war devoured the country. The problem was that in contrast to the American Republicans who asked Richard Nixon to resign, Somocistas would not advise Somoza to do so.

The administration's operational preference was that *others*, not the United States, should intervene or use force. The mindset was morally and politically flawed. It was contributing to a war, it misunderstood realities of client-state politics, and it did not fully grasp the negative impact on U.S. domestic politics that the constitution of anti-American regimes could have in the president's reelection.

I had been instructed to have frequent contact with the Nicaraguan president to learn as much as possible about his intentions. He received me on August 26 for slightly less than an hour.

The State Department, I said, wished to learn his opinion on the situation and the courses of action that the government was planning to take. Somoza's reply: "I'll break the strike. I cannot give up power under pressure because the government will collapse and anarchy will follow. Under existing circumstances, I am not prepared to remove anyone from the military [i.e., his family]. When people are trying to destroy you, you must maintain your cohesion and defend yourself. I will not resign, because this will break the 1972 pact between the parties. The opposition is a disorganized minority that does not control the radicals. I will never give up power to a group of people who can't control the situation; this will result in anarchy." But he added that in spite of pressure from the National Guard, he would not reimpose the state of siege (this seemed to have become a matter of principle). He was going to leave *La Prensa* free and use only the Radio and Television Code to curtail the "Communist" propaganda in support of the stoppage.

Somoza planned to jail any of the leaders behind the strike that he could catch, although the government had not issued any arrest orders. He was going to apply to the strikers the measures proposed by the Central Bank. As if betraying his initial statements, however, he commented that the measures would not be really harsh—he was only going to call in loans to the government and his personal private bank for those firms that had closed. "But I am not afraid nor cornered," he added. As of that morning, only in Esteli and Jinotega were over 75 percent of the businesses closed; in all the other cities, at least that proportion of businesses remained open. "I'm going to defeat the strike. Ambassador, these people are a bunch of imbeciles. They don't control the Communists; they are paper tigers. What I should be doing is negotiating directly with the Communists instead of these people. At the appropriate time I will prune these people." He smiled: "Isn't this what politics is all about?"

"Look, Ambassador," Somoza continued, "the United States has always been a mediator here. I have told you that I am willing to negotiate all of the demands of the opposition. It is not that I don't want to establish the grounds for the future of Nicaragua; it is the opposition that does not pay attention to the United States! I cannot accept the wild demands for my resignation and my son's leaving the National Guard. What is all this nonsense toward a twenty-six-year-old boy?"

Somoza reminisced about better, more vigorous times. When his father was assassinated, he had gone to the officer corps and told them that his position had depended on their loyalty to his father, not him; they had to decide who should be their leader. Everyone, including the older men present, decided that he should be their *jefe*. The situation was different now. He was willing to make changes in institutions within a time frame, but he could not purge people under current conditions. What the future Nicaragua needed were two separate leaders—a civilian leader and a military leader to replace him and maintain the army under civilian control, he said.

As we have been seeing, it was impossible to effectively break this deadlock without a firm U.S. initiative. In the face of an opposition still too weak to overthrow him, Somoza was unwilling to go beyond offers to negotiate, without making these offers credible. The opposition would not unite into a more solid organization nor negotiate with him. In the absence of a more active American policy, chronic violence would continue, with anti-American sentiment increasing on all parts. The embassy suggested that an international mediation be organized as soon as possible to give impetus to a negotiated settlement, confronting Somoza privately with demands for changes that, if not rapidly forthcoming, could lead to an American boycott.

Somoza had no plan to meet the impasse with massive repression nor any proposal for a package to phase out the regime. His bottom line: "I will only make concessions if the rebellion stops and a united opposition sits down and negotiates with me a future regime." His demand was an impossibility.

Somoza's Unchanged Prescient, Tragic Choice

I did not give up attempting to establish grounds for a resolution. On August 29 I invited to dinner Julio Quintana, the foreign minister—who had some credibility within the Somoza camp and among prominent oppositionists to succeed Somoza. I told him, "Dr. Quintana, I am not authorized to propose any specific political plan to your government. I have no instructions to raise this issue with you, and I am speaking as if I were a private individual, a foreigner who lives here and sees the dramatic deadlock around a point d'honneur. Do you think the president would be willing to exit before 1981?" Quintana told me that he would back a U.S. initiative to solve the crisis. Then he left the residence and apparently immediately reported our conversation to Somoza.

The threats against the private sector and an uprising in the city of Matagalpa (see later in this chapter) produced their effect in Washington. I was ordered to present a pro human rights démarche to Somoza, asking him not to take reprisals against the opposition. I thus went to see the general the next morning to deliver the démarche. Under the instructions I told Somoza, "If you react in a repressive manner, it could worsen the situation. I have been asked to inform you of my government's position. The State Department wants you to know that the best hope for a peaceful, democratic solution, which we are sure are objectives you share, would be for you to implement your announced intentions to effect a genuine reform of the political system and respect human rights."

Somoza agreed that he should not overreact; he had shown this, he said, negotiating the National Palace attack and by not jailing any strike leaders. However, he wanted a clarification of the second part of the statement. Then he turned irate. "What is this that you are telling my people that I have to go? How many times must I tell you that you can't do this?" Raising his voice, he dictated "instructions" to me: "Tell the State Department and the Department of Defense that if you ever come to tell me that I have to leave before 1981, you are the one who will be kicked out of Nicaragua."

Adopting a heroic pose, he stated that the honorable way was for him to go down fighting. He would do so, even as the "pirate of the Americas," condemned by the Organization of American States. (This is precisely what happened the following June.) He was not going to allow the gutless liberals in the U.S. government (who did not dare overthrow him) to have an easy victory by shortening his term. And he challenged us: "Why doesn't Carter resign? Tell him to come get me."

Calmly, I responded, "If I were to ask you such a thing, it would be under instructions from Washington, and not for personal reasons. I hope you understand that."

Somoza calmed down and engaged in a personal tirade against his foreign minister. He scorned "that ambitious, old man, etc." This man dismisses everybody; who does he have high regard for other than dead heroes such as his father, I thought to myself.

Somoza obviously feared that after my conversations, initiatives could take place among his followers to weaken him—"the American ambassador says Somoza must leave" was apparently too much of a threat for him. But his fears were unfounded. The Somocistas realized that any suggestion to the general that he compromise on his tenure would only result in a major confrontation without the benefit that I had of my government's protection.

Somoza elaborated on my relationship with the opposition. When accepting the new ambassador he knew that he or she would be instructed to have broad contacts with the unarmed opposition. Somoza still had had the option of procrastinating in accepting a new envoy, to keep only an American chargé d'affaires in Managua for some time. He wanted me to know that he was aware that my activities gave the impression that the United States did not back him and hence was encouraging the rebellion against him. Indeed, he had told me so at the outset of my mission.

Replying to Washington's démarche, Somoza said that he would not overreact. The Guardia Nacional would not shoot at anyone who did not first shoot at them. He then asked what reforms the United States wanted implemented. At my urging, he said, he had announced his intention of leaving the presidency in 1981, stepping down from the National Guard, and his willingness to change the electoral law so that all groups could participate in the elections at the end of his term. Yet the opposition refused to talk to him. What concessions did he have to make?

"The unarmed oppositionists do not understand that I am still young, only fifty-two; if I left tomorrow," he said, "I will be called back like Perón.[76] I have been very good to everyone, including the Conservatives and the businessmen. The problem is not my resignation but to find some leader who can replace me."

Somoza was very critical of the archbishop's going to Matagalpa to "impose a cease fire" on the National Guard. He considered himself a realist. When he had not been able to defeat adversaries he had dealt with them; why were the unarmed oppositionists so stupid that they did not recognize his strength and negotiate?[77] "I have insecurities of my own. I have the right to guarantees by leaving this country when it is at peace." Messianically, he added, "On three occasions, I have reconstructed this country out of shambles."[78] He could do it again and restore order, if only the U.S. government backed him until 1981. He was politically so isolated. It was very sad indeed.

Anastasio Somoza Debayle had informed me of his unchanged tragic choice: he would leave power before 1981 only if physically forced to do so. He would never propose any other real alternative. The subject was closed. A few weeks after this conversation, other envoys, American and Latin American, suggested he give up power. He refused, although earlier he had told the New York Times that if the United States asked him to resign, it would have serious political implications.[79]

More Trouble in Early September

The last nine days of August had been eventful: the National Palace occupation, a work stoppage, a popular uprising in Matagalpa. As the new month began, the rebellion in Matagalpa had collapsed, while Somoza adopted a firmer stance toward the continuing (but only partial) stoppage, and opposed any international initiative to settle the crisis.

The embassy's Political Section, strictly speaking, had only two officers; CIA staffing was similar. We did not have enough personnel to cover everything effectively, especially those events occurring far from Managua, a problem raised in Washington. Jack Martin felt comfortable with his office, and I was happy with his overall performance, so I had not insisted on an increase in staffing. I thought we were all well informed on the big picture, and officials in Washington had not moved to allocate more personnel to the embassy. In this instance we were expecting uprisings in several cities, but the embassy did not gather much information on Matagalpa. Fortunately, American journalists had been attracted again to Nicaragua and covered that city's rebellion. A couple of them told me critically about the absence of embassy personnel there. It was not a lack of information that impeded an effective policy.[80]

On a Sunday night in Matagalpa several hundred people rebelled.[80] The ragtag insurgent armed groups, called by the people the "kids" because of their youth ("*muchachos*" was being used to refer with sympathy to the growing number of revolutionaries), were poorly armed. Barricades were hastily put together along key thoroughfares with sandbags, tires, and rocks to block the National Guard, and the rebels' fire paralyzed the city's small Guardia Nacional garrison. The rebels remained in control of sections of the city for almost five days. Eventually National Guard reinforcements were mobilized and sent to the city. The two hundred to three hundred government troops were better equipped. There were two days of heavy fighting before the greater fire power of the National Guard succeeded in restoring army control.

In the face of army superiority and the shortage of homemade firebombs and ammunition, the insurgents dissolved Thursday under the cover of the night. The rebel force wore masks to conceal their identity; most of them were believed to have returned to their homes or to have left the city, some taking to the neighboring hills. As earlier in Monimbo, now in a larger city, a most dangerous pattern had been repeated: a rebel force took over a town (or large parts of it) and disbanded itself without being destroyed or captured by the government's forces.

The violence resulted in hundreds leaving the city with their possessions. Some feared the insurgents' destructive acts and house-to-house searches for arms; others feared army reprisals and worried that Somoza would order retaliatory bombing. At least four hundred women and children took refuge in a city church. Initial estimated casualties were fifty dead and over two hundred wounded.

The city was returned to government control. But the uprising had been relatively successful. First, there was the sympathy for the youths, who were not viewed as "Communists," not even as Sandinista old-timers, but as *muchachos* who had recently joined the exciting and just revolution to see an end to the dictatorship.[81] Recruitment and participation in revolutionary activities were taking place independently of the top Sandinista leadership, yet these largely autonomous groups and actions were part of a rapidly expanding revolutionary movement led by the FSLN.

Second, the bulk of the rebels had adequately protected themselves in buildings, had hidden their identity, and had escaped unharmed.

Third, they had not actually taken over the Guardia Nacional *cuartel* (the typical military headquarters or fort) but had nonetheless paralyzed it and temporarily occupied large sectors of an important city. What if similar operations were *simultaneously* carried out in many cities and towns? Revolutions are also a learning process. What if the cause recruited more and better armed individuals? Would *cuarteles* fall then? How long would it take for the limited number of Guardia Nacional troops (about eight thousand) to recover the lost territory, especially if captured arms were distributed among a populace wishing to defeat the government and its brutal army, to end the turmoil and achieve a just peace and better society? Increasing numbers were showing their availability to participate in a revolution.

An Expectation for U.S. Action

As the embassy expected, the violence placed U.S. policy once more in disrepute. No one in Nicaragua could understand why the United States did not act decisively to end the growing violence. No accepted ethical reason could justify the inaction explained by Washington on grounds that it could "not intervene."

The American journalists who had descended on Nicaragua got involved in the problem. I received many of them, to be informed that the citizens of Matagalpa wanted them to tell what they had seen and "tell the United States that the Nicaraguans don't have anything against the American people. What we protest against is only the policies of the State Department in supporting this tyranny." A civic leader went to the point: he appealed to the president of the United States to stop the bloodshed.

In the face of the local dynamics all our efforts were forgotten, as if the "United States really backed Somoza." American journalist Tom Fenton told me that embassy initiatives to get Somoza and the opposition to work out a compromise were not known by the public.

I began to have more contact with the excellent *Miami Herald* journalists. Don Bohning, the Latin American editor, cogently dealt with the situation:

> As so frequently happens the role of the United States is seen as crucial in resolving Nicaragua's continuing turmoil. So far Washington has done nothing and pleased neither side.
>
> Its stated position is to encourage democratic progress and a peaceful solution to Nicaragua's problems. That's not enough for the broad-based opposition seeking the ouster of [the government]. [On the other hand] Somoza has said he will leave office when his term expires not before. [He] is showing signs of increased irritation at Washington's policy or lack of it. He was quoted telling that the . . . Administration is "in the hands of leftists, of Communists." . . . He added, however, that one should not think he is without friends in the United States. "My friends have told Carter not to continue on this course. The battle is being fought in the United States."[82]

Notice the impact that the approval of the loans continued to have in Somoza's mind: he thought he could defeat the administration. "The dilemma is apparent. The opposition blames the United States when it fails to bring Somoza down. And Somoza blames the United States for not supporting him as it had done for so many years in the past."

Bohning went on to report a population "already near a state of insurrection" and indicated it was unlikely that the government would fall soon (the strike stalling, with major banks and most gasoline stations and transportation facilities still functioning, and also a number of other commercial establishments). "Washington, meanwhile, only watches an unfolding drama that it has helped set in motion through the human rights policy, taking no responsibility for the outcome."

What was the United States to do? On September 6 the *Miami Herald* editorialized: "Best Course: Hands Off Nicaragua." The days of sending in the marines were properly over, said the paper. The option remained that the United States join the Organization of American States to attempt to resolve the impasse and allay further tragedy. Six days later, the paper editorialized again, "Somoza Should Call Election Now," using the general's claimed democratic beliefs and his education in the United States to appeal for an early election supervised by the OAS. Yet the *Herald*'s staff had reported Somoza's "streak of stubbornness" and the widespread demand in Nicaragua that Washington obtain the strongman's resignation.

The Government's Counterattack

On September 3 *Novedades* published Somoza's statements that he was no dictator—60 percent of the people were with him—and that he considered himself safe vis-à-vis the United States, which would not "force" him to abandon power.

The following morning we learned that several politicians and private-sector leaders had been jailed. The first three names were of people that I felt close to: Adolfo Calero, Coca-Cola manager and member of the Conservative Party in the FAO; Pedro Quintanilla, of the Liberal Constitucionalista group, also in the FAO; and José Francisco Terán, INDE's vice president. I had met with Terán and INDE president Manuel José Torres, two days earlier. *La Prensa* had suggested that the United States was about to change policy, and they had come with a few prominent businessmen to express the desire that we mediate the conflict.

The Ministry of Labor had declared the illegality of the strike and announced that the closed businesses be fined. Now the government had rescinded INDE's legal personality for backing the strike and was arresting oppositionists to intimidate and break the stoppage. I do not have precise numbers—perhaps 40–60 so-called strike leaders and 300 other activists were jailed. The government announced the arrest of 200 grassroots "agitators" accused of throwing bombs and barricading streets in Managua. Apparently the objective was to impede a Matagalpa in Managua. As of September 5, Somoza stated, 135 people were still in prison. Numerous politicians and business leaders went into hiding; some UDEL leaders were detained in provincial cities.[83]

The arrests were, nonetheless, selective and limited. They did not decapitate the opposition leadership. The numbers were far too small in the light of the size of extant opposition to have a serious demobilizing impact. Many important organizers of the stoppage were not touched. The extensive nature of the rebellion already implied a need to arrest or kill literally thousands to decapitate the movement, a very massive well-organized repression involving the elite itself to deflate the situation. Order had escaped from the government's hands.

The State Department's reaction was immediate. Spokesman Hodding Carter stated on September 5 that the arrests constituted a "repressive measure that cannot contribute to the goal of a peaceful and democratic solution" to the violence. He also denounced Somoza's accusation that there were Marxists in the administration. The policy remained, however, one of "non-intervention": it was hoped that all sides would seek a peaceful, democratic solution and reject violence.

Somoza's Denouncement of Foreign Mediation

Somoza gave a press conference on September 5. There was a new agenda: Venezuela had asked the Permanent Council of the OAS for a meeting to discuss Nicaragua. Somoza placed this initiative in the context of the various foreign interventions suffered by Nicaraguans despite their "vocation for peace and independence." The Venezuelan petition was proof that President Carlos Andrés Pérez was continuing to promote subversion with the purpose of creating enough chaos so that there would be an excuse for the OAS to engage in a military intervention similar to the one in the Dominican Republic in 1965, Somoza said. He denounced "before the world" this Venezuelan "intervention" and made it responsible for the massacre that it would provoke. Somoza was not giving up—others had to, or they would be responsible for the consequences of the fight.

Venezuela immediately responded: "We do not accept that world attention be diverted from the Nicaraguan tragedy to which our countries cannot remain indifferent. Even less can the international organizations remain indifferent; the catastrophe predicted by Somoza could only result from a leader disposed to utilize the army against his own people, and a people disposed to immolate itself for its liberty and dignity." Venezuela denied promoting disturbances.

In the question-and-answer period, Somoza remained unperturbed, even blasé, minimizing the size and power of his adversaries. An inquisitive journalist asked why, as Charles De Gaulle had done, Somoza did not call for a plebiscite to determine the people's will. His reply: the constitution does not allow it.

That same day Somoza called to see me. He urgently wanted to solicit U.S. support against the Venezuelan OAS initiative to convene the meeting of foreign ministers. I had told him that as far as I knew, Washington was backing Venezuela. Remember, the new man in charge of Latin American operations had just ended a friendly tour as U.S. ambassador to Caracas. I had just received a cable outlining the administration's formal position and explained it to Somoza. The United States did not interpret the OAS convocation as involving the Rio Treaty's "threat to peace" provisions, but rather Article 59 of the OAS Charter because the Nicaraguan situation was a "matter of common concern" to the nations in the area. The United States did not seek a hasty vote nor wish to prejudge the outcome of the debate but felt that the organization should consider the matter because the situation was sufficiently serious.

Somoza replied that my presentation seemed "reasonable" but that the United States was being "duped" by Venezuela. He was not concerned that there would be a meeting of the Permanent Council, but he was against a meeting of the Organo de Consulta (Consulting Body) because it was all powerful. By taking this "extraordinary" step, the United States was opening the door to an intervention in Nicaragua, which his government would not permit. The OAS would divide itself and break down, Somoza warned me.

Somoza elaborated. "While the OAS debates our case, this will incite the opposition to violence so that in the face of these problems, a Communist threat included, the OAS will intervene and change the government here. Venezuela and your government will be responsible for the bloodshed here. The president of the OAS Council [at that time U.S. ambassador Gale W. McGee] would vote in favor of intervention, and I will have to reconsider our relationship with the United States."

"Ambassador, I want you to know that while the OAS is meeting, there is going to be a massacre here. You already have encouraged violence here. Your human rights policy has led a bunch of imbeciles to believe that you are going to overthrow me. Do not contribute more to the tragedy of this little country."

"How, with the international campaign against my government can I maintain law and order?" he asked. "I could stage an auto-coup and leave the country, but this will only result in chaos. I have just met with the National Guard—the officers are aware after the National Palace that the Communists are the only organized opposition; they will not permit being defeated by the Sandinistas because they know that their survival is at stake, that they will be destroyed as in Cuba." Indeed, the Guardia Nacional fought until the end. In listening to Somoza, I felt that he had gotten from the military officers the message he wished to hear—that he had to stay.

I simply encouraged his acceptance of OAS involvement. "You will excuse me, Presidente, but I think you are being too pessimistic. First of all, you will have some support in the OAS. Second, the meeting would provide an opportunity to candidly discuss the problems you have raised: the movement of people across international frontiers, the Marxist-Leninist threat of an insurrection. I think these matters should be discussed. Actually, Nicaragua could use the debate to clarify issues and problems, and propose solutions." If only Somoza would use the opportunity to propose alternatives other than his 1981 fixation, I thought.

Why, I asked him, did he oppose an OAS mediation, not to physically occupy the country as in the Dominican Republic, but to guarantee elections, for example. Both sides would compromise under the mediation. Somoza stubbornly dismissed this possibility, stating that Latins did not know how to compromise and did not understand free elections. I am not certain what Somoza had in mind; perhaps he felt that the FSLN would never submit itself to a neutral, fair electoral process. Or was it a lapsus linguae? We do not understand free elections, so at the appropriate time I will manipulate them.

Somoza had tried, he said, to make peace with Venezuela. He had traveled to see Pérez, but traditional hatreds, the old hatred between Betancourt (the mentor of Pérez's party) and Somoza's father, prevented any understanding. He sensed that the United States was using others to interfere in Nicaragua because of an unwillingness to take responsibility. Nothing constructive could come out of any OAS initiative other than backing him to end his term, although he knew (as we did) that several cities were on the verge of a major confrontation and bloodshed. The United States had to defuse the time bomb that was Nicaragua backing him.

In contrast, the nation was eager for mediation, or even better, for an arbitration that would shorten the president's term and lead to an eventual electoral solution. INDE had taken the initiative within the private sector, making broad contacts and keeping in touch with me.

On September 2 I visited Archbishop Obando. His mediation in Matagalpa had failed because he had no contact with Somoza, and the Sandinistas had no clearly visible command structure during the operation. He had discovered a popular uprising without any tight organization or a Marxist-Leninist-indoctrinated commitment: an expanded, heterogeneous Sandinista movement had developed. Monsignor Obando suggested that INDE make contacts to float the idea that the FAO and the interest groups ask for a mediation. He was willing to return early from his trip to Panama if needed. The old FSLN leaders now had an available mass of people to call to fight, and many different voices were encouraging and calling for rebellion.

That same day strike leader Alfonso Robelo came to see me. I hadn't seen him for a while, busy as he was participating in developing the revolutionary coalition in tactical collaboration with the Sandinistas. Robelo was still free to foment revolution and visit the U.S. embassy. He explained why his Movimiento Democrático Nicaragüense (MDN) had participated in organizing the stoppage. A lot of pressure had been building in the provinces to do something; Somoza had to go in order to calm down the situation. Robelo's people felt that they could not exercise leadership without militant anti-Somoza demonstrations. Nonetheless, he added, the MDN would welcome a mediation, although the Group of Twelve opposed such a formula—they maintained the FSLN line that Somoza resign prior to any concessions.[84] We understood that Robelo was playing it both ways: he was collaborating with the Sandinistas, but if the United States got Somoza out, he was with the United States.

I told Robelo that the stoppage would not succeed because the president retained Guardia Nacional loyalty, that the need was for a visible political leadership of moderates in the opposition with a position of their own. The democratic opposition should be prepared to ask for a mediation without demanding that Somoza resign first. I was in fact advancing what I would soon be asking the Nicaraguan opposition to do.

Robelo was troubled by the incapacity of the stoppage to change the government. He told me that he had been maintaining contacts with the FSLN to ask whether this would have negative effects on his political future. Would he be unacceptable in a transitional government? Younger Nicaraguans who had not lived through the U.S. occupation still felt that the U.S. government was the potential strategic kingmaker. Might other leaders be more acceptable to the United States?

The lack of support in the OAS for a meeting of foreign ministers—the Venezuelan initiative—helped bring about a mediation effort by the newly inaugurated Costa Rican president, Rodrigo Carazo Odio.[85] The United States still preferred that others take the initiative in Nicaragua. On September 6 the embassy was informed that Washington would back the Costa Rican effort as an appropriate expression of joint concern by Nicaragua's neighbors. The tactic was to postpone the discussions in the OAS to see if this new initiative gained strength. The Venezuelan president had agreed. The Venezuela–Panama–Costa Rica triangle (and Cuba) remained engaged to change the Nicaraguan government. For one thing, Edén Pastora (Comandante Zero) was in Costa Rica and was in contact with the Venezuelan president and Panamanian general Omar Torrijos; funds were allegedly being funneled via the Twelve. There was sufficient information about the "conspiracy" that Washington periodically made *private* representations to the governments involved without the conspiracy being dismantled. Those U.S. officials who claimed ignorance of the anti-Somoza international coalition had no excuse. Nonetheless, the administration continued making public statements that it would not deliver an ultimatum to the dictator. Any U.S. effort had to be ultimately understood as a gentlemanly initiative seeking a relatively consensual solution to the problem.

First thing in the morning of September 7 I met with Somoza to convey the instructed message: the administration welcomed the Costa Rican plan and, if asked, would so state. I said that an outsider to the conflict could help the polarized parties seek a peaceful, democratic solution. The United States, I said, is concerned as well with the detention of opposition leaders, specifically those who had employed only nonviolent instruments of protest.

Somoza replied that he had imprisoned a few leaders so as to give them an excuse to come to terms with his formula. It was a supremely unrealistic assessment of the situation: the businessmen, like children, would stop their protest because daddy Somoza scolded and punished some of the kids.

It seemed to me that such measures angered oppositionists and did not permit them to save face, whereas the mediation proposed by Carazo could permit all parties to save face and could provide a workable political settlement. "I am sure you agree," I said, "that it is important to strengthen moderate groups here. A mediation can break the stalemate and achieve this."

Somoza was unhappy. It was impossible that a man like Carazo, "who is not my friend," could mediate. What Carazo had to do was simply kick out the Sandinistas from Costa Rica. I replied that it was dangerous for Somoza, without any knowledge about the terms of the mediation, to reject it a priori. Somoza asked what I knew about the nature of this mediation. Would Carazo hear his case and the opposition's case and make a decision binding on all?

Somoza remained unpersuaded. Former U.S. ambassador Turner Shelton was a mediator here, and I was, in a way, mediating now, he said. I interrupted him. The embassy had not been mediating, only advising moderation and suggesting negotiations; something different was needed to break the impasse. Somoza replied that in the past Central American presidents had met to solve common problems, that a new modality was being suggested now. Before giving a final opinion he had to explore what the regional consensus was. There was a proposal for a meeting of Central American presidents to discuss Common Market issues, which might be a forum to discuss Nicaragua as a matter of common concern.

It was the messianic Somoza again; he would victoriously leap over all the reefs. His formal reply was (1) that he wanted a definition, specifically for the Nicaraguan opposition, of what the United States meant by "peaceful, democratic change"; when the opposition understood that this did not mean his "overthrow," the opposition would change its tune; (2) that the situation would calm down and was under control; (3) that he hoped the United States would abstain in the OAS meeting, as a trade-off for Nicaragua's years of friendship. He could not be persuaded that we were fair "mediators" because of our human rights policy.[86]

Perhaps Somoza had become concerned that, after all, the U.S. government might have the "balls" to present him with an ultimatum; if only more "normal" people ruled the United States, not the crazy "leftists" and "mystics" who were in office, this is what they would do, he might have thought. Perhaps he felt that if a mediation occurred he might be placed in the difficult position of not looking flexible enough to accept anything other than his own 1981 solution. He continued intensely discussing the international situation: the United States does not have the needed votes in the OAS; you are going to be defeated; the organization will break, he warned me. There were no grounds for OAS mediation in Nicaragua.

I proceeded with my act of calmly telling him that I thought that it was only natural to work out a compromise. Somoza knew that I believed in the advisability of a pre-1981 formula, and I had difficulties representing Washington's case because it was partly due to U.S. policy that he found himself in the current difficulties. However, I told Somoza with great conviction that I could not understand why the Nicaraguan government did not want the issues of the country discussed in an international forum. He had just said that the government of Venezuela was responsible for destabilizing Nicaragua, and he had previously blamed the governments of Costa Rica and Panama for doing the same thing. In this light it was only logical for the United States to be concerned with and wish to openly discuss the Nicaraguan difficulties. What the United States government wished to see was a peaceful democratic solution. This was only possible through a mediation or the good offices of a third party, because Nicaraguans had proved incapable of starting the process themselves, I told him.

In spite of the evident dangers and costs of revolution in Nicaragua for its neighbors, Central America was not ready to undertake a coherent political initiative. Only Costa Rica had an elected government with proper civil relations with oppositionists; serious problems of violent politics were faced by Guatemala and even more so by El Salvador. Because the human rights policy was considered to be destabilizing, relations between the United States and these two countries were, to put it euphemistically, not warm. It was only years later, under Republican administrations and after millions of dollars in U.S. assistance that followed the very costly Nicaraguan fiasco, that democratic forces gained measurable strength in Central America, eventually strengthened by the collapse of the Soviet Bloc. Ironically, it was during the later years of greater involvement of U.S. interventionism that Central American countries started to play more constructive regional roles, a phenomenon highlighted by the 1987 Nobel Peace Prize being awarded to Costa Rican president Oscar Arias Sánchez (1986–90).

The Costa Rican government was aware that the initiative could not be construed as a "dump Somoza" movement. Yet there was the belief that the general had to leave in perhaps no more than three months if the crisis was to be defused. But as an articulate Costa Rican ex-foreign minister saw, not only did Somoza have to be persuaded to resign, but the viability of a new government also had to be assured.

The impression that I got from Honduras was that the government was lukewarm—if all other Central American governments participated, they would attend. A consensus had to be built in the Armed Forces Superior Council, the political sovereign body of the military regime.

There were reservations in El Salvador. Somoza had to be included in the talks, and a Foreign Ministry spokesperson thought that Somoza felt an inherited, family right to rule. But it could send emissaries.

In Guatemala there was skepticism. In the prevalent local inchoate politics, the Congress had adopted a resolution repudiating the Nicaraguan ruler. But the highly partisan conservative press was against "intervention." At one point the Guatemalan government proposed that a group of Central American ex-presidents meet with Somoza, but Costa Rica was skeptical about this plan. It was reported that the Venezuelan OAS initiative would also be opposed. The alternative to Somoza might be worse.

Somoza must have made his position known to the Central American governments. On September 12 he declared that the Carazo initiative was dead and that his troops might enter into Costa Rica in hot pursuit to follow up a border incident there. Costa Rica would increasingly face the problem of how to deal with the mass of Nicaraguan émigrés coming into the country determined to use it to oust Somoza.

More Pressure for Mediation

The Nicaraguan foreign minister, Julio Quintana, was in Washington involved in the OAS dealings and along with Somoza's brother-in-law and ambassador to the United States, Guillermo Sevilla Sacasa, visited Viron Vaky, the assistant secretary for Latin America. Vaky went to the core of the problem, transcending human rights considerations against repression, which did not foster adequate institutional solutions. There was wide opposition in Nicaragua, not simply by Communists. The recent repression of moderates was deplorable because it only served to weaken the responsible opposition and legitimize the extremes. There was also a need for some outside catalyst so that a workable arrangement to solve the crisis could be achieved; therefore, he urged the Nicaraguans to very seriously consider accepting foreign mediation.

The Nicaraguans hesitated. Negotiations were necessary—after all, the Somoza camp had been talking about them—but they preferred that negotiations be undertaken by a distinguished, prominent Nicaraguan third party. Notice the absurdity of the procrastination: no Nicaraguan party was available, of course. Some third party involvement was desirable, but they did not like the term "mediation." It had to be called something else, less threatening, not considered binding. Then there was the problem of the opposition, which was disorganized, fragmented, and did not provide an alternative to the government.

Vaky stated that the United States did not have a concrete formula, but the solution would require "heroic" decisions and "sacrifice"; all opposition factions had to be included in the negotiations. He did not like the term "dialogue" because decisions had to be made. There was a need for a political agreement and to develop a workable national consensus between now and 1981.

Quintana did not face the real issue. His insouciant response was that he was willing to establish a commission for negotiations, and he would talk to Sergio Ramírez (of the Group of Twelve); Somoza had to be included in the negotiations. The opposition was in a good bargaining position, and a Nicaraguan Catholic Church or civil leader could perform the function. The Inter-American Human Rights Commission (of the OAS) had been asked to visit Nicaragua. Simply bullshit, of course.

Reading the report of the meeting, I was happy. I was not surprised when on September 10 we received new instructions superseding the previous ones of "neutrality." I was to seek support from oppositionists for a mediation and move toward organizing a group of leaders who could represent and articulate such support. I was told to intensify doing what I had started to do on my own.

The "Final" Mass Uprising

On September 10 Reynaldo Antonio Téfel—the important activist with strong revolutionary involvement—called me. Exuding apocalyptic hope, he said, "This is it." The previous night, the Sandinista general offensive had started. The mass insurrection combined with the still ongoing business stoppage would overthrow Somoza. Calls for "final" uprisings are recurrent and central in some revolutions. In fact, a coordinated rebellion of large geographical span involving several cities and towns had been launched. It did not prosper in Managua and was minor and short-lived in seven cities. However, in Masaya, Leon, Esteli, and Chinandega the recent scenario of Matagalpa had been substantially repeated. The uprising was very serious. It showed just days after Matagalpa that not only had the revolutionary spirit spread to manifest itself relatively spontaneously, but that the Sandinista movement—divided though it still was—had the power to summon increasingly large numbers into a coordinated uprising. History was being made by ordinary people, not only by elites.

This time the government reimposed the state of siege and censorship. One by one, the four cities were opened and "recaptured" by the National Guard, but it was not until September 19 that *Novedades* published Somoza's statement that the movement had been "crushed."[87]

We never knew how many had been killed—perhaps three thousand. Corpses were burned to prevent disease, and we were involved in cases in which bodies never appeared. Five Red Cross workers were caught in shelling and killed. I saw the extensive physical destruction—commercial city blocks were burned by the rebels, and much destruction was caused by the fighting and reestablishment of order. There was also substantial rioting with looting.

The bulk of the National Guard was not trained in the use of modern arms; there was just one armored battalion (controlled by the family) that had only several hundred men. Somoza Jr.'s recently formed small unit was the only better trained and equipped combat elite corps. Obviously, the government retained the resources to militarily defeat an uprising of the size that it faced. On September 12 Somoza predicted that it would take about a week more to clean up the resistance and reestablish army control.

The capabilities of the insurrection had dramatically increased, however. Troops were pulled out from Jinotepe to reinforce the Rivas garrison close to the Costa Rican border and repel a possible invasion (looters became active in Jinotepe). The invasion did not yet take place—reportedly there were only five attempts to cross the frontier by heavily armed Sandinista guerrillas. The uprising had prospered in only four cities, and although groups had taken them over as the National Guard remained hemmed in the *cuarteles*, none of the latter had yet been captured. Although the Sandinistas had improved their weapons, they could still not overrun the National Guard with their current firepower. The initiation of a popular revolt in Managua was rapidly suppressed by the Guard. But it was predicted that another insurrection would take place. The revolution had followed an incremental pattern with augmented periodic offensives.

What if more people, better armed, rose in more cities, coordinated with an invasion from Costa Rica? How many *cuarteles* would fall then? It took Somoza ten days to stop this revolutionary wave. How long would it take him next time? What would be the costs of such operations?

Less than a year before, in October 1977, the new Sandinista strategy of organizing for a short-term victory had begun. It took the form of armed attacks against a few military units. Noteworthy was the predominance of this strictly military dimension: the virtual absence of participants other than a small number of armed combatants. The belief of the Sandinista command that it would succeed showed the misperceptions and false expectations that also fuel revolutions. The October plan proved to be *loco* (crazy). But this had not led to re-equilibrate Nicaragua. After Chamorro's murder masses of people started participating in demonstrations of opposition, breaking the day-to-day routine with activity in the streets that did not involve armed combat. In this September uprising the *Miami Herald* published a vibrant photograph demonstrative of the kind of revolution now being conducted, one not characterized by a large, well-equipped revolutionary army engaged in large-scale combat by columns (with the support of terrorist sabotage).[88] The photo's caption: "Men, women and children lay barbed wire and other obstacles in a street of Leon." You could see unarmed citizens, including playful children, placing improvised obstacles on a street. The *Herald* did not publish pictures of combatants shooting at the *cuartel*, nor of "masked" snipers resisting troops, but of unarmed people giving support to the insurgents improvising barricades in the streets.[89]

U.S. journalists did not resist describing a callous Somoza, contemptuous of his opponents and with egomaniacal confidence in himself. When asked about reports of hundreds of civilian dead, he said, "It is unfortunate that the guerrillas enter private homes. We regret the action we must take but we have to neutralize the guerrillas—if the guerrillas want peace we'll give them peace. If not, we will give them no quarter. The events are the most violent and bloodiest in the country in 50 years." When asked that if the crisis continued, might it result in irreparable harm to the country, he reportedly said no.[90] For the dictator, the test of support was not elections or opinion polls but the failures of attempts to overthrow him.

"Civic" Oppositionists in the Violence

Some FAO leaders were involved in the violence. I spoke with Alfonso Robelo. The cadres of his MDN, which had been formed as a purely civic movement, were active not only in the strike but in the armed insurrection as well—a process of radicalization had gained strength in the entire opposition. Rafael Córdova Rivas, head of the movement founded by P.J. Chamorro, was also involved in the uprising. Córdova told one reporter: "Any government in the Americas would have fallen already; Somoza has been able to hang on because of his economic power and aid from the United States."[91] He opined about a future government: "The FAO [is] capable of forming a democratic government that might include Sandinistas but not be dominated by them." He felt the FAO could avoid a power vacuum. It was asking for an international mediation to change the government: "without negotiating with Somoza, we will only talk about the Somozas leaving the country." It did not matter what foreign governments felt was feasible.

But General Somoza retained the loyalty of the Guardia Nacional. Who was going to get him out?

Historian Richard Millett had this to say:

A decade ago, direct or covert action against Somoza might have been considered in such situation but changes in public attitudes, combined with the Administration's determination to keep as low profile as possible makes such moves at this time extremely unlikely. . . . Efforts to promote negotiations have met with virtually no success, leaving State Department personnel frustrated and generally ineffective. . . . There probably is a fear that even an open call by the United States for a change in government might be ignored by Somoza and the Guardia. As long as the use or even the threat of force to back up such a call is ruled out, the result might be to leave the . . . Administration looking foolish and impotent in the face of yet another international crisis.[92]

Millett was absolutely clear about the dilemma facing the United States. The result, of course, was precisely his final scenario.

Involvement of Venezuela, Panama, and Costa Rica

The predominant tactic developed by the majority of the unarmed, non-Marxist opposition was to use the FSLN to help them change the government, while hoping that ultimately an international action would kick Somoza out, and thus that a regime not dominated by the Sandinistas would result from the struggle. Obviously a highly heterogeneous coalition had been formed. On the other hand, the involvement of non-Marxist Venezuela, Panama, and Costa Rica in the anti-Somoza cause diminished the salience of the Cuban influence. Northern neighbor Honduras was more cooperative toward Somoza. For instance, on September 15 Minister of Defense Lt. Colonel Diego Landa was reported to state that Central American armies might go to Somoza's aid under the regional mutual defense pact and to mention the armies' concern with their own internal stability because of the events in Nicaragua. On September 19 *Novedades* reported that eighty-three guerrillas had been detained in Honduras. But the role of the other three Latin countries in the campaign was better known; at this time the U.S. press reported on their recruitment, training, and supplies, including bases in Costa Rica. The Sandinista offensive still underway, it came to our attention that the FSLN wished to form a provisional government in Costa Rica and that Panama threatened to recognize it. Panama also placed restrictions on the departure of Nicaraguan officers who were training in the Canal Zone; they had been called back to face the uprising, but they would have to leave from an airport chosen by the Panamanians to irritate the Nicaraguans.

As the front-line state, Costa Rica was directly involved. Peñas Blancas, the town across Nicaragua's border, was a natural focus of Sandinista and

Somocista activity, and there were mutual accusations of territorial violations. The Costa Ricans were uneasy. Democratic Costa Rica had "abolished" its armed forces: there were now only small police forces in the country, and the government made appropriate noises about neutrality, pacifism, and lack of involvement in exporting the revolution. You may remember reports of Costa Rican officials denying the existence of Sandinista activities, or excusing themselves by stating that just as the Nicaraguans were incapable of controlling the movement of their citizens into Costa Rica, Costa Rica was unable to control it in the opposite direction. In any case, movement of Nicaraguans across the border was a fact, and the democratic regime faced serious problems in controlling it in the light of the numbers involved, the tradition of giving political asylum, and Somoza's unpopularity in the country. During the uprising, Costa Rica claimed international propriety. For instance, it reported on September 15 that nine heavily armed Nicaraguans had been held for questioning at Peñas Blancas. That same day, the Nicaraguan government stated that fourteen Sandinistas had been deported by Costa Rica. But a few attacks were launched from Costa Rica as part of the uprising. Now, as if Nicaragua were the true aggressor, on September 12 a frontier incident led Venezuela and Panama to come to the aid of Costa Rica. Planes and helicopters from the two countries were offered; Venezuela also offered tanks and Panama a company of infantry.

The Venezuelan president was reportedly furious. There was no climate in the OAS to "intervene" in Nicaragua. It was proving difficult even to convene a meeting of OAS foreign ministers. We learned that he was "desperate," accusing the U.S. government for its incapacity to resolve the crisis because it maintained assistance to Somoza. He threatened to go public in a letter to the president of the United States. Apparently the U.S. mission in Caracas calmed him down. It was also reported that Panamanian strongman Omar Torrijos wanted to invade Nicaragua.[93] The Venezuelan, Panamanian, and Costa Rican rulers met.

At 5 a.m. on September 18, I was awakened by a call from Somoza. He said that there continued to be attacks from Costa Rica, and he wanted to invoke the U.S.-Nicaragua military assistance agreement in order to have the actions stopped in the frontier. I told him that I would inform Washington and get back to him. The Nicaraguan Foreign Ministry issued a communiqué interpreting the events. The statement referred to the "aggression" as a "flagrant violation of the most elementary norms of hemispheric international law" and protested the "Marxist-Leninist-inspired systematic propaganda," which pretended to make it appear that Nicaragua was the "aggressor," when international "terrorist forces of several nationalities that operate with the complicity of the

Costa Rican Government, are the ones that have been criminally assaulting Nicaragua with military attacks from its territory."

The American diplomatic strategy was twofold: use the Sandinista offensive and these international complications to obtain in the OAS the convening of the foreign ministers (this meeting would be "kept open" so that it could be reconvened at any time to deal with the Nicaraguan problem), and use the "good offices" of the OAS to obtain a cease-fire and peaceful democratic solution in Nicaragua. On the other side, make bilateral representations to the governments involved against Nicaragua to "cool it," not engage in military actions, and support a mediated solution.

By September 19 we were informed that President Carazo was cooperating to reduce tensions. He would not accept foreign troops nor tanks; international support would be welcomed only if required to defend Costa Rica—three larger airplanes that would be interpreted as having offensive purposes had already left the country. In principle, Venezuelan aircraft would remain farther away from Nicaragua in Panama, not Costa Rica.

6. Mediation

To mediate is to reconcile. And reconciliation is the only stable base of peace.
Pablo Antonio Cuadra,
prologue to *Agonía en el Bunker* by
Miguel Obando y Bravo

We already know that when the interests of the U.S. are involved they forget this principle [of non-intervention]. In any case, this would not have needed an armed intervention but a simple warning to the dictator that he could not go against the whole of his country.
Carlos Andrés Pérez, *Newsweek*, October 9, 1978

The Embassy Organizes the Mediation

A few hours after the beginning of the "final" uprising we received instructions to get the opposition to ask for a mediation. On September 11, 1978, I got positive responses from Archbishop Obando y Bravo and the economic sector: crystallize "soonest."[1]

My objective was to obtain an invitation without preconditions. However, my tactic was a low-key approach to gain as much enthusiastic, unconditional support as possible and to have the dissident parties subsequently eliminate themselves from the process if they so chose.

La Prensa's initial reservation sustained the doctrine of self-determination to mean both the right of constituting sovereign states independent from foreign dictates and the right of having a representative government freely elected; the problem was compounded because a supportive clientelistic relationship had existed between the United States and the dictatorship. La Prensa stated that "any 'mediation' which did not assume the necessary retirement of the Somoza family from power, in addition to being an intervention in our internal affairs would be useless because it would not help solve the conflict." It criticized the United States because "under the pretext of the principle of nonintervention, [it] refuses to clearly break the ropes that tie it to the Somocista dictatorship."

Next to the editorial was an article titled "Democratic Organizations, Watch Out: A Friendly Initiative That Arouses Suspicions." With the mixture of fantasy and fact that I had learned to live with, the article opposed a mediation because the anonymous author believed it was a U.S. plan to keep Somoza in office until 1981 and lead the country to an electoral solution that excluded the left. There was, however, ambiguity toward the United States: a pre-1981 solution was necessary because the next elected U.S. president could be an ultra-rightist Republican.

That same day, La Prensa published a communiqué from the FAO. It was a restatement of the solidarity of all opposition groups, armed and unarmed, to establish a government of national unity so that Nicaragua again could become a republic. The document recognized the role that the (Sandinista) Movimiento del Pueblo Unido also played in the strike called by the FAO and private sector and was supportive of the Sandinista armed insurrection.[2] The marriage of convenience between the unarmed and armed opposition was celebrated in public.

I expected that a stumbling block to obtaining the invitation without pre-conditions would be placed by the Twelve. I had met members of the Twelve even before talking to the president of Nicaragua, but I suppose because of the sensitivity of some of them that the FSLN would disapprove of contacts with an American embassy, the group had been keeping away from me.[3] The embassy had been falsely accused by some of the Twelve of being behind a "capitalist plot" to abort the overthrow of the government. Actually, my objective had been to maintain contact with all groups, the Twelve included, while advocating Washington's policy preferences.

There had been an initiative by a few of the Twelve to meet with me on "neutral" grounds. I arranged a meeting with Emilio Baltodano, Miguel D'Escoto, and Sergio Ramírez at the residence of a long-time embassy employee, Juan Manuel Siero. I wasn't interested in protocol but rather in showing them the embassy's open door to them. I went in my limousine with only an improvised small American protective detail, no Nicaraguan security personnel. I had not seen D'Escoto since our 1977 meeting in Washington.

"What is this that I have been hearing about complaints coming from you about the embassy? I certainly have not been supporting Somoza," I stated. They were hesitant, but their response was positive. With the current administration there had been a substantial improvement in U.S. policy, they said.

Once the ice had been broken, the three indicated they opposed negotiations. The FSLN was the key force—the Sandinistas were not seeking to establish a Marxist-Leninist regime, I was told. (But they don't intend to establish a democratic regime, I thought to myself. My doubts were supported by the recent FSLN public statements during the takeover of the National Palace signed by the more moderate Tercerista faction).[4] Their idea was that only after Somoza left would the Nicaraguans work out a government of national unity among themselves. (Incidentally, later, on September 30, Nicaraguan desk officer Daniel Welter informed us that two members of the Twelve had visited the State Department: the FSLN would lay down their arms if a FAO provisional government was constituted by the United States. Indeed, among Nicaraguans, only the Somocistas did not want the United States to "intervene.")

On September 14 I met for breakfast with Emilio Alvarez Montalván and Conservative legislator Eduardo Chamorro Coronel. The moderates had prevailed in the FAO. They would support an international mediation without preconditions. At 10 a.m. I received the FAO report. A political commission, an executive organ that took the form of a troika, had been formed by Rafael Córdova Rivas, Alfonso Robelo, and Sergio Ramírez. Córdova Rivas, through UDEL, represented the historical "real" opposition; Robelo, through the MDN, the presence of the business community in the FAO; Ramírez, a member of the Twelve, was the FSLN spokesman. The need for this organizational development in the still otherwise factionalized opposition had been reinforced in the light of supporting a mediation; thus the new U.S. policy was helping to organize the opposition.

The FAO's agenda was centered around two points. First was a humanitarian mediation. There should be an immediate cease fire ("today") supervised by the International Red Cross; the government should stop its military operations, especially bombing cities to recapture them. Second was a political mediation. The FAO would accept without any preconditions an international team to assist in negotiating a solution; it was not necessary that Somoza resign first.

As the quality of the mediating governments was important, they should be democracies, semi-democracies (e.g., Mexico), or opposition-friendly strongman regimes (e.g., Panama). And the security of the opposition leaders should be guaranteed. The lack of success in overthrowing the government and the fear that Somoza might launch an intense wave of repression to decapitate the opposition—I thought—had contributed to the acceptance of mediation. I was told that Sandinista spokesman Sergio Ramírez had changed his mind partly because his father had been captured by the Guardia. Some leaders already were in hiding, and there was an obvious need for the FAO to have guarantees that they could meet to deliberate. In sum, the FAO felt that the state of siege should be lifted as soon as possible, restoring freedom of association and expression.

Washington was informed of the developments. That same night we got the response: in a "flash" cable I was asked for a formal statement from all opposition groups to the effect that they were petitioning for the humanitarian and political mediation. IN DE's president, Manuel J. Torres, brought me their petition. As Washington was seeking an international mediation, I had asked that the petition not be addressed to our government but as broadly as possible.[5]

The crux of the document read as follows:

URGENT MESSAGE OF THE NICARAGUAN PEOPLE
To the Organization of the United Nations
To the Organization of American States
To the Sister Republics and Peoples of the Americas
To the Inter-American Human Rights Commission
To the International Red Cross
To All the Peoples of the World

The Catholic Church and other Christian churches of Nicaragua, the Broad Opposition Front, and the organizations of the Private Sector make a most urgent appeal to the governments friendly to the Nicaraguan people, so that with a humanitarian spirit and one of solidarity, they develop an effective and immediate action directed to mitigate the suffering of our population, victim of the terrible effects of an unequal struggle, which already has taken an enormous balance of deaths and destruction in the principal cities of Nicaragua.

It also cannot be delayed the offering of an immediate mediation to obtain the political solution of a permanent character, that will preserve the dignity and claims for which so heroically is struggling the Nicaraguan people.

Managua, Nicaragua, September 15, 1978

The Embassy in the Violence

The uprising posed problems for U.S. citizens in Nicaragua. Embassy intelligence had been expecting the major offensive, though we did not predict how extensive it proved to be. Americans were not targets of Sandinista nor National Guard operations.

We believed the armed offensive would not prosper in Managua, but we did not wish Americans to be trapped in cities overtaken by an uprising. To this effect it was decided that all Peace Corps volunteers were to be brought back close to Managua, where other U.S. government operations were located. Our options with U.S. citizens not linked to our government were more limited. We had encouraged close ties with the American community at large: I had given a large reception at the residence for them after public order had begun to decay, and they were encouraged to register with the embassy, since we ultimately had in mind the possibility of an evacuation. However, we did not have the legal authority to prohibit American citizens from doing business in the country, nor could we order them to leave.

An evacuation seemed premature. Americans who had chosen to remain were obviously taking some risk. The consequences of deciding to recommend that they all leave the country seemed drastic, spreading panic. What would be the reaction of Nicaraguans that we were leaving their country to their fate? Nor did the option of informing U.S. citizens that our intelligence expected uprisings in specific cities seem prudent. One had to weigh the risks to our citizens; my wife and our child also remained in Managua, and our intelligence was correct about no direct threats. Only one American was injured in the September uprising, in Managua, the victim of an isolated expression of "Sandinista" hatred.[6]

We decided that we would not evacuate personnel. Yet two days after the initiation of the offensive I was informed that a few members of the embassy staff, all career or permanent bureaucrats, wished to evacuate their families. The head of one of the non–State Department sections sent me a memo simply informing me that he was taking his family out of the country and would return in a week. (He was reprimanded by Washington for leaving the post.) Interestingly, the initiative to evacuate was centered in the USAID Section. It was ironic that the move to leave the country was concentrated in a unit so prone to claiming that their activities were apolitical, only technical, that Nicaragua was an optimal place to continue and expand U.S. programs. Their political insensitivity had suddenly changed.

As the move to evacuate involved mainly the USAID unit, other units became critical of it. This internal memorandum sent to me is illustrative: "I hope you will give your attention, taxed as it must be, to a budding disposition of some in the Mission to characterize the AID people who have left as being 'Nervous Nellies,' to use Lyndon Johnson's phrase."

No one was talking about closing embassy operations, only that an evacuation of dependents be ordered so that the U.S. government would underwrite the expenses. The initial position I had taken was that decisions would be made on an individual basis. On September 16, however, we decided to support the departure of dependents who wished to leave. Only a few left the post.

The fact that Somoza had yet to be persuaded to accept mediation made me especially sensitive about acting realistically toward the crisis. I did not wish to order the evacuation of American citizens because it was (correctly) predicted that the uprising would not last long. I could imagine Somoza's laughter, observing the return of the Americans who had been pulled out by the U.S. government. What really was needed was to deliver an ultimatum to Somoza, not engage in theatrical tactics of support-withdrawal.

However, on September 14 the embassy received a flash cable stating that Washington was thinking of instructing me to evacuate and ordering me to discuss with Somoza the possibility of evacuation from areas that were still not under National Guard control. A Foreign Service officer who had served some years back in Managua was sent to help us out.

I did not like our visitor's first statement to me. He said he had come because the embassy had to work harder, report more to Washington, formalize our organization better. The deputy chief of mission had to be utilized more effectively, and we had to control our personnel better to avoid casualties. We should have evacuated; embassy reporting had underestimated FSLN strength.

Now, I thought to myself, what American "casualties" was this man talking about? This official did not know more than I nor have greater expertise about revolts. His comments reflected on the quality of the embassy's career bureaucrats whom Washington had assigned to it. Apparently the violence increased tensions within the embassy and between it and Washington.

Hope and Anger

Typical of revolutionary situations, Managua was full of rumors. A very prominent politician assured me that Monsignor Obando y Bravo had left for political exile in Costa Rica. Many felt an urgent need to leave the country—a Latin American ambassador came to see me for help evacuating the citizens of his country; my wife was hysterically approached by a few Nicaraguans wanting U.S. visas. I received a telephone call from Leon from a citizen who spoke until the line was interrupted. His last message: the National Guard's air force was attacking the city and producing innumerable casualties; there were muchachos (Sandinistas) everywhere; the entire commercial sector had been burned by the populace because the Sandinistas had not been able to control them, I was told.

A somewhat different story was conveyed in a visit by a former prominent collaborator of Somoza who had left Leon that same morning. He said several private residences had been looted and burned. My informant wanted me to be absolutely clear that the insurrection was led by Communists. His great fear was that the FSLN would bring peasants into the city to plunder. The army had to restore order, and Somoza had to be asked to resign to reestablish a viable political order.

It was difficult to get an accurate picture. A state of siege finally had been declared, and the media was being censored; some days La Prensa was not published. There was also anger in our contacts. One of our officers reported a conversation with one of Somoza's closest military advisers, who was extremely bitter: U.S. policy was responsible because of the withdrawal of support; what the Latin countries needed was an iron hand. He didn't think he would be allowed to go to exile in Miami, but this did not matter. He would "die fighting." Months after the revolution, I found this officer pleasantly walking one of the streets of Miami.

There had been another influx of U.S. reporters in search of stories. On September 16 I met with a large group of them in the chancellery, as usual under "deep background" rules—the meeting could not be divulged, the sources could not be cited even indirectly. Several journalists were incensed with U.S. policy. How could I sit in my office and do nothing to stop Somoza's genocide, one of them asked. I informed them about Washington's policy. The tone of some of the statements was quite emotional and confrontational, to the point that Miami Herald's Don Bohning later commented to me about the "lack of professionalism" of some participants. Irrelevant remedies were suggested, and no one precisely stated how we could give Somoza an ultimatum that would stick. As discussed in chapter 1, increased regime crises tend to be accompanied by intensified international clientelistic and interventionist pressures.

Totally unexpected was the discovery that the Peace Corps volunteers had never been relocated to the Managua area. I had thought they were all fairly safe. This was one of three serious disappointments that I had about my judgment of the public servants with whom I worked in Nicaragua. On September 13, I discovered something truly incredible—a volunteer had been allowed to return to Leon.[7] I had a very serious conversation with the Peace Corps director, a Latino whom I personally liked and had misjudged to be an administrator cooperative with our mission. He was recalled from Nicaragua at my request.

On September 15 I went to see Somoza, under instructions to seek the evacuation of American citizens from the three remaining cities. I had decided on my own not to attend the diplomatic corps ceremony to "salute the president" that had taken place on the Nicaraguan Independence Day. The situation was far too serious for me to lend myself to be a party to the government's propaganda.

The previous day I had received a very bizarre telephone call from Somoza: jokingly he asked me if I had declared war against him. I answered no and asked why. He commented that the United States was blocking a credit from the International Monetary Fund. He had seemed genuinely surprised with the extent of the disorders, almost admiring the Sandinista "trickery," now enjoying commanding the inexorable defeat of the uprising. The FAO's position had also been conveyed to me: a cease fire rather than reoccupation of the cities by the National Guard. Part of my instructions was that the government should work on this with the Sandinistas.

I presented the evacuation petition in the best possible light. I delivered a written Diplomatic Note requesting the evacuation of not only all Americans in Nicaragua but their families as well. The instructions provided that I suggest to Somoza that a cease-fire be worked out so that all civilians who wished to depart the critical areas could do so.

The general replied: "This is what I have done. I have held back the Guardia Nacional for the last couple of days to allow people to leave. I am now in the middle, however, because the army is already in the process of pacifying Leon—I expect to have it and another city today under government control. If we soon have our towns back as I expect, there should not be any need to evacuate," he concluded.

I suggested, following the instructions, a cease-fire to allow the International Red Cross to supervise an evacuation. If the Sandinistas refuse to allow this operation, I explained, it would be their responsibility before the entire world; if the Guardia went into a full attack, there might be many casualties among innocent civilians. Somoza said that as a result of my earlier call about the safety of Americans and the need to allow them to escape from the cities, he had issued orders to the Guard to assist in their evacuation. But the issue of the cease-fire was a very serious and problematic one: he had to consult his cabinet, which was at the time in his office waiting for him.

A confident Somoza took well the representation as a humanitarian initiative, which, of course, he would not implement. He elaborated: the archbishop had gone to Matagalpa and asked the Guardia commander for a four-hour cease-fire; this was immediately granted. However, Obando returned with a paper demanding that the Guardia give up entirely. "I assure you that people have had the opportunity to leave the cities. The majority who wished to leave have already done so. But the Sandinistas have not decided yet to retreat and allow free traffic through the cities. I cannot give a belligerent status to the Sandinistas," Somoza said. Following the instructions, again I asked him to act benignly toward political and business leaders, suspending arrest orders and releasing those engaged in unarmed opposition from prison. The conversation was brief. It was obvious that no real evacuation would take place. When I asked him about possible housing facilities for citizens who might seek refuge in Managua, he did not answer. His plan was a step-by-step move north to successively take control of each city.

On September 16 we were officially notified that the National Guard command in Leon was ready to help us evacuate our people. Leon had just been recaptured. Evacuating Chinandega should be possible the following day, but we would probably have to wait two more days to evacuate Esteli. The Nicaraguans were only going through a ritualistic cooperation. However, to comply with the spirit of Washington's instructions, a convoy was immediately organized by Colonel Francis Matthews, the gentlemanly head of the embassy's military mission, to go to Leon. The result: they brought back a Peace Corps volunteer and accompanied a family of four who came to Managua in their own car. There were no American fatalities.

The FAO's Troika

It was not only Somoza who still refused to accept a mediation. I received a telephone call from Alfonso Robelo, who said a wave of anti-American sentiment was developing because the United States was not acting decisively to solve the crisis. There was an urgent need for the mediation; and he conveyed a mild threat that if it were too slow in coming the FAO troika would repudiate the document that it had signed the previous day.

Robelo wanted a political victory: the strike ended because the mediation arrived. On the one hand the private-sector strike was conducted in cahoots with the left, but as a leader of the private sector, Robelo ultimately preferred the United States as his ally and backup. He was holding the view that he could pressure the United States to follow his desires.

Ramírez had launched himself in a Sandinista career. He might have been representing the mediation to his constituency as a means to avoid the complete military defeat of the armed offensive and a practical, less costly way of getting rid of the Somoza family.

Córdova Rivas—whom I considered a genuine, good-natured man—carried the frustrations of too many years of uncompromising opposition and was inclined to take emotional, not always wise positions (occasionally in the form of a personal broadside involving me).

Though more moderate voices were found within the FAO, and although the troika's composition revealed the minority position of the FSLN in the FAO— their presence was through only one representative—the Broad Opposition Front was not reflecting in its new formal three-man leadership a spirit of negotiations with mutual concessions for a successful mediation. In fact, within the FAO the overwhelming sentiment was for the mediation to come and serve as the mechanism for the mighty United States to quickly depose Somoza and retire the family to some foreign country.

On September 21 the "final" uprising was over, and the following pronouncement was made:

OFFICIAL COMMUNIQUE OF THE BROAD OPPOSITION FRONT (FAO)
The Broad Opposition Front (FAO) named a Political Commission to represent it among other activities in a possible mediation realized by Democratic Latin American Governments, in search of a permanent solution to the Nicaraguan dramatic problem.

Somoza's response to the possibilities of a mediation was the Genocide ordered by him and executed by his son against the civilian population of Matagalpa, Masaya, Leon, Chinandega and Esteli.

On the Conference of Foreign Ministers of the OAS meeting to analyze the situation of injustice and violence that lives Nicaragua, we feel it pertinent to clarify again that a mediation in the case of Nicaragua can only take place to obtain a permanent solution, and that this can only be obtained with the definitive eradication of the Somocista dictatorship, especially after it has been proven before the entire world, that the Somocista dynasty and the officers of the National Guard who accepted and executed the order of Genocide are war criminals against their own people.

The Broad Opposition Front (FAO) was consenting to a mediation for humanitarian reasons, but will never permit that such an instrument be used to prolong the political life of the staggering Somocista dictatorship.

The Struggle Continues!

Long Live the Heroic Nicaraguan People!

Long Live a Free Nicaragua!

> Broad Opposition Front (FAO)
> Political Commission
> Sergio Ramírez Mercado, Alfonso
> Robelo Callejas, Rafael Córdova Rivas
> Information Committee of the FAO
> Jaime Chamorro C.

The September uprising had failed to unseat the government, but its human and material toll had resulted in a general, increased alienation—intense, verbally expressed hatred—against the regime.

The Archbishop Suggests an Army of Peace

I visited Archbishop Obando on September 19. Saddened by the costs incurred and the promise of more to come, he opined that ideally un ejército de paz (an army of peace) would be deployed in the country to pacify the spirits and bring about his formula of mutual concessions to culminate in a general election. He remained interested in promoting a mediation, even though Somoza still refused to accept one.

I wished to provide as many options as possible to Washington. It could be the SEDAC (the Episcopal Secretariat of Central America and Panama) or the Episcopal Conference of Nicaragua and some foreign representative who would mediate, he suggested. There was a need to talk to Foreign Minister Quintana, to *Novedades*'s Luis Pallais, to Somoza's nephew, the congressman, to see if the president can be influenced, he suggested. We agreed to make contacts.

The following day, Monsignor Obando, Monsignor Pablo Antonio Vega, the vice president of the Episcopal Conference of Nicaragua, and Manuel J. Torres, INDE's president, sent a letter to Somoza. It was a call to reason and proposed high-level negotiations between the parties aided by governments of the hemisphere. A signed copy of the letter was forwarded to us. It was not that an American mediation was not welcomed, rather that apparently Washington still hesitated to lead one. Somoza did not have the courtesy to answer the letter; he had his secretary of the presidency reply. The president was willing to negotiate but without any mediation: "He considers that Nicaraguans have the civic and moral values to jointly find the solution that the Fatherland demands in these moments."

There were other voices for moderation amid the increased frustration and rancor produced by the violence. On September 19 another document by Humberto Belli elaborating on the archbishop's position was brought to our attention. "The just desire of vengeance is profoundly against the Gospel," Belli said. The martyrs of the struggle had no passions now; they could not from their heavenly status desire ill to anyone: "There is no justification for the sacrifice of one more innocent person to punish a culprit." Belli empathized with the government, the FAO, and the FSLN.

Somoza feared humiliation, the loss of self-esteem in being forced out of power; his Liberal followers feared that they would be swept out of their public jobs by a new government without being able to find any alternative employment; and the military feared not only widespread purges but also physical reprisal—imprisonment, death.

The FAO had its own fears of falling into a trap, in which a moderate stance would result in their losing momentum, to be then tricked by Somoza's intention to prolong his family's domination. The FAO also feared losing out completely to the more militant FSLN and to an undemocratic Communist solution.

And the FSLN feared that the maintenance of the army would result in keeping intact the nation's socioeconomic structures and that the sacrifice would be wasted; that a Somocismo without Somoza triumph would be to the detriment of the popular masses, the dominant elites keeping their privileges.

Belli observed that the intransigence was fueled partly by misperceptions about the strength of the adversary. A substantial proportion (17 percent) of the economically active population was employed by Somoza's public sector; Liberals had well-entrenched patron-client (*cacique*) loyalties; the government machine could not be simply swept away. By contrast, the government underestimated the opposition, taking the absence of a well-organized structure with a clear leadership to deny the extensive disaffection with the rulers, which was still rapidly rising. Elements of the middle stratum up to the upper classes were joining the guerrillas.

It was evident to pragmatic idealists such as Belli that to avoid a slaughter the parties had to stop expecting the unconditional surrender of the adversary. There was a need to develop a scheme of mutual concessions that would reduce threats and fears, to build *puentes de plata*, elegant exits. To overcome the impasse, Belli proposed outside mediation to form a *gobierno puente* of transition that would organize the elections that would peaceably decide the government. His detailed plan for democratization in phases was imaginative: it provided guarantees to Liberals and an electoral mechanism that could contribute to strengthening a democratic center. It should have been attractive to the Somocistas. But all parties had to give something to obtain something in return. And Somoza had to shorten his term.

We received a few other proposals: all included Somocista presence in a transitional government. The president rejected them all. It was not the weight of general cultural traditions nor the weight of socioeconomic structures, but the insufficient support for representative democracy that impeded the solution.

Nicaraguan public opinion still wanted a clear, forceful action from us. On September 16 I met with a few sisters of the Teresiano religious order. They were American citizens and wanted me to know that anti-American sentiment was developing and gaining substantial strength because of U.S. inaction. We cabled Washington stating the necessity for the mediation to materialize soon. But Washington was using the OAS, which moved slowly and would not lend itself either to deploy military forces or impose a binding arbitration.

The Administration States How Far It Will Go

The *Washington Star* revealed the administration's intentions: "The U.S. has decided, in effect, to seek the resignation of . . . Somoza and thereby encourage a moderate leadership to take power before the country is completely engulfed in civil war." However, the article continued, "ideologically, this administration will not directly call for a resignation because that would be interference in another country's domestic affairs." It would not go beyond "urg[ing] the

Government to accept a mediation and seek an enduring resolution to the crisis . . . and to be prepared to make concessions and sacrifices to bring an end to the suffering."[8] Somoza had been publicly told once more that only oblique language would be used by Washington.

The administration was adhering to the position of the U.S. Congress limiting the deployment of troops and the employment of covert action abroad. The political costs of intervening in Nicaragua were increased because Somoza claimed to be a friendly American client only seeking support to end his term. But how much pressure would the United States have to put on Somoza to have him compromise? Would a "simple warning" suffice, as the Venezuelan president claimed? In any case, no one in Nicaragua agreed with the administration's public statements of policy. Apparently Washington was not going to please Nicaraguan aspirations.

Somoza Calls for the U.S. Marines

On September 19 I returned to see Somoza. We talked about an hour and a half. William J. Jorden, the outgoing U.S. ambassador to Panama, was being sent on a mission to several countries to seek support for the mediation. Somoza wanted me to know that the OAS was not going to approve the mediation. We were going to fail, and a number of very intelligent individuals thought that the Jorden mission was only going to complicate the situation further. "I cannot accept a mediation by your government because I must mistrust it. What the United States wants to do is overthrow me," Somoza continued. "I talked with Carlos Andrés [Pérez] and told him that I was willing to talk, that I would be willing to discuss even the opposition's desire to shorten my term, but that I wanted him to tell the opposition to talk to me and respect my life and property." Instead of doing this, "Pérez has sent military equipment to Costa Rica and is trying to overthrow me. Carazo is also an enemy of the Somozas; how can he be a mediator? I don't like the term 'mediation': it applies to people with the same status, and the opposition here is illegal; it is composed of a group of self-appointed leaders without organization nor electoral strength."

"There is a lot of chaos now," I said. "The only way to solve the problem is if the government and opposition negotiate. You know, Mr. President, that I have been many months here trying to get everyone to talk and negotiate, and I have been unsuccessful; it is apparent to me that there is a need for the mediation or the good offices of an international force. Only with this presence can an umbrella be created that will permit people to negotiate without losing face."

Somoza then invited Luis Pallais to join the conversation. Luis stated that if Somoza left, there was a danger of a coup d'état; there was a need for a constitutional solution and that meant Somoza had to remain in office until

1981.[9] I told him the only way to get negotiations going was if there were no preconditions, either on the part of the government or the opposition. There must be some way to work a satisfactory constitutional solution.

Both Pallais and Somoza said shortening the presidential term was "retroactive" and therefore unconstitutional because the president had been elected for that full term. As a lawyer, I thought the position absurd: in criminal law many countries hold the principle that legal changes should apply only to benefit the culprit. But even contracts—and this is how Somoza viewed the constitution—can be changed with the consent of the parties.[10] As the archbishop publicly stated, "No justification or appearance of a constitutional legality can be above the Common Good."

But I was not about to enter into a discussion about this and so went on: "I am very concerned by the differences that exist between us with respect to mediation. The economy is in ruins, the polarization is immense; the best course of action is for our two governments to walk hand in hand trying to achieve a political settlement that sticks."

"I have been trying to do this all along," Somoza answered. "I do not oppose the good offices of the United States, but if what mediation means is that you are going to impose your conditions, I must fight and force you to send the marines. I have repeatedly asked you what I must do to continue getting aid. If I give these concessions, will you give me aid? You told me that I should make concessions based on a spirit of patriotism. Then the opposition doesn't want to talk to me, and I have to go all around your people [in the State Department] to obtain the little aid that I have been able to get.[11] I have asked you, Ambassador, to talk to the opposition to pressure them to negotiate with me and for you to mediate the conflict, and you told me it was impossible." Obviously the unprecedented situation of an opposition that would not talk to him continued to make Somoza feel that he could not work out any elegant solution.

He then showed me a cable reporting the investigation on Nicaragua being sponsored by his friends in the U.S. Congress: he was taking the fight there. Somoza's congressional friends wished to obtain support to force the resumption of military assistance to Nicaragua, stop the anti-Somoza international axis, back the Nicaraguan government (at least) until 1981. The Nicaraguan government had charged that invasion attempts took place from the south with the aim of establishing a provisional government in a "liberated zone" that would be recognized by the friendly governments; in the United States the press reported that the FSLN maintained a "command center" in Costa Rica.[12] As one of our military officers said, if the Sandinistas had been successful in a southern drive, it would have taken much longer for the National Guard to reestablish order. This is precisely what took place in the next revolutionary uprising.

Some of the presentations on Capitol Hill were disappointing, not suitable for a well-informed body.[13] A congressman, one of Somoza's cronies, claimed that "Nicaragua has a constitutional government, and Anastasio Somoza is its constitutionally elected president. In that respect, it is no different than the United States." He accused Panamanian strongman General Torrijos of having a "Communist philosophy" and said that "the best known Sandinista leaders are Costa Rican and Mexican, not Nicaraguans." The internal Nicaraguan debate with its falsehoods and paradoxes had been transferred again to the U.S. Congress, though few attended the sessions.[14] Only 78 of the 435 House of Representative members signed a letter to the president urging him to make a public statement in support of the Somoza government.

There were other voices. Senator Edward Kennedy said the United States should use available relief resources. He called on the Nicaraguan parties to make the concessions necessary to negotiate peace and said that all assistance should be terminated to the Nicaraguan government, the U.S. military mission should be withdrawn, and the administration should deal with the problem of the American private mercenaries working for Somoza.[15] Senator Frank Church, on the other hand, stated that "It is a national mutiny in which almost every sector of the country has united against a dynasty which has plundered the country for nearly half a century. The longer Somoza resists the will of his people and uses his armed guard to quell resistance, the more likely it is that another Castro-type revolutionary government will eventually emerge." Interestingly, the pro-Somoza legislative group cited cases of successful Marxist-Leninist revolts, not any of the successful transitions to democracy also part of the historical record.

In the meantime the "human rights" issue was intensively reactivated: there were dramatic stories about atrocities committed by the unsophisticated, traditionally brutal National Guard. One of the pieces by Karen DeYoung was exemplary.[16] She vividly reported the executions in Leon of "at least 14" unarmed young men who had not participated in the uprising; their only crime was their age, which led to their generalized classification by the Guard of being "Communists." The accusations of "genocide" made Somoza believe he would be leaving power at a very inauspicious time for him and his men.[17]

The OAS Decides on Mediation

The Nicaraguan issue was international. First, there was the problem of Nicaraguans crossing into Costa Rica and using it as a base to invade their homeland. The problems faced by the less anti-Somoza (more "non-interventionist") Honduran government placed the situation in relief. Among the reported three thousand refugees who had already arrived from Nicaragua there were Sandinista activists, creating a potential source for Honduran involvement in the conflict. The moderate military government wished international assistance to meet the refugee problem. At the same time, the Nicaraguan dictator was increasingly unpopular in Costa Rica, so it was politically costly to control or repress his opponents and physically difficult to control the border. Although Costa Rica did not want war, the easiest course was to favor an early replacement of the Nicaraguan strongman for a more "normal," less "old-fashioned" regime.

Faced with these realities, the United States was seeking to convene (under Article 59 of the OAS Charter) a meeting of consultation of foreign ministers of the OAS on a basis of open standing, so that it could be called into session any time. If successful, the initiative would convert the OAS into a monitoring agency of Nicaraguan developments. The U.S. agenda included as well an OAS presence along the Costa Rica–Nicaragua border to avoid the potential for a major international conflict, humanitarian relief for refugees that had moved into Costa Rica and Honduras, and a mandate for the Inter-American Human Rights Commission to investigate allegations of indiscriminate killings.[18]

Venezuela and Panama continued pressuring, however. A few weeks after arriving in Nicaragua I had cabled Washington suggesting that our policy be coordinated with Venezuela. I did not know then of President Pérez's radical intentions, only his role in Venezuela's successful democratization. I thought he was in a position to know and advise about Nicaragua. Later exchanges had indicated his militancy. Now, after William Jorden's visit, Pérez's position was obvious, as shown in his letter of September 20 to President Jimmy Carter.

Mr. President:

I have had the opportunity of talking today with your special envoy Ambassador Jorden. From this conversation I have obtained nothing that would permit me to be optimistic about the attitude of the United States to meet General Somoza's bloody regime. . . .

The number of deaths, the massacre and genocide have devastated the people of Nicaragua. The Somocista Dictatorship unleashed a war to death against the Nicaraguan people, to the point that I feel profound sorrow and shame for these events, which in some form imply an international complicity that involves us all.

I hope that you had the opportunity to read the anguished message of the bishops, of the sectors of the private economy, of the parties and groups of democratic opposition, in which they implore the world to save them from extermination.

It is evident that in its most overwhelming majority the people of Nicaragua cry out to the democratic world for pity and help.

I sincerely believe, friend President, that the case of Nicaragua places your human rights policy in dramatic danger, [a policy] which so many hopes arose in Latin America, and to which Venezuelans gave their most sincere backing.

On the eve of the meeting of the Organ of Consultation of the Organization of American States, I petition you that the attitude of your illustrious government be as decisive as necessary to avoid so much suffering to the Nicaraguan people, and preserve the so seriously threatened peace in the region.

As I opportunely informed your Ambassador and Assistant Secretary of State Vaky, breaking my sincere and very deep peaceful sentiments I sent war planes to San Jose to dissuade Nicaragua from an invasion of Costa Rica, an exemplary nation of peace which has no army, and which now is submitted to the aggressions and humiliating insults (vejámenes) of the Somocista dictatorship.

Signed—Cordially yours, Carlos Andrés Pérez

The Venezuelan president was unhappy: Ambassador Jorden offered him a "mediation" plan that the Nicaraguan government could ultimately reject.[19]

Venezuela and Panama were persuaded to go along with the mediation though they were not optimistic. General Torrijos, who had reportedly continued to meet with Sandinista leaders, believed that Somoza was crazy, that he would not compromise, and that there was a need for action. Indeed, on the diplomatic front Panama and Venezuela made common cause with Cuba in the United Nations Assembly on September 25, with violent verbal attacks against Nicaragua's human rights performance.

On September 18 the Permanent Council of the OAS finally called the Meeting of Consultation of Foreign Ministers for the 21st. Many of the nations voting for the resolution made it clear that they were against "foreign intervention" (including from the OAS), but conditions in Nicaragua affected regional peace, thus creating an urgent situation.[20] Warren Christopher represented the United States in the meeting. There was an immediate need to put an end to the bloodshed and killings, and Christopher emphasized the human rights violations of the National Guard. He called for an immediate visit by the Inter-American Human Rights Commission and also requested support for the humanitarian involvement of the International Red Cross and United Nations agencies, including medical and food assistance to the refugees.

Using the petition for mediation that we had obtained in Managua, the deputy secretary considered that the OAS should offer its "good offices"; the United States was willing to participate. The question facing the OAS,

Christopher stated, had been raised by Archbishop Obando y Bravo: "How to contribute now, with generosity, to end the mourning and anguish, the massacre, and the hatred, so that it will be possible to return peace to the Nicaraguan people." The administration had come a long way. But only if the Nicaraguans voluntarily accepted the recommendations of a mediation would a peaceful solution be possible.

On September 23 the Seventeenth Meeting of Consultation passed its resolution. Politically there were not great differences between it and the American proposal. The session was adjourned, but the Seventeenth Meeting would be kept "in session as long as the present situation continues." This implied that Washington intended to use the body throughout the crisis. Crucial was the resolution's statement on the mediation:

> To take note that, without prejudice to full observance of the principle of nonintervention, the Government of Nicaragua has stated that it is willing in principle to accept the friendly cooperation and conciliatory efforts that several member states of the Organization [of American States] may offer toward establishing the conditions necessary for a peaceful settlement of the situation without delay.

General Somoza remained the Achilles' heel of the entire enterprise.

The Nicaraguan delegation had intensely lobbied so that a resolution not be passed. But given the support for only a "friendly cooperation and conciliatory efforts," Somoza thought he did not have to fear the mediation that much. Anti-interventionist sentiment was expressed as well in the OAS by some leftist governments that repudiated the Somoza regime and what it stood for (e.g., Jamaica). The OAS had been an inadequate mechanism to change Latin American governments: the use of U.S. troops remained a necessary condition to change recalcitrant governments under Reagan, Bush, and Clinton.

William Jorden's Nicaraguan Mission

That Washington had sent Jorden to all the countries involved except Nicaragua was interpreted by Somoza as a "slap in the face"; in order to soften the president's stance, the United States should send Jorden to talk to Somoza, Luis Pallais told me. We immediately informed Washington, and Jorden arrived in Managua on September 23.

Jorden's message was that the United States was extremely concerned that what the Somozas had built in Nicaragua would end up being destroyed. The problem was not only the Sandinistas; a very broad opposition movement had developed. Although the Sandinistas were militarily defeated in this uprising, they were going to return to action: their movement was growing, recruiting people, obtaining increased support. The extant political deadlock played into the hands of Castro and the Communists. Venezuela and Panama were seeking Somoza's overthrow through an impotent Costa Rica. It was evident that no dialogue or negotiations could emerge within Nicaragua. There was a need for outside assistance, friendly good offices so that some kind of agreement would be reached. The only way to achieve this was for an outside mediation without preconditions. The mediation would try to minimize differences and help work out a compromise. The possibility of Somoza's departure from office before 1981 had to be considered, yet his views would carry tremendous weight. The United States would not impose a solution. This was the promise.

Jorden informed Somoza that the United States, the Dominican Republic, Honduras, Colombia, and Guatemala could serve as mediators; the U.S. delegation would be headed by former assistant secretary of state William Rogers.[21] Somoza objected to him on grounds that he was an "adversary to his family," and said that he would think about it and reply soon. The strongman continued to say that he was the only, irreplaceable leader. Oppositionists were, pure and simple, dismissed as nonentities or Communist murderers.

There were other signs of difficulties facing the mediation. Divisiveness remained within the Broad Opposition Front, even though it had its executive triumvirate.[22] The day after Jorden's visit, Alfonso Robelo came to see me. The strike still had not been called off; in the face of business sentiment, he had tried to get a vote so that the FAO would formally call an end to it, but he had been defeated 7 to 5. (On September 25 many businesses reopened in Managua.) Robelo was working in coordination with Sergio Ramírez (the Group of Twelve's representative in the troika), for he attributed his defeat to the latter's absence—Ramírez was hiding, fearing that the government might take action against him. Robelo reported jealousies within the FAO because the Sandinistas had proclaimed that the troika would constitute the provisional government. (Another version was that the FSLN backed the Twelve as the provisional government). The violence was going to return, he said. The FAO could not sit down and negotiate directly with Somoza. Robelo's thesis was that the United States should declare the government illegitimate and demand Somoza's resignation, that this would not fail.

On September 25 Jorden returned to obtain Somoza's reply. The president would comply with the spirit of the OAS resolution and invite mediators for a dialogue. But with the exception of the United States, the countries that Jorden had earlier proposed were unacceptable. Somoza's list: Argentina, Brazil, Guatemala, and El Salvador.

Washington proposed a new list of countries: the United States, Colombia, Dominican Republic, El Salvador, and Guatemala; if Colombia was not acceptable, then either Honduras or Costa Rica were.[23] The State Department was deadly serious; if Somoza insisted on his position, the United States would not participate. I was instructed to discuss the panel with the opposition as well. My own appreciation from the tone and content of my telephone conversation with Washington was that the assistant secretary did not realize how much Somoza enjoyed demonstrating his power in negotiating, that in a mediation he would try to engage in these tactics all along. I did not yet know that a bluff to obtain the general's immediate resignation under the guise of OAS "mediation" was planned.

On September 28 Somoza informed me that Colombia had to be dropped because of its role in a United Nations "anti-Nicaragua" statement. On the 29th, Jorden returned proposing Costa Rica instead of Colombia, but the Costa Rican president did not wish to participate, and a panel of three was suggested. Somoza accepted this idea, so El Salvador was dropped from the remaining short list. The United States, Dominican Republic, and Guatemala formed the final team, which Somoza publicly announced September 29.

Opposition Shortcomings Pose Hurdle to Mediation

The problem was not settled. The FAO had to accept the mediation team. Washington had chosen not to have Jorden discuss the matter with the opposition, so the embassy was taking care of keeping them informed. On September 26 I had briefed representatives of the FAO, noting the confidential nature of our conversation. The United States would take a central and active role. The mediation panel would include an equal number of representatives from the nondemocratic camp and from ours, so that it would be acceptable to Somoza. I asked the opposition three things: that the FAO reiterate its support for the mediation, accept the panel of countries, and be willing to deal with the mediators upon their arrival.

On September 28 I met again with the opposition. I had not insisted in any of my meetings that the FAO troika be present. My tactic was that the FAO would decide who should maintain contact with the embassy, thus avoiding interfering in their internal delicate balance, which could only be counterproductive. At the same time, because I knew that the FAO's internal organization was precariously held together, I kept contacts with individuals with whom I had been working, regardless of their position in relation to FAO structure, to maintain our influence. Specifically, I kept in touch with La Prensa, INDE, and Conservative Emilio Alvarez Montalván. Now I also met with, among others, released prisoners Conservative Adolfo Calero and Liberal Pedro Quintanilla.

My contacts indicated that there was strong support for mediation. For instance, I was reassured that La Prensa would welcome it. Archbishop Obando supported it. Yet there was malaise within the FAO: one or two individuals told me that it might break down. This was precisely Somoza's hope and expectation.

To my surprise, on September 29 Robelo telephoned me. Rather than meeting with me, in the light of the approval of assistance to Somoza by the U.S. Congress, the FAO had canceled our noon meeting. I tried to explain that no new assistance had been approved and clarify the nature of the congressional discussion on aid for Nicaragua. But he refused to talk and angrily and abruptly ended the conversation. Personally I felt that the U.S. ambassador deserved more courteous treatment—Washington's policy had helped construct the framework that had permitted Robelo's meteoric political career, and I had promoted INDE's cause when he presided over the organization. These gentlemen are mistaken, I thought. They hold an unrealistic idea of the nature and possibilities of the mediation.

Tomás Borge had just made radical statements from Cuba[24]: the Sandinistas would support a provisional government only if it confiscated Somoza's property and dismantled the National Guard; the mediation was a desperate attempt of the United States to find a nonrevolutionary solution; the Sandinistas only supported the Group of Twelve; Panama, Venezuela, Mexico, and Costa Rica were against U.S. policy; Cuba was providing only "moral" support to the revolution so as not to provoke American action; the FSLN had not been defeated, the dead were civilians, not Sandinista cadres; the termination of the uprising was only a tactical retreat; the FSLN would launch another offensive from Costa Rica soon. Notice the open "international intervention" component of the revolution.

Thus I understood FSLN pressures on the FAO. The Sandinistas still were not unified, which affected the Group of Twelve presence in the FAO. In order for the troika to form part of a projected future provisional government, it had to be receptive to radical stances. The OAS resolution talked about a negotiated compromise, not the overthrow of the government. Could there be any confidence that reasonable interests of the Liberal Party and National Guard would be respected by a government of the FAO troika?

On September 25 the Washington Star published an interview with Robelo. He discussed his possible role in the FAO's provisional government if the Sandinista offensive had triumphed and the impossibility of Somoza reequilibrating the polity with any semblance of a civilized regime. These were among Robelo's statements:

Somoza's resignation is the solution. At the beginning, we thought there could be an agreement between the forces opposing Somoza and the forces that had backed him . . . without Somoza himself, [in] a national government. But this was before the National Guard committed genocide in [the rebellious cities]. There is absolutely no possibility of any kind of mediation or agreement between the opposition and members of the National Guard who carried out genocide. . . . But we do still hope there are some officers in the Guard who may not have been involved in the genocide and with whom we may be able to work. Anyone suspected of or denounced for being in the fight is summarily executed [by the Guard]. [Reconciliation is not possible], no, certainly not now. . . . I do not foresee a government without the participation of the FSLN.[25]

He publicly suggested a program of massive purges of the National Guard. If Robelo meant what he had told me—his concern that the FSLN dominate the opposition or the new government—he was not taking a prudent position, for there were two possible armies, the National Guard and the developing Sandinista force. In order to avoid the dominance of the Sandinistas, the opposition had to accommodate the National Guard. Robelo was suggesting forming a government of national union that excluded the Somocistas, who still controlled the state. This could only be accomplished if some army imposed the formula.

Moreover, although Somoza had accepted mediation, his public statements remained highly conflictive. Indeed, Somoza arrogantly had reiterated his position: the opposition needed time to organize a real political party that would be able to compete in the 1981 elections; this is what they should be doing rather than devoting their energies and resources to organize violence. Insultingly he accused the unarmed opposition of being cowardly. Where were they during the uprising? "Probably in the safety of their homes, or with their families in the safety of [exile in] other countries," he said.[26] But Somoza was not one to brag about bravery: he often spoke protected by a bulletproof box and was physically protected behind an army of bodyguards.

Upon being notified of the meeting's cancellation, political officer Jack Martin and I rapidly made contacts to neutralize any movement against an unconditional invitation. I personally spoke with Adolfo Calero and Pedro Quintanilla so that they could clarify in the FAO's next meeting the misunderstood issue of the loans.[27] Although the FAO had "learned" that the U.S. Congress had approved new financial assistance for Somoza and thought this was "unacceptable," in fact the case was very different. Senator Frank Church's amendment to the Foreign Assistance Bill for 1979, which required that the president make a special certification to the Congress that any assistance would be for promoting democratic progress in Nicaragua, had been eliminated in a conference committee of both the Senate and House of Representatives. This was simply committee work. No loans had been approved, and the 1979 economic assistance had not been approved yet by the Congress.

On September 30 the troika visited my office. They agreed with our agenda but wished to add a postscript. I urged them to drop their wording to the effect that "without the lifting of the state of siege" (and a few other conditions) "negotiations cannot continue," which appeared to be establishing preconditions for negotiations, and to deal with the problem in a twofold way. One issue was the acceptance of the mediation; the second was the establishment of their own policy priorities, some of which would subsequently have to take the form of demands to the mediators and the Nicaraguan government. No preconditions could be attached to the first. They were free, however, to make policy statements separate from the acceptance of the mediation, as Somoza had been doing.

The battle had been won. A few hours later, from my office, Emilio Alvarez Montalván checked with La Prensa and Adolfo Calero, his group's representative in the FAO's meeting. "Yes, the FAO has accepted your formula, they will issue two separate statements." History had been made: the chance had been given to work out an honorable compromise. It was now up to the mediators to make their efforts a landmark in Nicaraguan history. I had worked very hard and felt very relieved. My conscience was clear: my Nicaraguan mission had ended properly.

In the end, we never knew the number killed during the uprising. Figures were imprecise: many bodies had been burned and buried. Perhaps 3,000 had died. Figures about displaced individuals were also rough estimates; we heard 30,000 people were homeless. A firm of American lawyers visited us right after the events because of the insurance claims exceeding $60 million. Certainly the human needs were very serious. On September 21 we presented a check for $25,000 to Ismael Reyes, president of the Nicaraguan Red Cross; USAID-Washington was asked to send down experts immediately to assess the tragedy.[28] This was only a token gesture. The International Red Cross representatives spoke to us of a need for $445,000 for Masaya alone, where a total 25,000 individuals needed some form of assistance.

The costs of the uprising—including costs to the unarmed oppositionists—had contributed to the acceptance of the mediation. After all, many had expected that the National Guard would not remain so monolithic behind Somoza.[29] This did not mean that its acceptance implied support for the violent route had ended for good. Contrary to Somocista interpretation, the Sandinistas had not come out tarnished with a general image of brutality, a semiotics employed by the government to promote the inhibiting effects of violence.[30] Don Bohning observed: "As opposition despair grows, even some who are wary of the Sandinistas' Marxist orientation are coming to view them as the lesser of two evils and perhaps the only alternative for ending the Somoza dictatorship." The opposition had not yet crossed a point of no return, the belief that violence was absolutely necessary, that the sooner the apocalypse came the better to obtain a quicker relief. But it was clear that if the mediation failed, war would be inevitable. The violence option was not restricted any more to a small minority with millenarian or messianic ideological visions to achieve social change.

Although in a sense the opposition had been militarily defeated, it had gained politically because of the resulting increased revulsion against the government.[31] The *Miami Herald* predicted that in the absence of a settlement, the FSLN would recruit more men, funds, and military equipment. It was unlikely that Somoza could remain in office three more years.[32] *New York Times* correspondent Alan Riding reported to me that the mood among the people was not fear, but anger against the government: the FSLN still did not have the resources to win, but there would be a different story if the Sandinistas acquired more men and better equipment. Unfortunately, predictably the next uprising would be far more costly.

The Mediators Arrive

Reflecting the spirit that prevailed in the OAS, the mediation was named Mission of Friendly Cooperation and Conciliatory Efforts. It had no mandate to work out a binding solution. The team was formed by William G. Bowdler of the United States, Ramón Emilio Jiménez of the Dominican Republic, and José Alfredo Obiols of Guatemala and arrived October 6.

Bowdler was a career diplomat who had spent much time in Latin America. In addition to minor posts, he had been ambassador to Guatemala, El Salvador, and South Africa. At the time he was director of intelligence and research at the State Department. Jiménez was a retired vice admiral and the foreign minister. He was knowledgeable of the democratic compromise that had been worked out earlier in the year in his country and was a participant in the mutual guarantees worked out to achieve that transition, being a carryover of the departing Joaquín Balaguer administration in the cabinet of the new government. Obiols was a former vice foreign minister of Guatemala.

The mediators' activities would test the capability to easily change foreign rulers; they were faced with the incapacity of important Nicaraguans to recognize and accept Pablo Antonio Cuadra's epigraphic nature of a mediation; and, above all, they had to deal with the personal shortcomings of a dictator. The acceptance of the mediation had raised hopes among the general public: people were calmer, and the censorship of the state of siege reduced the level of open agitation as well. Yet there was no sufficient climate for compromise.

Somoza would not accept that a mediation meant mutual concessions; rather, he interpreted it as an opportunity for the opposition to "climb down the coconut tree" and stop making absurd demands so that an electoral solution could be achieved at the appropriate time. He expected more trouble: violence had been going on in the country for fifty years, he said, as if dismissing it; the mediation would serve to expose and defeat the Venezuelan president and Costa Rican ex-president José Figueres.

The day of the mediators' arrival and the next, Somoza held press conferences. His message was clear: he was willing to discuss anything the opposition wanted, but "it's not mediation, it's friendly cooperation," he insisted, implying the OAS representatives' powerlessness to obtain his resignation. He was going to retain martial law and double the size of the National Guard to 15,000 to cope with the international subversion. "My U.S. teachers [at West Point] taught me that the best defense is a strong defense." He was preparing himself for war. "The election will be the first Sunday in February in 1981, not before, because that's the way it's in the Constitution." And he dismissed the opposition for failing: "Let them stop the foolishness."

Indeed, the feasibility of a moderate government was based on its early formation. Adolfo Calero, later a leader of the anti-Sandinista (Contra) Nicaraguan Democratic Force (FDN), was poignant: "The viability of a moderate opposition, of the FAO itself, is contingent upon an early Somoza departure—otherwise its prestige would vanish, and the armed Sandinista-led route prevail. The [FAO] envisions a provisional government that would run the country while political parties prepare for elections [to take place in two or three years]. The opposition will need [that time] to organize for elections."[33] (The latter point was precisely Somoza's contention.)

The FAO's Comisión Política, or troika, had far-reaching ideas. Two days before the mediators' arrival I received a manifesto with their demands. For a start, they felt the need to justify participating in the mediation and accuse the United States for sustaining the "genocidal" government. They would deal with the United States as a necessary fact but did not intend to "dialogue, pact or enter in *componendas* with Somoza or the Somocismo."[34] Before arriving, the mediators had been told by the FAO that to succeed they had to unilaterally change the government, to entirely restructure the state and exile the Somoza family; if not, there would be a violent revolution. No consideration was given to the actual mandate of the OAS, nor to how the mediators were going to reorganize the National Guard and form a new government with the FAO and without the general.

Some oppositionists dealt with the topic, referring to the OAS intervention in the Dominican Republic, in which American troops had successfully invaded the country. Luis Pasos Argüello sent me documentation legally justifying such OAS action as a case of "collective action," not "intervention." Incidentally, the opposition's strategy of seeking some form of foreign intervention reinforced Somoza's perception that Nicaraguans could not defeat him, hence his emphasis in changing U.S. policy.

We did not want the mediators to be surprised. Before the mediation began, Jack Martin drafted with my assistance a cable entitled "Mediation: A Difficult Road." The message expressed our belief that Somoza would continue to insist on his position, and that he had successfully suppressed within his military and party any leaders who demonstrated a potential for independent action. We could not expect pressure from them on Somoza to depart. "The quandary is that, in order for these institutions to become revitalized, it is essential for Somoza to relinquish the total control he now exercises over them. However, Somoza justifies his continued domination on the grounds that no one but he is strong enough to hold these institutions together and in line." This was, of course, the old Somoza Doctrine.

An analysis of the opposition followed: any intermediate solution (i.e., not Somoza's immediate departure) was unstable because of its unacceptability within the FAO; Somoza's continuing in office would split the FAO. The popular support and legitimacy of moderate traditionalist groups was seriously weak—they lacked "significant organization and rank-and-file support." "The strongest group in the opposition, in terms of organization and capacity to act in the short-run (not to be confused with a long-run ability to capture votes in any free electoral process) is the FSLN."

We dealt with the FAO's troika and warned about possible problems. "The troika has demonstrated a willingness to act independently of FAO instructions, and a greater preparedness than the FAO itself to threaten to abandon the game whenever events not to its liking occur."

Finally, we addressed the constitutional issue: Somoza could always resign; his term could be shortened by partial amendment. As time went on, less time was available to make constitutional changes a reason for Somoza's dilatory tactics.

These were the conclusions: "It is difficult to see how an end to the violence is possible if Somoza is unwilling to surrender power. Only the moral weight of the international presence in favor of a partial solution (other than immediate resignation) might lend such a solution sufficient support to maintain a semblance of peace. But, in this case, the U.S. will have undertaken a very significant commitment to insure that such an agreement is (nationally and internationally) fulfilled."

Hours before the mediators' arrival, I spoke with Luis Pallais. By now he was the only one close to the president with whom I could discuss issues with any hope of influence. Luis complained about the excessive demands that the FAO's troika was making. Unfortunately, most of the more reasonable members of the FAO did not have the guts to exercise leadership, so they were relegated to secondary roles, thought Luis. It was just too much for the Somocistas to accept the troika's position that they relinquish control of the state, give absolute control over it to the FAO, and exile the Somoza family. It served as an excuse for their immobility and no compromise initiative.

I told him the mediation was serious, the White House was fully involved in it, the mediators were not coming to make a courtesy call. The mediation would specify the objectives for a solution; it would be very dangerous for Nicaragua to break its ties with the United States.[35] I was undecided between two interpretations of Somoza's attitude. Maybe he just did not mind taking his partisans—and the country—down with him in his sinking enterprise, stating that "others were the cause of the tragedy." Or maybe he did not realize the seriousness of the situation: his conceit sustained the notion of his irreplaceability and that people would soon realize that he was much better than his opponents, who would make some fatal error. Or perhaps it was a combination of both.

We were faced with a paradox. There were strong reasons to believe that Somoza would not relinquish power in the absence of an imminent or serious threat against him. Neither the U.S. government nor the OAS would do so. While the chances of a mediated compromise were consequently perceived by the embassy as very low, if the opposition demanded the total surrender of the Somocista group and total power for itself, it was certain that the mediation would fail. Despite the odds, I was firmly committed to obtaining the mediation's success in order to try to avoid an even costlier outbreak of total war.

Formal Instructions to the U.S. Mediator

The objective was to achieve an enduring, peaceful, democratic solution. The instructions for the U.S. mediator stated: "To the greatest extent possible, allow the solution to emerge from the play of the positions taken by the two sides. While the U.S. role in the mediation will be important, perhaps central, it should be carefully calibrated to permit the parties to express their views fully and to reflect the international character of the mediation." The U.S. mediator was to assist in obtaining a compromise between the Somoza camp and the FAO on a transition to free elections, its mechanisms, and timetable. Democratization required the preservation of the National Guard to maintain law and order; however, Washington thought that it needed an "acceptable new leadership"; other institutions of government (e.g., the judiciary) might also need to be reformed.

How was the transition to be achieved? "If necessary . . . persuade Somoza and his close relatives to step down in advance of 1981 and not run for office. Consult with Washington on what steps may be desirable and appropriate. . . . Their departure from the country would be preferable but this decision should be a function of the negotiating process. Should Somoza express a desire to come to the U.S., indicate that entry could be considered." No ultimatum was considered; the document's tone was to persuade, not dictate. The instructions ended by indicating that Washington was prepared to provide humanitarian assistance to Nicaraguans affected by the violence and that "once agreement is reached on a transition, [Washington is prepared] to consider resumption of economic and military assistance."[36]

I went to the airport to receive William Bowdler on October 6. The ambassador projected self-confidence and serene determination. He knew what had to be done, and in a meeting with the embassy's core staff he conveyed the message: they were coming to obtain Somoza's resignation and form a transitional government. His statement contrasted with the softer tone of his formal instructions.

It was expected that the Dominican mediator, Foreign Minister Jiménez, would actively participate to achieve this goal. Guatemalan ambassador Obiols's position was more doubtful, for his government was rightist and authoritarian, not close to the United States. In fact, Obiols proved to be trustworthy and easy to get along with; he performed a very constructive role.

Bowdler was in a hurry and showed no interest in any conversation with me. Despite my attempts to offer insight on the personalities involved, he had made up his mind and would try first to organize the opposition as a coherent alternative to Somoza. The mediators were on their own. The embassy's role was essentially only supportive.

The three mediators began work right away, first visiting President Somoza, then Archbishop Obando y Bravo. They were immediately faced with a "respectful" petition of several business chambers requesting, in order to obtain a propitious climate, that a minimum of freedom of expression in the media be restored so that the public could be kept informed. The reimposed state of siege was still in effect, which technically also implied that the FAO could not assemble to participate in negotiations. The mediators spoke for over an hour with the president, who reportedly said Nicaragua's political system was similar to Mexico's. Somoza said he would not lift the state of siege but was not entirely closed to the idea that greater freedom of information be restored.

The next day, October 7, the mediators met with the FAO's troika. They were quite negatively impressed: the representatives gave an ultimatum, refusing to negotiate until constitutional guarantees were restored. The troika made their plans clear. They could promise that no work stoppage would be called by the FAO but not that the Sandinistas would not carry out military actions. However, the Twelve's representative in the troika dismissed the notion on grounds that it would be a tactical error. Indeed, at this time there was no climate for another uprising—it had been too costly, and there were hopes that the mediation would triumph.

The mediators—the panel, as they became known in official circles—then visited La Prensa, where the issue of restoration of constitutional guarantees, including their freedom to publish, was raised. The mediators were on the right track: if censorship was lifted, the press had to act responsibly.

The mediators were feeling their way. Bowdler knew that there was no precedent for this OAS enterprise. He did not like what he had heard from the troika. We talked on October 7. He wondered if it would not be advisable to try to divide the FAO, whether La Prensa would take a more reasonable line than the troika, if the mediators dealt directly with the factions that formed the FAO.

I commented that the need for freedom of the media was deeply felt by all. This concession had to be obtained from Somoza. Perhaps the formula to begin the negotiations was to also get the freeing of prisoners who did not participate in the violence, while keeping a more limited curfew, as the troika could not promise that the FSLN would not attack. The FAO, on the other hand, should ask all Nicaraguans, including the FSLN, not to participate in disturbances of public order and should ask the media to moderate their verbal aggressiveness. Based on my experience, I also suggested that the panel meet freely with other oppositionists than the troika and that a rule of confidentiality be established so that the mediators could engage in private negotiations without their positions being immediately published.

The FAO troika's intransigence was a serious problem for the mediators, so the panel returned to Somoza, who had adopted the "Cabinet principle"—he would consult with his ministers and reply. Knowing the nature of the group, Somoza was going to get "more pro-Somoza" opinions than his own, but this provided him with excuses of representing his people while going through perfunctory motions.

Somoza returned with his position: (1) on October 13, when the thirty-day state of siege ended, he would lift media censorship; (2) starting tomorrow, October 8, the censors would be removed from *La Prensa*, and prisoners would start being presented to the courts; (3) the state of siege would not be lifted because of the possibility of crop sabotage. I learned that Somoza observed to the mediators that he was making these concessions to them, not to the FAO—such was the animus.

The concessions did not change the troika's position of no negotiations until all constitutional guarantees were fully restored. The mediators had three options: (1) pressure Somoza so that he would comply; (2) leave the country temporarily until the opposition's formal representation changed its mind; (3) initiate individual direct contacts with members of the FAO to determine who would wish to participate in the negotiations.

La Prensa took a constructive position. It is true that they published incendiary information on events that had taken place during the days that the paper had not appeared because of the censorship. Some of the headlines were even imprudent: "International Reaction against Somoza Grows: A Tribunal Proposed to Judge Him [as a war criminal]." But *La Prensa* wanted a peaceful solution and backed the mediation. In its first issue the headline was "Mediation Advances: Arduous Work of Ambassadors." The editorials supported both the mediation and the FAO. The need for moderation was acknowledged: "[Although we] have the obligation to report [the recent events], we have stripped ourselves of every spirit of revenge, so as to, without hatreds or sectarianisms, promote the conciliatory effort that with the help of friendly countries is taking place in Nicaragua."

On the mediators' next visit, Somoza told them of his desire to participate in the negotiations himself—not through proxies—and, wishing to indicate "reasonableness," said that he was planning to reduce the number of hours of the curfew.

Somoza must have been happy: he was deliberately trying to project an image of the smart, reasonable leader. If the mediators were fair-minded, he must have thought, they would realize the incapacity of his opponents, who were unwilling to make any concessions. He was counting on the FAO to collapse into factionalism. But the president certainly was not giving any indication that he intended to leave power—in fact, that same day he publicly committed himself to double the size of his army (embassy staff was reporting a slow increase in recruiting). Two days later, he gave another speech.

Somoza's messianic, charismatic self-conception reached its climax. "We are creating 21,000 new jobs. There is no other government today that can say this is happening on its soil. They are all cornered, against the wall, because no one planned like the Liberal Party planned—its directors, and above all, Anastasio Somoza, who most affectionately loves the Nicaraguan people. Thank you." Statements such as this one were perhaps behind the spreading rumor that Somoza was again drinking very heavily and going insane.

The opposition's intransigence was obvious. It was blocking any progress in discussing substantive formulas to solve the crisis. Opposition inexperience partly resulted from Somoza's previously successful will to conquer his opponents and concentrate all power in himself. The issue was not Somoza's talents, nor his other contention that the opposition needed time to mature in organization: Nicaragua needed a respite from his rule precisely so it could grow.

Informed conservative Americans continued to insist that he yield power. On October 14 my immediate Republican predecessor, James Theberge, stated:

> The holding of early national elections (in 1979) and a rapid transition to a democratic government is perhaps the most desirable and realistic option. I believe it is in the best interest [of all] that we use our considerable influence to achieve this objective and not permit the Marxist Sandinista guerrillas, who are hostile to the United States, to seize power and impose a repressive, Castro-style dictatorship. [Somoza] is attempting to preserve power in the face of widespread popular revolt against over four decades of family rule. [37]

However, within the Somoza camp it was felt that, barring a U.S. ultimatum, they had time, even though the mediators' presence made them uncomfortable. They continued with their intense partisanship. It was the same capacity to "ideologize": to label those with whom one disagrees as symbols of opprobrium and to disregard fact in the advocacy of sentiment, common to far too many actors in the ancien régime. It was as if the Somocistas could not understand that a new game with new actors and a new situation had materialized.

I met with Luis Pallais, who referred to Somoza stepping down before 1981 as "his last resort concession." As to the eventuality of the president being "forced to resign by the intervention now present in Nicaragua," Somoza had told him that in that case, he would spend several million dollars to get Pallais elected. The Somocista command felt that they had great political space for maneuvering and retaining control. The recent carnage and their lack of contact with the nation's social forces seemed meaningless. They were still "the majority."

Negotiate a Compromise

I was getting impatient with the lack of progress. On October 9, the mediators had a conversation in which the president reiterated his unwillingness to accept "retroactive" political changes. This continued inflexibility on the basic issue of his earlier retirement was combined with periodic minor concessions: now all the political refugees in the embassies but two would be given safe conduct to leave the country.[38]

Although I talked to Bowdler over breakfast every morning, in the face of the impasse and the danger of mediation collapse, I sent a memo to him. "I think that it is going to be extremely difficult to get Somoza to resign and to persuade him to accept de facto constitutional changes"; it is "very important that we straighten out our constitutional arguments as soon as possible," so that the mediators can immediately start to persuade Somoza that the natural "recommendation of any mediation will have to be something other than 1981, a compromise, and that there are constitutional grounds for such an understanding." At best, I thought that the mediators might be able to reach a solution in which both parties made concessions as part of the process of providing mutual guarantees. This was the spirit of the formal instructions to Bowdler, what Ambassador Jorden had suggested to Somoza.

There is no contradiction between my disappointment that Washington was unwilling to put serious pressure on Somoza—recall the administration's reluctance until recently even to "mediate" the conflict because of its interventionist implications—and my concern that the mediators present a demand to him that implied the total defeat of his people. Again, certainly, the latter kind of formula would never be acceptable to the dictator, and we had to try to avoid the mediation's breakdown and total war. It was not because of my personal preference that no ultimatum to Somoza was being planned at the administration's higher level.

Aware of the impasse, La Prensa's Danilo Aguirre presented a memo to the mediators, showing how to change the government within the extant constitutional system. The solution was Somoza's resignation and family vacation as soon as a legal fallback position was available. The presidential term could be reduced to four and a half years, to terminate on April 30, 1979 (slightly earlier than the ultimate success of the revolution). If absolutely necessary, the president would serve his reformed term until then, with fundamental reforms being simultaneously implemented (e.g., reform of the National Guard and the courts, to make them professional democratic institutions). After such date, a new executive would be constituted by a triumvirate composed of a representative of the ruling Liberal Party, one of the FAO, and one appointed by the Catholic Church.[39] Under the triumvirate electoral reforms would be implemented to establish the basis for a free democratic election in 1981.

It was considered that if Somoza accepted leaving office by April 30, the progress toward democratization would be sufficiently evident to weather the criticism of advocates of a more radical, immediate solution. But if this option was unacceptable—and notice Somoza would have ruled over four years during this term—then the mediation would have to use its "resources" to obtain from Somoza a non-all-out war solution (i.e., a United States ultimatum). Thus it should be on the record that within the FAO there were reasonable intellects committed to avoiding the certainty of a revolution's cost and uncertainty of its democratic outcome.

I saw advantages if the mediation would move to explore a position "neither today nor 1981" and start working out the legality of such a formula. However, Bowdler was set on obtaining Somoza's resignation and establishing that the state would be reorganized with a set of "institutional" or "constitutional" acts of an executive formed in a de facto manner by the mediators. He had in mind using the Dominican model of 1965, when foreign troops occupied Santo Domingo, not the constitutional agreement worked out there earlier in the year.

On October 11 Bowdler told me that his priority was to develop opposition organization so that chaos did not overcome the country when Somoza resigned. That same day he addressed the embassy's Country Team, where he expressed his desire that our personnel make no comment about the mediation—any statements, especially to the press, should come only from the mediation or the ambassador.

The following day he and I met with our USAID and military personnel with new instructions: no disbursements should be made in the pipeline of any of the ongoing assistance programs. The idea was to put pressure on the government. Unfortunately, it was only the mediation's bluff: Washington was not even committed to end our assistance.

Beginning October 10 I met with a series of interest groups to elicit their support. My presentations were initially formal: a summary of U.S. policy since the Ford years, embassy communications urging all parties to dialogue and negotiate a compromise disregarded, suggestions of an international mediation to start negotiations without preconditions—although the FAO had not yet decided to negotiate. Regional international realities indicated that if a compromise were not achieved, massive violence would overcome the country.

I asked the groups to participate in the mediation by publicly and privately encouraging the parties to negotiate a compromise. The replies had nuances according to the special interest involved. The Asociación de Instituciones

Bancarias de Nicaragua, for instance, was particularly sensitive to the pending International Monetary Fund credit. Of all groups, the coffee growers seemed most conservative, with their priority on being able to harvest and sell the crop. As noted, the agricultural sector had not been active in the rebellion. However, practically all immediately committed their support right there in my office and subsequently took public stances for the suspension of armed actions and government repression "to promptly obtain a political understanding in the national interest and harmony," as one of the documents stated. Actually, some representatives said that they had not given a blank check to the FAO and criticized the troika's intransigence, stating that they wished the mediation to continue regardless of what the FAO decided to do. A sense of calm had been brought by the OAS-sponsored team. Make active contacts with FAO and Somoza followers to influence them and facilitate a reduction of distrust between the factions, I suggested.

Business interest groups were becoming more active in and expanding the umbrella organization, Consejo Superior de la Empresa Privada (COSEP). Groups that had kept themselves at the margin of the political process wished to participate as well in some capacity (e.g., as observers) in the mediation.

Of interest was the statement by the Association of Cattle Growers. It appealed to the tradition under the Somozas to "dialogue," "negotiate understandings," and it depicted the situation as deplorable that foreigners had needed to come to help solve the crisis. The association came out in favor of "improving" the country's democratization within the legal system, but it supported the mediation and called for a compromise. In short, more groups outside the government understood that the 1981 formula was not workable.

By October 11 I had learned that changes were taking place in the FAO. A member informed me that the size of its plenary assembly would be doubled to thirty members, and that on October 13 the plenary would meet to decide that the troika should resume the discussions with the mediators. Indeed, on that day it was unanimously decided that the discussions should be continued by the troika. The plenary had dropped the demand that Somoza lift entirely the state of siege.[40]

Although the decision that the troika would meet with the mediators could be interpreted as a victory of the moderates, the message given by the troika on October 14 was clear: the OAS panel would have to oust Somoza. The continuation of the family in the country was not negotiable. The United States should stop all its assistance to Nicaragua and the military assistance or sales by its allies (e.g., Israel). The troika would not present any concrete plan until they obtained assurances that the Somoza family would be exiled. Such a position reinforced the strongman's conviction that his opponents were not really operating under democratic premises of fair play, that Nicaragua was "not ready for New England democracy." He would not consider legitimate, opposition fears that if he remained in Nicaragua he would be able to summon the National Guard to restore him to power.

The mediators asked about the role of the Guardia Nacional and Liberal Party in any transition. One of the troika denied that the Guard had any legitimacy to participate; only Liberals who were not Somocista had a role to play, another said. The demand was clear: the United States must eliminate the state's structure and give them all power. How could this be achieved?

Negotiations were also challenged internationally. Venezuela and Panama had accepted the mediation but gave signs that they would give up if it did not achieve a solution soon. On October 10 Costa Rica alleged that some of its citizens had been kidnapped inside Costa Rica by the Nicaraguan Guard and had been "tortured."[41] Costa Rica was going to take the "violation of national sovereignty and human rights" to the OAS. The pendulum of public opinion moved against the Nicaraguan dictator even more. Something had to be done. If no satisfaction was forthcoming, Costa Rica would withdraw from the OAS and take other actions.[42]

Guatemala was unhappy with Costa Rican diplomacy. The Foreign Ministry threatened to withdraw Ambassador Obiols from the mediation if the anti-Somoza diplomacy continued in the OAS. Although its president, General Romeo Lucas García, had come to think that it was unlikely that Somoza could last his entire term, he was unwilling to go beyond suggesting to Somoza that he negotiate an honorable exit. The Honduran military junta reportedly held a similar position.

The end result was only a pro–Costa Rica resolution passed in the OAS by a majority; the United States voted against Nicaragua. The votes were not there—as Somoza knew—for any collective action against him.

The FAO's Formal Demand

Eleven days after the mediators' arrival, the FAO's Comisión Política finally presented a scheme for a transitional government. Briefly, a three-year provisional government was proposed: it would be constituted by a Junta, a Council of State, and the Judicial Power, and it would establish the bases for a "republican" and "democratic-representative" system of government, that is, a Western-type democracy.

The Junta would be the executive, composed of three individuals all appointed by the FAO. Initially the Council of State would perform as the legislative branch and would consist of a thirty-member body, two from each of the fifteen organizations of the FAO. A year and a half after its establishment, the Junta would call a general election for a National Constituent Assembly, which would both promulgate a new constitution and become the provisional legislative organ until the inauguration of the new constitutional order three years henceforth.

The Council of State would reorganize the judiciary appointing the new judges, and the Junta would reorganize the National Guard, creating a National Police as well. The commitment to competitive electoral processes was included. A year and a half after its inauguration, the provisional government would call an election not only for the Constituent Assembly but for all mayors and municipal assemblies as well. The articles of the extant Nicaraguan Constitution that were not in opposition to the new rules would remain in force.

The troika was asked about the participation of the ruling Liberal Party and other sectors in the provisional government. The National Guard would definitely participate in determining its future through consultations that would take place around its reorganization: it had not been given a formal role in the government in order to establish the principle that it was an apolitical, professional institution subordinated to the executive. It would remain operating as an institution—only the "bad officers" would be weeded out.[43] And the FAO would accept all of Nicaragua's international obligations and honor international human rights conventions. The FAO representatives explicitly were asked, "What if Somoza says no?" They replied that then there would be fighting.

The U.S. mediator, hopeful that he could get Somoza's resignation, reported that this had been one of the best meetings held so far with the opposition, even though stumbling blocks remained: the FAO did not wish to negotiate with the Liberal Party, and the representatives of the Group of Twelve were particularly prone to threaten that if the opposition plans were not implemented, violence would follow.

To the point, Obiols, the Guatemalan mediator, personally commented that the FAO's proposal was one in which it attributed to itself total political sovereignty to staff and reorganize the entire state—it was as if they had vanquished Somoza's army in the September uprising. The FAO was to appoint the new government without any representation of the party in power, even though "national reconstruction and reconciliation" were the stated goals. Also, there was still an "unmentionable": if General Somoza did not comply, would the United States dispose of the family and followers and give total power to the FAO?

When the mediators met again with the troika on October 19, the following statement (which I abridge) was given to them from the FAO:

> The FAO considers that the first step to obtain the success of the mediation is to fulfill the first point of our initial positions presented on October 14, 1978, that is, the definitive separation of the Somoza family from all political and military office, and their departure from the country. The FAO is willing to continue the mediation once the Somoza family is separated from power, and when it is outside of the country.

The document asked that all types of foreign assistance be suspended. In the meeting the troika expressed the willingness to follow a constitutional solution provided that the core demand be implemented.[44] They refused to negotiate any solution with any government representative.

The problem with the FAO's approach, however, was obvious: the mediation did not have the mandate to forcefully change the government. Thus naturally it had to conduce negotiations, and its success was to work out mutual concessions in that context. To avoid breaking up the opposition's formal unity, the FAO was being allowed to exercise a fertile, fanciful imagination. Somoza must have been enjoying the mediation's difficulties, I thought, in his belief that the FAO would prove itself "unreasonable" in demanding his party's total surrender and would disintegrate. I found the situation far too awful.

There were oppositionists who realized still that the mediation was not simply to get the dictator and his family to leave the country and constitute a new government totally controlled by the opposition, even if they expected that the United States would exert maximum pressure to obtain an agreed-upon change in government.

I met with Danilo Aguirre and Alberto Saborío, expressing my concern that Somoza was being violent and intransigent in his speeches, even daring the United States to send the marines. The FAO had voted 11 to 4 for the immediate resignation formula, but Somoza was going to say no, so they again raised their constitutional solution to end the regime in April 1979 as a position for the mediation to be able to return to the FAO. It was becoming increasingly clear that the mediation would have to make a proposal of its own if the impasse was to be broken. One morning the CIA chief of station came to see me: "What we need here is covert action to undermine Somoza's National Guard and Liberal Party support. Otherwise we cannot win," he said. It seemed more ethical to deliver an ultimatum than to plan the assassination of a dictator, but there are actions between extremes.

The mediation was left only with exercising economic pressures on the government to obtain its collaboration. The U.S. Treasury had postponed badly needed International Monetary Fund (IMF) credit. La Prensa was publicizing the suspension of USAID disbursements.[45] From Washington came another signal of pressure: Nicaragua would receive an increase in its export quota of cattle only if the mediation were successful. The minister of finance, retired general Samuel Genie, came to see me to protest *La Prensa*'s articles and seek a clarification of policy. Genie, who had headed the secret police, was a serious, courteous officer who always manifested his absolute loyalty to Somoza. Nicaragua, he said, was making payments on time into their bilateral projects—what was the delay?

We did not have instructions to formally suspend any money in the pipeline; the instructions to embassy personnel were to respond "no comment" when asked. We could not give a blunt and decisive message, such as that the U.S. would boycott the economy until a constitutional transition was worked out. The structural constraints of our assistance programs were once more manifest: formal bureaucratic deadlines had to be met internally and in public presentations. We again saw the potential for disruption that the system posed in its lack of synchronization with local realities. Public discussions were now taking place in the Congress about economic assistance with figures that made no sense in terms of the extant situation.[46] If a new government was not inaugurated, major violence was predictable, thus making inoperative any budgeted amounts; conversely, if the crisis were resolved, one would hope for a much larger American assistance to the new government. In fact, a total economic boycott was not even contemplated in Washington.[47]

On October 20 the Catholic Church issued a message. First, constitutional arguments of legality could not be above the common good (i.e., a transitional government without the Somozas had to be formed soon). Second, morality had to prevail: the leaders should not "fall in the temptation of retaliation, rancor, and vengeance." In the spirit of the post–Vatican II social reformism, a "new sociopolitical order" had to be installed, "affirming the national identity versus a constant and permanent foreign intervention." It was as if Monsignor Obando had started to distrust the mediation, as if a (final) foreign intervention to end all intervention by forming a popular and progressive new regime were being demanded more angrily.

Meanwhile, Washington was telling other countries of the need to support the mediation. Panamanian Torrijos and Venezuelan Pérez were contacted, and Pérez was asked to convince the Group of Twelve to maintain FAO unity and to negotiate a solution with the Liberal Party. Pérez's position was that the crux of the problem was to devise the mechanism to get rid of Somoza; once the opposition and Somoza knew this, negotiations would then be possible. However, in his opinion, the confiscation of Somoza's properties was inevitable, which handicapped the role for his Liberal Party. In short, the United States had to orchestrate the change of government. The mediation would propose a formula for "national reconciliation" based on Somoza's immediate resignation and the formation of a provisional junta.

Unfortunately, we could not be optimistic. The mediation had concentrated efforts that obtained from the FAO a proposal for a transitional regime that reasonable men had to judge unacceptable to those in power. The general was making statements that "proved" his obsession to never relinquishing control of the state.[48]

The Opposition Splits

On October 25 we learned of the withdrawal of the Twelve both from the FAO and the mediation. It was sad that after all our efforts, they would break with the hope of a peaceful settlement. I understood their position, however. There were no signs that the mediation could obtain the formation of a new government in a reasonable time frame, thus in the group's mind war was inevitable unless U.S. policy changed. They had tired of playing Somoza's mediation charade and wished to influence the U.S. government attacking its policy.

The Twelve's merit had been their sponsorship of a role for the Sandinistas in the country's future regime. Despite the presence of intellectuals in the group, its platform had remained rudimentary, with no discussion about a new social order beyond their original position: a democratic regime with civil liberties, a new system of property starting with an agrarian reform within a mixed economy, and nonalignment in the international arena ending the dependency on the United States. The Twelve's priority had been to terminate the dictatorship.

Their linkage with the FSLN, however, posed problems. As we saw, Sandinista propaganda had indicated the continuation of authoritarian Marxist-Leninist roots among top core leaders. Indeed, some members of the Twelve vocally claimed that they were trying to "moderate" the Sandinistas.

In any case, because of their political demands, the Twelve's spokesmen in Nicaragua had not been facilitating a compromise with the ruling group. Ironically, the devastation finally brought about by the coming all-out war marred the efforts to perpetuate the future Sandinista regime, given its economic vulnerability and consequent dependency on the wealthy foreign democracies. And the Twelve's ideological-social heterogeneity, including the substantial presence of the haute bourgeoisie in it, added to the Sandinista regime's incoherence.

When announcing their decision, about half of the Twelve who were in Nicaragua obtained political asylum in the Mexican Embassy. This represented an implicit recognition that they had been operating under the assumption of

American protection, and that now they felt that they could not count on it.[49] But there was melodrama in their entering the local embassy: it was not Somoza's style to capture prominent citizens in the presence of an OAS team in the country.

Some observers gave the Twelve's departure more importance than it actually had. The door for a solution remained open. Group of Twelve participation in the mediation suggested that the FSLN did not have yet the strength to overthrow Somoza. But given the constraints established by Washington on itself, a solution was possible only if Somoza stopped stalling and took a bold initiative rather than his 1981 obsession.

These are parts of the Group of Twelve position:

To Our Nicaraguan Brothers:

We, the members of the Group of Twelve, wish to inform . . . that we have decided to withdraw from the Broad Opposition Front (FAO) and not participate more in the conversations of the so-called "Mediating Comission."

[We] considered that in spite of the unforgivable delay [of the mediation to arrive before the killing of thousands of Nicaraguans], we had the duty to confront the United States with the fact that, thanks to the support that they continue giving to the Somocista dictatorship, and which they have kept for almost half a century, the dictatorship continues to be sustained; that until that support was radically cut, the blood would continue to run; and that for Nicaraguans to obtain an immediate exit of Somoza, his family and the Somocismo, it was necessary that the United States withdraw immediately from him that assistance, and impede those countries under their sphere of influence to continue arming Somoza. Also, that Somoza should be notified that never again would he receive any assistance. It was not in any way to open the door to an [American] intervention, rather on the contrary, to cut the intervention that signifies supporting an immoral regime like Somoza's.

The Mediating Commission is making suggestions that signify leaving practically intact the corrupt structures of the Somocista apparatus, suggestions that also imply a dialogue with Somocista representatives.

Nicaraguans must insist today more than ever, that until the National Guard is profoundly restructured; until the Somocista party is dismantled; and until the immoral capital of the Somoza family is expropriated, it will be impossible to eradicate Somocismo from our country with what it represents: genocides, assassinations, robberies, disloyal [business] competition, tax evasion, in sum, the demoralization and bankruptcy of our country.

The mediation is impudently intervening. We Nicaraguans should not tolerate in any form that under an untrustworthy promise of Somoza's exit, the United

States assures beforehand all the mechanisms so that the military dictatorship survives, and the clamor of the oppressed of our land continues being drowned in blood.

We know that we are not alone. We have on our side the solidarity of democratic countries, such as Venezuela, Costa Rica . . . Panama [sic] . . . and the solidarity of hundreds of thousands of Latin Americans and within the United States itself.

And finally, we wish to tell our people, that our backing of the Sandinista Front of National Liberation continues as unshakable as the first day; that the message that we have carried through so many places continues to be the same: it is the Nicaraguan people who are the only ones who can decide the course that our fatherland takes, and it is the people who will walk to its liberation.

How could the group have grounds to accuse the United States of working to perpetuate the "military dictatorship"? The basic problem could not be the advocacy of a social order opposed by the United States (then ruled by an administration sympathetic to Third World socialist experiments). The problem, according to their statement, was different. They did not wish to negotiate with the ruling group nor give it representation in the new regime. They sought to dismantle the ruling Liberal Party and the National Guard, exile the Somozas, and confiscate all their property.

The document claimed to reject ("with all our forces") foreign intervention. In fact, it referred approvingly to the backing of a few regional countries. Illustrative, from his exile in Costa Rica Twelve member Carlos Tunnerman said in an October 26 interview that a military offensive would be launched from there to liberate Nicaragua; he referred to the military activities along the border and the constitution of a new provisional government.

One thing is certain: the measures against sharing representation in the state suggested by the Twelve were not taken in the successful Dominican democratization earlier that year, nor in the mediated democratic transition that finally began to take place in 1990 in Nicaragua.

The FAO immediately made its position known. Although regretting the Twelve's withdrawal, it reiterated its support for using the mediation to obtain a "true, permanent, democratic, profound and rapid" solution, to form "a National Government of a provisional character which will establish the bases . . . for a system of government republican and representative-democratic."

La Prensa published the entire manifesto of the Twelve and gave it balanced coverage, but backed the FAO: "Without Somoza and No Pact nor *Componenda*; FAO: There Is No Retrogression." [50] The mediation had lost strength because of the confidence that the FSLN had publicly manifested in the Twelve; to maintain the confidence and backing of Nicaraguans the mediation had to achieve a rapid eradication of the dictatorship as a system. The FAO's objective was social democracy: "A solution to the political problem is necessary, to initiate the solution of all the other economic and social problems, which constitute the substratum of the injustice and, consequently, of the nonconformity and the protest." Thus La Prensa still backed the peaceful route, but it carried on its front-page two pictures of Nicaraguan guerrillas marching in "some place of Central America" with heavy military equipment—a warning that war might take place if the mediation failed.

That same day, the Comisión Internacional de Cooperación Amistosa y Esfuerzos Conciliatorios—the mediation's technical name so that there be no mistake about its limited mandate—presented to Somoza the FAO's position "as the beginning of a new stage in the negotiations that will permit a peaceful, permanent, and democratic solution to the current situation in which Nicaragua lives." Somoza told the mediators that he would answer in a few days, but he later called Admiral Jiménez to present the names of the three representatives of his party appointed by him to negotiate with the FAO.

The withdrawal of the Twelve increased the chance of working out a compromise. At this moment Somoza could have taken the initiative, dropping his politically uncreative, purely defensive strategy of gaining time, rather than using the mediation to strengthen the longer-run position of his group by shortening his tenure. Never had his regime faced such a challenge. But he was impervious. He publicly dismissed the situation: "When anybody has any other countries backing them, naturally there is always a possibility of violence. [But] the National Guard is well prepared to take care of anything." [51]

The Miami Herald, on the other hand, projected scenarios of war: rebel raids from Costa Rica, photographs of well-equipped guerrillas in "a jungle" with "heavy machine guns for use against the National Guard"; Red Cross volunteers starting to give lectures to the population on first aid; new recruits of the National Guard with their heads shaven and exercising for combat training; soldiers patrolling the cities in convoys of two or three jeeps and armored cars protecting cuarteles of provincial cities. [52] Although there was the opinion that large-scale armed operations would not be launched soon, we were uneasy. We tried to persuade a group of American religious activists, who were in Managua praying for peace, to leave the country for their safety. Participants of the mediation who lived in hotels moved to safer residences. [53]

We were involved in the international conspiracy. Immediately after the decision of the Twelve, our ambassador visited the Venezuelan president to ask him to influence the opposition so that there would be a chance to negotiate a settlement. Carlos Andrés agreed, and on October 27 I received Washington's request that I assist in obtaining exit visas for Alfonso Robelo and Jaime Chamorro Cardenal. [54] They would go to Caracas at the same time that "Comandante Zero" and Carlos Tunnerman. (Comandante Zero was a symbol of FSLN non-Marxist pluralism. He was appointed vice minister of defense and Jefe Nacional de las Milicias Populares. The Comandante defected in 1982 and fought again against the Sandinista government. Tunnerman, one of the Twelve, eventually became Nicaragua's Sandinista ambassador to the United States.) I spoke with the pertinent Nicaraguan official and was informed that the trip was cleared: Somoza knew that the two were going to talk to his "enemy." As I understood it, the Venezuelan president would meet with representatives of the FAO, of the Twelve, and the FSLN to persuade them to allow the mediation time to work out the formation of a new government. Bowdler was asking for two, preferably four, weeks to settle the problem. [55]

In Panama, General Torrijos was delivering a pro–Comandante Zero line to U.S. functionaries. American officials were invited to meet with both of them (around October 30), but instructions were given to the U.S. ambassador in Panama not to meet with any of the FSLN leaders.

While Costa Rica's president was formally projecting to our embassy an image of "discretion"—he was not in the same league as Pérez and Torrijos, not financing nor having direct contact with the FSLN leaders, and was dismissing the importance of the Sandinista presence in his country—Carazo still supported a change of regime with sufficient guarantees to Somoza and the opposition.

Of Nicaragua's other neighbors, only Honduras gave indications of international "neutrality," whereas the Guatemalan president and foreign minister felt that the U.S. policy was "unrealistic."

In effect, U.S. continental diplomatic resources were being spent with virtuosity but ineffectively because it was expected that diplomatic action would change the government. In fairness, the panel had felt a need to commit itself to opposition forces simply to get them to make a constitutional proposal beyond the United States ousting Somoza and giving total power to them. Bowdler informed me that on November 2 he would try to "bell the cat" and ask Somoza to resign. The Dominican mediator was also planning to see Somoza alone to suggest that he resign; the Guatemalan would wait for Somoza's reply before any decision was made. The Guatemalan government was inclined to a greater "evenhandedness," but Ambassador Obiols knew that Somoza had to go, and he acted accordingly. It was hoped that as a professional military man, Admiral Jiménez could influence Somoza.

Unfortunately, it was not clear yet the extent to which Washington would apply sanctions against Somoza. When I compared the more drastic measures sought by Bowdler with the information coming from Washington, the mediation's outcome looked very uncertain. I was soldiering on and to maintain morale did not share this appraisal with the embassy. Only the bilateral military assistance had been totally suspended and the IMF financing postponed, not eliminated.[56] It was absolutely clear that to avoid a U.S. diplomatic failure it was necessary to make Somoza know of the administration's commitment to seeing him leave office fairly soon and at least to realize that a serious boycott of his government would otherwise be implemented. As subsequently shown, Washington gave the opposite impression to Somoza.

The FAO Becomes More Moderate

On October 27 the FAO's second proposal, elaborated with the mediation's input and submitted to Somoza, was made public. It contained concessions to the Somocistas. First, it proposed a broad general amnesty that would cover the government's supporters and oppositionists. Second, although the National Guard would be restructured, the FAO recognized it as "the Armed Force of the Republic." The National Guard would participate in its own reorganization and the to-be-created National Police would be staffed principally by members of the Guard. Contrary to FSLN aspirations, no military role was given to it, in or out of the state. Third, the Liberal Party–dominated Congress would remain standing until the election of a National Constitutional Assembly in September 1980.

The proposal chose what it considered to be a "rapid constitutional" process to adopt reforms. This and other constitutional problems could have been legally resolved, however.[57] The document's "indispensable condition [was] the definitive retirement of General Anastasio Somoza Debayle of the Presidency of the Republic, the National Guard and any other public function; as well as the definitive separation from the National Guard of members of his family. And departure from the country of Somoza and his relatives with military posts, because their presence in Nicaragua constitutes a factor of permanent disturbance." How would the Somocistas negotiate and formally agree to the ostracism of their leader?

Although the Congress was to remain in operation, it would coexist with a Council of State and the Government Junta.[58] One could foresee serious difficulties between the opposition-dominated legislative Council and the Somocista Congress. The Council would consist of two representatives from each of the groups in the FAO (Novedades interpreted this to mean thirty-two oppositionists in the Council) and only two from the government camp.

Progress had been made in the direction of providing guarantees to the ruling group, however. Somoza was being offered the continuity of the National Guard and Liberal Party. Somoza appointed Foreign Minister Julio Quintana, Alceo Tablada Solís, and Orlando Montenegro Medrano as his representatives to the mediation. On October 27 they met with the OAS panel. Although Quintana had expressed an interest in the notion of a constitutional assembly, there was no progress at all in the conversation. The government's message did not change. Moreover, the Somocistas told the mediators that there was "no problem." The crisis was externally created, and they did not see any great dissatisfaction with Somoza nor a need for an urgent solution. Their assertions were incredible.

Novedades was especially vitriolic: the army had already won the battle against the Communist mob attack; the opposition consisted of "minigroups" seeking power "without recourse to voting," and the government was the elected majority; the alleged purpose of the FAO was to destroy the National Guard and the Liberal Party.[59] Somoza's inner circle pretended that the "friendly" mediation would be used to devise constitutional changes for 1981, which would be ritualistically adopted by a rubber stamp Congress in which practically all the opposition was not seated.

The yearning for political change with peace continued to have fairly wide support, however. Not only Conservatives but also Nicaraguan Communists represented by Luis Sánchez Sancho, of the Partido Socialista Nicaragüense, remained in the FAO. The party deplored "the inconsistency and lack of confidence in the democratic route and popular will, of those who have decided to abandon the FAO that nevertheless remains unyielding in the struggle for an authentically democratic solution—without more spillings of blood."[60] The Socialists called for opposition unity behind the mediation. After all, Western European Communists were following the path of alliances and elections.

But there was a sense of urgency. Our CIA chief of station reported that if the mediation did not deliver a solution soon, the Group of Twelve would be vindicated, and the more moderate elements would be weakened. Jaime Chamorro Cardenal summarized well the national sentiment: "If we see that [peacefully] it is impossible to obtain [the democratization], we will accompany the Twelve [ending the mediation]; if we obtain [the peaceful democratization], we hope that the Twelve will accompany us in the task of transforming this country."[61]

November started with a session between the OAS panel and Somoza's three representatives, who said that they would study the FAO's proposal and respond by November 6. That day the official answer was delivered. The proposal was completely rejected on the usual grounds. These days Somoza was publicly quite vitriolic against the United States. The rumor spread and was published that I had left in protest for Washington after his speech in which he threatened that he would fight the United States. Doña Hope, Somoza's wife, called me. She was traveling to the United States and was extremely worried that a confrontation was going to occur, judging from "Tacho's" anti-American speech.

But the government introduced the notion of a referendum later used by the mediation: a "well-supervised" national plebiscite for each of the opposition groups could take place; those groups that obtained "significant popular support" from the voters would then acquire the standing to "participate at the high level in the decisions of the [government] until the 1981 elections," a reiteration that the opposition had no important number of votes and should accept Somoza's rule. [62]

The Liberal response was accompanied by two long studies, one on Nicaraguan history, the other on the unconstitutionality of the FAO's proposal. The latter document also reflected the thinness of well-trained intellects in legal and political matters remaining in government circles. The scholastic component of a legal tradition prone to prove and refute issues based on nomenclature and definitions was apparent. [63] But the legal analysis was not only "metaphysical" or a prioristic, but also crude; I had never seen such primitive legal analysis. In large portions of the document the FAO's proposed articles were simply contrasted to the existing constitutional ones, inferring their "unconstitutionality" purely on the basis of these differences. Several reforms were also rejected for being "unnecessary" simply because the institutions existed regardless of specifics or praxis. How could one expect to make sense with individuals who presented such rebuttals?

Although not yet creating a fatal problem, the inability of the mediation to obtain Somoza's resignation continued to erode the FAO—a few other small groups announced their withdrawal. Unfortunately, however, such defections reinforced Somoza's intransigence in the hope of seeing the FAO disintegrate.

As practically all my contacts told us, after Chamorro's murder the only "rational" or civilized course was for Somoza to step down soon and for a new government formed. Yet some political issues remained. Even if Somoza vanished, what would be the behavior of the Liberal-controlled Congress and of the National Guard? This and other issues were raised by a group of very competent young independent Nicaraguans, one of them a very prominent key official of the future Sandinista regime. [64] They sent us a working paper dated November 6.

In sharp contrast to the Nicaraguan government, our friends believed that if the "fragile truce" being kept by the mediation terminated, there would be a catastrophic breakdown. "Previously friendly" regional governments had decided to provide material assistance to oust Somoza. Moreover, the mobilization of resources by the government to contain the opposition and impose order—given the size of opposition already developed—would have a "devastating impact" on the society. In short, already the government could not impose a half-civilized, unilateral order. In contrast to the FAO, the drafters also discarded the notion of the facility and terminal nature of a clean uprising, as well as the expectation that the U.S. government would readily constitute a new government.

The document dealt with the operational problems of both establishing a new regime and maintaining it. Given the pressing circumstances and the democratic objective, a provisional government would be formed, with the principal purpose of holding free elections as soon as possible. Only those institutions that impeded the rule of law or were undemocratic would be modified and repealed at this initial transitional phase. Only partial constitutional reforms would be enacted initially.

First, there was the need to obtain for the new government as broad support as possible, including of the National Guard and the Liberals. The FAO's proposed representation of only two Liberal members in the transitional regime simply could not be acceptable to the government camp. The National Guard required guarantees for the officer corps.

Second, the government had to be "viable." Adequate popular support required Somoza's resignation from office and the family's "return" to private life. The phrase "family exile" was not used—it was too explosive.

Also, the revolutionary foreign axis would have to end. Under OAS auspices the new government would be supported by and receive assistance from the United States, the axis, and the Central American Common Market to control the recurrence of violence.

Under "viability," the form and composition of the provisional government were discussed. The new formula: (1) the executive, a president, and his cabinet; (2) the Council of State with legislative functions. The president would be appointed by mutual agreement between the government and the FAO. The council's composition was dramatically altered: one-third would be representatives of the Liberal Party, one-third from the FAO, and the other third selected by mutual agreement from a broad list of citizens of recognized independence and honesty from various sectors of the nation. Thus a government of "national unity" was proposed to enhance its acceptability. [65]

The provisional government had to be "stable." It had to be absolutely clear that the regime would be transitory and would be replaced by a freely elected government; democrats would then be willing to accept this brief interim rulership to subsequently obtain their proportional share of power as determined by the people. It was hoped that the Sandinistas would incorporate themselves in the civic political process, fully participating in the elections.

The presidential form was considered more stable than a junta. The arrangements to constitute the government would take place at a single occasion upon congressional acceptance of the president's resignation. (History later proved the destabilizing potential of the dual transfer of power carried out in 1979. Parliamentarians were dissatisfied about the notion of leaving office; it was therefore unwise to submit the mediation's pact to possible subsequent veto or change.)

Finally, there had to be a sense of trust that the new government would implement the agreement, the mutual guarantees. The document lamented that guarantees of the nature of financial contracts could not be provided. However, the endorsement of the international mediation, an immediate program of foreign assistance, and periodic inspection tours of the OAS Human Rights Commission could provide reliability to the agreement.

In sum, there were two possible constitutional transfer dates: January 1979 or, following a more restrictive interpretation, April or May 1979 (at about the time that the final successful uprising was initiated). Indeed, Nicaragua counted with many capable individuals.

The U.S. initiative with the Venezuelan president following the Group of Twelve's withdrawal from the mediation had culminated in meetings in Caracas. Reportedly, Carlos Andrés Pérez also had called in core FSLN revolutionary leaders. Pérez's message: the mediation had to be given a chance. A deadline of November 20 was proposed for Somoza to resign or establish a date to resign—if not, violence would be resumed.

Actually, although the violence had subsided and a semblance of more civility had emerged, Nicaragua was not pacified.[66] Alfonso Robelo reported numbers of hard-core Sandinistas: 600 in Costa Rica, 300 in Honduras, between 300 and 400 in Nicaragua. These numbers were small, but the National Guard was also small, and there was already a populace "trained" in urban uprisings in the poor barrios and beyond. Nonetheless, in Managua we were not receiving intelligence on estimates of FSLN strength in the bordering countries.

Carlos Andrés Pérez was encouraged by the negative findings of the visit of the OAS Inter-American Human Rights Commission. He still did not think that

Somoza would depart without the use of force. He also wished to impose economic and military sanctions (including a boycott of oil and arms exports) and was advocating the formation of an inter-American military force to change the Nicaraguan government. His priority was to get Somoza out—now or never—preferably without a revolution taking place. But if the mediation failed, he would back the armed route. On the other hand, from Guatemala we heard that the foreign minister had raised with U.S. officials the idea of some military intervention to prevent the outburst of all-out war.

Somoza, on the other hand, remained hopeful of regional support. On November 4 he went to Guatemala. Perhaps the Guatemalan mediator would not go along with asking him to resign, thus breaking up the mediation? It had been agreed that the three mediators would meet with Somoza to explore his resignation. With great expectations on my part this took place at noon on November 7. The president cleverly did not receive them alone—Foreign Minister Quintana was with him. The plan was to tell Somoza that the Nicaraguan people wished him to leave office and that the mediators awaited his reply by the following day to proceed with the negotiations.

Some dramatic moments were reported: the voice of one of the mediators faltered as he represented the general wish of Nicaraguans, and that Somoza referred to "all those cadavers on my conscience." Bowdler told the president that the team would be willing to wait for a reply more than twenty-four hours. As I recall, it was a polite meeting. The presence of Quintana reduced the tension, for he was very supportive of the president: the Congress (i.e., the Liberals) would not accept Somoza's resignation, he said.

The plan was for Bowdler to meet with Somoza the next day as a follow-up, using these points: the United States believed that the package solution offered by the FAO plan provided the basic elements for reconciliation and peace; Somoza should accept the fundamental elements of that proposal and negotiate the subsequent details with the FAO. Some Nicaraguans and I could not see how Somoza would agree with the offer and leave power for exile, with only token representation of the Liberal Party in the new government. Thus I gave a one-paragraph memo to Bowdler suggesting that he not discard the option of telling Somoza, if necessary, that the mediation would like to have his approval to proceed with the negotiations, on the assumption that he would relinquish power prior to 1981 (the sooner the better). It was necessary to get a pre-1981 commitment from Somoza; in its absence the mediation was a waste of time. Bowdler seemed to me to have become too committed to and caught by the FAO's position. Though he needed to keep opposition support, the first priority was the Somoza term, not pleasing the dreams of total control of the FAO's majority.

On November 9 the president of the United States gave a press conference in Kansas City. He had this to say:

Question: *Concerning Nicaragua is the U.S. going to act to prevent further blood-shed and repression or do you feel that your hands are tied because you don't want to interfere in the internal affairs of another country. What can you say?*

Answer: *We are participating actively and daily in the negotiations to bring about a settlement in Nicaragua. I get daily reports from Mr. Bowdler. We are working in harmony with two other Latin American countries in this effort. . . . [I]n the last few weeks since these negotiations began, the bloodshed has certainly been drastically reduced. It is one of the most difficult tasks that we have undertaken. We proposed others to be the negotiators at first. All sides [however] wanted the U.S. to be negotiators. So we are negotiating actively now to reach an agreement to control bloodshed, to minimize disputes, and to set up a government there that will have the full support of the people.*[67]

You can observe the theme of the human rights policy, of moral international leadership, without really "intervening." Ideally, others should be more involved than the United States in sorting out problems.

On November 10 General Somoza, who traditionally saw U.S. envoys immediately, finally received Bowdler. The report that I saw mentioned a vacillating Somoza when faced with the statement that for the good of his people he should resign. On the one hand obstinate Somoza still maintained that the Liberal Party was the majority, that the opposition was disorganized and weak, that the United States was giving moral encouragement to the opposition; and he did not like the proposed transitional government. Somoza mentioned that I had already told him about a pre-1981 exit, thus he had been expecting Bowdler's representation. On the other hand Somoza talked about his 1977 illness and said that his resignation was an issue that he faced everyday. But, he stated, he did not resign because of his obligations.[68]

Plebiscite

Although it had serious problems of its own, the idea of a plebiscite appealed to me, not in its Somocista form, but as a mechanism to test whether the people wished Somoza to leave or remain until 1981. Its advantage was that one had been proposed by the government, so they could not argue that it was unconstitutional in principle. It could give Somoza an opportunity to leave power with dignity on democratic grounds. However, Bowdler rejected the idea because he felt the FAO would never accept it.

I had breakfast with Bowdler and his two American aides. The ambassador asked for their opinion on the plebiscite. They objected to it: Somoza might "win" it because of his machine's dominance; it would not serve to renovate the Liberal Party away from the corrupt machine; it would not be legally binding. I replied, "The problem is that without a threat of American force, we can't dismantle the regime. How are we going to persuade these people? If Somoza is a democrat he can accept defeat with dignity. The problem is to construct a mechanism for change. So far neither Somoza, the Guardia Nacional, nor the Liberal Party have been persuaded to accept the FAO formula sponsored by you. Referendums can work and be binding to the parties. Corrupt electoral machines can be and have been defeated with appropriate controls."

On November 11 we got formal instructions from the assistant secretary in the light of the visit to Managua planned by the Congressmen John Murphy and Charlie Wilson, Somoza's friends. We were to tell them that U.S. opposition to the IMF loan had been decided only on technical grounds, and that the current USAID pipeline had not been suspended; only two new loans (approved at the request of Wilson against embassy position) were not being implemented, also on technical grounds.

There was nervousness in Washington. On November 13 the local USAID director and I were cabling, "explaining" the delays in disbursement; these were only in three loans, but it was not "inordinate" because the hold-ups were due to lack of Nicaraguan procedural compliance, we wrote, following instructions.

Clearly Washington's message to Somoza now was very far from the ultimatum scenario that everybody in the field thought necessary to succeed. A reversal of any psychological pressure on the dictator was taking place. Washington had returned to its equivocations, lying about the policy orchestrated on behalf of the mediation's success. The administration had caved in, mortally wounding the already sick mediation, suggesting that assistance would continue as normal. Somoza was right: his enemies were some lower-level officials, and he could win appeals through his friends.

When the congressmen came to my office, I was most uncomfortable because of the instructions. I felt I had to deal in generalities with them. They mentioned that Somoza would not resign, that he felt he had majority support, and hence there was a need for a referendum before the president would step down. What a lost opportunity to reply, "Yes, this is what should really be done," to test if he truly does have majority support, among other rebuttals that occurred to me. The two subsequently held a press conference, although Warren Christopher tried to persuade them not to. Their public message to Somoza was that he could do as he pleased and need not fear the United States.

At the same time, we received information in Managua that the Guatemalan foreign minister had expressed his concern to the U.S. secretary of state that the mediation was being used to oust an "elected" president; apparently the Guatemala government was responding to the earlier mentioned Somoza initiative to influence it. Recent Guatemalan governments were being spuriously elected. Would Guatemala pull out of the mediation? Could Somoza bribe key Guatemalans?

If this was not enough bad news, intelligence reported that Nicaragua was obtaining Argentine and Israeli arms. On November 10 our military attaché informed me that he had seen substantial new armament, which might confirm the purchases.

On November 11 *Novedades* carried news of Somoza's press conference. Of interest were the headlines: "Somoza Submits His Permanence to a National Plebiscite: That the People Decide Who It Wishes." But this was not his purpose. Later, the editor explained to me that Somoza was very upset with this headline. Luis Pallais was indicating that he had done this on his own to influence Somoza to compromise.

The FAO's response was immediate: reiteration of the deadline for the mediation to obtain the resignation and exile of the ruler. The *New York Times* reported that "both the Government and the opposition seem increasingly resigned to a violent solution," and that the Sandinistas "may have as many as 2,000 men under arms."[69]

Once more the dictator was toying with the world. The *Washington Post* discussed the policy: the United States would not intervene in the situation nor press for a plebiscite not agreed to by the parties; only (minor) diplomatic measures would be taken if Somoza did not cooperate with the mediation; there was a strong probability that the mediation will fail, with the likely result of war.[70] One obstacle was the Carter administration's unwillingness to deploy troops and employ covert action to unseat Somoza; a second obstacle was that no real diplomatic pressure could be used. I could not understand—what a bizarre, extreme, doctrinaire philosophy of "non-intervention."

While the American mediator was in the United States, we wished to start preparing the ground in case a plebiscite became the only and last option. On November 14 we cabled the assistant secretary for Latin America and the U.S. mediator to keep them posted on our conversations. I invited one of Bowdler's aides to join the meetings because he continued to oppose any referendum; he still did not realize that Somoza was not going to resign when asked again.

Our first talks were with Ernesto Cruz, Mariano Fiallos, and Eduardo Montealegre Callejas. I opened them stating that Somoza's departure had to be considered in terms of his being forced from office by external or internal force or "voluntary departure" accepted by him to avoid incurring higher costs;

and that without credible force his resignation was not forthcoming. The only option left, consequently, was the "honorable" exit.

Our visitors expressed this common opinion: two months previously Somoza had been publicly insisting that any plebiscite was unconstitutional, whereas now his position is that it is legal. It might be easier for him to leave as a "democrat," after the people have decided in a vote, and thus he says, "as always, I abide by the popular will, so I leave power." Any "reasonable" leader would accept such a solution, we speculated. Indeed, this could be an elegant exit. He was being given the last chance to save his ship.

The "National Consultation" would have to be simply worded: "Do you support the Liberal Party position (mark the Liberal red box) that President Somoza should govern until 1981 or the FAO position (mark the blue box) that he should resign now?" The problem was to convince the two parties. My guests concurred that there would be problems obtaining FAO compliance for several reasons: (1) the belief that the mediation, if pressured, could not fail in getting Somoza to step down; (2) the feeling that Somoza's delaying tactics were eroding their credibility and popular support for not being sufficiently anti-Somoza; (3) the belief that if the mediation failed, direct U.S. intervention would take place to avoid a (Marxist radical) Sandinista victory serving them Somoza's "head on a platter"; (4) the opposition's hesitation to test its popular support against the money and corrupt "machine politics" of Somoza. Note that in spite of the public indications that Washington was not going to intervene, the unarmed opposition continued playing the game of forcing an American intervention. All my visitors believed that Somoza would surely lose a properly formulated and supervised national consultation.

On November 15 three Conservative members of the Congress visited us: Julio Molina, Carlos Solórzano, and Arnulfo Rivas. We discussed the mechanics of a plebiscite (which had been first proposed by Molina). The legislators were so confident that Somoza would be overwhelmingly defeated that one of them said that they could give him a 60 percent margin. The possibility of congressional action to oust Somoza was raised. Again we were told of the availability of some Somocistas to defect: fifteen Liberals had privately "guaranteed" their votes to declare Somoza "incompetent." They asked if the mediators had contemplated such action as a contingency, and whether we could give guarantees to the dissenters.

I could not speak for the mediation, so I asked what type of guarantees they wanted. Physical protection from the National Guard, one of them replied. There would also be a need for the United States and the OAS to recognize immediately the government appointed by the Congress to replace Somoza, and provide it with assistance.

An authentic referendum faced difficulties other than Somoza's undemocratic mindset. Emilio Alvarez Montalván said, "The problem is that especially the rural people do not have the experience nor preparation for true democratic voting—they have never participated in true elections. Somoza has a good chance to manipulate a victory and this would not solve the problem."

We were working to give Somoza an honorable option, but this worried the opposition. Some feared that he could always rally a sufficient number of people to win an election, given the nation's undemocratic traditions and the government's disproportionate resources. This was a broadly shared "secret fear" on the part of many democrats wishing a peaceful solution. Was Somoza's proposal a propaganda ploy in the conviction that the FAO would refuse to accept an electoral test, given the actual lack of faith in it within its ranks?

Alvarez prepared a working paper that raised the problem that the referendum could further divide the opposition. Paramount was the need to obtain FSLN "neutrality" so that it would not violently boycott it. Alvarez also mentioned the psychological costs to the opposition: the plebiscite would require an at least implicit "understanding" with Somoza. But the plebiscite could serve as an opportunity to mobilize the FAO and better organize itself, thus increasing its capability to govern the country. It will be difficult, the document concluded, to get Somoza to accept an electoral consultation controlled by a foreign force. The Somozas had *never* accepted internationally supervised elections.

That the mediation itself was a bluff became perfectly clear in a *Miami Herald* article. The front-page story was that the administration had refused to seek an embargo of Israeli arms to Nicaragua. The administration "would not be unhappy to see Somoza removed from office," the article said, but it would not apply pressure on him. [71]

At this time the Nicaraguan government launched a continental lobbying effort, sending an emissary throughout the Americas to seek support for its plebiscite, even though it was not truly willing to submit itself to one.

Other formidable obstacles were found with the Nicaraguan opposition. The FAO thought a plebiscite would take too long, even if it was not rigged. "The American mediator urged opposition groups to [draw a plan] for the upcoming transition [government], [while] say[ing] they'll negotiate the resignation question directly with Somoza. The Americans keep saying they have plans, but they won't tell us what they are. They've nevertheless committed themselves to getting rid of Somoza. The U.S. can hardly call itself a superpower if it fails against a tiny Central American dictator." [72]

La Prensa was critical as well.[73] "The simple fact that [Somoza] proposed [a plebiscite] is sufficient to discard it, for Somoza knows [the resources] that he has to win [it], terror." It went on: "To arrive at having [a real popular consultation] we need in Nicaragua much schooling and many years with honest exercise of the suffrage."

This was an instinctive reaction of many in a "democratic" opposition, which did not have any electoral organization and little recent experience in these matters, and which felt that nothing but the total defeat of the quasi-devil "monster" was satisfactory. Poor uneducated masses can, however, throw governments out via elections.[74]

U.S. efforts to rally support in the OAS for the plebiscite also faced difficulties, a point worth raising because the organization took an anti-Somoza position a few months later at the denouement. According to our cable traffic, a significant number of the Latin American foreign ministries were not very interested in the issue; at this time the majority had not adopted a position against the Nicaraguan government. The overrepresentation of dictatorships with serious human rights problems of their own and stressful relations with Washington resulted in a lukewarm reception in the OAS of the Inter-American Commission on Human Rights report against Somoza.

The Venezuelan president had a negative attitude and was doubtful that the FAO or the FSLN would accept the plebiscite. Panamanian strongman Omar Torrijos vocalized his anti-Somoza position: he was personally afraid of Somoza, whom he called a "madman with ties to the mafia"; he considered that the Nicaraguan National Guard was too weak to withstand a popular insurrection, and he was skeptical about the plebiscite. Somoza's exit by January was too late, he thought.

In contrast, the Costa Rican president was positive—a plebiscite might break the impasse. He maintained the nationalist position: Costa Rica would defend its sovereignty (now that Costa Ricans had been trained in anti-aircraft defense, they would start shooting Nicaraguan planes that violated the airspace, he said). Carazo continued, however, to misrepresent to American diplomats the FSLN presence in his country as only about fifty well-armed men. Certainly there were many more than that. A member of the cabinet estimated that there were about six hundred Sandinistas in the country. He reported that the traditional national distaste for the Somozas had resulted in considerable popular support for the insurrection: "If we put Comandante Zero under custody for any length of time we'll have massive demonstrations here against the government," the official reportedly told our embassy.

Indicative of Castroist influence in a future Sandinista regime, on November 17 it was reported that Fidel Castro was making a "determined effort" to obtain the unity of the three FSLN factions under his "experienced revolutionary tutelage." The U.S. government wished to obtain Havana's cooperation for its Nicaraguan policy.

Upon their return, the mediators immediately went to work with the FAO skillfully seeking those conditions they thought necessary for a viable referendum. As the FAO still refused to negotiate with the Liberals, the mediators had to obtain the FAO's position first and then go to Somoza to iron out differences. Obviously the minimum basis for an understanding would have to be that Somoza would resign if he lost the vote, and his party and the FAO would need to negotiate a transitional government for that eventuality.

But the FAO showed reservations, demanding that the Somoza family be out of the country during the plebiscite. Obviously, any other formula than Somoza's resignation ran counter to popular sentiment. Yet it just did not make much sense for Somoza to accept being exiled prior to and during the consultation. FAO leaders also feared that if they accepted a popular consultation, the FSLN might physically target them—hence their demand that Venezuela, Panama, and Costa Rica support the referendum and restrain the Sandinistas.

The Mediation's Proposal

As if meeting the FAO's deadline, precisely on November 21 the OAS panel made public its proposal to government and opposition. The Comisión, acting according to its mandate, without breaking the principle of non-intervention, was suggesting a formula for conciliation to avoid irreparable damage to country and region.

Given that the basic difference consisted of who would preside over the Government of National Unity that Nicaragua needed before the next scheduled elections, the commission proposed that the parties consider and accept the plebiscite they were proposing. In an act of self-determination, the Nicaraguan people would decide whether the National Unity government would be headed by Somoza or not.

In order to obtain a free impartial consultation, a very large international presence was proposed to administer the plebiscite, as well as a very drastic limitation of National Guard activities and those of the key local functionaries, the *jueces de mesta* and *capitanes de cañada*. Case studies indicated that an incumbent could be defeated without such extensive international controls and safeguards, but the proposal was oriented in the right direction: organizing an authentic test of popular sovereignty and preference.

The point that if Somoza lost he had to leave Nicaragua with his family was included in response to the FAO demand that prior to any consultation this take place. Opposition understanding of national popular sentiment was being reflected in the inclusion of undiplomatic, psychologically and symbolically costly items technically unnecessary to form a new government. The text, however, did not mention "exile" nor the length of absence from Nicaragua for the strongman. (Some Latin American dictators have returned to power after temporary exile, Somoza knew. In a messianic mood, he had told me more than once that he would be called back and could return like Perón if he resigned.)

In the following days the mediators intensified their contacts.[75] The situation in Costa Rica had taken a serious turn for the worse; after a border incident that nation broke relations with Nicaragua and made statements to allow Sandinista guerillas use of its territory. Time was running out.

On November 22 we met with La Prensa. Our visitors were on the defensive. A referendum was an unpopular idea. The OAS human rights report had clearly stated the nature of the regime; why compromise with Somoza rather than have him resign as was morally and politically sound? It was so difficult to obtain support within the FAO.[76] I recall Danilo Aguirre saying that just as the people informed the Inter-American Human Rights Commission against the government, they would vote against Somoza, but to provide a spirit of fairness and impartiality Somoza would have to be away when voting took place. It would be a tragedy, I said, if the FAO did not "return the ball" to Somoza to maintain the pressure on him and keep open the possibility of a peaceful settlement. My own view was that the FAO could not lose in accepting a well-supervised referendum, for under the worst scenario that Somoza rejected it, this would seal his downfall. We were, in fact, acting perhaps now even more as "advisers" to the opposition.

That same day we spoke with Rafael Córdova Rivas, one of the original members of the FAO troika. He said that the mediation had no prestige because it had only obtained the lifting of press censorship. I replied that the mediation arrived after the opposition had been militarily defeated and there was great repression and fear of more—it also obtained the end of the curfew and of the national radio propaganda chain, and although there was repression, in my opinion, it was not as bad as it could be.

Córdova went on. "In order to return to the mediation the FAO needs to be given a 'pearl,' such as lifting the state of siege and decreeing an amnesty. Then the Archbishop could ask the FAO to resume the talks. We feel defrauded; in Caracas [with the Venezuelan president] we reached an understanding that a deadline would be established to the mediation." The problem was that if they accepted the referendum, Robelo's MDN and the Partido Liberal Independiente (PLI) would leave the FAO; the plebiscite was so unpopular that (Marxist leader) Luis Sánchez Sancho had been purged as an adviser because of his acceptance of it in principle. Córdova Rivas said the ideal would be to accept the referendum, but with Somoza being absent from the country for sixty days. This Bowdler conceded, in part: two weeks before and one week after the vote. I was not impressed with the mediator's verbal offer. I felt that it should be easier for Somoza to abdicate in the face of an unfavorable referendum than to simply resign because he was asked to do so by his adversaries, but I could not imagine that he would agree to leave the country prior to a popular consultation. This symbolized his defeat prior to the vote.

Why had the mediator made what appeared to be a commitment to a ridiculous demand? Under an egoistic assumption that it was easier to explain in Washington that the mediation had failed because of Somoza's intransigence than the opposition's fear of him. The altruistic assumption was that it was better not to further divide the FAO by imposing unpopular conditions, especially if (what seemed likely) Somoza would accept nothing but his 1981 package.

Córdova insisted that the three Somozas had to be out of the country during the election. "This country is 'magical'; if the 'sorcerer' is in the country people feel that they will be defeated—that is why caudillo Emiliano Chamorro had to leave Nicaragua to have the 1928 free election, stated Emilio Alvarez Montalván, who accompanied Córdova. [77]

The government really *did not wish* to negotiate. The president, I was told by a Somocista, continued to hold cabinet meetings. He had just referred to the beginning of a new phase of mediation and said that many would die. He, the party, and the army would not give up power. A member of the cabinet, loyal to Somoza but an informant of the CIA as well, summarized the situation: "Somoza says that 2,000 more people will die but that the government will survive." Revealing was the conversation in Washington between Congressman John Murphy and one of the undersecretaries of state. Murphy thought Somoza could not turn over the country to a fragmented and incapable FAO. Somoza had support—he had just gotten three thousand voluntary enlistments in the National Guard, whereas the Sandinistas did not have the base for a successful insurgency. Somoza would not agree to a "Somoza yes or no" vote. This was the only meaningful issue for a referendum.

Unacceptability of the Mediation's Proposal

Seventy-two hours after the proposal's delivery, both the government and the FAO rejected it. The government was stuck with its fallacious legal ideas—it was formalistically dismissed because it was not contemplated in the Constitution, although neither was the Somoza plebiscite plan (which was typical of the old-fashioned *caudillo* patterns of *imposición* and *continuismo*). [78]

In contrast, the FAO was not as negative, but it found difficulties with the mediators' proposal: "The plan presented by you eludes the fact that the permanence in the country of [General Somoza] and his relatives holding military posts impedes any national democratization process." Still this relatively more moderate opposition accused the government and petitioned the OAS to "judge and condemn the President of Nicaragua . . . and others [in the government] responsible of the violations of human rights and the crime of genocide." The opposition was still after a humanitarian intervention. La Prensa referred to the desire of public opinion that the United States request an Inter-American Peace Force to oust Somoza and avoid the pending bloodbath.[79] Reports from U.S. embassies, however, indicated that indifference toward the Nicaraguan issue prevailed among most OAS governments.

Guatemalan representative Alfredo Obiols was particularly critical. He had been approached to defect in favor of Somoza's plebiscite, but he realized his responsibility. The dictator would have provided him with a handsome financial compensation for such action, I thought. Bowdler, on the other hand, reassured me that Washington continued committed to a popular consultation, that if the FAO endorsed the plebiscite he would be authorized to present a démarche to Somoza to the effect that unless he agreed to it, U.S.-Nicaragua relations would be "very strongly affected." Actually the FAO was tactically divided. The reply to the "Plan Washington," as the plebiscite was already locally known, had been a difficult decision, Adolfo Calero informed me. Alfonso Robelo and Virgilio Godoy threatened to leave the FAO if an absolute rejection was not approved.[80]

Public support for the democratic consultation was not forthcoming, and the mediators were contemplating giving a forty-eight-hour ultimatum to the parties. If their plan was not accepted, they would end their mission.[81] Thus I asked Danilo Aguirre to come to the embassy to talk to the mediators "to build up their morale." On November 25 my wife, Joan, talked to Sonia Chamorro, the wife of La Prensa's director, who told her that La Prensa would accept a plebiscite with conditions.

On November 27 the mediators reiterated the same "proposal of conciliation." Noting that both the Liberals and the FAO had not closed the route to peacefully settle the crisis, the panel asked them to reconsider their positions, while warning of the costs if a compromise was not accepted.

The frankness of the statement is noteworthy: (1) their proposal was not unconstitutional—Article 187 allowed for the voluntary resignation of the president; (2) Somoza had stated that if the law did not prohibit something, it was not illegal, and the plebiscite was not prohibited by the constitution or the law; (3) *Novedades* had interpreted the government's plebiscite as a test of Somoza's permanence in office; (4) the current problem was fundamentally political, not juridical, thus a political innovation had to be adopted; (5) a *Consulta Popular* was an excellent democratic and honorable method, so that the Nicaraguan people themselves freely decide on the fundamental question of Somoza's permanence in office.

But the unfortunate limitations of the mediation were recognized: "The Comisión considers necessary to repeat that because of the policy of its governments, its [OAS] mandate, and the personal convictions of its members, it does not have the capacity to impose solutions, rather only to propose the viable alternative to obtain the earnestly desired peaceful and democratic solution to the Nicaraguan crisis."

The mediators gave the parties seventy-two hours; if a positive response was not forthcoming, they would terminate activities and leave the country. Bowdler's hope of obtaining the resignation so emphatically expressed at the beginning had not succeeded. The bluff had not worked.

The Foreign Minister Understood

On November 27 Bowdler and I met with Julio Quintana; at his request a lunch was organized for the three of us at the residence of the CIA chief of station.

Quintana employed the old arguments: the unconstitutionality of the mediation's proposal; if Somoza left, the Sandinista threat would increase (i.e., the perennial historical excuse that a member of the Somoza family was the only one who could maintain the National Guard functioning while never trying to solve the problem); Nicaragua could be ruled only by a "firm hand" (i.e., the "*caudillo* theory" of government); the mediation was sponsoring the FAO's interest and threatening Liberal Party and Guardia Nacional interests.

Bowdler went to the point: "The problem can't be solved until Somoza goes." As long as he was in control, the army could not evolve, nor could democratic opposition mature. He had not allowed it, and now it was just too late.

I pointed out that during my tenure the FSLN had dramatically increased its strength because of the general anti-Somoza sentiment in the country; post-1958 Venezuela shows that a country without a democratic tradition can break with the pattern of dictatorship.

Quintana replied that it was up to the United States and Bowdler to convince Somoza of the need for a negotiated solution; after all, Somoza would want to live in the United States, he said, adding that personally he was very concerned that our government might pull out, leaving Nicaragua to be attacked by forces aided by foreign countries. He felt the only course open to Nicaragua was to compromise or risk isolation and a multilateral attack; this would be madness and would not provide a viable solution.

Some members of Somoza's entourage understood the scenario that faced them. But as in any classic tragedy, they instead kept telling "The Boss" that he had to stay, building up his own perception of irreplaceability.

I interjected: the men surrounding the president should not keep spoiling him—loyalty cannot be misguided—all the pacts and previous changes in the constitution were to maintain Somoza's control over the National Guard and the country; this cannot go on.

Bowdler insisted that it was up to Somoza to negotiate a solution; the FAO's plan was merely a starting point; Somoza would remain in office until a settlement had been negotiated and its implementation begun, Somoza being a key actor in the solution. Quintana said that he was encouraged by Somoza's "flexible" attitude earlier that morning and urged Bowdler to have a "man-to-man" informal talk with Somoza.

The next day I found out the nature of Somoza's new "flexibility." A Liberal senator came to my office to inform me about developments: Somoza had spoken twice with his staff on the previous day and had said that if the plebiscite took place they would all be lost (i.e., they could not win it, and a FAO government would be constituted); he had said that there were two better options—a constitutional assembly or (even) his resignation. Notice that Somoza would not accept the only advantage that a referendum could provide him: his "democratic exit" once the people decided. He just could not act democratically. (Unfortunately, FAO rhetoric reinforced his authoritarian mindset and fear of an opposition victory).

Somoza was seeking a mechanism so that his people would remain controlling the state, and he would remain on top of them. The constituent-assembly formula fits a Latin American pattern: the caudillo had such power over his followers that he could continue ordering them around even if he did not hold office.

The Mixed Political Culture and Intervention

There were level-headed democrats within the unarmed opposition who still realized that their cause and democracy's would only be strengthened with a peaceful resolution. But their actions were affected by the presence of undemocratic forces in their environment. The FAO had to contend with Somocista support for strongman rule. Would they be loyal to a democratic regime? The factions to gain the most politically with the violent route were the armed ones known for their authoritarian flirtations. Would the FSLN use violence to stop a referendum? Given their extant support, they could seriously hinder conducting a successful plebiscite that would defeat Somoza. (This did not mean that the nation's majority already favored the violent route—Somoza's state was still far better "organized" at this time than the opposition, though the ruler himself privately recognized that he would lose the proposed consultation.) And there were the reservations among democrats whether an inexperienced, uneducated populace would be able to make the "reasonable" choice in a consultation.

Slowly La Prensa turned more favorable. Its November 28 headlines read, "Mediation's Document Was Well Received: FAO Studying It." The mediators' statements that neither the plebiscite nor Somoza's resignation were unconstitutional were built up, as well as Somoza's contradictory position toward the referendum. But the editorial indicated the unarmed opposition's insecurities. La Prensa's rejection of violence did not mean a condemnation of those who were pursuing such route, for Somoza had forced them into it. Indeed, the paper had to be very careful not to deflate the opposition's momentum, fearing that Somoza would again regain strength with a loss of credibility of the opposition's viability. It thus faced the difficult task of rallying public opinion for the mediation while maintaining the "Somoza Beelzebub" imagery. "A plebiscite could only be carried out in a society with an acceptable cultural level that is not the case of Nicaragua. The truth is that here it is not a plebiscite that is needed, because the problem is not only Somoza, but rather of a structure which could very well continue operating without him."[82] Nonetheless, the acceptability of a referendum by the FAO was gaining support. Alfonso Robelo reported that the president of Venezuela had told the opposition that they should accept it. The two large-scale non-Somoza financial groups, Banco de América and Banco Nicaragüense, would finance the FAO's campaign. Pressure remained on the FAO, however, to pull out of the mediation. Sentiment within the Group of Twelve was also violently anti-American.

Obviously the United States had played a role in the pseudo-democracies of Nicaragua, but the case of democratic Costa Rica placed in relief the importance of local factors. Nor could the United States be blamed for the nature of the authoritarian rule under the coming Sandinista dictatorship. Nevertheless, for the nation's majority—given democratic deficiencies—the regime had to be changed through U.S. actions. As we saw, lack of democratic consensus can promote clientelistic dependency. Evidently the notion so prevalent in Washington that anti-American feelings could be explained by past U.S. interventions and would be intensified by future ones was unrealistic.

Somoza Is Not Deceived

On November 28 Bowdler received guidelines from Washington for his intended private meeting with Somoza. The points: he should tell Somoza that the United States wished either his prompt resignation after negotiating a transition or his acceptance of the mediation's plebiscite. If he refused, our relations with Nicaragua "would be very strongly affected." A 1981 solution required an unacceptable price in violence and repression; Somoza did not have the capability to secure order in the country. Somoza was being warned, not betrayed. But there was no ultimatum. The policy's logic resulted, in fact, in threatening an American withdrawal from his country.

To the FAO, the U.S. mediator was to represent the great likelihood that it would win the plebiscite and the advantages of a democratic popular decision. If the FAO accepted the plebiscite, we would pressure Somoza to accept it, as well as to lift the state of siege and decree an amnesty. The consequences of a Somoza acceptance of the referendum and a FAO "no" would be extremely serious. The mediation would not be able to assist the FAO in the future. The FAO was being told again that the United States would pressure Somoza. However, it was being misinformed in that it was not being told the minor nature of those pressures.

Bowdler spoke with the president to deliver the démarche, and Somoza took it matter-of-factly, which was one of his poses when he sought to project the image of an experienced, burdened statesman. Somoza stated that he preferred a plebiscite because his resignation was not a graceful exit; however, he could not accept an "up-or-down" vote, only one measuring relative party strength. Alternatively, an election could take place for a Constituent Assembly that could subsequently decide whether he should remain in office. The dictator, the megalomaniac little god, was after a mechanism to retain control.

In suggesting a Constituent Assembly, however, Somoza had opted for the most "unconstitutional" of all formulas—the constitution explicitly prohibited its total revision at this time, as he had said. Indeed, the problem had not been to maintain constitutionality but to avoid submitting his tenure to a popular consultation that he privately acknowledged he would lose.

The embassy had sent a cable on November 28, drafted by Frank Tucker, our loyal deputy chief of mission, recommending what to do if negotiations failed: total withdrawal of the Military Advisory Mission (Milgroup); total suspension of USAID, including all pipeline projects; total withdrawal of the Peace Corps. (USAID estimated that it could reduce the local mission to approximately eight officers for ninety days, then to zero. At the time there were still twenty-three Peace Corps volunteers in the country, all in the relatively safer areas.) Washington would not accede to implement this limited package.

After meeting with Somoza, Bowdler informed his superiors that the pressures were insufficient to compel the dictator to agree to step down. The

Central American Stabilization Fund had authorized a $20 million loan, which had boosted his morale.

On November 30 Bowdler told me that Assistant Secretary Vaky had reported the high-level unacceptability of withdrawing the remaining four U.S. military officers. Only two would be removed, and the USAID office would not be closed. Why was Washington unable to take a firm stance? We were becoming clowns in Nicaragua, alienated from the government, the opposition, the entire nation.

The Parties' Counterproposals

The mediators' proposal was answered. The government proposed a plebiscite to determine Somoza's continuation in office, to be followed by an election of a National Constituent Assembly to decree a new constitution and to form a provisional government.

The FAO also accepted a plebiscite, but with its own conditions. Importantly, its spirit was not of conciliation: *before* the plebiscite, the president (and his relatives in the National Guard) had to temporarily leave office and the country, and an acceptable new head of the Guard would be appointed.

It was preposterous to expect that to change the government, the opposition had to win *two* popular consultations: first the plebiscite and then the election to a Constituent Assembly. It was unrealistic that before losing in the vote, the Somoza family would have to leave the country. The FAO considered it was a necessary condition in order to increase the chance of popular acceptance of the plebiscite.

In the midst of the impending chaos, the Somocistas seemed unperturbed. The Liberal Party was going to celebrate Somoza's birthday. The rites of deference and subordination to him could have taken place in a rudimentary, absolute patrimonial monarchy. Consider these statements:

> While newspaper headlines scream imminent catastrophe, economists and bankers predict financial collapse, and guerrillas and government troops arm for a resumption of civil war, officials of . . . [the] Liberal Party are preoccupied with a more traditional concern.
>
> Tuesday is the President's birthday. As in the past, it is planned to be a day of celebration in government and party circles. Celebrations in Managua call for . . . a ceremony in honor of . . . Somoza.
>
> The most complex preparations, however, involve the selection and purchase, with "voluntary" party and business contributions, of the President's birthday present. Considered Nicaragua's best kept yearly secret, the present is chosen by a Party committee that struggles to come up with a gift suitable for a man who appears to have everything.

*The birthday preparations lend an additional element of surrealism to what is
already a dreamlike atmosphere here.* [83]

In his speeches accepting homage, Somoza concluded: "They can say that this
country has been controlled by the [Liberal] party during many years. . . . They
can say that we have done our whim, but the people are behind that whim. [84]
They can say that they need a change. Let them win it with a popular vote! Let
me tell you that the best gift that you can give me is the good will that you have
for me. [I am willing] to do whatever is necessary . . . to maintain our thesis:
what we elected in 1974 is good and valid until 1981."

A New Mediation Proposal

The mediators used the acceptance in principle by the government and the FAO
of the idea of a plebiscite to make a new proposal on December 2. They kept
the key issue, that the people should decide whether Somoza would continue
in office. But the new document proposed the formation of a Government
of National Unity to be presided over by General Somoza if he won the referendum or by a citizen agreed upon by the two parties prior to the popular
consultation.

The mediation had come close to the alternative proposals that several moderate Nicaraguans had made, not disenfranchising the government's forces.
Now the mediators were offering mutual guarantees. They proposed in this
spirit that the cabinet of the Government of National Unity be formed by
three groups, with its members being drawn equally from the FAO, the Liberal
Party, and politically independent citizens agreed upon by the government and
opposition.

The mediators called for direct negotiations to work out the details under
their sponsorship. Also, in order to give a more national dimension and help
tackle the intransigence, it was proposed that representatives of the Catholic
Church and the private sector (i.e., COSEP) "be present" in the negotiations.

The document was reasonable. It is true that it stated again that if Somoza
lost the plebiscite he would resign and (temporarily) leave the country. But it
was appropriate that the strongman take a "vacation." And by suggesting that
the Liberal Party hold a third of the positions in the cabinet—the same as the
FAO—and by not dismantling the National Guard, General Somoza was being
made an offer that he could only refuse at his peril.

In these first days of December, our activity consisted of persuade, persuade,
persuade. In retrospect, sadly the feverish exercise in diplomacy seems very
futile, even ridiculous. Conditions in Costa Rica did not augur peace. President
Carazo had started to present to U.S. diplomats a different and new picture
of militarization: he had just received knowledge of two Sandinista training

camps in the north of the country with five to seven hundred heavily armed men, and a few days later a third camp was "discovered." Also, he had told Edén Pastora (Comandante Zero) to refrain from invading Nicaragua but felt that he could not do much. The Costa Rican police force was too weak to dismantle the FSLN camps. The international dimension was also exemplified by the formation of the "Panama Brigade" to join in the fight in Nicaragua. Volunteers from several countries were joining up to fight.

At the same time, the United States had intelligence of Panamanian arms shipments to Sandinistas in Costa Rica, with Costa Rican government knowledge of it. The Venezuelan president had given money and possibly arms to Pastora. The link was thought to reflect a disappointment with, and pessimism about, U.S. policy, while reducing Cuban influence. One would think that an opposition that would converse with the population would realize the unpopularity of the government—Somoza himself kept saying that he would lose a referendum. Wouldn't the FAO lose its raison d'être with the failure of the mediation—the only possible means to peaceably obtain Somoza's relinquishing of control? Yet the FAO continued to resist the plebiscite.[85]

Why? The Guatemalan mediator commented, "There is a need to separate his followers from Somoza, yet the FAO is not being helpful in its intransigence against giving a substantial share to them in the transitional government. But Somoza has such control over his people that he can try to use them to come back at any time." It was this sacred bond that served as the fundamental inhibitor of more creative initiatives on the FAO's part. La Prensa's editorial on December 4 in response to the new mediation proposal was revealing. How could the FAO negotiate with a party that had never shown any independence from Somoza, especially when the dictator had demonstrated little interest in conducting a true plebiscite? Patrimonial regimes make peaceful democratic passages highly contingent on the will of the leader. In the case of Nicaragua, Somoza's continuing behavior "confirmed" the perception that the strongman had to be "forced" out. A significant share of the state could not be given to a party in vassalage to Somoza. Now the FAO refused to participate in direct negotiations unless the government made three prior concessions to them. A small group withdrew from the mediation and the FAO; three other factions demanded that the mediation's December 2 proposal be entirely withdrawn.[86]

Conversations on December 3 and 4 between the mediators and FAO representatives underlined these problems. From the first meeting, the FAO had always talked about preconditions for negotiating with the government's representatives, and there was strong opposition to sharing the state with the Somocistas. This involved the fear that a "pact" would once again result in triumph and trickery by Somoza. These intense feelings prevailed even though the mediators represented that the proposed "Government of National Unity" had no Somocista precedent—it was a government of democratic transition, not of subordination to the Liberals. My own interpretation was that the mediators remained reassuring and flexible. But the FAO was highly divided. Of necessity, the proposal had limitations, including its "undemocratic" dimension of allocating one-third shares to the two sides regardless of the outcome of the plebiscite.[87] For a start, the point was to combine domestic and international pressures to obtain acceptance of a mechanism to form a new government not controlled by Somoza.[88] Second, limitations to majority rule are not uncommon in democratic forms of government. Unfortunately, a termination of regime without the costs of revolution required Somocista collaboration or for the United States to change the government. Such a miracle belonged to the realm of voodoo politics, if only because of those who governed the United States.

Under these conditions, on the evening of December 5, 1978, the three mediators met for a couple of hours with Somoza, expressing their strong annoyance with the obstructing tactics of his party and asking him to deliver the concessions demanded by the FAO. The president agreed to lift the state of siege, draft a new law to regulate radio and television broadcasts, and introduce a bill in Congress for a general political amnesty. Once more he showed his notable flexibility, except in abandoning his control.[89] However, Somoza expressed several concerns: the FAO was too immature to form a government; lifting the state of siege could increase the danger of a Sandinista invasion from Costa Rica; it was difficult to separate political from common crimes for the purpose of an amnesty; the National Guard could rebel if he pardoned the Sandinistas who had been captured by them.

In return for the concessions, he asked the mediators for a guarantee that the FSLN would not attack. Somoza also expressed reservations about the proposed transitional government, seeing in it a veto power by his opponents (the oppositionists made the same complaint about Somoza's veto power), and the problem of conducting a plebiscite without any prior registration (those under eighteen might vote, and the young were presumed to be largely against the government). In my opinion Nicaragua deserved a more developed, self-confident unarmed civic opposition and a new government committed to democracy, free from its fraudulent "democratic" baggage.

The Formal Replies
The FAO and Liberal Party answers to the December 2nd proposal were dated the 5th and 6th, respectively. The Liberal Party was courteous: they were al-

ways willing to "dialogue" and would do so to establish the basis for the plebiscite, while maintaining that the people are the "source of all political power" and the "spirit of constitutionality." The document also referred to the three concessions that the president had made to the mediators so that the oppositionists would accept negotiating the conditions of a plebiscite. Thus, ironically, the Somoza camp had saved the mediation.

In contrast, the FAO's initial response was negative: only if Somoza already fully implemented their three demands would they consider negotiating. They could not "conceive the possibility" that the people would vote to maintain the general in power (provided that "indispensable" guarantees were operative). But they would not negotiate.

The mediators visited a FAO meeting and spoke forcefully of the need not to lose momentum and to work out a solution that could only benefit the FAO. But the FAO was still afraid of Somoza, of his treachery. They thought they had to show intransigence so as not to lose popularity to the FSLN. "How are these people going to govern Nicaragua?" the American mediator asked me. Given Somoza's unwillingness to step down, the mediation itself was taking the FAO on a road to political failure, a fact that was obscured to us in Managua hoping for the best, seeking the meditation's success. Yet we learned later that the majority sentiment had prevailed in the FAO and that negotiations would start.

The Sandinistas had also taken their position. Very significantly, for the first time, the three factions signed the same communiqué, formally repudiating the mediation and any plebiscite. They had given up on U.S. policy. Their goal was to overthrow the dictatorship via violent revolution or a popular mass uprising and the "dissolution" of the National Guard. As in Cuba, the old order would be destroyed, replaced by a new and revolutionary sovereign armed forces.

The document, subscribed to by the Dirección Nacional and Estados Mayores of the FSLN, explicitly asked the FAO to withdraw from the mediation and denounce the plebiscite "as a trick of Somoza and the imperialist policy of the American Government that today like yesterday tries to impose on us a traitorous and subservient government." It concluded the following: "We condemn the plebiscite and reiterate that the only solution to the crisis . . . is the constant armed action that the insurrectionist people today spread throughout our entire territory. Against the Somocista Plebiscite, the Sandinista Insurrection. Against the Imperialist Trick, the Sandinista Insurrection. Viva the Gobierno Democrático Popular. Death to the Somocismo. Patria Libre o Morir."

This communiqué had less of the Marxist-Leninist phraseology than usual, though it expressed venom against the (vende patria) bourgeoisie and referred to the "popular democracy" term of Communist countries. The FSLN had continued respecting the physical integrity of both Nicaraguan and foreign businessmen. (Since May, for example, five foreigners had been kidnapped in El Salvador, and the revolutionaries had just murdered a Japanese businessman.) Yet it was widely believed in Nicaragua that a total Sandinista armed victory would result in an anti-American regime influenced by Marxism and Leninism.[90]

Indeed, judging from the document, the Sandinista common denominator was an intense anti-U.S. sentiment: the plebiscite was allegedly a maneuver and trap of the *imperialismo yanqui* to establish a reactionary government "submissive" to U.S. designs. Little did they understand the intentions of the American government.

The FSLN also threatened to use violence against an OAS-sponsored transitional government not of their liking and rallied support for their growing rank-and-file Movimiento Pueblo Unido (MPU). A more confident Sandinista movement—all factions definitely committed to immediate regime overthrow—called for strengthening the revolutionary struggle, joining an FSLN-dominated political front to channel mass direct action in support of the physical revolt.

Direct Talks Begin

The animosity was such that even with the moderating presence of the OAS commission, the unarmed opposition had only most reluctantly finally decided to sit in the same room with the Somocistas. This places in relief the difficulties I had in getting the parties to negotiate without any foreign mediation after P.J. Chamorro's assassination.

The first meeting took place December 8, at the Dominican Republic embassy.[91] The mediators sought to establish rules quickly to achieve a national agreement (in eight days), with the intention of holding a plebiscite on January 1. The team meant business. An agreement was required on the mechanics of the referendum (*consulta popular*), its object, its conditions, and its consequences. They suggested that their November 21 proposal serve as the base of the discussion of the first three themes and their December 2 document for the fourth.

Despite good intentions, the mediation was still faced with the FAO's demand for the implementation of preconditions. It was finally agreed that two mixed FAO-Liberal subcommissions would be established to reform articles deemed to curtail freedom of expression and review the amnesty case by case. The FAO presented language for a general amnesty, which Foreign Minister Quintana offered to speed up, beginning the following Monday, December 11.

Apparently the mediators were encouraged by the cooperative spirit of the Nicaraguan foreign minister (not his companions) and by the opposition's demand that only some (but significant) articles of the radio and television code be repealed. The FAO's interest in the pardons was understood, for colleagues were still being held in jail without charges.

There was another proposal in the interest of an honest plebiscite: local officials—*jueces de mesta, jueces de cantón,* and *capitanes de cañada*—would be relocated to the capital before and during the voting, which I thought unnecessarily restrictive. Such extreme measures to dismantle the government's machine were not adopted in several cases of authoritarian regimes that lost elections.

Unfortunately, Somoza's intentions were still to negotiate an understanding that included the Constitutional Assembly option to avoid entirely losing his control. This he stated openly in a press conference.[92] Somoza said that the effort to oust him was only a facade: the opposition's objective was to destroy the army, not just obtain his resignation. He was now making public his version of a "prisoner dilemma": If I am sacrificed, you, my followers in the army and party, will also be destroyed, and a Castroist-inspired revolution will triumph, which proved to be a self-fulfilling prophesy.

Internationally, the Nicaraguan regime found itself increasingly isolated. For example, on December 8 it was censured in the United Nations; only Paraguay joined Nicaragua in voting against the motion. The situation in Costa Rica had not improved.[93] The U.S. embassy in San Jose appraised the situation: the president did not control events, and there were freelancing activities of cabinet and lower-level government officials sympathetic of the Sandinistas.

This did not mean that appearances of neutrality would be totally abandoned. Periodically the Costa Rican government announced clean-sweep operations against the FSLN. But the local press was not helpful in maintaining a neutral image. It reported the existence of Sandinista camps with photographs and interviews; advertisements to join armed brigades to overthrow Somoza were also published.[94] Years later José Figueres, the key statesman, explained to me in a visit to the United States the all-out international effort, including Cuba, in which he participated to overthrow Somoza using this southern front.

Some incidents exemplified the climate of psychological warfare that involved us: on December 15 a cable from Panama reported that the FSLN had rented a dwelling overlooking my official residence and office, planning to attack them. There were rumors of other plots against us.[95]

Somoza found only comfort in the electoral defeat of Carlos Andrés Pérez's party, hoping that the new president to take office in March 1979 would restore the good relations. But serious armed clashes were already taking place at the Costa Rica–Nicaragua border.

Misunderstandings in the White House

On December 9 the president of the United States made the following statement:

> We have had remarkable good progress in Nicaragua. Instead of violence and thousands of people losing their lives . . . last night the FAO, representing the Sandinistas, and the Somoza Government, have decided to sit down and begin negotiating today, not on how to stop massive bloodshed, but on the terms of a plebiscite to determine the Government of Nicaragua in the future. We can't say we have reached complete success, but we are willing to get in and use the tremendous influence of the United States in a beneficial way.

The president was being excessively optimistic about the progress that had been achieved and was confusing the relationship between the FAO and the FSLN.[96] President Carter elaborated:

> In international affairs, our country has injected itself, I think wisely, into regional disputes where we have no control over the outcome. But we have added our good services, in some instances with almost no immediate prospect of success. My own reputation has been at stake and that of our country. In Nicaragua, I think instead of having violent and massive bloodshed, we now have the parties negotiating directly with one another for the first time on the terms of a plebiscite and whether or not there should be a general amnesty.

In contrast, at the same time the president went on to express public U.S. support for the autocratic shah of Iran and confidence that he would maintain power in Iran, as well as asking other OPEC nations not to raise the price of oil.[97]

I did not know the source of Carter's optimism about Nicaragua. Was it that officials in lobbying for continued support for the mediation were presenting a far too rosy picture to the White House? What kind of information was the Latin American section of the National Security Council processing for the president? Later this same month, when negotiations broke down and we met in the White House, I discovered that the president's White House aide, with whom we discussed the problem, was unprepared for the collapse of the mediation—they had been getting very favorable reports, he said.

Carter's comments reflected his noble idealism; he was placing his own "reputation at stake." His contradictory position—he spoke of America's "tremendous influence" but said that it had "no control over the outcome"—reflected the popular mood that a new order with a decline in, and limitations to, American power had developed, a world of greater interdependence, as opposed to the *dependencia* view popular in Latin America. In Managua there was the belief that U.S. policy was advocating total defeat at great human costs.

La Prensa now published a letter to the president of the United States by Thomas Walker, a political scientist writing on Nicaragua. Walker had been happy with the good standing that I had with Chamorro, but as American policy muddled after the sudden crisis, he increasingly became critical.

He thought Washington should recognize and back the FSLN to achieve a social revolution that would result in human development, a healthy nationalism, and a friendly progressive government. By siding with the Sandinistas, the president had the opportunity to initiate processes that would end the hatred of Latin Americans for the United States.

However, Walker misunderstood U.S. policy. He recommended that the U.S. government immediately establish communications with the FSLN, terminate all forms of economic and military assistance to Somoza, end any other form of supportive interference, and urge all Latin governments to do the same. These measures would result in a brief civil war, after which the United States would have the opportunity of establishing friendly, healthy relations with a new, reformist-socialist Sandinista government.

Walker's prescription was for a special kind of U.S. "intervention," which the Reagan administration would ultimately adopt: the assistance to armed movements. The White House had other instruments to terminate the Nicaraguan government more likely to result in maintaining U.S. prestige and influence. It was far more preferable to act in accordance with the vast majority, who sought a viable U.S. ultimatum. Soon this thesis of assisting the Sandinistas to minimize the costs and time frame of an inevitable war and obtain Somocista defeat acquired enormous support.[98]

Little Promise for Mediation

We could not be optimistic. A referendum still had to be accepted and not subjected to threats of violence that would make it unviable. It was crucial to maintain momentum.

The government's propaganda was disquieting. On December 12 *Novedades* devoted four full pages (including the first) to photographs of the president's visit to his son's military academy and elite corps. Somoza appeared with his son and his half-brother, General José Somoza, in most of the pictures. The readers were informed of the family's absolute military control and activities to prepare to defeat the next expected popular uprising. This was a provocation. There had been no progress in the old demand of ending family control over the National Guard.[99]

The situation had become so sensitive that it was difficult to handle my relations with the Somoza family. On December 13 the president's father-in-law was buried in Managua. I did not attend the funeral; instead I sent a message and flowers and subsequently sent word to Somoza that his office had not answered my inquiry about diplomatic corps presence at the funeral. The fact was that few ambassadors attended.

Two days later, Pallais met with the U.S. mediator. Somoza's wife was an American citizen, so the entire family (including those who had resigned their U.S. citizenship, such as Anastasio Jr.) were eligible for permanent residence in the United States, in case the president lost the referendum. But Pallais insisted that the question of Somoza's exile had to be treated as a "personal decision"— that Somoza would voluntarily decide to leave temporarily, to return when propitious to do so, not a departure from Nicaragua formally and publicly agreed upon in the negotiations as a formal point of the popular consultation. He would not be expelled from his country. The point could not have been made more clear.

The Private Sector In

On December 13 William Baez Sacasa informed me that the FAO had reservations about business community participation, for it could give an image of conservatism to the negotiations. However, the need to support the only possible peaceful solution and the ongoing mobilization of the left had induced the business sector to accept participation as "observers and witnesses" in the mediation.

This was part of COSEP's statement:

Nicaraguan private enterprise believes that to develop a strong private enterprise, which provides abundant employment, it is necessary that an adequate political organization exist that has the backing of the nation's fuerzas vivas, which Somoza's government does not have. [100]

Remarkably, in my first three months in the country a number of my business contacts had few expectations that the regime would change, partly based on tradition—the custom of family rule, the Somozas' resources and expertise—and the country's low educational and economic level, indicating a lack of preparation for democracy. Now virtually all business leaders felt that the president should resign as soon as possible. Only very rarely did I have contact with any Nicaraguan (or American) supporter of Somoza.

In spite of the hurdles ahead, I made contact with the Nicaraguan gran capital (big business) to ask it to be prepared to help finance the plebiscite's political campaign. I also suggested that the private sector might take some initiatives to counter the virulence of radio programs. Audiences should be exposed to more programs that reasoned the issues. I was promised action on both fronts.

The Catholic Church Out

The archbishop decided against participating in the negotiations. The Presbyterial Council was opposed because many parish priests in the barrios, members of the clergy organizers of religious base communities, and heads of Catholic educational institutions were siding with the FSLN position of no role for the Liberal Party and the National Guard in the new government. Within the Church the process of popular conversion to "Sandinism" had expanded and solidified. This led me to talk with Monsignor Obando on December 14. He had an usually large number of visitors, including the rector of the main public university, who was facing an internal political crisis, and representatives of COSEP. The archbishop was a very popular, respected national leader, indeed. I told him that the United States would not intervene to oust Somoza on philosophical grounds; hence, in order to achieve a peaceful solution we had to provide Somoza with an exit—perhaps the plebiscite would fulfill this role.

Obando y Bravo's reply was that a civil war was unacceptable. "We must try to solve the problem in a civilized, Christian way. A new uprising will be costlier than the September events and may not defeat the National Guard. I hesitate to participate in the mediation because a sector of the Church does not want it. Nevertheless, I will be as helpful as I can so that reasonableness prevails."

That same day, El Centroamericano, the responsible daily from Leon, published an interview with the archbishop in Honduras. He said, "We asked for the OAS mediation to come in the midst of the September uprising to avoid further bloodshed, but it came too late and the killings have filled with hatred the hearts of a people that has always been a good people." Many oppositionists felt that Somoza was engaged in a public relations effort, stalling only to gain time. The government's repression had become more acute. "It seems that the opposition has very good intentions to deliver the common good— social services, work, education, health, and above all liberty and the Christian evaluation of a life to be happy here and the life after death." Monsignor Obando was skeptical of the mediation's ability and did not wish to commit himself to an unsuccessful enterprise. After all, he had been one of the first to diagnose that the solution was for Somoza to end his rule and had publicly asked him to do so.

The Catholic hierarchy was also faced with its own radicalized, revolutionary liberation theology current. Clergy commitment to a violent revolution was dramatized December 11 by the media, which reported the combat death of a Spanish priest, Gaspar García Laviana. La Prensa published his public letter from a year earlier that explained his "inalienable" revolutionary project. Taking up arms was his best contribution to the Nicaraguan people and the Catholic Church, he wrote, so as to fulfill his religious consecration to "serve the people of God." The priest was "liberator" and "redeemer" of the people, seeking liberation through revolution and martyrdom. The Catholic Church, he wrote, has to participate in a "Christian revolution to overthrow an assassin regime and construct a new society, where the Christian ideals of justice, love, and peace are lived."[101]

The same interview with Obando provided a measure of the archbishop's internal position. He was asked if it was licit for priests to participate in politics. He replied that there were two aspects to politics, in a broad sense and in a strict sense. The first referred to the pursuit of the common good—all human beings, the church included, should participate in such politics. However, priests should not participate in the second type, partisan politics to conquer political power, because they are leaders of communities in which the Catholic faith coexisted with different legitimate party preferences. (This was precisely the Vatican's thesis that the clergy should not belong to movements seeking to control the state nor be officials in governments.) But, the hedging archbishop added, neither should judges nor the military participate in such politics.

Monsignor Obando's thought was progressive, in agreement with post-Vatican II Latin American Catholic developments. "If we try to evangelize, I believe . . . that the evangelization consists of bringing the good message to all men. This means that one should try to change the sinful structures and the [social] structures which impede the transformation of man."

The archbishop treated kindly Father Ernesto Cardenal, who was also actively involved in the Sandinista camp. Indeed, the top hierarchy, while not yet proclaiming a theological right or duty to participate in the violence, did not condemn the cleric revolutionary activists. This is of historical interest, because after the revolution the archbishop faced the rebellion of Sandinista priests and nuns and was portrayed by some sources as a very traditional prelate. Actually, he was also opposing the unjust dictatorship that was allowed to follow.

On the Threshold of Revolution

The Somoza government had no sensible plan to remain ruling. It was undermining itself. With the amnesty already taking place, significant numbers of the active oppositionists were being allowed to return to their revolutionary activities and show their resilience. Lifting the state of siege allowed incendiary media broadcasts and the spread of information for opposition activities to increase. That is, Somoza's concessions to the FAO-mediation interest were facilitating militant opposition, increasing its opportunity to organize, mobilize, and augment its power.

One of the paradoxes of revolutionary situations is that although in fact these reductions in government *control* occur, and opposition costs for collective revolutionary action are diminished, the pattern of sanguinary government "repression" continues. Thus the government does not gain resources or support while still being condemned as the source of the social strain. The situation is defined as one of wanton government cruelty, and the government's evident yet inadequate control tends to make people see it as more illegitimate and relatively less threatening; its repression is less intimidating and less effective. The ultimate result is that peaceable alternatives to change government are perceived as closed, and public opinion sees drastic opposition measures more favorably, becoming anxious to settle the crisis.

The generalization of the advocacy of, and belief in, violent activism "to solve the problem once and for all soon" is one of the social-psychological components for moving the revolutionary process toward culmination. The U.S. press revealed this mood among the public. A Nicaraguan named Carmen was described saying she was not partisan: "she likes motorcycles, Travolta-style dancing, and blue jeans." But this was her definition of the situation:

> I just want to live in peace, but you can't any more. I'm not interested in politics, but why doesn't Tacho [Somoza] just quit and get out? Can't he see that the whole country is going to hell? And why doesn't the [FSLN] give out rifles to everyone to shoot it out and get it over with? I might even take one myself.[102]

Revolutions are not made exclusively by ideological fervor but also by the spreading commitment of individuals with diverse motives and interests.

The danger of the emerging situation was brought to my attention on December 12 by Mariano Fiallos, the able analyst and politician. "Ambassador," he said, "the left has launched an intense campaign against the 'new American intervention.' The plebiscite is represented as a formula to keep Somoza in power. It is essential to move rapidly if the mediation is going to succeed and not lose credibility."

I asked the U.S. mediator to join us. Fiallos continued: "Somoza's machine has been substantially weakened. For instance, in Leon, the three Liberal party chiefs are not in the city any longer; neither are key men in place in other areas such as Masaya or Chinandega. The Movimiento Pueblo Unido [MPU] is actually replacing Somoza's political organization." With the lifting of the state of siege, our visitor added, the MPU was organizing meetings in the barrios and even some small street demonstrations. The people were slowly, once again, losing their fear of political activity. The FAO might have the support of the middle and upper classes, but the MPU was organizing and had the people in the barrios.

We were rapidly moving toward a point of no return in making the all-out effort to overthrow the government. There seemed to be even greater psychological revolutionary tension than actual violence. It rattled nerves. Rumors of imminent attacks spread. There were indications that a new phase with increased violence had started. For example, on December 14, the *Miami Herald* signaled the beginnings of the increase in urban and rural armed actions by small groups and a few columns, which would grow into a significant number of larger-scale military operations by bigger combat units at Somoza's downfall.

Prompted by a bureaucratic requirement—sending to Washington the mission's "goals and objectives" for the following year—on December 13 Jack Martin, the embassy's intelligent and capable officer, and I sat down to draft a document. This gave me the occasion to look back on our activities since my arrival and gage the future. I had no expectation that the administration could be influenced to change its course. But it was an opportunity to be on record. I recall Francisco Aguirre of *Diario Las Américas* insisting repeatedly that I keep documentation of my position. This would be a final, in a sense farewell, statement. It was clear that the mediation was about to end, and I should not take responsibility for the future outcome.

The following were some of our considerations:

> Nicaragua per se is not strategically important, and the U.S. does not have any major economic or commercial interest in [it]. However, political developments in Nicaragua have implications beyond its borders especially in the Central American region, and it has come to be a major focus for the global human rights policy of the US Government. In March, Deputy Secretary [Warren] Christopher judged that "Nicaragua may well present a crucial test for our Latin America policy, affect not only Nicaragua, but our interest in the promotion of human rights and political independence, as well as the avoidance of instability in the Central American region." This is still true. U.S. interests are clearly to promote peaceful democratic change [here]. Such change would promote regional stability, with attendant implications for economic cooperation and development, and would promote U.S. economic, commercial and human rights objectives while benefitting the Nicaraguan people.

We proceeded to summarize developments: "1978 represented a year of deteriorating political, economic and social conditions. . . . Popular repudiation of the government, civil insurrectionary activism, and guerrilla operations all increased while respect for human rights and the economic situation deteriorated especially toward the end of the year. This possibility was foreseen in last year's goals and objectives statement. However, the speed and depth of political polarization was greater than originally anticipated." (We had not foreseen Chamorro's assassination and its immediate consequences of fueling a national rebellion.)

We then referred to the plan of action that Washington had traced for my mission:

> The goals and objectives of the Embassy outlined shortly after the Ambassador's arrival in September 1977 were primarily to promote democratization and improvement in the human rights situation, while maintaining neutrality through "correct relations" with the Government of Nicaragua and widespread contacts with legitimate opposition forces [i.e., unarmed groups]. As conditions deteriorated in early 1978 as a result of the assassination . . . Embassy instructions were altered to emphasize that while we were to maintain neutrality we were also to encourage all factions to negotiate a democratic and peaceful solution to the crisis. However, faced as it was with local pressures to intervene on the side of each party, the Embassy was instructed to avoid acting as negotiator or guarantor for any agreements.

We had in mind the limitations imposed on us that we not become a "hub of political activity." Despite these restrictions we had performed our instructions:

> Embassy believes that it effectively implemented instructed policy of neutrality and promoter of democratic change through its broad contacts with [the government], opposition, Church, human rights and private sector leaders. The test of this was evident when the deteriorating conditions reached the point in late July–early August, when it became evident that the [United States] could no longer maintain its low-profile, neutral posture. Under new instructions [from Washington] the Embassy brought together in less than a week representatives of a broad spectrum of the society to request a U.S. Government–sponsored outside mediation, without which the U.S. would have had much less opportunity to influence the course of events.

Symptomatic of our understanding that Washington remained concerned with the more elementary problems of human rights abuses and our desire to make it known that we were aware of this, we wrote: "Although we would expect changes in command and control of the National Guard [if the mediation succeeded forming] a new government, we would not expect a total volte-face with regard to human rights attitudes. We will have an important role in monitoring human rights compliance as well as freedom of the press, governmental honesty and related issues, and in signaling deficiencies as they arise."

We dealt then with the political fundamentals:

The upcoming key policy-level issues are directly related to the current mediation initiative[,] whether it succeeds or fails in producing a Government of National Unity. If a new government does emerge, there may be continued instability and the threat of further guerrilla attacks and/or a military coup, especially during its initial period. The U.S. will be expected to assist governmental stability in terms of reopening the military and developmental assistance faucets. Secondly, incremental flows, probably outside normal budgetary procedures, should be considered to prime renewed investment and to assist alleviation of the foreign debt situation. The U.S. may also have a major role with regard to third countries, especially Costa Rica, Venezuela and Panama in attempting to interdict FSLN re-supply and safehaven assets, and other efforts to reduce its continued revolutionary activities to the status quo ante or less.

On the other hand, if the mediation were to fail, we may expect the belligerency/public order/economic situation to resume its former alarming deterioration. In that case, the U.S. would be challenged to the dilemma of how to check the slide toward anarchy and wide-scale insurgency on the one hand, and increasing repression by [the government] on the other. The hope of a majority of Nicaraguans in such a situation, would be direct intervention either by the OAS or even by the U.S. unilaterally. If such direct actions were not forthcoming, the credibility of the U.S. would be undermined not only in Nicaragua, but also within and possibly beyond the hemisphere.

The key issue is whether the current political crisis can be overcome so that significant progress can be made. . . . With the current high-level focus on the Nicaraguan issue in Washington, the Embassy believes there is full understanding of the need for timely action, if the mediation succeeds, to begin to generate an improved climate in which the ground lost can be regained, and in which further progress in attaining our goals and objectives can be made. Similarly, if the mediation breaks down, the anticipated further violence and deterioration of public order will require immediate U.S. policy reactions.

Thus Washington was told that even if the mediation succeeded, a successful policy demanded that it get substantially involved in the transition. The extant political fragmentation of the opposition and the threat from within the opposition to continue with violence, as well as force and instability from and within the state, posed problems for the immediate future. Precedents for these problems were found, of course. However, the point was made because the administration was so reluctant to prop up regimes facing insurgencies.

We also addressed the desire of the vast majority of Nicaraguans that we take a forceful stance to change the Somoza government and avoid the impending war. The principle of non-intervention, although in general a prudent rule with wide acceptability, is not and should not be considered an absolute prohibition for all circumstances. If Somoza did not compromise and took the country to war, American prestige, morally and pragmatically, would suffer excessively. Washington should not allow itself to be defeated by a capricious, confused, provincial little man.

As we expected, the embassy's statement had no impact. The next day the man in charge of Latin American operations, Viron P. Vaky, as if replying to our formal position, made a public presentation articulating the prevailing Liberal Hour, even if he privately had warned of the costs of revolution in Nicaragua.[103] I certainly did not find fault with all his facts and ethical principles: Latin American nations were industrializing; they were more developed and capable of better articulating their self-interest—in spite of the inevitable areas of U.S.-Latin America conflict of interest, these were positive changes. A new era of economic and political cooperation for democracy was being envisioned in Washington, in which our neighbors would exercise greater sovereignty over their economies, and the United States would be more responsive to the economic demands of the North-South dialogue.

Differences in power existed, so relations tended to be asymmetrical. But Latin Americans were prone to misunderstand the nature of the U.S. form of government, with its decentralized structures of authority and the autonomy of private citizens to engage in their own activities, which have important effects that cannot be controlled by the U.S. government.

A new, less interventionist internationalism was transforming the relationships, such as the cooperative enterprises of the Panama Canal treaties and the OAS mediation in Nicaragua—it was "inconceivable" that the United States would use its military power to intervene in the internal affairs of any other American republic, the assistant secretary stated.

Vaky also referred to the "hegemonic presumption" error, that the United States had the capacity to determine all fundamental events and hence was responsible for conditions and problems in the area. This "paternalistic" assumption was invalid.

The assistant secretary recognized that Latins expected the United States to use its power differential. But the administration did not want to exercise it, wishing to relinquish any hegemonic position in hemispheric affairs so as not to be responsible for the realities. The Nicaraguan case was presented as exemplary. In contrast to the past, Vaky said, when we would be inclined to impose a solution or unilaterally intervene in Nicaragua, we were now using the multilateral persuasive means of the mediation. The philosophical inadequacy of policy was evident, and it disappointed all those involved in Nicaragua. There was nothing any of us could do in the field to change policy.

The Talks Resume

There really had not been any significant progress. Somoza, I thought, was still hoping to see the FAO further split, thus perversely "proving" that there wasn't a "viable alternative," as he kept telling his contacts. The Sandinistas were more defiantly committed to the insurrection, the MPU repudiated any plebiscite, and so did the Group of Twelve. On December 18 those of the Twelve who were in political asylum in Managua's Mexican embassy published a virulent communiqué or manifesto: the honest groups in the FAO should break with the mediation and join the struggle for "liberation" and "profound and real change." The government remained in power simply because of the U.S. "criminal" military, political, economic, and diplomatic assistance to the "genocidal" Somoza. Of interest was the accusation of "deceit" against the mediation. The U.S. mediator had committed his government to change the Nicaraguan government, if the opposition proposed a plan for a transitional regime without Somoza that would avoid a power vacuum. This had been trickery on the mediation's part, for they had done so, and nothing had happened. The Twelve did not acknowledge that, given the lack of coherence of the opposition, the mediation had needed to take the initiative and help organize the FAO around a plan to constitute a new government. The signers of the document had feared for their lives and now voluntarily left the embassy, while the government took no action against them.[104]

Rallying in favor of the electoral consultation was not helped by the Catholic Church top hierarchy. On December 17 La Prensa published an interview with the archbishop, who was noncommittal about the plebiscite. The church favored a peaceful solution, not one imposed by arms or terror. He did not know if the church's position would improve or deteriorate with a Sandinista government. He would not criticize Father Gaspar García Laviana, the Spanish missionary Sandinista guerrillero who had just been killed. (In fact, with the advent of FSLN rule, very conflictive relations developed between the Catholic hierarchy and the new government.) And the FAO still lacked a wholehearted commitment to a plebiscite. Nonetheless, American experts came to Nicaragua to study the mechanics of a fair plebiscite. Only one small faction (the Conservative Zancudos) had participated in elections; it was deemed that the various groups would have to work together to ensure opposition representation in every district. Several Nicaraguans expressed the need to use international and national notables to get people to vote. A public relations firm advised them that instead of the almost one dollar customarily given to voters, on this occasion a Nicaraguan flag or an instant picture of the voter might be given as a gift, to entice participation of the masses.

It was bizarre that U.S. electoral experts were carrying out these contacts without meeting with the Nicaraguan government at all. Luis Pallais visited me to complain. But such was already the deep lack of cooperation between Somoza and the mediation.

On December 16 the second session of talks took place, this time at the Guatemalan embassy. This and the subsequent meetings of December 17, 18, 19, and 20 were attended by representatives of Somoza, the FAO, and COSEP. But from the beginning, two problems were insurmountable: the FAO's demand that if Somoza lost the vote, he and his family would go into exile, and the FAO's unwillingness to participate in a government under Somoza if the president won.

Ramón Emilio Jiménez, the Dominican foreign minister, repeatedly made efforts to move the talks and conciliate differences. The Somoza camp was the most intransigent. Indeed, he proposed the alternative that if the FAO lost, then it would not participate in a coalition government but would commit itself to act as a democratic, loyal opposition respecting the popular vote. The FAO accepted this formula, but the Somocistas claimed that opposition participating in the government under Somoza was the test of the FAO's willingness to reconcile itself with the Liberals.

The Somocistas also proposed that the Group of Twelve and the FSLN be invited to participate in the talks. Their real message was that an understanding with the FAO was meaningless, and the war inevitable—there is no alternative but Somoza or revolution. The tragic strategy was to make unviable any other option but Somoza (or the Sandinistas if they defeated the National Guard). The FAO's position was to invite FSLN participation once the political compromise was worked out.

In contrast, despite the pressures to end negotiations and the risks of implementing an agreement with the Liberals—given their disciplined organization and their continued loyalty to Somoza and hence receptivity to arrange his continuation in power—the FAO had proved their awareness of and sensitivity to the costs of the alternative route, plus their apprehensions that it not lead to a democratic regime. It was impossible for the FAO representatives to forget or repress the rancorous widespread mood of public opinion.

It was the moment for maximum pressure: resignation or acceptance of the referendum. The U.S. mediator cabled Washington that General Dennis P. McAuliffe should now come to present Somoza a firm démarche to end the obstructionism, and that we should immediately begin the pull out the entire U.S. Military Mission and suspend all economic assistance projects. The mediation's tactic was to make a "reasonable" final proposal acceptable to the FAO and place the pressure and burden on Somoza so that he would be responsible for the mediation's failure and be left in a perilous position of further isolation.

McAuliffe, the head of the Southern Command based in the Panama Canal, had been very useful in helping me maintain relations with U.S. military personnel in Nicaragua under adequate cooperation. Such personnel typically sympathize with the local armies, and these were under the attack of the human rights policy. [105]

On December 21 McAuliffe was in Managua, where the situation had further deteriorated. Before he and Somoza talked, Bowdler and I spoke with our visitor. The general was going to tell Somoza that the U.S. Department of Defense and the Joint Chiefs were very concerned with the situation; there was consensus within the U.S. military that with him in office, there could be no peace in Nicaragua, and consequently he should give a solution to the crisis, such as accepting the plebiscite.

We eagerly waited for General McAuliffe's return. The result: "no runs, no hits," he said using baseball lingo. Nothing was accomplished. A cable was sent to Washington with my concurrence recommending the need for a new approach to tell Somoza that if he did not cooperate, the United States would have to withdraw from Nicaragua. [106]

In the face of the intransigence, on December 20 the mediators presented their "last and integral proposal." They claimed it combined elements of the positions of the two parties, and the agreement—the Acta Compromiso—could be signed by tomorrow (mañana mismo); otherwise the mediators would leave the country, to return only if called by both parties.

The principal element was the constitution of the National Reconciliation Government by March 3, 1979. On January 5, the process for the plebiscite on Somoza's tenure would begin. The vote would take place February 25. If Somoza lost, on March 3 the Congress would appoint his successor and enact the constitutional amendments required to form a new government (according to the one-third formula) to be constituted on May 1. This government would rule with the extant Congress until the election of a Constituent Assembly on November 1. Noteworthy, the basis for a government with mutual guarantees was established in the requirement that key executive positions would be staffed according to Liberal and FAO agreement. The National Guard would be maintained as an ongoing institution under a new director and reorganized by itself through a Consejo Técnico de Oficiales under the cabinet, where the Liberals and the FAO were equally represented.

The proposal posed problems for Somoza, however. First, it stated that to ensure a fair plebiscite, the president, prior to the vote, would remove his half-brother and son from their command positions in the National Guard and appoint them to posts abroad—Somoza would have to sacrifice his family prior to the plebiscite.[107] Second, Somoza would not only resign if he lost but would also agree to go into "voluntary" exile until May 1, 1981 (for the remainder of his current term). Third, prior to the vote his electoral machine would be temporarily exiled within Nicaragua: the *jueces de mesta, jueces de cantón,* and *capitanes de cañada* would be moved to Managua so that they could not influence the voting process.

In all fairness, the goal of obtaining FAO approval for the proposal and diminishing public opposition to the plebiscite resulted in the inclusion of "objectively" and technically unnecessary points for an impartial consultation that the opposition could win. But stipulating Somoza's absence from Nicaragua seemed pertinent to pacifying the spirits so drastically altered after Chamorro's death. And by now it had become clear that the strongman would not accept any fairer mechanism to end his rule at this time. Obviously the proposal would be unacceptable to the Somocistas. National opinion was such that Somoza could not have won any reasonable consultation. Once he lost the vote, public pressures would be such that he would have had to relinquish power and go into exile in some foreign land.

The mediators asked for formal replies by the next day, and they got them. The FAO said yes. Although the democratic opposition's "aspirations had not been fully met," it considered that the proposal permitted a peaceful transition. *La Prensa* encapsulated the mood: "Somoza is against the wall. The new document . . . offers feasible conditions for a plebiscite. It permits the effective implementation of the sixteen point program proposed by all the organizations of the FAO." The daily explained that the FAO had ended with the tragic history of "pacting" with Somoza, considered that he had been exposed "knowing that he will certainly lose" a popular consultation, and called "now more than ever" for an "invincible anti-Somocista unity of all opposition forces."

La Prensa was irritated by the Sandinista-inspired, pro-revolution radio campaigns against the FAO. The amnesty was a plus for all. The shifting position on intervention/non-intervention taken by some advocates of revolution was apparent. For example, Sergio Ramírez had been one of the FAO's negotiators who had requested consistently that the mediation obtain Somoza's resignation. Now his position had changed against the mediation's "intervention" because he did not agree with Liberal participation in the transition government.[108]

The government's response was no. The headlines of its daily read: "Antipatriotic Proposal of the OAS Commission. Intervention! Violation against the Dignity of the Republic and the Patriotism of Nicaraguans." It claimed that the FAO wished to "liquidate the Liberal Party that represents one million citizens and the National Guard to replace it with a Red Army."[109]

These reactions were supplemented by a long counterproposal of December 26. The Liberal electoral machine would not be dismantled, nor would the Liberal-dominated Congress, which would elect the new president. The opposition's influence in a future government was delayed until a new Constituent Assembly would be elected six months after the plebiscite. This was the old formula that to end Somoza rule the opposition had to win two elections (the plebiscite and the majority of the Constituent Assembly). Obviously the objective of the dilatory game was to destroy the FAO's prestige. The passage of time without any results confirmed the thesis that only violence could defeat the dictator—precisely the Sandinista historical belief. Somoza's actions irresponsibly called for a revolution to destroy him and his followers, which is what they got.

Washington's only reaction was that the mediation should not close the door to further negotiation. All along, first the embassy, now the American mediator, had not been given the instruments to solve the crisis. Nor were the top officials in charge of policy weighing the reactions of the other countries in the mediation. Admiral Jiménez refused to continue playing Washington's game and did not return to Nicaragua after the events.

Reactions to the mediation's proposals by the American press were not all realistic. The press, nonetheless, perceptively reported the movement toward the "point of no return," of generalizing the belief in the necessity of violence (the sooner the better) among public opinion: "one moderate business leader [said] last week, 'If the choice is between selling out to Somoza or a civil war, we'll reluctantly have to pick the latter.' "[110]

The Archbishop's Christmas Message

Monsignor Obando y Bravo had not come out in support of the referendum, but in this last December under Somoza family rule he still advocated peace. It was, however, a call to Christian activism to construct a new just social order with a good government: "Let us not adore the God of sloth but the God of liberation," he preached.

By contrast, well-known members of the clergy were declaring the mediation's failure and calling for armed action—including the future Sandinista cabinet ministers Ernesto Cardenal and Miguel D'Escoto. Clerics propagandized messianic-millenarian themes in anticipation of, and to incite participation in, the FSLN "final offensive." The apocalypse was unfolding with great individual suffering. But this was not hopelessness: personal sacrifice and immolation resulted in personal aggrandizement by liberating the people and self. Everything was to be given up for God to share in his millennium.

Consider the propaganda:

> We live under the sign of terror and death. . . . Besides the murder of the people by [Government] bombings, besides the destruction of the cities, besides the merciless persecution of the youth who are tortured and castrated in the basest manner, besides the atmosphere of fear and insecurity, besides the sleepless nights and constant worries. . . .
>
> The political climate of Nicaragua is grim. Even the sermons of the Archbishop are censored. In Esteli a priest was shot and we also are awaiting our hour. In a humiliating and violent manner, soldiers broke into my church and searched through everything. I am the victim of constant psychological torture in the night. . . .
>
> The hour of martyrdom in Latin America has already broken upon us. But from our suffering and blood, a new church will arise.[111]

In the Hands of a *Medio Loco*

Just before returning to the United States for a policy review meeting, I had breakfast with Ernesto Fernández Holmann, the financier who had been periodically advising the mediation. He coolly outlined the alternatives:

1. The United States directly negotiates with Somoza, telling him what is not negotiable (e.g., his resignation, a free election) and obtains from him his plan to exit. This would have to be backed with an American military threat to Somoza because he is willing to be left with arroz con frijoles ("rice and beans") because of economic crisis and physical destruction.

2. The United States uses covert action and buys the vote of Liberal congressmen to rebel and impeach Somoza and/or through the military mission conspires against him. Ideally the Somocistas are told that if Somoza doesn't leave, the United States will use force against the government thus inducing them to act to avoid a "greater evil."

3. The United States withdraws from Nicaragua. This is the worse scenario, because it will not change the government and will leave a chaotic legacy behind it, as American influence on day-to-day events disappears. [112]

My visitor concluded: "I fear Somoza because he is *medio loco*. You should give him time to react. Sometimes he has late reactions and this could be the case with the visit of General McAuliffe."

A sense of personal responsibility, of not leaving Nicaragua in chaos, made me indefatigable. On Christmas Day I had breakfast in Miami with Luis Pallais. Pallais was concerned about McAuliffe's visit. "El Jefe told me that he had not asked him to resign," he said. Pallais then elaborated on five options. The last was for the president to appoint "a *ministro de gobierno* as his successor, leaving him in charge by departing for the United States. [113] Would the FAO accept Foreign Minister Quintana as the new head of the government? The only other alternative would be Congressman Francisco Urcuyo Maliaño." [114]

I told Pallais that the best solution was for Somoza to resign. "Not only are there problems of a satisfactory international control to make a referendum credible, but there is also the free media agitating and Sandinista pressure on the FAO. They continue to insist on absurd things. For Somoza himself, it would be best if he resigned. He has been sick, he wishes the good of Nicaragua. If he resigns, he would leave the Liberal Party and the *Guardia* in a much stronger position to bargain." This was precisely what Somoza tried to do the following June, when it was too late.

The Presidential Review Committee

At 3 p.m., December 26, the Presidential Review Committee (PRC) meeting took place in the White House. Secretary of State Cyrus Vance presided over the meeting. I had never before met the top While House aide. Neither had I met the general who represented the Defense Department, nor the deputy chief of the CIA, who was also there. Symptomatically, National Security Adviser Zbigniew Brzezinski was not present—Robert Pastor continued to represent the National Security Council. [115]

The secretary of state summarized three alternatives: (1) curtail relations with the Somoza government; (2) send Bowdler to see Somoza again to try to change his position and report back; (3) accept Somoza's forthcoming counterproposal if it was positive.

Surprisingly, the discussion about imposing sanctions on the recalcitrant dictator was still open. An important number of those present explicitly stated that the United States should not get involved in ousting Somoza. The president would not do this for ethical reasons, which was a reason to favor a plebiscite to resolve the conflict.

The idea that the possible punitive actions against Somoza (those that the administration might be willing to employ) would probably not have substantial effects was also discussed. The majority of those gathered did not wish to exercise American power and apparently held a sense of powerlessness and lack of confidence in policy success.

Robert Pastor was one of the articulators of a formula of defeat. He was against adopting sanctions. The president should be allowed all options, he stated (as if his government had not been involved in, and committed by, the mediation). In Pastor's view, it was preferable that Somoza not resign if this was perceived as having been pushed by Jimmy Carter. He felt that given more time, Somoza would cooperate with the administration.

The majority felt, however, that some measures would have to be taken to maintain U.S. credibility in the face of defeat (e.g., pull out the Military Mission and the Peace Corps, one half of the USAID personnel, some State Department officials). The majority feeling was that the response should be graduated to give alternatives to the president to choose policy. The decision was to announce measures against Somoza only after the mediation gave its report.

The administration had to be ready to face the unfolding failure of the mediation with the press and the Congress. Secretary Vance's prescription was to start background meetings with both to prepare for the problems ahead and the actions to be taken after the mediation's report. Top officials must be aware that the U.S. government is made responsible by various publics of foreign crises.

I felt that officials in the White House viewed themselves as protectors of the president's interest. It was in his interest that there be "no problems," that there be "peace." Resources are limited; one has to economize the allocation of time. The team most representative of the prevalent spirit of the administration had been stating, from the very beginning, the relative unimportance of Nicaragua and of the Communist challenge in the region.

Obviously the mediation was about to end. I was extremely concerned that the White House would not even show strong displeasure with the strongman. The FAO had made an act of faith and collaborated with us. Now Washington would prove them wrong, thus further weakening the FAO's position. This would deflate U.S. prestige and seriously reduce our capacity to influence subsequent events.

From the assistant secretary's new deputies I found out what was going to happen. One of them told me that in a week or so we would make payments in Nicaraguan accounts, and suggested that the USAID disbursements that we had been withholding in Managua be made at the time that any decisions to cut back operations (to show Washington's displeasure) were announced. He was describing a continuation of the pattern of half-measures. As if there had not been any need for sustained pressures, a Foreign Service bureaucrat told me that he did not understand why in Managua we had not made disbursements when Somoza made the concessions that led to the beginning of the government-opposition talks.

I foresaw that loans, such as the one pending in the International Monetary Fund, would soon be approved. How was I going to explain to Nicaraguans the capitulation of the United States? We were going to become politically irrelevant. As the man in the field, I would be responsible for failure, the scapegoat.

In Search of My Exit

Others would oust Somoza and blame us for the cost they had to incur to do so. I felt that I could not continue representing the administration. I was very apprehensive about any design to make the embassy the scapegoat for the failure of others. I never forgot Bowdler's involvement in messages criticizing the embassy for insufficient anti-Somocismo. There was a different source of his failure and the failure of the U.S. policy: it was the higher-level officials who soon promoted Bowdler. From Washington I spoke with my wife, so that she could seek her position back at the university.

On my return trip to Managua I stopped in Miami, but Mayor Maurice Ferré was out of town. I spoke with Luis Lauredo, who had also been instrumental in my appointment. I asked him to assist me in working out an "amicable divorce" with the administration. As the first Cuban-born U.S. ambassador, I sought a dignified exit. I was quite frank: "I am very sorry that I was sent to Nicaragua, because I have not been useful to you. My presence in Managua is divisive within the Cuban-American community because of its support for Somoza and what is needed is unity."

Lauredo promised me that he would explore the situation and see to it that I would be financially accommodated in my transition back to the University of Illinois. There were surprises ahead as to how I would exit for good from Nicaragua.

Can the Mediation Be Revived?

On December 29 I returned to Managua. Two days earlier Bowdler had arrived to visit Somoza in the newly built Presidential Palace. Since the mediator's arrival I had not spoken at length with Somoza. The building of the palace, however, reminded me of the construction of a new one by Fulgencio Batista in the last months of his regime prior to his ouster: that building had symbolized to the public the Cuban dictator's desire to remain ruling. Somoza was confident: the quarrel was only with members of an administration, not the American people, and the OAS would not violate Nicaragua's sovereignty against his tenure.

In the meantime, Somoza moved in Central America against the mediation and Costa Rica. Tensions increased. On December 27 he accused Costa Rica of complicity in Sandinista attacks. He publicly said that until the FSLN problem was settled, the southern border would be closed, and he warned that if the OAS did not head off the guerrillas' raids, his troops might invade Costa Rica. The result: the OAS Permanent Council resolved (on December 30) to reaffirm the proscription of threats and use of force among member states, to notify the Nicaraguan government to normalize commercial traffic and the transit of people across the border, and to petition the formation of a commission of civilian observers so that it could travel as soon as possible to the frontier.[116] The OAS had postponed the monitoring of armed activities between both countries. A source of the delay now was Costa Rica's objection that one of the assigned observers was from the pro-Somoza Paraguayan government.

The United States, by contrast, was in favor of urgently sending the OAS observers. However, our embassy in Costa Rica was reluctant to have a U.S. congressman visit with Sandinistas in his planned trip to the country, not only because this could bolster the FSLN but because it could compromise the local government proving the harboring of Sandinistas. Such was the prevailing schizophrenia. (Novedades published several photographs of FSLN training camps in Costa Rica; Somoza's daily alleged the presence of guerrillas from Panama in them.)

In his last months in office the Venezuelan president sent another message to the president of the United States, complaining about the lack of anti-Somoza action in the face of the failure of the mediation. Pérez visited the Dominican Republic and urged that the OAS "energetically act now" against Somoza.[117] But neither the United States nor the hemispheric body would act effectively.

After his brief visit to Managua, Bowdler went to the Dominican Republic to meet with the other two mediators to draft the report on their mission. On December 28 I learned of his instructions: the report should be written to inform the OAS; the United States did not wish to push for a resolution critical of Nicaragua; a move against Nicaragua in the OAS on the basis of Somoza's lack of acceptance of its last proposal could be interpreted as transgressing against Nicaragua's sovereignty; the Costa Rican government could use the initiative to urge collective actions against Nicaragua. The United States would later use the discussion of the Inter-American Human Rights Report to debate Somoza's refusal to carry out a fair plebiscite.

On December 29 the embassy received a copy of the American mediator's message to Washington from the Dominican Republic, explaining why Somoza's counteroffer (which included the notion that even if the opposition won the plebiscite, it could not form a government yet) should be rejected and the mediation terminated. The project had failed.

There was little left for me to do. Dissatisfied with the mediation's prospects, the Dominican foreign minister did not return to Nicaragua. For its own reasons, the Guatemalan government subsequently withdrew its representative. After an initiative by some oppositionists that I reported to Washington, I was explicitly forbidden to attempt undermining Somoza's position within the National Guard to facilitate a coup. Once again my hands were tied. According to the new, explicit order, I could not even discuss the possibility of a coup d'état with any Nicaraguan.

Before my final departure in February, I witnessed Somoza's escalated challenge to his opponents: the promotion of his twenty-seven-year-old son to Lieutenant Colonel as a prize for his role in suppressing the September uprising. I felt as if I had been slapped in the face by Somoza. The promotion was an insult to the entire community, an indication of his desire to continue the dynasty. This act, in my opinion, was a final symbolic step on the ladder toward successful revolution. The feeling that he would never be willing to step down, that he listened to no one including the United States, further spread and solidified. I asked myself: who is this spoiled, conceited man, who, when faced with internationally supported, broad-based national repudiation, considered the state to be bequeathed to his son? Why is he willing to take his country into an all-out war? Why can't other Nicaraguans aspire to rule their nation?

I never talked to General Somoza again. As he had told me in August, Somoza would go down his "honorable" way, fighting while being collectively declared the "Pirate of the Americas." The months of mediation had not moved the strongman an inch.

7. Partial Withdrawal

With the collapse of the mediation, after the OAS team's final visit of January 1979, U.S.-Nicaragua relations entered a new phase that I would call "partial withdrawal." A package of sanctions to pressure the Nicaragua government to negotiate had never really materialized beyond the few improvised, piecemeal measures reported in the previous chapter. Despite resistance, however, the old spirit of the human rights policy of suspending some programs with target dictators was revived. The following actions were announced: formal termination of the military assistance program and withdrawal of the military advisers (only four officers still remained); suspension of the new package of USAID programs (for approximately $12 million); reduction in the number of state and USAID functionaries in the embassy (by twenty-two); and withdrawal of the remaining Peace Corps volunteers.

The ambassador was not withdrawn. The objective was to show displeasure with Somoza while still maintaining a presence in the country. The measures were quite limited—for instance, the much greater USAID pipeline was maintained. It was essentially a return to the initial policy of so-called neutrality: not backing Somoza while also not siding with any viable alternative.

A sense of duty in a situation in which one crisis followed another had inhibited extricating myself from Managua. My Miami contacts succeeded. Following the mediation's failure Washington informed me that I would be replaced in Managua, and arrangements would be made to accommodate me until I could reincorporate myself into my permanent job.

Suddenly we obtained reliable intelligence that a Sandinista faction intended to assassinate me; the plot was conceived to trigger another explosion for the dissolution of the regime. We knew that the source was reliable because in the past it had given the local CIA information about terrorist acts that had subsequently taken place. The residence had been chosen because it still remained insufficiently protected and unfenced. Ironically, it took time to determine the location of the planned "murder, not kidnapping," and the first reaction was to keep me in the residence.[1]

When an official's life is threatened, a possible action is to remove him or her from the scene to have more time to evaluate the threat. Thus I was told by Washington to momentarily withdraw to the United States. While I waited to leave Nicaragua I decided, but shared with no one, that I would use this opportunity to not return to the post and to terminally disassociate myself from the adventure. I was both relieved to be separating myself from a fiasco but intensely saddened by the tragedy of Nicaragua.

I still vividly recall my last hours at the residence. Reservations had been made under a different name on the Pan American morning flight. Two cars left the residence: one with a bodyguard more or less my same height as a decoy went to my office; the other to the airport with me. As I entered the airplane surrounded by very heavily armed men, led by Msgt. Peter Delandero, the able head of our U.S. Marines, the flight attendant became faint: she thought it was a skyjacking. . . .

I left Nicaragua on February 26 1979 and never returned. Embassy affairs were left in the hands of the deputy chief of mission, who during my tenure had been involved in the administrative side of operations, not the political. In not returning to Managua I had a sense of loss of the loyal officers with whom I had had the privilege to serve. But at the same time I had a sense of fulfilled duty; others should take responsibility for the mediation's failure and future events.

It took time for the administration to decide to implement the sanctions, limited though they were; they began to be carried out just before my departure. I recall Washington's eagerness to find out about local reaction to the measures. It was zilch. By the time the sanctions were publicized, Nicaraguans had other concerns. Limited punitive action historically has proved ineffective in many theaters, but in Nicaragua the adoption of no sanctions while not supporting the government could have only been psychologically more disastrous, further eroding the U.S. position with the local opposition and public opinion. Although U.S. policy failed, our position within Nicaragua could have been worse if no action had been taken at this point. Nicaragua did not experience the intense anti-U.S. backlash of Iran. That the U.S. government was incapable of ultimately preventing the deterioration of relations with the Sandinista regime is another matter.

Crazy Enterprises

From the day that I left Managua, I had nothing to do with Nicaraguan affairs— my comments must now be interpreted in this light. The policy of partial withdrawal, compounded by subsequent administration action, only produced more disappointment.

There were not many alternatives left. The administration could have sided with the revolution, as a few individuals with access to the State Department urged during these months. But this violated any commitment to peaceful change, entailed the use of "covert" operations against the administration's philosophy, would have been met with problems in the U.S. Congress, and was seen by some key functionaries leading toward the installation of an adversarial regime aligned with Cuba. In fact, if the administration had been willing to use covert action, other routes could have been used with less cost to change the government than a violent revolution.

The direct unilateral use of U.S. force was also precluded by the prevailing philosophy. Given the extant sentiment in the Organization of American States—reflected in Guatemala's recent defection from the mediation—the multilateralization of a forceful U.S. intervention to oust Somoza and block a full Sandinista military victory would have required forming an axis outside of the OAS—for instance, joining Venezuela, Panama, and Costa Rica in their anti-Somoza activities. The nature of such operations and the costs in terms of domestic congressional politics were beyond the administration's Liberal Hour to explore; Somoza's was a "friendly" government, and its collapse was not yet imminent.

Why not support the Nicaraguan government until 1981? This retreat was too much to swallow. It already entailed assisting a very repressive campaign against the population by the government, more so than the repression that had originated the anti-Somoza human rights campaign to begin with. And the Somoza regime had been mortally wounded: its dynastic patrimonialism was an anachronism, and it was desperately isolated—it called for regime change, not re-equilibration. I must emphasize that interpretations at this state that "Washington pursued every route short of armed intervention to frustrate a revolutionary victory" are incorrect. As we have seen, the necessary U.S. political-military counterinsurgency resources were not allocated to Somoza to remain ruling. Such support to Central American regimes had to wait until after the revolutionary victory in Nicaragua, especially to the Reagan years.

In sum, it would be incorrect to argue that, because at this phase the United States did not act to remove Somoza, the administration "supported" him. Nevertheless, there was now an anti-revolution, and in this sense a "Somocista," tilt in the policy. All in all, it was a pathetic enterprise, one that would not create any friends for our nation. We had been displaced as a decisive force. Not having succeeded in sponsoring change by persuading Somoza and being tokenly anti-revolutionary evidenced the lack of realism of a sanctimonious and absurd policy. The United States was not using significant resources to stop the revolution, while it successfully antagonized the people of Nicaragua.

The Somocistas were also engaged in a "crazy enterprise." By stubbornly acquiescing to General Somoza's unshakable search for his unrealistic, "theoretically" best possible outcome, they had taken a large step toward obtaining their worst possible outcome—indefinite exile for the leadership and long prison terms for thousands of the followers.[2] The mediation had offered them intermediate outcomes—after all, it had proposed the dismantling of neither the National Guard nor the Liberal Party. Although Somoza may not have willfully gambled the destruction of his followers, clearly the costs of defeat were not the same for the leader as his followers. The Somocistas had, in fact, opted for an unviable "all-or-nothing" strategy.

The consequences of the mediation's failure were far reaching. It had again served to raise expectations that the United States would change the government, but with its rejection, hopes for any peaceful solution were dashed. The political space for maneuvering virtually collapsed, leaving only violence.

Nicaragua was at a point of no return. By involving not only the political opposition but also the key economic and social groups that could be the only sources of support of a Nicaraguan-type conservative regime (the clases or fuerzas vivas), the mediation had, in fact, further isolated the president. Somoza had been left alone with his small National Guard, his bureaucratic Liberal cadres, and a few friends and associates. Thus as this Sandinista belief in violence to solve the impasse became quite generalized, the Sandinistas became the undisputed leaders of the opposition. Somocista hidebound sectarismo strengthened their greatest enemy. The widespread expectation of another wave of violence further reinforced the opinion that violence was required—the sooner the better to end the crisis and pacify the country.[3]

Certainly the unarmed opposition had also been involved in another "crazy enterprise." Their unrealistic demands that foreigners give them absolute control of the state played into the hands of Somocista intransigence. The unarmed opposition's interest was a settlement that avoided a war, which could only displace their leadership, be extremely costly, and increase the uncertainty of democracy's victory. War could be avoided only by negotiating a settlement that included a role for the Somocistas. Unfortunately, civilized national democratic convivencia eluded the parties mainly because General Somoza with the support of his small group of followers refused to compromise. He "proved" to all of us that it was a waste of time to negotiate intermediate outcomes with him.

I left Nicaragua thinking that a new, more violent stage of the conflict was already on its way, that a coup d'état was not likely, and that a revolutionary victory was possible if proper international assistance was forthcoming.

New Developments

After my departure and total disengagement from policy the Sandinistas continued making sustained efforts to build the broadest possible coalition under their leadership. Although the United People's Movement spoke of radical political and social change, it also claimed a pluralistic, democratic program.[4]

But there were important additional developments in the international front. Although with the advent of their new administration in March the Venezuelans appeared to change militancy, Panamanian and Costa Rican involvement continued, thus reinforcing perceptions that a revolutionary regime aligned with Castro was not inevitable. Cuban involvement, however, dramatically increased. According to the State Department:

> By the end of 1978, Cuban advisers were dispatched to northern Costa Rica to train and equip the FSLN forces with arms which began to arrive directly from Cuba. FSLN guerrillas trained in Cuba . . . return[ed] to Nicaragua via Panama.
>
> In early 1979, Cuba helped organize, arm, and transport an "internationalist brigade" to fight alongside FSLN guerrillas. Members were drawn from several Central and South American extremist groups, many of whom were experienced in terrorist activities. Castro also dispatched Cuban military specialists to the field to help coordinate the war efforts. Factionalism threatened Sandinista unity again in early 1979, and Castro met personally with leaders of three FSLN factions to hammer out a renewed unity pact.
>
> When the insurgents' final offensive was launched in mid-1979, Cuban military advisers . . . were with FSLN columns and maintained direct radio communications to Havana. A number of Cuban advisers were wounded in combat and were evacuated to Cuba via Panama.[5]

The added international support that the embassy thought could lead to successful revolution was developing.[6]

The violent revolutionary level further escalated. A few weeks before the May-June final offensive, I accidentally met William Bowdler in Washington. He told me that the Nicaraguan government was making noises toward talking. Months later, after the revolution, I had a conversation with Luis Pallais, who referred to this meeting in the State Department to explore the possibility of another OAS initiative. According to him, the U.S. showed interest in a Nicaraguan, not American, initiative in that body. Upon his return to Managua, Pallais raised the issue; however, in a discussion with Somoza and members of the cabinet, a Nicaraguan proposal to the OAS was vetoed on the grounds that Somoza would probably have to relinquish his sovereignty. According to Pallais, only two cabinet ministers were receptive to the initiative. General Somoza's entourage remained unwilling to manifest that their interests could be represented by anyone other than him.[7] The working out of a realistic solution—consonant with Nicaraguan and international conditions—remained impossible. This political incapacity was also extensive in the National Guard.

During this phase Somoza's perception of reality unfortunately was still conditioned by his few U.S. Congress supporters. The administration had as a priority to obtain from Congress the implementation of the Panama Canal treaties; again Somoza's friends were in the strategic committee needed to obtain passage of this legislation, and he was well aware of the precedents of administration retreat vis-à-vis this congressional "connection." In late spring 1979 Panamanian support for the Sandinistas was discussed in the U.S. Congress in an effort to defeat administration proposals.

Some Somocistas were unrealistic about the prospects of remaining in power. There was the sense that there was time, and some even thought that in the event of an uprising the U.S. government would rescue them rather than allow a Sandinista victory. Defections are supposed to take place when, in the face of growing opposition, ruling group interest is perceived as threatened and generates the notion that the leader has served his purpose, and it is appropriate now for him to go.[8] However, opposition partisan rhetoric, proposals, and weak organization were not helpful in persuading that the alternative FAO-Somocista cooperation was feasible. But principally the Liberal Somocistas were not democrats. They strongly identified with their leader and his aura of superiority over them, had internalized norms of loyalty and subordination to their leader, and were incapable of changing the leadership.

Regime dynamics were affected by the ruler's social psychology (and that of his intimate circle) and by situational factors. Only after sustained U.S. initiatives had Somoza stopped ruling in late 1977 as a dictator with state-of-siege powers; he had just shown his true authoritarian colors—he could not be trusted. On the other hand, the sudden explosive growth of the opposition that had taken place since early 1978 reinforced opposition intransigence lest it return to its immediate prior impotence. No one would talk to Somoza; it was not the best moment for him to step down.

His opponents "knew" the Somoza personality factor and the political, cultural, and structural conditions that resulted in his unshakable control of his followers. As Conservative Horacio Argüello, my first official contact with the opposition, told me, "Somoza will never leave power unless forced to."

8. The Failure of U.S. Policy

The Final Uprising

In my months in Nicaragua there were recurrent calls for a "final" revolt. We have analyzed the main components of the events: armed actions intended to take over cities by taking control of their *cuarteles* (military bases); the taking over of city sections by popular uprisings that built barricades on the streets and involved unarmed and armed men who blocked off all traffic; fairly extensive general strikes; and incursions by armed men crossing international borders. The September uprising witnessed a combination of these events, especially of the first three, and although no military base was successfully taken over, for several days the National Guard was unable to recapture the cities involved. Now at the end of May, early June, the uprising combined all these activities and had much greater military weight. The revolt spread through the nation to involve more cities and towns, and military columns engaged in urban and rural areas. An outright invasion was launched from Costa Rica. The increased government repression had not succeeded. The revolution with the greatest popular participation of contemporary Latin America had been unleashed.

The previous September no city had been entirely captured by the insurgents, and no uprising by the populace had touched Managua. The picture was now different. With their increased numbers and materiel the insurgents captured a few cities, and the revolt included sections of the capital, where Somoza's general military headquarters were located. But before the president's resignation, the uprising in Managua had been contained, and his main headquarters fell only after his exit and the subsequent collapse of the National Guard. The invasion from Costa Rica did not progress, though it occupied vital government resources.

During the preceding period of U.S. inaction, the entire opposition had opted to go all the way and to back an insurrection rather than remain Somoza's "prisoners." This culminated in June 1979 in the formation in exile of a revolutionary junta based in Costa Rica that was intended to replace Somoza.

This Junta de Reconstrucción Nacional was presented as the executive of the future government.

Symptomatically, the Junta was composed of five members: its majority was formed by a Sandinista military commander and two spokespeople for the FSLN, who had been aligned with them throughout the entire process. This contrasted with the earlier situation during the mediation, when the unarmed opposition had had the upper hand. In the Junta the FAO representatives were the minority: Violeta Barrios de Chamorro, Pedro Joaquín's widow, represented *La Prensa* and the tradition of Conservative Party opposition to the Somozas; and Alfonso Robelo, of the MDN, gave a conspicuous presence to the private sector. This Chamorro-Robelo presence furthered the claim about the coalition nature of the revolution. The understanding was that after victory, a democratic, internationally nonaligned regime with political pluralism and a mixed economy would be established.

In October 1977 the civic opposition and the Catholic Church condemned both government repression and opposition violence. Now the Episcopal Conference also justified the insurrection. In revolutions, fear does not disappear from the picture. But with the growth in networks of opposition, the principles of power and safety in numbers gained strength: the opposition had outpaced the government's repressive capacity.

Also, as the government was taxed, it tended to become more indiscriminate: troops became less disciplined, more arbitrary and brutal, exemplified by the filmed murder of ABC correspondent Bill Stewart in early June. As in Cuba, a stage of truly wanton, anarchic government violence developed. Rather than intimidate, the government repression produced greater outrage.

International Clientelism Does Not Die

Once the carnage started to unfold, the U.S. government sought to "mediate" again, once more relying on the OAS. On May 20 Mexico broke diplomatic relations with Nicaragua; eight days later, the Andean Pact nations—Venezuela, Colombia, Ecuador, Peru, and Bolivia—condemned extant conditions and sent a mission to Managua in search of a solution to the war. On June 4 Gale McGee, the U.S. ambassador to the OAS, was quoted as saying: "We condemn [foreign] intervention in the Nicaraguan situation, if such be proven."[1]

On June 18—and I rely on the notes graciously made available to me by Luis Pallais Debayle, who was personally involved in all the conversations—what the Nicaraguan government considered an American "ultimatum" was delivered by the State Department in Washington to Pallais and Guíllermo Sevilla Sacasa, the Nicaraguan ambassador to the United States. The Nicaraguans never talked to any official higher than the assistant secretary level.

In several ways the new initiative followed the old mediation. Once again the president was asked to resign—this time to answer by the following day—in order to form a Government of National Reconciliation, as the alternative to the FSLN-dominated Junta de Reconstrucción Nacional in Costa Rica. The expressed objective was to maintain the National Guard as a viable institution and to keep the official Liberal Party alive. It was stated to the Nicaraguans that the United States, operating through the OAS, would seek to stop the war.

Although the goal was to pack the new transitional government with "moderates," for the first time the United States already talked to the Nicaraguans about direct Sandinista military presence in the provisional government. The Sandinistas would be asked to depose their arms.

The Nicaraguans argued that General Somoza's sudden departure could create a leadership vacuum and drop in morale leading to the collapse of the National Guard, that (as in September 1978) a military victory should precede negotiations, and that Nicaragua needed military resources, especially ammunition. Notice the stubborn irreplaceability of the leader theme. The United States was unwilling to prop up the regime, however. The Somoza family had to leave the National Guard and the country, and any subsequent U.S. military involvement would be channeled through the OAS. On June 19 Somoza dictated his answer: he resented the ultimatum. If the OAS provided for an orderly transition with guarantees, he would carry it out. He and his family needed visas and guarantees that they could remain in the United States without being extradited back to Nicaragua.

The end was near. Somoza was aware that he had to leave. In fact, the conditions that he sought (and continued to seek during the following weeks) had been essentially met by the mediation.[2]

The Nicaraguan leadership had started to learn about what a well-known American columnist described as an "inglorious attempt to rob the rebels of victory by backdoor maneuvering."[3] As in earlier periods of Nicaraguan history, the United States was seeking to be the kingmaker in a situation in which a revolution had become legitimate. Constituting a government along the State Department's lines was a very precarious effort, to say the least. Precedent during the mediation suggested that the Sandinistas (and their fronts) would fight to defeat the American plan now backed by guns. The American plan had no credibility, unless support was provided to the Nicaraguan National Guard.

Notice the ungraciousness of American claims: the administration had been unwilling to take responsibility for replacing Somoza, yet it intended to form the next government of Nicaragua. These clientelistic policies could only be resented. We were witnessing that despite the rhetoric, the combination of foreign legitimacy crisis and the perceived probability that an anti-American regime allied with adversary nations would take root tends to foster clientelism. For in spite of ambiguities, American influential sectors and the public are not entirely indifferent to shifts in foreign spheres of influence—and presidents' wish to be re-elected.

Defeat in the OAS

On June 21 the U.S. secretary of state appeared before the OAS to propose the establishment of a transitional government, which would be a clear beak with the past. On the same day the United States proposed a resolution, the crux of which was the creation of a special delegation of the OAS that would work to constitute the Government of National Reconciliation, command an international military force to pacify Nicaragua, and channel humanitarian assistance to the war-torn country. The U.S. proposal was resoundingly defeated—it did *not command a single vote!* Two days later, and in the face of the gruesome events being reported by the media throughout the world, with the support of the U.S. government, the OAS approved its final resolution. Among other points: the "horrors," the "great suffering and loss of lives," were the result of the "inhuman behavior" of Somoza's "dictatorial" regime; the solution to the civil war fell exclusively to the Nicaraguan people, a curious point in the light of the intervention by several countries that had been going on and had not been effectively dealt with by the OAS. The OAS suggested as bases for the solution the immediate and definitive end of the Somoza regime, the constitution of a democratic government with participation of the principal opposition groups, the respect of the human rights of all Nicaraguans, and free elections as soon as possible to establish an authentically democratic government.[4]

Somoza's scenario in his August confrontation with me had come true. Indeed, he was going down as the "Pirate of the Americas." With this OAS resolution, the U.S. government sealed the boundaries of its subsequent policy. Somocistas had been left "*solos,*" (alone), as his handpicked successor of only hours wrote.[5]

In choosing the full-blown multilateralism of the OAS, the administration had foreclosed establishing a government not dominated by the Sandinistas. (I would not have backed at this moment a unilateral U.S. intervention to pacify Nicaragua—it would have been too costly and unprincipled; the moment for a credible ultimatum had been earlier). There was a tradition in the Americas of opposition to multilateral peacekeeping forces. Multilateral OAS "peacekeeping" forces only had materialized ex post facto, after physical interventions not involving the collective body but member countries (e.g., in the Dominican Republic in 1965).[6] Thus OAS approval of the American proposal could not have been expected. Those in the U.S. government who knew better seemingly felt forced to conduct a desperate effort to avoid the inevitable. Zbigniew Brzezinski, the national security adviser, reportedly fought unsuccessfully for a U.S. unilateral intervention in support of maintaining a viable National Guard; he wished to avoid another major policy defeat after Iran.

In fact, it was remarkable that in June 1979 the Organization of American States had come so far to condemn the Nicaragua government and explicitly declare the need to change it, in contrast to its September authorization of the mediation. But the situation had changed: a much publicized, cruel war was underway. The Somoza regime was a peculiar one within Latin America; area elites could understand the rebellion against a dynasty, largely viewed on the continent as an index of "Central American underdevelopment."

As I read about these events, they did not make any sense. Neither did they to journalists who had covered Nicaragua during my tenure—I received a call from the *Miami Herald* to ask me to assert in Washington that the path taken to "stop" the revolution could only be politically harmful. It was a desperate call from friends.

If the United States had not taken any formal position to stop the revolution, and the revolution then turned "sour," our government would have been blamed for the outcome. However, its ineffective stance did not entirely assuage such claims but, as history showed, did further antagonize the future rulers of Nicaragua. More importantly, we had helped them believe that a combination of stratagem and tough politics was the best strategy to adopt toward a disliked United States, which did not help future U.S.-Nicaragua relations.

The Attempt to Form a Non-Sandinista-Controlled Government

On June 25 the United States communicated its formula to the Nicaraguan government: the president steps down and he, his family, and other closely associated individuals leave Nicaragua; Somoza could not negotiate the transition, though his views would be considered. Immediately after his resignation the Nicaraguan Congress would convene and elect a new president, who would dissolve the Congress and name a provisional government, an Executive Committee, dominated by "moderates." This committee would subsequently announce a change in the command of the National Guard, call for a cease-fire, and negotiate with the Sandinista Junta, already recognized by Costa Rica, Panama, and Grenada. The objective of the negotiations was not to completely defeat the uprising but rather to form a new, more broadly based transitional coalition government. After the date was set for Somoza's resignation, all the steps would take place within twenty-four hours; the United States would work with the Executive Committee and help, as best it could, with the reorganization of the National Guard; within hours Lawrence Pezzullo, the new U.S. ambassador, would go to Managua to implement the plan.

On June 27 Pezzullo arrived in Managua. Somoza knew that he was defeated. He referred to his personal fear of assassination.[7] He was abandoning his supporters to their fate, while he was flying to safety. Wouldn't one of them try to stop his cowardly act?

The U.S. strategy consisted of a bluff comparable to the mediation. In this case, it tried to stall Somoza's departure and use it to negotiate a cease-fire under terms favorable to impede a complete takeover by the Sandinista-dominated Junta and a total Sandinista military victory. I should note that as there was an ongoing war, there was significant public dissatisfaction with this policy that was prolonging it. In the United States many viewed it as a callous, self-serving tactic.

To constitute the transitional government, the collaboration of regional regimes was sought in negotiating the cease-fire. (This included a secret visit to Washington by Panamanian strongman Omar Torrijos). The United States was no longer the hegemonic power; it had to depend on many foreign voices. One of the concerns was that other Latin American governments—whose foreign offices have an agenda of their own—undercut the initiatives by recognizing the Sandinista-dominated Junta. Such was the perceived divergent diagnosis about realities between the United States and several Latin American "rightist" authoritarian governments.

The constraints on U.S. policy were severe. At no time did the administration commit itself to unilaterally coming in and militarily assisting the discredited National Guard. Indeed, Somoza was informed about the changing of the Guard's name and its reorganization into a new entity—old Sandinista demands during the mediation. His statements notwithstanding, he never was promised that the United States "guaranteed" the Guard's integrity.[8] And although the National Guard still was fighting, the Sandinistas already controlled vastly more territory than in September: to recapture the territory would have now taken far more time at far more cost. The logic of the American strategy of negotiating a cease-fire and reorganizing the army at this point necessarily had to lead to the heavy inclusion of Sandinistas in a newly formed institution.

In sum, after the defeat of the U.S. proposal in the OAS, U.S. strategy was two-pronged: negotiate to minimize the possibility of a Marxist-Leninist-oriented (i.e., "hard-core" Sandinista) government and maximize the survival of National Guard cadres. Somocista expectations that the United States would rescue them with military assistance and rob the Sandinistas of a victory in the ongoing bloodbath only indicated their stubborn lack of awareness of political realities in Washington. They had never paid attention. The United States was substantially abiding by the spirit of the OAS resolution. Nevertheless, other foreign parties continued to provide support to the insurrection.

From Ambassador Pezzullo's arrival until Somoza's July 17 departure, twenty-one days lapsed. The formation of a transitional government that would "break with the past" and be "packed with moderates" did not occur. On July 14 the U.S. mediator communicated in Costa Rica to the Sandinista-dominated Junta of National Reconstruction that it would be recognized, sealing the revolution's victory.[9]

Some interpretations place the blame on the American negotiators. One version was that if the United States had been firmer in these negotiations, it would have been possible to stop the revolution. We know, however, that in December 1978, in the much more favorable climate of the mediation, unarmed oppositionists were most uncomfortable with constituting a government that included Somocistas; more than ever they now blamed the National Guard for the macabre state of affairs. Who were the Nicaraguan oppositionists willing to form a transitional government not supported by the FSLN in the ongoing war? Indeed, Pezzullo has reported his unsuccessful contacts with Nicaraguans: the embassy's friends were not available to form a government in defiance of the Sandinista Junta. One of my regular contacts asked Pezzullo, "Is the United States prepared to send in troops to stop the fighting and support this transitional government?" No, was the answer. Our friend replied, "Then it won't work." He also expressed the lack of credibility of the U.S. government left among oppositionists. "You raised our hopes during the mediation, but you failed us. . . . It is too late to be devising schemes."[10]

Problems remained. Would the National Guard accept the proposed coalition government? There was a deep conviction among Guard officers that the Sandinistas were their enemy, "Communists," the "devil" incarnate. Nicaragua's past history consisted of a struggle between highly *sectarias hegemonías* that exercise power at the expense of dominating opponents. The Guard had reasons to fear reprisals and its total displacement from power. This proved the case, although the United States in the negotiations with the Sandinista Junta obtained a pledge that the safety of members of the National Guard, who respected the cease-fire, would be guaranteed, and that the newly organized army would include members of the Guard. However, the latter—

politically the most important point—became moot with the collapse of the Guard after Somoza's exit.

Somoza resigned, leaving Nicaragua on July 17 with the cabinet, top National Guard staff, and directors of the Liberal Party.[11] That same day, after accepting Somoza's resignation at 1 a.m., the Nicaraguan Congress appointed its president, Francisco Urcuyo Maliaño, as the successor; the new command of the National Guard was also in place. But contrary to the understanding with the United States, Dr. Urcuyo refused to resign. Ambassador Pezzullo abandoned Nicaragua with his embassy in protest.

Urcuyo must have been aware that the plan agreed upon between Somoza and the United States was for him to leave office immediately after his congressional appointment. But apparently he did not wish to be historically responsible for recognizing the FSLN victory. Somoza's one priority was to get out of Nicaragua alive. Seemingly, he would not negotiate for the U.S. government a binding agreement with Urcuyo that he hand over power to the Junta, though Pezzullo felt that he had agreed to do so. Once again Somoza had outmaneuvered a U.S. mediator.

On July 18 Deputy Secretary Warren Christopher called Somoza, who was already on his Miami island. Feeling threatened with expulsion by the U.S. government, Somoza phoned Urcuyo and asked him to resign. On July 19 the Sandinista revolution triumphed: the command structure of the National Guard had collapsed, and with it the National Guards who remained in Nicaragua— thousands of Somocistas left the country when they could—became prisoners of the Sandinistas; they were now the new, collectively defined, "criminals" of the reconstituted state. A reversal of roles—yesterday's groups backed by the state's legality becoming the criminals of the new regime—was dramatically illustrated in Nicaragua.

The National Guard's Disintegration

A closer look at the military situation hours prior to the evaporation of the National Guard is warranted. The Guard had been fighting: the invasion from Costa Rica had been checked, although the need to divert troops to the southern border meant that it would take longer to control the uprisings in other parts of the country. Managua had not fallen, but the insurrectionists had taken neighboring Masaya. Since July 7 Nicaragua's second largest city, Leon, had been in rebel hands; several other cities and small towns had fallen. The Sandinistas kept up their military as well as political pressure. It was announced that their Junta would fly from Costa Rica to Leon to establish their government in the liberated city. Did the confusion inherent in the described last-minute, erratic actions precipitate the collapse of the Guard? How much of a role in the disintegration was played by the growing awareness that international pressures were for the Guard to technically fall under the Junta controlled by the "enemy"?

It is noteworthy that the revolutionaries had supply and organizational problems of their own. The revolutionary processes had exhibited significant spontaneity. For example, the uprising in Monimbo that subsequently served as a model has been called an "unexpected explosion" by Sandinista sources because it occurred independently of any FSLN plan. The decentralized participation of small groups and their imitative chain reactions of participation by other groups were present in the uprisings. The revolution was largely improvised and learned behavior. Nonetheless, there was organization, even if loose, in the final uprising: it was initiated by Radio Sandino's call for the uprising of May 25 and sufficiently coordinated. Still, as noted by Sergio Ramírez, the "great majority, and until almost the end, of the members of the Dirección Nacional of the FSLN [the maximum revolutionary leaders] were outside of [Nicaragua] and did not have effective control over the rebels, every time more numerous."[12] Indeed, it is remarkable that with the disintegration of the National Guard a new state was reconstituted by the top FSLN leadership that was accepted by the people. States are valuable entities. The intervention of other states in constituting foreign governments—Nicaragua showed—contributes to their maintenance.

Our military officers in Managua had considered the National Guard's counterinsurgency capabilities limited given its training and size (at the time it numbered perhaps around eight thousand). Most important in the Guard's collapse, however, was the highly centralized and authoritarian command and control structure successfully kept by the Somozas. Hear Somoza's son assess the situation on June 29, in a conversation with our ambassador:

> I've been in the firing line with the people that are under stress at this stage; and my best, my very best observation on the subject [i.e., the viability of the Guard after the departure of the family] is that . . . what you would need here . . . would be almost an immediate injection of American officers that have served here and have had contacts with the Guardia Nacional and have had relationships. Because, unquestionably, in certain strata of the Army—basically coming from the top major colonels right now, down to those that are the senior lieutenant colonels right now in th[at] strata . . . their leadership has always come directly from above. . . .
>
> I interject that and I would say that to cover that vacuum, to cover that vacuum that will exist if most people in the government have to leave, I would make

the suggestion to have a team of [U.S.] officers ready to come in . . . to the new
government of whatever. Because I know that they will be looking towards this as
a possibility of sounding out or finding buts.

I know this has been sort of traditional in a certain way, but I think that it's
an idea that you should play with, put in your scenario; because, to be very, very
frank . . . the leadership as it exists now emanates from three different people you
see; from the President, or from yours truly, or from General José Somoza.[13]

The deliberate system of making the Somoza family irreplaceable in the
Guardia Nacional, which for decades had served to justify the need for the
family to retain its control, contributed to the absence of established alternative
cadres and clear command roles to immediately lead the institution.

A sense of the climate that prevailed among the newly established command
of the National Guard was provided to me in two retrospective conversations
with General Federico Mejía González, who, in the final hours, was promoted
to general and appointed to head the Guard. (General Mejía was related to
Colonel Bernardino Larios, the only top officer of the Guard who had defected
to the opposition in 1978. In conjunction with Larios's defection, Mejía had
been imprisoned for twenty-two hours by Somoza—notice the internal control. Colonel Larios, who was later jailed by the Sandinista government, was
at this time in Costa Rica collaborating with the FSLN command. Mejía had
been appointed by Somoza to head the Guard following U.S. wishes because
of Sandinista interest; Mejía was acceptable to Somoza though.)

This is Mejía's story. Upon his assuming the headship of the Guard, the
fighting was ongoing. General Mejía was faced with demands for logistical
support from all the key military units. There had remained hope within the
Guard that once it was renovated, passing in control to the colonels, the
United States would assist them in recapturing the lost territory. There was
also hope that materiel would come from other friendly sources. However,
Nicaraguan commanders rapidly learned, directly or indirectly, of U.S. refusal
to assist; expected supplies from Argentina, Israel, and Guatemala were not
forthcoming. The word spread that U.S. "instructions" were not to defeat the
Sandinistas. The U.S. embassy urged Mejía to go to Costa Rica to negotiate
with Comandante Humberto Ortega Saavedra (who became head of the new
army after the victory). General Mejía hesitated to go to Costa Rica: he feared he
could be made a prisoner there. Mejía and Ortega unsuccessfully held several
phone conversations to arrange form, time, and place of the meeting.

Mejía received other international calls. Among them were calls from
Ramón Emilio Jiménez—the Dominican foreign minister who had served as
one of the OAS mediators and presided over the OAS Consultation Meeting

(technically still in session)—and the president of Costa Rica, who urged him to accept and receive the Junta de Reconstrucción Nacional. This was interpreted as an international demand to surrender and the institution's downfall. General Mejía resisted handing over the state to the Sandinista-controlled Junta and sought the formation of a government headed by the archbishop.[14]

On July 18 three key commanders, the chief of the Nicaraguan Air Force and two members of the General Staff, left Nicaragua. That same day, Sandinista Comandante Humberto Ortega phoned Mejía to inform him that he was aware of the defections and to take a bolder stance: the FSLN was no longer interested in a cease-fire but wanted the surrender of the National Guard. At 7 a.m. on July 19 General Mejía left Nicaragua, persuaded that he headed a lost cause against the "Communist enemy," that resistance would only result, instead of "in 40,000, in 100,000 dead." Before this decision, he envisioned his army shooting at unarmed, enraged, improvised columns of civilians in an uprising against Managua's military base, the largest in the country and the location of his general headquarters.

The merit of this story is that it conveys the alienating sentiment of abandonment and futility that prevailed at the very top of the Guardia Nacional. An army is militarily defeated if it stops working (fighting) and accepts the conditions of the adversary (revolutionaries). One element is the material resources available to the organization to continue functioning, and another is the will to continue functioning (fighting). There is no need to physically destroy or capture a military organization in order that it discontinues to function.

Contradictory reports have been published.[15] As I see it, it was not that large parts of the National Guard had been physically destroyed or captured, thus resulting in paralysis, disorganization, and surrender. Psychological disorientation, intimidation, and fear, and a sense of powerlessness and futility contributed to a reorientation and decision to disband to minimize personal and group losses.[16] The paralysis resulted from the perception of the Guard's command that they lacked the support to continue fighting. They were faced with the awesome task of re-occupying a vast territory, with insufficient resources (without external sources), to recapture control of the country at a reasonable time and cost; with abandonment by their leaders—who had been their political cause; and international pressures (including that of the United States) to stop fighting and "submit themselves" to the control of a new government of their "enemies." This was the equation of the "output failure": the perceived incapacity to activate the support considered necessary to continue functioning.

Actually, during this phase the United States had launched itself to work out the establishment of a consociational regime between two enemies, in the absence of the requirements for its success.[17] There was strong reason to believe that the FSLN was not really interested in working out rules for such a coalition with the armed Somocistas: they had shown this throughout their history. The widespread premise was that the Guard could not compromise with the FSLN because the goal was to destroy it. History proved this right. Latin American precedents were considered. Where social revolutionaries constructed their own armed forces they consolidated themselves in power (Cuba in 1959); where they did not, they lost power (Chile in 1973).

In short, General Somoza of all people bitterly claimed that if U.S. diplomats had allowed him during this phase to leave earlier, the outcome would have differed . . . There are subtypes of revolutions. In contrast to Bolivia in 1952 and Cuba in 1959, the Nicaraguan military did not stop functioning because they split and fought among themselves when faced with widespread societal opposition, or because they were not committed to undertaking the increased costs of fighting under their leaders; rather, in comparative relief, under particularly adverse national and international pressures, in Nicaragua the head was severed from its body.

Epilogue

Lessons

What "lessons," if any, were learned and applied by the U.S. administrations that followed Nicaragua's revolution and Carter's electoral defeat? The Reagan administration, inaugurated in 1981, repudiated the human rights policy, returning to favor realpolitik.[1] Reagan blamed Carter's human rights policy for destabilizing the international environment in a manner unfavorable to the United States, with its moralizing interference bringing about undemocratic, cruel, anti-American revolutions. The post-Vietnam lack of consensus on foreign policy had grown. Reagan's team claimed a new nationalistic realism that had to opt for lesser evils to protect the nation's security. Reagan still considered Communism a serious threat: the United States had to intervene in some theaters and prop up friendly governments—even with dictatorial-supporting, anti-revolutionary, counterinsurgency, "anti-terrorist" policies in order to safeguard the nation. In short, there was a return to the strategic security rationale of the Cold War.

The U.S. international position had declined from the lack of will to use power because of the prevailing non-interventionist pacifist mood. What became known as the Reagan Doctrine sought, while avoiding a large-scale war, to destabilize and change hostile governments and support friendly ones. Once again the interaction between the conceptualization of the national interest and Latin American realities had resulted in a policy change. Reagan wished to re-establish friendly ties with the Latin countries—mostly ruled by anti-Communist dictatorships that had been alienated by the human rights meddling of the prior administration—except for Nicaragua, which already had established close ties with the Cuba-Soviet axis and was promoting the export of revolution. Reagan sponsored an anti-Marxist Nicaraguan force, the Contras, while also deploying U.S. troops in Honduras and assisting, as allowed by Congress, the governments of El Salvador and Guatemala. Noteworthy again were the zigzags in U.S. policy: both realpolitik and democratic crusades had failed to produce relatively stable, friendly environments.

In 1983, for the first time in almost twenty years, American troops successfully invaded a Caribbean country, Grenada. Reagan had been elected despite the post-Vietnam climate of non-interventionism. The weight of public opinion in the U.S. political system produced effects. Public opinion had considered that Carter's foreign policy had failed: Iran, Nicaragua, the Soviet invasion of Afghanistan. Americans do not like to view their country as a loser. Carter's defeat was attributed to an inability to grasp the realities of both the international environment and the exigencies of the American political system.

But, interestingly, by his second term Reagan came to adopt a pro-democratic crusade for Latin America, continuing into the Bush administration, that included the kind of anti-Communist, interventionist counterinsurgency dimensions found with Kennedy's democratic reformism and abandoned by Carter. Why did this take place?

First, Reagan encountered strong congressional opposition, especially for his Central American policy. The post-Vietnam mood was still alive in the Congress, and while the U.S. public did not favor "other Cubas" in Central America, it did not wish another involvement as in Vietnam.[2] Human rights advocacy remained the law of the land. The repulsive, repressive patterns of the Latin anti-Communist allies could not be condoned. Further, the Cuban and Nicaraguan adversaries were not democrats. Thus, in order to obtain the needed domestic support—and make policy more palatable to allies—a pro-democratic packaging seemed warranted. As most Americans believe that poverty and social inequality are the root cause of violence, the Reagan team accepted the promotion of social reformism.

Second, the realpolitik support of friendly dictators had proved once more that it did not guarantee success. The Philippine events culminating in 1986 dramatically demonstrated the dynamics of increased tyranny and ungovernability and the pressures to intervene to which authoritarian regimes can be susceptible. The Reagan administration had been supporting the Marcos dictatorship, yet contrary to a naive realpolitik conceptualization, the regime entered into crisis. It was not sufficient, as some Reagan spokespeople had suggested, to back friendly dictators to obtain an international environment to the liking of Washington. In the eternal need to oversimplify, the U.S. government was again preaching pro-democratic themes to further national interests. The obvious instability of authoritarian rule strengthened the inclination toward a preventive pre-crisis, pro-democratic U.S. diplomacy.

On the whole, Reagan's foreign policy was successful. However, despite the change in rationale, the Republican team faced difficulties generating support domestically and in Latin America. As in earlier years, Latin America was unwilling to join a pro-democratic continental campaign under U.S. leadership. Nor did the majority of these countries help to make the OAS the effective multilateral channel to terminate dictatorships. Although a body of

Latin America opinion continued to view negatively U.S. realpolitik friend-
ship with some dictators, and in several countries domestic groups sought
American clientelistic assistance to determine their governments, most Latin
American nations pursued foreign policies independent of the United States.
The incoherence and inconsistencies in U.S. policies, especially in Central
America, intensified by the executive-congressional divisiveness that prevailed
in Washington, reinforced this.

A unified Latin American bloc of governments did not materialize. An
innovation did take place, however: the proliferation of ad hoc regional sub-
blocs with a wider dimension than earlier ones, such as the Legión del Caribe.
Focusing on Central America, the Contadora Group (1983) and what became
known as the Arias Costa Rica Plan (1987) were formed. They sought Cold War
disengagement, an end to external subversion, and regional peace exclusively
through diplomatic means, favoring détente while opposing Reagan's use of
force in the Nicaraguan Contra war. The Latin Americans advocated democracy
and respect for human rights, which played a key role in Nicaragua's democratic transition. The fact is, however, that in Nicaragua the country's 1990
democratic transition was viewed, even by Sandinista leaders, as resulting also
from the high costs produced by the Reagan-supported Contra insurgency.[3]
Apparently that "bite" proved important to end the Sandinista dictatorship,
which subsequently contributed to democratization processes in Nicaragua's
neighbors.

Why this search for Latin America's autonomy? Beyond authentic nationalism and ideology, when upholding the principle of "non-intervention" against
the United States, Latins try to gain leverage that can be used to their material
and spiritual advantage. This is facilitated when the United States faces a
clientelistic crisis posed by adversarial regimes, which opens possibilities for
exercising domestically popular, independent leadership roles by the Latins.
There are great differences within Latin America. Some countries have special
relations with the United States; their governments can face internal political
problems and instability of their own, challenges that can be considered ame-
liorated by nationalistic stances, not being U.S. minions. Then there is also the
case of perceived national impotence to solve some problems beyond giving
diplomatic support to the United States. This tends to foment attitudes among
some leaders that others should solve the problems. The inclination of some
to rely on U.S. government leadership while being publicly critical of it should
not be considered pure irresponsible demagogy.

It is only natural that there should be areas of conflict of interest in U.S.-
Latin America relations and that in the face of extant power differentials in
them Latin Americans would be sensitive to maintaining their autonomy to

articulate and defend their own interests.[4] To this day within Latin America there are important movements for foreign policies independent from the United States. This should be expected and not necessarily seen as illegitimate by Americans.

Clientelism, then, had proven throughout the years to be a principal instrument to influence and cope with unstable, "unfriendly," international environments and with management problems faced by the United States and other countries, such as the Soviet Union. In addition, other nations were also involved in interventionist patterns. Yet the fact that American public opinion favored peaceful relations posed serious constraints on the Reagan administration. It had to find an equilibrium between the costs of being a "policeman of Latin America" and a "midwife to democracy." In spite of its nationalism, the administration wisely did not exclude the use of multilateral policies, though it did not refuse to intervene unilaterally. American force was to be used cautiously. There was the brief invasion of Grenada, but in the face of the longer commitment to support the Nicaraguan Contra war, the overthrow of the Panamanian dictator waited for the Bush administration. Following congressional directives, only a small number of U.S. military advisers were deployed in El Salvador to train local fighting forces. At the same time, though the pro-democratic crusade targeted authoritarian regimes of the left and right (e.g., Nicaragua's and Chile's, respectively), priorities were established to avoid reckless involvement.[5] Democracy means self-government, not government by foreigners. This limits the capacity and willingness of the United States to impose it even with Latin American cooperation.

The senior Bush years (1989–93) saw the culmination of ongoing trends. Some Latin American countries and the Soviet Bloc were involved in Central America in clientelistic patterns. Other than Spain, Western European nations had had a minimal presence in Nicaragua before the revolution. Now they acquired a new influence, providing significant assistance; noteworthy were the activities of Nordic European countries and the European Union. Along with the customary OAS participation, other international organizations, such as the United Nations, played a role in Nicaragua's pacification. Furthermore, a series of international public financial institutions (IFIs) and an increasing number of nongovernment organizations (NGOs) contributed to Nicaragua's democratic transition of 1990 with a broad range of innovations, from efforts to build local organs of civil society to monitoring elections.[6] Other "security" issues also acquired salience in U.S.-Latin America relations. There was the war against drugs, which took the extreme form of the 1989 American military invasion of Panama to depose and imprison its dictator, Manuel Antonio Noriega, accused of involvement in the sordid traffic.

With the collapse of the Soviet Union (1991) during Bush's term, the United States became the world's sole superpower. A greater "globalization" and multilateralization of clientelism took hold amid reservations of U.S. public opinion. It seemed not to matter much that under the Republicans U.S. troops had invaded two countries in the hemisphere, as if a return to pre-FDR years, although the occupations were now brief. Indeed, far greater positive Latin American cooperation with the United States in promoting democracy began to develop.

Since the early 1960s, a decline in economic clientelism had been taking place, strikingly shown by the formation of the Organization of Petroleum Exporting Countries (OPEC), which included Venezuela. In the 1990s a resurgence of economic liberalism or neocapitalism occurred in Latin America. Superseding the previous diagnosis that underdevelopment was caused by their economic ties with developed economies, their *dependencia*, Latin American governments sought closer economic integration with First World economies such as the United States. This culminated in the North American Free Trade Agreement (NAFTA), formalized by Bill Clinton. As part of this increased economic globalization, international financial institutions advocated the democratization of the structures of recipient nations to achieve more openness and accountability. Never before had so many multiple international actors promoted democracy with various forms of "intervention," including economic incentives.

The overall international success of the Republicans notwithstanding, the new democratic administration inaugurated in 1993 had not learned from experience. It was not that Republicans had not made mistakes, but that the gestalt of the incoming team was that of "another Carter": preaching human rights, moralistic interference with threats of implementing some sanctions, backing off, retreating at the crucial moment. The Reagan experience showed the unsustainability of realpolitik prescriptions as an absolute, universal principle. Clinton's early years, on the other hand, indicated the shortcomings of campaigns for democratizing reforms, especially those for which the United States is incapable or unwilling to use force to back policy.

The vacillating spirit of Clinton's policies received strong criticism from the secretaries of state of the preceding Republican administrations. "Empty threats send a message to American adversaries worldwide." "When you make a threat and you do not do it, then you lose tremendous credibility very easily." "We made a mistake early on . . . in saying we were going to go in there and then backing off."[7]

The climate in the United States (and internationally) was of profound dissatisfaction with policy; all administrations, of course, can back down—

Reagan, for example, had to withdraw the U.S. Marines from Lebanon after the destruction of their Beirut headquarters in October 1983. It was the Clinton administration's overall ineffectual moralizing and preaching that made the difference. It placed in relief the validity of some of the criticisms of realpolitik advocates against do-gooder, unrealistic policies.

Fortunately the Clinton administration changed course after an initial phase of counterproductive ineffectiveness, as with the unfulfilled trade sanctions against China, the withdrawal from Somalia, and the early retreat in Haiti. The crucial event was the invasion of Haiti by U.S. troops in 1994. Showing the willingness to use force, the administration began to overcome its extremely poor performance in foreign affairs, to the point that it was not a reelection issue in 1996. In abandoning its initial non-intervention and moralistic meddling, the administration left the route to political disaster. As in some domestic issues, Clinton had cleverly become "Republicanized."[8] Other foreign interventions followed. Once again, a prudent projection of force to "defend national interests"—despite divisions in this regard in the United States— seemed ultimately necessary to avoid domestic political defeat in the United States.

Especially in Haiti, it was possible to observe once more a strengthening of clientelistic politics, in which local factions asked foreigners to intervene and form coalitions with them to determine their government, thus breaking the sacredness of the sovereignty of the so-called nation-state, allegedly in pursuit of greater political and economic justice. In Haiti it was also possible to see the U.S. government involved in a very poor country, an involvement disproportionate to any realpolitik strategic or economic interest; in fact, the United States incurred economic costs with the invasion and its aftermath.

As in the Nicaraguan case that I have reported, Haiti showed again that in some countries dictatorships are difficult to dislodge and that a big power cannot always determine the local government of a tiny, weak country, without using military force. Above all, Haiti showed the risks of following humanitarian democratic crusades: to avoid the failure of policy, a foreign power might feel forced to intervene militarily, even though it does not wish to and its people do not favor it.

As many of us expected, with a Sandinista military victory a Marxist-Leninist-influenced, authoritarian regime was constituted. But as Sergio Ramírez has commented, "The great paradox was that in the end Sandinism left as a legacy what it had not sought: democracy, and could not leave what it sought: the end to backwardness, to the poverty and the marginality."[9] The Direccón Nacional of the FSLN was composed of nine comandantes, three representatives from each of the factions, and it became Nicaragua's new political sovereign. Yet in 1990 the revolutionary government gave a free election. In contrast with the past history of *hegemonías* the losers were not entirely displaced from state positions, nor did the winners gain absolute control of the state. A new democratic learning experience was initiated that survived despite its instabilities.

The Sandinista vice president provides a pertinent inside story.[10] He traces to two months after victory the privately held decision of the top FSLN leadership to consolidate itself in power by forming a Marxist-Leninist party. The party's goal was to achieve a socialist society based on the dictatorship of the working class that would replace, the sooner the better, the current first phase of alliances with the bourgeoisie. The FSLN Dirección Nacional considered itself in a fight to the death against Yankee imperialism and in alliance with the Soviet-Cuba socialist bloc, which it aspired to join as a member as soon as feasible. A basic part of the hegemonic plan was to transfer to the state the key means of production. In the meantime until conditions were favorable, the revolutionary regime would deny to friends and foes the Marxist-Leninist project and publicly uphold the Tercerista program that had been vocalized by the Twelve: political pluralism, a mixed economy, and international non-alignment. In contrast to the Cuban model, which the Nicaraguans did not plan to reproduce exactly, but with which they sympathized and which was influential in Nicaragua, the FSLN Marxist-Leninist revolutionary party did not materialize beyond the intentions.

A fundamental, distinct component of Cuba's 1959 revolution, its initial crypto-Marxist agenda notwithstanding, was the concentration of absolute power in only one leader, an unusual type of leader, who sought to project himself as a Weberian charismatic ruler and who received wide popular acceptance that he be so with the victory. Remarkable was the very rapid centralization of personal authority in Castro, the prophetic messiah with *fortuna* on his side. In the first year in power, as a means of rallying absolute control for himself, Castro discarded the role of elections and purged the revolution's just-appointed prime minister and then the president.[11] By early in the following year, close links were established between the regime and the Soviet Union—this included Nikita Khrushchev's threat to give Cuba military protection if the United States intervened in the island's affairs.[12]

The escalation of conflict with the United States rapidly accelerated—in January 1961 diplomatic relations were totally severed between the two countries, and in April the failed Bay of Pigs invasion took place. At the end of that third year Castro's regime proclaimed itself Marxist-Leninist. As he demonstrated his absolute power, the revolution's original party—the 26 of July Movement—disappeared, and Castro took over the leadership of Cuba's small but well-organized Communist Party. Indicative of the regime's Marxist-Leninist totalitarian character amid the frenzied popular mobilization, Castro also broke with and suppressed the Catholic Church. As a consequence of the October 1962 missile crisis, U.S.-Cuba relations entered an enduring phase characterized by the lack of U.S. support to movements to overthrow the Communist regime. The United States had made the Cuban policy exception: in the future "no other Cubas" became the new policy.[13]

Nicaragua's revolution contrasts sharply with Cuba's model. It did not rapidly abandon a democratic pretense nor consolidate its control over the population. The FSLN never achieved the control of Fidel Castro's government. A set of domestic and international factors differentiated Nicaragua from Cuba.

To begin with, the FSLN did not develop Cuba's centralized charismatic leadership. The Dirección Nacional remained functioning during the Sandinista's time in power, the preeminence of the Ortega brothers in it only gradually developed, and Daniel's leadership was much more limited than Fidel's. Raúl Castro's subordination to his brother was not reproduced in the Humberto-Daniel relationship.[14] Second, the regime operated with less control over a relatively more pluralistic civil society. Recall the extremely broad revolutionary coalition that materialized to overthrow Somoza. While acute conflict developed between the government and the top Catholic hierarchy, in contrast to Cuba there was never a total break in state-church relations with the corresponding religious suppression. In fact, priests held cabinet positions during the entire Sandinista experiment without renouncing their Catholic beliefs—greater ideological pluralism than in Cuba was maintained in Nicaragua.[15] Similarly, the economy did not fall under a comparable ownership-control of the state. Nicaragua's state was a dictatorship with its consequent serious limitations to political pluralism, but it did not achieve Cuba's totalitarian heights.

The favorable conditions to establish a Marxist-Leninist regime were not perceived to materialize. The revolution was faced with Ronald Reagan's electoral victory of November 1980 and with it an aggressive, anti-Sandinista U.S. military policy: the administration's firm commitment to the new so-called Contra war. Nicaragua's geography facilitated regime destabilization: it was not an island, but a nation with a history of porous borders. Provocative Sandinista policies (e.g., the assistance to El Salvador's Marxist guerrillas) notwithstanding, a proclamation of a Marxist-Leninist regime would have been exceedingly risky.

Other international factors were operative. The cost of the victory against Somoza had left Nicaragua in a precarious economic situation. Although close ties with the Cuba-Soviet axis were established, even before the accession of Gorbachev in 1985 it was clear that Nicaragua could not count on major Soviet support, in dramatic contrast with what had been the Cuban experience. Wealthy social democratic capitalist countries were helping Nicaragua financially and were available to provide diplomatic support in the fight with the United States—thus the inclination not to exalt Marxist-Leninist virtues when talking to such audiences.

Some Latin American countries also played an important role. In 1983 Panama and Venezuela, which had been active in Somoza's overthrow, were joined by others, forming the Contadora Group to mediate the international Contra war. In sharp contrast to Cuba, *after* victory the Sandinistas continued to promise elections. That same year, in response to Contadora's initiatives autonomous from the United States, the Nicaraguan government agreed to advance elections to 1984. With international assistance the institutional organization to conduct fair elections was being developed. Nonetheless, the Sandinista victory did not stop the U.S.-supported war—opponents considered the elections flawed.[16] And the political and economic dysfunctions generated by the contradictions inherent in the FSLN project of societal transformation produced opposition against the government, including growth in its armed form.[17] At the same time, the mandatory draft to fight the Contras produced popular dissatisfaction with the FSLN.

In the meantime some democratic progress was taking place in Central America. In 1982 constitutional elected government was restored in Honduras, and with the election in 1985 of Vinicio Cerezo, Guatemala began a period with elected civilian government. In 1987 a new peace initiative, the plan led by Costa Rican president Oscar Arias, took place also independently of the U.S. government. In contrast to the earlier discussed Costa Rican initiative of 1978, now Central American presidents coherently acted in coordination to pressure the Nicaraguan and U.S. governments to end the war.[18] The plan contemplated among other items a cease-fire leading to demobilization; an end of military assistance to insurrections, including hosting bases for attacks against neighbor countries; reducing the size of the armed forces; free elections. As the Reagan administration was ending, the Soviet Union—with Gorbachev's changes taking place in European Communism—and the United States agreed to support the Central American initiative to end the war.

Central America would gain from a peace accord. Costa Rica was faced with hosting massive immigration from Nicaragua and with the dangers of involvement in the war. El Salvador had priority in avoiding FSLN support for its insurrection. Guatemala held similar concerns in trying to consolidate the democratic regime. Honduras faced the political tensions of the presence of

U.S. troops in its territory and of the launching of the Contra war from inside its borders. All the countries were concerned with the imbalance posed by Nicaragua's militarization and the economic problems being created to the Central American Common Market.

In sum, the revolution had resulted in a vulnerable regime that had a priority in economic reactivation and its survival, while better organizing the masses politically and militarily. A quick transition to a democratic regime was blocked by the weight of the new ideological influences and traditional reservations about democracy's viability in Nicaragua.[19] But faced with war, the FSLN had felt the need for coalitions and international support and to make concessions to survive.[20] The regime had much to gain by accepting the Arias plan. There would be great benefit if the Contras disarmed. The economic situation was disastrous. The regime had lost internal support. If it won an internationally supervised election, the regime would be fully legitimized, and the war would end.

Thus, in contrast to Somoza's decision, elections were advanced, and contrary to Sandinista expectation, they lost. Violeta de Chamorro, Pedro Joaquín's widow, became the opposition's candidate.[21] Her motherly figure symbolized pacifying Nicaragua, national reconciliation, repairing relations with the United States, getting substantial foreign assistance to create a better nation. The stalemated, cruel, "low-intensity" Contra war had not sufficed. The role played by multiple international political influences was essential in this democratic transition.

This book has focused on foreign relations between legally sovereign states that are supposed to have their own governments, not the politics of empire. Americans do not have the vocation for the latter, especially with its costs in the contemporary context of mobilized societies. We have focused on a special or particular type of interstate relations: international clientelism. Should the United States intervene or not (unilaterally or joined with others) supporting or opposing with various means foreign governments? Should the principle of non-intervention, of the absolute sovereignty of states to determine their own governments be a sacred prohibition? Should nations seek to constitute and maintain client-states? Although not a universal pattern, to this day foreign public and private actors are clientelistically involved in a number of countries.

In discussing the nature of client-states we have in part traced their dependence on foreign support to the absence in them of broad domestic support for their own regimes. Feeling compelled to exercise influence in their international environment, U.S. governments seek friendly, cooperative relations with other governments. Such "normal" ties involve allocating various resources to them. Given the shortcoming in domestic support, these transfers tend to be interpreted as helping to determine the client's government, "intervening" in its otherwise internal affairs. Hence, some forms of clientelism seem inevitable when they partly result from the projection of power or influence in an unstable, nonconsensual regime environment. In fact, as discussed, a tendency of client-state politics is for local factions to look for international alliances, collecting support from foreigners in their pursuit of their own partisan interests to form or sustain a government. In polarized clientelistic settings strong interventionist demands are unleashed against the neutrality of key international actors. In Latin America, not only did the United States intervene, but so did some of its friends and foes as well.

Practically from their beginning, U.S.-Latin America relations were conditioned by the related problems of institutionalizing democracy and the propensity to experience regime overthrow in Latin America. With a measure of independence from Latin American realities, the different intervention objectives of American governments were rationalized under two ideal-type banners, democratic crusades and realpolitik. Domestic and foreign realities rendered untenable the search for an absolute, universal or permanent doctrine of American international policy.

It is intriguing that since early in the nineteenth century pro-democratic interventionist rationalizations were recurrently used. As we saw, during the period of maximum U.S. military intervention in Central America that ended in the 1930s, the economics of "Big Stick" diplomacy was partially masked by democratic international treaties. Despite its democratic conceptual links, Theodore Roosevelt's corollary to Monroe, with its unilateral U.S. physical interventions, was highly feared and resented in Latin America. The corollary's goals were overshadowed by the perceived arrogant, paternalistic, go-it-alone attitude of the United States, and its bellicose claim to the right to use preemptive force in defense of the national interest in Latin America's supposedly independent nations. The principles of non-intervention and national sovereignty guide wise, prudent rules. Economic clientelism proper is the least justified form of intervention. In my view it should be considered an absolute prohibition.[22]

The unilateral deployment of U.S. troops was not sufficient to exercise U.S. regional leadership and obtain politically supportive, friendly ties in the Americas. To achieve these goals a Pan American movement was developed with inter-American conferences, in which the region's sovereign states participated under the cloud of long, recurrent U.S. interventions in a few countries. The result of this diplomacy was incorporated into FDR's Good Neighbor policy and culminated in the formation of the Organization of American States.

By treaty, Monroe was multilateralized, and the principle of non-intervention by American countries in each other's affairs was established, as were the principles of collective defense of the Americas. By the Truman years the United States had exchanged the expediency of unilateralism for the principle of non-intervention protective of weaker parties and for a system of multilateral collective defense against both inter– and extra–Western Hemisphere foreign interventions.

The constitution of the OAS and U.S. participation in it serves to test multilateralism. In the past a spirit of non-intervention to forcefully change regimes fairly consistently prevailed in the body. This reflected a relatively broad, though not universal, view of political values, interest, and responsibility in Latin America. Yet the organization performed useful consultative functions and policies. It contributed to foster measures of regional solidarity and successfully mediated various conflicts.

Faced with the realities of non-intervention sentiment within the OAS and the need for action felt by some U.S. administrations, the United States did not choose to withdraw from the body nor to formally repudiate multilateralism ideologically as the preferred option; this was deemed too undiplomatic, counterproductive, and unnecessary.

Indeed, in the most serious Latin American crisis that faced the United States in the previous century, the OAS provided legitimacy to American resolve. In the 1962 prelude to the Cuban Missile Crisis the organization supported "the member states to take those steps that they consider appropriate for their individual or collective self-defense, and . . . to counteract threats or acts of aggression, subversion or other dangers to peace and security resulting from the . . . intervention in this Hemisphere of the [Communist] powers."

Alternatively, when considered necessary by Washington to the nation's security, the U.S. government occasionally circumvented the OAS, even unilaterally deploying American troops. Noteworthy was the pioneering case of the Dominican Republic in 1965. Faced with a de facto U.S. invasion, the OAS accepted the fact, and a transitory force from six Latin American countries (plus the United States) temporarily occupied Santo Domingo, until the formation the following year of a new Dominican government. The OAS facilitated the handling of the conflict and the early withdrawal of U.S. troops and consolidation of a new regime. In sum, while the OAS did not impede the occasional but brief U.S. physical interventions, it served to restrain the arbitrary use of force. Its existence helped to avoid American unilateral and long occupations of countries. The principle of non-intervention did not prove to be an absolute prohibition, but it served functions, such as tempering the fanciful changes in foreign policy fads of U.S. and Latin governing circles.

In January 2001 George W. Bush became president. Candidate Bush had projected radical departures from his predecessors: a conservative realpolitik nationalism, inclined to isolationism and unilateralism in world affairs. An arrogant leitmotif, that the inordinate superpower status of the United States allowed it to act alone—"you don't like it, that's too bad" attitude—was manifest.[23] In Bush's new "realism," the national interest, not humanitarian nation-building involvement nor the moral interests of the international community, would be the paramount standard. The climate of greater isolationism was evident in the professed lesser inclination to intervene in other countries and participate in pro-democratic campaigns and in an aversion to binding international treaties. A new international division of labor to reflect America's power would be pursued. No U.S. ground troops would be deployed for peacekeeping, humanitarian interventions, or nation building, rather only for big wars. It was for the lesser regional powers to engage their troops. In sum, in the imagery of the incoming team there was "more arrogance, more unilateralism" and less language of partnership, mutualism, and combined actions with allies. Predictably such symbolism would prove insulting and be resented, even feared, and would result in less international cooperation with, and favorable attitudes toward, the United States. The message was not conducive to the exercise of American world leadership; it was dramatically different than senior Bush's.

The unexpected, tragic September 11 events had profound effects, however. War was declared on the Taliban government hosting the al-Qaeda terrorists involved in 9/11. A logical link was established between rogue states (e.g., Afghanistan) and anti-American terrorists. What if the former possessed weapons of mass destruction (WMD) and made them available to terrorists? This was interpreted as a need for a change in doctrine from deterrence to preemptive war in order to safeguard national security. By his January 2002 State of the Union speech, the president had adopted a highly interventionist posture. Not only was the United States engaged in a global fight against terrorism, but it was also up against "an axis of evil." Bush accused Iraq, North Korea, and Iran of arming themselves with WMD and pledged to disarm them by military means if necessary—the sooner the better. But there was a new moral dimension in the messianic message: in its new interventionism, the United States would now fight for "non-negotiable" democratic values. Thus another cycle of replacing a realpolitik banner had taken place. And despite the U.N. Security Council authorization of the use of force in Afghanistan and multilateral involvement in its pacification, Washington was thought to have changed to a bellicose interventionist unilateralism. Perhaps the swift military victory—not the pacification nor its corollary nation-state building and consolidation—in Afghanistan reinforced the administration's spirit that it could go it alone. The increased military gap between the American capacity to wage war, with its new low U.S. casualties due to its smart weapons, and the capacity of others, evident in the most recent wars, combined with Washington's unilateral instinct, produced increased fear and antagonism within the international community. The U.S. capacity to lead became widely questioned by early 2002.

The task in Afghanistan had not been completed; the Israeli-Palestinian violent conflict—with its strategic importance in the war against terrorism—had escalated without the re-engagement of Washington necessary to solve this crisis. As if confirming the administration's belief that its use of military power is the basis of true security, in February 2002 the secretary of state was supporting the need for "regime change" in Iraq. But, he added, "democratic, representative government" should be established there. That year the UN adopted resolution 1441 demanding that Iraq open its weapons facilities to inspectors or face "serious consequences." In March 2003 the United States and Britain declared war on Iraq without an explicit approval of, and substantial opposition in, the international community, on grounds that it had WMD and links with al-Qaeda, thus posing an imminent threat to international peace. Ironically the Iraqi genocidal dictator was overshadowed by fairly widespread views that the United States had become a global aggressor. And in Iraq, changing its earlier tune, the Bush administration became the principal "nation builder" in a country in which knowledgeable observers considered it most difficult to establish democratic stability.[24]

Returning to our Latin American survey, after the Second World War, more than one U.S. president sought to destabilize and change hostile regimes in the area using covert force or deploying U.S. troops. In the face of the perceived lack of receptivity for the use of force in the OAS—and more so in the UN—and a belief in the urgency of obtaining a regime change, troops were unilaterally deployed, bypassing extant international organizations. Even then, although all the invaded Latin countries were quite small—and incidentally culturally closer to the United States than Islamic countries—which facilitated the exercise of American influence in them, the U.S. administrations sought regional support for the successful consolidation of the regime change and the also desired quick pullout of American troops. The U.S. anti-Communist clientelism also involved several administrations in the sponsorship of counterinsurgency—that is, "anti-terrorist" campaigns. At the same time, American-led democratic crusades encountered regional resistance and failure, which in part led to dropping the policy. It was only in the 1990s, with the proliferation of democracies in the region, that broader legitimacy for pro-democratic clientelism materialized.

In the post–World War II period the United States did not adopt a unilateralist *doctrine* in its Latin American relations. The earlier, more frequent, and prolonged unilateral physical interventions of the gunboat years had not fostered international support nor a spirit of inter-American cooperation. Therefore, Theodore Roosevelt's corollary to the Monroe Doctrine, formally claiming the right of the United States to use preemptive force in defense of its national interest, was eventually deemed counterproductive and unnecessary, too undiplomatic; it was buried for good and replaced by the Good Neighbor policy and other more recent doctrines.

As you can see, I have found disquieting the contemptuous tone of some of the Bush administration's representatives, as well as the doctrinaire tendency to oversimplify and disregard historical precedents. In the immediate aftermath of the military "victory" in Iraq, the rhetoric from the administration suggested a temptation to unleash American forces again in the region. As we have argued, the American public favors peaceful relations: this ultimately limits its support for a policeman-of-the-world role. Nor do U.S. governments have the resources to impose democracies, especially in regions unreceptive to such form of government. Tinkering with authoritarian regime reform or change in those conditions can provoke instability and even revolutions not necessarily sympathetic to Washington. The overall success of recent Democratic and Republican administrations was partly based in a prudent international projection of force. No administration should expect to be surrounded by domestic and foreign sycophants: there is a legitimate need to advocate restraint in the use of force in the international community.

The United States and the world community are facing two very serious challenges: international terrorism and the proliferation of WMD. These are complex, distinct though related problems that need to be tackled by the workings of substantial international cooperation, including treaties.[25] Given its resources and political character, the United States has to play a leadership role in the world community. This cannot be adequately achieved by misguided, unrealistic, and divisive claims to exercise a global hegemony based on the "superpower" assumption, nor by using an intellectualized preemptive unilateralist language. Historically such attitudes had proven alienating to many in Latin America. It is true that, in a sense, in the capacity to launch war, in which the U.S. military excels, we might currently speak of unipolarity or only one superpower in this dimension, but not so in many other vital areas. However, even in the military dimension, the United States cannot simply act alone. It needs allies to legitimize its policies. Military interventions are not won when a regime is overthrown. As with Nicaragua, recent events in Afghanistan and Iraq show that the stabilization of a new, responsible regime is necessary for the success of peace. Multilateral international participation in such task is proving essential.[26]

With George Bush the semiotics of policy changed in directions unheard of in inter-American relations since pre-FDR years. It is not that the United States, in adhering to a cumbersome multilateral internationalism, should consider the unilateral deployment of troops an absolute prohibition—it should retain the right of self-defense. The point is that a more pragmatic, less doctrinaire foreign policy, forceful toward adversaries yet respectful of others, will be more ethical and successful.

Notes

Prologue

1. See the review of post-Skocpol conceptual developments in Meeks, *Caribbean Revolutions*, chapter 1.

2. Although it may be fashionable in some quarters to concentrate on socioeconomic inputs at the expense of political ones to explain revolutions, the need to stress the political inputs is recognized in some of the Nicaraguan Marxist literature; see Vilas, *Sandinista Revolution*, especially pp. 91–101. In his memoir *Adiós muchachos*, Sergio Ramírez, the Sandinista vice president, does not consider that the revolution resulted from an abrupt economic change or crisis. He writes: "the crisis of Somocismo had an essentially political nature" (p. 121). But as Nicaragua modernized, its long-term effects undermined support for the highly centralized, low participatory, old-fashioned dynastic rule. It is long established that economic crises play a fundamental role in the overthrow of some, not all, regimes; see, for instance, the documentation in Solaún and Quinn, *Sinners and Heretics*, chapter 5, and more recently in Meek's *Caribbean Revolutions*.

3. Particularly useful to my understanding of the Nicaraguan case were Tilly, *From Mobilization to Revolution*, and Easton, *Systems Analysis of Political Life*. See Tilly's polity model (p. 53) and mobilization model (p. 56) and Easton's input-output conceptual framework elaborated in that work.

4. For instance, see Easton, *Systems Analysis*, p. 155, and the application of Easton's concepts to Nicaragua by Fiallos Oyanguren, "Nicaraguan Political System."

5. A good example of this approach is Opp, Voss, and Gern, *Origins of a Spontaneous Revolution*.

6. There are several meanings or types of alienation that can find themselves leading to opposite behavioral results; for pertinent discussions see Seeman, "Alienation and Engagement"; Finifter, "Dimensions of Political Alienation."

7. Cohn, *Pursuit of the Millennium*, is a classic statement on the role of religious expressions in revolution; Ramírez, *Adiós muchachos*, emphasizes the presence of quasi-religious elements in Nicaragua.

8. Useful to my task were Turner and Killian, *Collective Behavior*, and Smelser, *Theory of Collective Behavior*. A survey of models that may be applicable to particular problems is found in McPhail, *Myth of the Madding Crowd*.

1. Introduction

1. Contrast, for instance, Kissinger, *Does America Need a Foreign Policy*, and McNamara and Blight, *Wilson's Ghost*. Background materials on the foreign policy issues discussed can be found in Beitz, *Political Theory and International Relations*; Galbraith, *Triumph*; Hoffman, "States and the Morality of War" and "Hell in a Very Small Place"; Kennedy, *Rise and Fall of the Great Powers*; Luban, "Romance of the Nation-State"; Nicholson, *Diplomacy*; Renwick, *Economic Sanctions*; Shadid, "Sanctions Yield Few Successes"; Ustinov, *Love of Four Colonels*.

2. By "regime" I mean not a particular administration (as in the Bush or Carter regime), but the form of government of a sovereign state determined by its operating political constitution.

3. I use these terms as ideal-types, abstractions that serve as points of reference to analyze reality; they rarely happen as scripted, given the mixed character of administration policies.

4. There has been an absence of consensus about U.S. government foreign policy objectives; see the review by Domínguez, "Consensus and Divergence." Prevalent goals have changed historically. In the early twentieth century "economic interventions" were common (e.g., the intervention against General José Santos Zelaya, Nicaragua 1909). By the Kennedy-Johnson years Cold War "security issues" had become highlighted (e.g., the attempts to unseat Fidel Castro). More recently there have been cases of humanitarian, pro-democratic interventions without evident economic or security concerns (e.g., the U.S. invasion of Haiti in 1994). But, unfortunately, it was not always easy to differentiate security from economic objectives, for as in Cuba some social revolutionaries can seek military alliances with threatening adversaries of the United States, while at the same time confiscating the property of American citizens. Regardless of the prevalent policy priorities, it is in the nature of the U.S. political system that its diplomats also continue to routinely represent material interests of Americans, if for no other reasons than congressional directives or initiatives.

5. Prominent Latin American politicians have held to this mirage. A pertinent example: Sergio Ramírez Mercado, the Sandinista vice president, wrote to the effect that as the United States did not obtain Anastasio Somoza's resignation when he demanded that we do so, this "demonstrated" that we "supported" Somoza. This was the case even though he was aware of our destabilization of the strongman and our representations to Somoza that he abdicate. As the United States did not use its power in a total break with Somoza to get him out—which Washington allegedly could easily accomplish—we backed him. See Ramírez's memoir, *Adiós muchachos*. Alternatively, Robert Dahl, the important American political scientist, despite the emphasis that he placed on the beliefs of the politicians in his much cited theories of democracy, has blamed the United States for the Central American authoritarian experience; see Dahl, *Democracy and Its Critics*.

6. In 1971 a dynastic succession actually took place in Haiti, but Haiti is outside the Iberian American family of nations.

7. This is known as "personal *continuismo*" of a strongman, the expansion of terms of office by the alteration of constitutions or electoral fraud, among other techniques. See Solaún and Quinn, *Sinners and Heretics.*

8. For example, in 1989 the unyielding Chinese Communist government successfully repressed the protesting pro-democracy movement, eliminating its challenge. In Poland in 1989, on the other hand, the Communist rulers were willing to give up power and negotiate a transition to democracy with the opposition. But also in 1989, in Romania, the intransigent Communist dictator had to be overthrown (he was executed) by a complex rebellion that involved the state's military organ. And in the East German transition from communism in the same year, the unarmed protests succeeded in terminating the regime also only after the dictator was forced out by his government's cadres. See Opp, Voss, and Gern, *Origins of a Spontaneous Revolution.*

9. See, for instance, Ian Kershaw's highly praised volumes on Hitler, *Hitler, 1889–1936: Hubris* and *Hitler, 1936–1945: Nemesis.*

10. In his organization theory Hirschman, *Exit, Voice and Loyalty,* also notes the nonmaterialistic and structural bases of loyalty that operate as well in democratic administrations. Sociology suggests the need to combine organizational principles worked out in small groups and those of larger scale formal organizations with their more formalized, hierarchical power structures; see the review in Jonathan H. Turner, *Structure of Sociological Theory.*

11. For general histories see Woodward, *Central America,* and Pérez Brignoli, *Brief History of Central America.*

12. After the "final" uprising in El Salvador in 1980, the Carter administration changed its "hands-off" policy, assisting in its last days in office the beleaguered Salvadoran government that was threatened with being overthrown. The Sandinista victory of 1979 had resulted in the rapid formation of a militarized alliance between the Nicaraguan government and the Cuba–Soviet Bloc, which was intervening in El Salvador in support of constituting a Marxist-Leninist-influenced authoritarian regime.

13. This was the period of more crass U.S. economic clientelism: the use of its disproportionate political-military power to achieve and sustain economic monopolistic objectives, especially in Central America and the Caribbean. The U.S. hegemony/Latin American *dependencia* has been considered the cause of underdevelopment, with exploitation, inequality, and mass poverty. See, for instance, LaFeber, *Inevitable Revolutions.* On dependency theory see Love, "Origins of Dependency Analysis," "Modeling Internal Colonialism," and "Raúl Prebish." LaFeber traces Central America's violent governmental repression and revolutionary processes of the post–Second World War years to the nature of the political-economic dependence on the United States; his is a defense of social revolutions.

14. The quotes on Monroe are from the 1975 *World Book Encyclopedia.*

15. On Tobar see Woodward, *Central America;* Grieb, "United States and Hernández Martínez"; Salisbury, "Domestic Politics and Foreign Policy"; Stansifer, "Application of the Tobar Doctrine."

16. On Franklin Roosevelt see the classic work Wood, *Making of the Good Neighbor Policy*.

17. The first long-lasting democracy was established in Chile, 1932–73.

18. Kennan, "Reflections," p. 53.

19. Politzer, *Altamirano*, p. 181.

20. Guatemala in 1954 and Chile in 1973 are often cited in blaming the United States for the "pathology of democracy" in Latin America. The overthrown Guatemalan regime was not building democratic consensus in its highly polarized society without democratic traditions. But President Eisenhower's realpolitik acted with precipitation. Those were the years of the very militant anti-Communism of Secretary of State John Foster Dulles and of McCarthyism in the United States. The Guatemalan government found itself isolated, the only opponent of the 1954 anti-Communist Caracas Declaration, which the United States sponsored and the OAS adopted, with Argentina and Mexico abstaining. A balanced synthesis of the Guatemalan events can be found in Amaro, *Guatemala*. For the absence of a definite democratic commitment by the Chilean Allende experiment, see the confessional statements of a principal actor in Politzer, *Altamirano*. Fermandois, *Chile y el mundo*, provides documentation of the foreign policies involved.

21. See Ameringer, *Democratic Left in Exile* and *Don Pepe*. For Cuba, including Fidel Castro's involvement in the legion, see Márquez Sterling, *Historia de Cuba*; Masó, *Historia de Cuba*; Suchlicki, *Cuba*.

22. For perspectives on the period see, among others, Cotler and Fagen, *Latin America and the United States*; Einaudi, *Peruvian Military Relations*; Lowenthal, *Dominican Intervention*; Mañón, *Operación Estrella*; Martin, *Overtaken by Events*; Moreno, "Sociological Aspects of the Dominican Revolution"; Needler, *Political Development in Latin America*; Skidmore, *Politics in Brazil*; Stepan, *Military in Politics*; Mitchell, "Dominance and Fragmentation." In Brazil, for example, the 1964 coup was not simply the result of U.S. government encouragement but must be placed in the context of its military professional doctrine of "Poder Moderador"—that is, that the armed forces view themselves as the ultimate political sovereign power, if needed to maintain "social equilibrium." Many other military organizations have held variants of this professional self-identity, e.g., Pakistan and Turkey.

23. In fact, some critics of the right and left considered that the Alliance for Progress had helped to increase the polarization within the region. See the useful presentation of views in LaFeber, *Inevitable Revolutions*, pp. 155–58, 184–85, 265–67, among others.

24. A remarkable story of this case of British and American economic clientelism can be found in Kinzer, *All the Shah's Men*.

25. By the Nixon-Ford years Central American economic dependence on the United States had declined, as evidenced by the destination of exports and origin of imports. In 1970, 1975, and 1977 a majority of the region's exports went to other countries than the United States, and in none of the five Central American nations did the majority of their imports come from the United States. Thus regardless of U.S. government objectives, American economic "monopolistic hegemony" had

waned. See Wilkie and Reich, *Statistical Abstract of Latin America*, pp. 438, 442, 443, 445, 447.

Economic realities may have been reflected in the prevalence of other than the radical dependency perspective to explain inter-American relations, reported by Domínguez, "Consensus and Divergence." Of course, the Nixon administration was involved in clientelism (e.g., in destabilizing Chile in 1973). The fact that, in contrast, it accommodated the Peru leftist regime initiated in 1968 but not the Chilean Marxist-Leninist-oriented one suggests the importance of strategic anti-Communist considerations over purely economic ones. Again, on the nature of Chile's revolutionary Allende regime see Politzer, *Altamirano*.

26. As predicted by the so-called bureaucratic perspective of U.S. foreign policy, there were divisions within the Carter administration. Secretary of State Cyrus Vance more fully followed the spirit of the human rights crusade. He adopted a non-interventionist vision, feeling that Soviet weaknesses would work themselves out in the longer term and thus did not require knee-jerk containment policies. In contrast, National Security Adviser Zbigniew Brzezinski remained a Cold War warrior. He saw in the human rights banner an attractive instrument to undermine Communist authoritarianism, while feeling that Communist advances had to be checked. Although Vance's perspective proved valid in the eventual collapse of the Soviet Bloc, in the short term Soviet advances (as in Afghanistan and Nicaragua in 1979) created disturbances in the American political system that called for administration responses. For the bureaucratic model see Lowenthal, "United States Policy." For these high-level differences, see Vance, *Hard Choices*, and Brzezinski, *Power and Principle*. Interestingly, the non-intervention of the U.S. human rights policy overlapped with the post-1968 "Brezhnev Doctrine" claiming the right of collective socialist intervention to keep the Soviet Bloc alive.

27. On the connection between the United States de-emphasizing the principle of containing Communism and its undermining the then predominantly anti-Communist Latin American dictatorships, see Levinson, "After the Alliance for Progress"; and on the relations between U.S. assistance and the birth of the human rights policy, see Schoultz, "U.S. Economic Aid."

28. See, respectively, Kirkpatrick, "Dictatorships and Double Standards," and LaFeber, *Inevitable Revolutions*, pp. 209–13, 242, 269.

29. Since the nineteenth century Americans had been involved in Nicaraguan politics. Still remembered, under the influence of Manifest Destiny, is that in 1855 an American, William Walker, launched an expedition in civil war–torn Nicaragua with fifty-eight soldiers of fortune to create a state with slavery. The following year, with the collaboration of some Nicaraguans, he controlled the Nicaraguan government and proclaimed himself president. He was finally executed in 1860 by a firing squad in Honduras. Walker met the combined resistance of Central American governments. A readable account of his exploits and of U.S. government opposition to the annexation of Nicaragua is Rosengarten, *Freebooters Must Die!*

30. On Zelaya see Stansifer, "José Santos Zelaya"; Munro, *Intervention and Dollar Diplomacy*; Teplitz, "Political and Economic Foundations"; Rice, "Nicaragua and the United States." On nineteenth-century social and economic history see Burns, *Patriarch and Folk*; Robert G. Williams, *States and Social Evolution*; Langley, *Banana Men*.

31. In 1934, after the U.S. Marines had left, Somoza tricked General Augusto César Sandino, the nationalist leader who had been fighting the marines from hideouts in the mountains, and had him murdered by national guardsmen. The Sandinista movement, the FSLN, took its name from Sandino.

32. Christian, *Nicaragua*.

33. See the debates in U.S. House of Representatives, Hearings before a Subcommittee on Appropriations.

34. A description of pre–National Guard patterns of expanding the military and private armies around the civil wars—with old and newly recruited, improvised unprofessional "officers"—in a state without a real standing national military organization is in Calero Orozco, *Sangre Santa*. I use the term "feudalistic" metaphorically, not to depict for Nicaragua the feudal order conventionally defined for medieval Europe in dictionaries: the system in which land, worked by serfs, was held by vassals in exchange for military and other services to overlords and ultimately to the monarch at the top of the pyramid; a part of this order was the decentralized nature of rulership, by which feudal lords kept relatively autonomous political jurisdictions over their own fiefdoms. What I wish to capture is the notion of a weak central state, without the constabulary force to impede the formation of improvised armies in various parts of the nation's territory. I clarify my terminological usage in the light of the Marxist controversy about the feudal, precapitalist nature (or not) of Latin American societies. Richard Millett reports the oscillating but small size of the Nicaraguan military during the pre–National Guard period; see his *Guardians of the Dynasty*, chapter 1.

35. See Weber, *Economy and Society*, especially chapters 12 and 13. By "patrimonial" I mean here a form of government, the outreach of patriarchal rulership by which a state is appropriated by a man and ruled as if his personal property; the state becomes the private patrimony of the ruler, as if his "private farm," and tends to adopt a dynastic character. Metaphorically this state is the outgrowth of the household of the ruling family. While Weber treats the patrimonial regime as a form of legitimate rulership, it usefully cannot be characterized as such in Latin America, where its most pristine type often took the form of the pseudo-democratic authoritarian regime with dynastic intent and has had serious legitimacy problems; such regimes have all perished.

　　The most enduring Latin American pseudo-democratic authoritarian regimes were embedded in nations that were relatively less developed socioeconomically— e.g., in Rafael L. Trujillo's Dominican Republic (1930–61); in the Nicaragua of the Anastasio Somoza García family (1936–79); in Alfredo Stroessner's Paraguay (1954–89). The heavy component of patrimoniality of this regime provides it with dynastic *tendencies*, as in the cited cases. For the Dominican Republic, see Balaguer, *Memorias de un cortesano*; for Paraguay, Stroessner, *Proyección internacional de Stroessner*. Even in Fulgencio Batista's Cuba, where the regime's propaganda did not work with dynastic themes or implications, it was rumored that the strongman intended to eventually leave his son in power, as the natural extension of Batista's private appropriation of the state. But not all dynastic Latin American regimes can be classified as pseudo-democratic—e.g., the Duvalier family in Haiti (1957–86), where there was no pretense of "electing" presidents.

Naturally, regime longevity tends to be increased by the acceptance of their dynastic component—they go beyond the life of their founders and as such are not purely "personalistic"; it is precisely the personalistic irreplaceability character of some patrimonial regimes that is most damaging to their endurance. For an exaltation of this trait of nontransferability found in the regimes of so-called traditional Latin American strongmen, see Vallenilla Lanz, *Cesarismo democrático*.

36. My subsequent comments draw upon the documentation found in the following basic works on Nicaragua: Millett, *Guardians of the Dynasty*, a book with a prologue by Miguel D'Escoto, the Maryknoll priest who became foreign minister of the Sandinista revolutionary regime; Dodd, "United States in Nicaraguan Politics"; Walker, "Nicaragua"; Fiallos Oyanguren, "Nicaraguan Political System"; Chester Y. Williams, "Presidential Leadership in Nicaragua"; Ameringer, "Nicaragua."

37. For the Sandino story see Macaulay, *Sandino Affair*. For the outline of Sandino's somewhat eccentric ideology see Hodges, *Intellectual Foundations of the Nicaraguan Revolution*, and Bendaña, *La mística de Sandino*.

In contrast to the post–William Walker Conservative hegemony, which lasted until the revolution of 1893, the period of Conservative Party rule during the U.S. occupation was more unstable. In my opinion this resulted not simply from a nationalistic reaction against the Americans; in the earlier period the Liberal opposition was discredited because of its collaboration with Walker. Also, after 1909 there was a greater balance of forces between Conservatives and Liberals, who were much more tempted to test their strengths and compete for power. In the absence of well-established rules of the game for competitive politics, the result of competition to control the state *tends* to be regime crisis, even near or total civil war. However, American diplomacy might have contributed to the Conservative Party factionalism that also furthered the instability of the period.

38. In the previous context, from 1857 to 1893 there was a long period of Conservative rule. After 1867 the polity moved into a system of orderly succession of leaders of the Conservative elite, as opposed to strongman rule. However, this regime was not a representative democracy but was of the family that I have called protodemocracy. These regimes are characterized by party *hegemonías* (hegemonies) and *party*, as opposed to strongman, *continuismo* (illegalities to remain in office). There was no neat law of historical development for Nicaragua, from lesser-developed personalistic dictatorship to oligarchical, protodemocratic, one-party rule to political democracy. On protodemocracy see Solaún, "Colombian Politics."

39. Contemporary civil service–type bureaucracies are a recent invention in the history of the advanced countries, though less developed incipient manifestations of them had existed. Max Weber appropriately deals with these modern bureaucracies as a type of (modern) legal authority, that is, as organizations that operate under, and are constrained by, the rule of law. Weber differentiates them from patrimonial bureaucracies typical of earlier patrimonial regimes. As he shows, patrimonial organizations are less efficient than modern ones in that they are ridden with "corruption." It is precisely with the development of postpatrimonial organization that the differentiation between the private and public domains increases in the state, and it stops being defined as a fiefdom of the rulers.

    A more readable statement on patrimonialty is Scott, *Comparative Political Corruption*. He clearly explains the origins of the modern conception of government corruption: the (mis)use of public office for private gain and breaking the formal rules of office. I paraphrase him: it is with the rise of the modern nation-state by the nineteenth century that the distinction between acting in a private and public capacity increases. Elaborate civil service legal codes are adopted, signaling the transformation of the view of government office and even kingship, from a private right into a public responsibility. Even in the modern private corporation a separation between ownership and administration took place, and management became "accountable." Before this modernization, public offices were viewed as a private domain—the sale of public office and patronage were legal practices. In many nations, however, modern patterns of administration, though formally adopted in the law, are not sufficiently socially sanctioned: officials feel that they are doing personal favors in making decisions, and citizens feel that they are asking for favors from officials. In some countries favoritism, gift-giving practices, nepotism, and other "corrupt" patterns permeate their public administration and to some extent are expected, considered acceptable, or even, in some cases, socially approved.

    Studies of modern bureaucracy question Weber's conceptualization of it as an ideal-type of organizational efficiency (e.g., Blau and Scott, *Formal Organizations*). Weber's model was historically conditioned—he was comparing modern with patrimonial bureaucratic organizations and hence argued, in this respect, for the superiority of the first, being the outcome of the Western rationalization and systematization of administration. Obviously, given their characteristic corruption, patrimonial organizations are less efficient than modern bureaucracies. However, Weber's paradigm is not useful when the research objective is to develop theories of efficiency for modern formal organizations, i.e., discover which organizations are most efficient among those falling within the same family of modern organizations.

40. Lenin, *What Is to Be Done?* makes a classic treatment of the lack of consciousness of the masses or false awareness of their class interest, a problem that can be faced by revolutionaries and reformers; in the 1920s there was little of a social revolutionary consciousness among the Nicaraguan poor.

41. Dodd, "United States in Nicaraguan Politics." A useful description of some of these early, quite common patterns for acquiring and retaining control of the state in most of Central America is in Stokes, "Violence as a Power Factor."

42. Prior to the foundation of the National Guard the local military practiced corrupt and abusive patterns, U.S. sources opined. See Millett, *Guardians of the Dynasty*. They were not overcome and were part of the "human rights" problems that we faced many decades later.

43. The most extreme example of such interpretation with which I am acquainted, combined with an attempt at a systematic theoretical explanation, is Payne, *Patterns of Conflict in Colombia*.

44. Bendix, *Force, Fate and Freedom*, and Ortega y Gasset, *Historia como sistema*. For a more recent view see the introduction in Kershaw, *Hitler: Hubris*.

45. *Caudillo* is the Spanish term for "leader," "chief," "commander"; it has come to mean "strongman"; *caudillaje* or *caudillismo* refer to the dictatorship or tyranny of a ruler or to bossism. See Deas, "Caudillismo, Coronelismo and Caciquismo." Manifestations of caudillo rulership vary, but a usual characteristic is a personalistic, extralegal (i.e., outside the rule of law) character. But in Nicaragua caudillo rule informally evolved into rulership by a family under the headship of the senior male, who was the dominant caudillo. For the initially socially progressive, reformist platform of Somoza García, and the support given to him by youthful progressive intellectuals, see Fiallos Oyanguren, "Nicaraguan Political System," pp. 37–39.

46. Millet, *Guardians of the Dynasty*, p. 176.

47. Millet, *Guardians of the Dynasty*, pp. 183–84.

2. The Somoza García Legacy

1. Although Nicaragua had achieved a relatively high ethnic homogeneity, it remained even after General Somoza García's death one of the poorest countries in Latin America. A socioeconomic profile of the social class and the urban-rural differences is in Fiallos Oyanguren, "Nicaraguan Political System," pp. 22–29. Socioeconomic underdevelopment—poverty—is conventionally viewed as an impediment to political democracy. Introductory texts establish the importance of personalistic-familistic cultural orientations and socioeconomic organization patterns. To cite only one, see Wolf and Hansen, *Human Condition in Latin America*. Both the Latin American and general sociological literature consider that these so-called primary-group orientations intensify social conflicts—e.g., Wolf and Hansen, *Human Condition in Latin America*, pp. 200–204; Simmel, *Conflict*; and Coser, *Functions of Social Conflict*.

2. I refer again to Weber, *Economy and Society*, especially pp. 1006–7, 1010–11, 1014, 1031–32, 1048, 1088–89, 1094, 1099. Nicaragua's was a neopatrimonial regime, that is, a regime with roots in traditional patrimonialism that had never developed into a Weberian legal-rational state but was mixed with some formal institutions of modern states. The regime was sufficiently bound in the exercise of power by traditions not to deserve Weber's sultanistic classification of pure, arbitrary, personalistic rule.

3. See López Gallo, *Las grandes mentiras de Krauze*, p. 64, for the use of this symbolism in another, more modern context. The political role of an ethos of friendship is found also in ancient societies. See, for instance, Taylor, *Party Politics*.

4. I have in mind administrative problems that I have encountered in my business— e.g., the impossibility of obtaining the admission of a student in some Latin American universities, unless a contact is made with someone who will personally see to it that the admission is processed; in such contexts without personal contacts, letters to many universities will go unanswered.

5. It has been argued that newly formed organizations are more subject to the influence of its first leaders; see Merei, "Group Leadership and Institutionalization."

6. Fiallos Oyanguren, "Nicaraguan Political System."

7. Somoza García continued to head the army, while periodically an assistant or yes-man was expected to temporarily hold the presidency. The case in hand was the coup d'état against Leonardo Argüello because he was not performing the latter role.

8. The reader interested in background information can look at Millett, *Guardians of the Dynasty*, pp. 201–13. Many Nicaraguans attributed fortuitous factors to Somoza García's appointment to the National Guard: his ties to the two Liberal leaders, Juan Bautista Sacasa and José María Moncada, and his position as Spanish interpreter for the American Embassy. I also heard allegations of an amorous relationship between Somoza and the wife of an American envoy, but storytelling was a pastime in the Old Regime.

9. While the cult of personality has varied in intensity, followers consider that these leaders have established a new "order" (regime). This realization is often mixed with paternalistic titles—for example, Rafael L. Trujillo was called "Padre de la Patria Nueva" (father of the new country) and "Benefactor de la Patria." For comparative examples of the fawning, see Galíndez, *Era of Trujillo*, and Stroessner, *Proyección internacional de Stroessner*. However, the consideration that the formation of a new political order follows constitutional change was also a French tradition—e.g., the "Fifth Republic"—though these changes did not use the above mentioned paternalistic dynastic symbolism.

10. That these apparatuses be built is not a constant of the pseudo-democratic genus. In Cuba, Batista did not form a truly national, well-organized, civilian party. Neither was he able, especially during his second period in power, 1952–58, to establish as firm a control over the military officers as Somoza García, which was maintained later by his son Anastasio Junior.

11. Fiallos Oyanguren, "Nicaraguan Political System," p. 44.

12. Chester Y. Williams, "Presidential Leadership in Nicaragua." In Nicaragua, the officers were taught and accepted a doctrine of "professionalism" that meant military subordination to the line of command, which was headed by a member of the Somoza family. However, the *objective* levels of professional development and expertise were very low, as Williams documents.

13. Millett, *Guardians of the Dynasty*, p. 207.

14. See Millett, *Guardians of the Dynasty*, p. 203. Actually, the occurrence of chaotic, violent politics during democratic periods in some not well institutionalized regimes

can contribute to undemocratic rationalizations—"democracy really does not work here; we can't have it among our people."

15. These data are taken from Chester Y. Williams, "Presidential Leadership in Nicaragua," p. 91; his chapter provides other interesting materials on the National Guard. The early appointment of the children of monarchs to the armed forces is, of course, nothing new.

16. However, Fiallos Oyanguren, "Nicaraguan Political System," chapter 5, reports Liberal Party resistance to the 1966 constitutional reform eliminating the prohibition of religious teaching in public schools; the Liberal secular philosophical antecedents had remained latent, to be reactivated at that point. Similarly, during my tenure Somoza, in his conflict with the Catholic Church, said he wished to rally the historical anti-clerical Liberal roots. Ideological dimensions did not entirely disappear in the old regime though machine politics appeared to have reduced their salience. See note 17.

17. The Nicaraguan machine approximated Scott's (*Comparative Political Corruption*) definition: a non-ideological organization interested less in political principle or issues than in securing and retaining political office for its leaders and distributing material goods to those associated with it (p. 108). Scott provides entertaining historical accounts of the rise of electoral machines in Britain, France, and the United States. The partisanship against "starved out" oppositions, the buying of votes, the offering of free drinks and meals—the patterns are reminiscent of Somoza's "realism": "My father told me and I later learned, politics doesn't work here like in New England; you have to give free *guaro* [the local popular spirits] to get the people to vote," he explained to me. Without adhering to a theory of inexorable historical development, Scott's accounts are helpful to understand Nicaraguan problems by comparisons with the obstacles also posed by poverty and tradition in the democratization of more advanced societies (i.e., Britain, France, and the United States).

18. Fiallos Oyanguren, "Nicaraguan Political System," p. 47.

19. Fiallos Oyanguren, "Nicaraguan Political System," pp. 45–46.

20. Fiallos Oyanguren, "Nicaraguan Political System," p. 47. I should note that although opinions were divided, the high investments the Somozas had in Nicaragua were viewed by many as an impediment to their abandoning control of the state. Millett reports that one of my predecessors "informed the [State] Department that the size of [Somoza García's] investments . . . made [him] unwilling to even consider the possibility of allowing anyone hostile to his interests to obtain the presidency" (*Guardians of the Dynasty*, p. 203).

21. For example, Kirkpatrick, "Dictatorships and Double Standards," interpreted the Iranian and Nicaraguan revolutions arising because of the "personal, hierarchical, non-transferable" character of the shah's and Somoza's authority. Contemporary organizational theory views personalistic authority as dysfunctional. But dynasties can function. Although the efficiency of the National Guard was low, it had been able to survive because of the effective carrying out of a dynastic pattern of suc-

cession and the historical weaknesses of insurrectionist groups: they had not been allowed to grow.

22. *Dictadura* means dictatorship, and *dura* means hard; *blanda*, meaning soft, implies a mild dictatorship. Thomas W. Walker, a promoter of the Sandinista revolution and critic of the Somozas, considered that on the average the dynasty had been relatively mild in the context of Latin American dictatorships; see his "Nicaragua." The problem of "constitutional fetishism" addressed in this section can be interpreted in the context of a tradition characterized by the prevalence of formality and subjectivism in legal matters as outlined by Karst and Rosenn, *Law and Development in Latin America*.

23. For comparable problems in the Roman Principate, see Griffin, *Nero*.

24. See the discussion on the inauthenticity and weakness of electoral mechanisms in Solaún and Quinn, *Sinners and Heretics*, pp. 106–12.

25. This and the following quote are taken from Fiallos Oyanguren, "Nicaraguan Political System," pp. 48–49.

26. Fiallos Oyanguren, "Nicaraguan Political System," pp. 48–49.

27. Fiallos Oyanguren, "Nicaraguan Political System," p. 44.

28. Fiallos Oyanguren, "Nicaraguan Political System," p. 52.

29. Fiallos Oyanguren, "Nicaraguan Political System," p. 52.

30. I am paraphrasing here Charles Tilly's model of political mobilization and control, *From Mobilization to Revolution*, p. 56. While the chronic normlessness of the regime resulted in political alienation and weak legitimacy, sentiments of powerlessness or lack of political efficacy (another form of alienation) contributed to political apathy favoring regime maintenance. For the various kinds of alienation that influenced the so-called rational behavioral choices of the actors, see Seeman, "Alienation and Engagement," and Finifter, "Dimensions of Political Alienation." For complementary works on social movements, see, among others, Gamson, *Strategy of Social Protest*, and McAdam, McCarthy, and Zald, *Comparative Perspectives on Social Movements*.

31. This is the terminology of another political mobilization and control classic, Easton, *Systems Analysis of Political Life*.

32. Millett, *Guardians of the Dynasty*, pp. 210–11.

33. The *mandamás*, or "superboss," has a connotation of being domineering, imperious, oriented by *machismo*. I have in mind a pristine orientation toward conquering, dominating, constituting subservient dependents.

34. For details, see Millett, *Guardians of the Dynasty*, pp. 202–13.

35. This system of guaranteeing to a cooperative opposition a fixed minority share in some offices of the state, regardless of the number of votes, was characteristic of some other pseudo-democratic regimes—e.g., that of General Alfredo Stroessner in Paraguay.

36. Fiallos Oyanguren, "Nicaraguan Political System," pp. 96–97.

37. Under the Somozas, the opposition went through phases of a fairly cohesive unity behind a strong, popular caudillo and periods of fragmentation with small, cadre "parties" and factions without any large-scale organization. Umbrella entities were

useful to provide a workable opposition unity; they continued to be formed beyond the Somoza years.

38. For supporting materials see Fiallos Oyanguren, "Nicaraguan Political System," pp. 97–100.

39. Fiallos Oyanguren, "Nicaraguan Political System," p. 99.

40. Fiallos Oyanguren, "Nicaraguan Political System," p. 102.

3. The Golden Years

1. See Chamorro Cardenal, *Estirpe sangrienta*.

2. Fiallos Oyanguren, "Nicaraguan Political System," p. 114. In this respect, the regime was deviating from the ideal-type pseudo-democratic authoritarian regime in which the rulers formally claim that it is a democracy. Notice the reference to the "We are not ready for more democracy" rationalization, a variant of the notion that socioeconomic underdevelopment impedes democracy. It, of course, serves as a self-fulfilling prophecy used by elites who do not break the vicious circle of authoritarianism.

3. Fiallos Oyanguren, "Nicaraguan Political System," chapter 3, where statistical data are readily found for the period.

4. Agricultural modernization became conspicuous in the Pacific and lake plains with the development of the technologically sophisticated production of cotton for export. This brought about a change in relationships between landowner and peasant. The old *colono* system (in which land is given to the *peón* in exchange for part of the crop produced on it) was transformed into a monetary (proletarian) wage relationship more integrated into the market economy. Some sources consider this type of social change undermining the old solidarity arrangements to be conducive to revolts. But others have claimed that small landholder peasants who possess and work the land on their own are more prone to participate in rebellions. See the review of the causes of agrarian revolution in Bermeo, *Revolution within the Revolution*, pp. 5–8. These inferences might be valid for particular cases. Slaves, serfs, and populations under semi-serfdom arrangements also have rebelled. Actually, successful revolutions depend on the behavior of not just one social class but of several social classes, and also on the actions taken by the state itself (and in some cases coalitions of states).

5. See, for instance, Teresa Hayter, *Aid as Imperialism*, on early criticisms, and on the Alliance for Progress the comments in chapter 1, note 23.

6. The Alliance for Progress themes about connections between social change and revolution were found in the social science literature; see Deutsch, "Social Mobilization and Political Development," a classic.

7. The nature and findings of the survey are reported in Fiallos Oyanguren, "Nicaraguan Political System," pp. 70–83. He compares his findings with the classic pioneering study by Almond and Verba, *Civic Culture*.

8. Fiallos Oyanguren, "Nicaraguan Political System," p. 82, wrote: "Nicaraguan political activities tend to be sporadic rather than sustained or permanent. This may

result from the lack of organizations available to sustain continuous pressure or action. So it is that action seems likely only when an effective grouping procedure is present to take up this absence of permanent group activity. In Nicaraguan history, this [collective] grouping seems a function of catalysts like [mobilizing] caudillos . . . or crisis events."

9. The national budget, including public autonomous agencies, grew from 4.8 percent to 19.2 percent of the gross national product from 1950 to 1966; there were net increases on a per capita basis as well. The foreign public debt grew from $2.6 million in 1951 to $74.4 million in 1966. Although the creation of new taxes was associated with turmoil, new ones were established, and government revenues increased. A few cases of demands for land made by peasants were muted in the 1960s, in conjunction with the creation of the National Agrarian Institute (IAN) to implement the new Agrarian Reform Law inspired by the Alliance for Progress.

10. The "liberal reform" of 1893 was led by a dictator, General José Santos Zelaya, and its modernization goals were the increased secularization of state and society— the separation of church and state, civil marriages, etc.—and the promotion of capitalistic economic development. Notice again that the reform lagged in developing political democracy; also its anti-clericalism coincided with the dissolution of communal properties. While studying with the Jesuits, it was brought to our attention that there was a "Black Legend," which misrepresented the role of the Catholic Church and the traditional regime as exploitative, when allegedly the anti-church "liberal" reforms were the ones that served the private economic interests of the landed elite and proletarianized the rural people. This was part of the earlier discussed ideological conflict over regime, which helped to arrest the development of stable democracies in some countries. The quote is from Fiallos Oyanguren, "Nicaraguan Political System," p. 150.

11. This took place in April 1959; the Fidel Castro regime had been in power since January, and agrarian reform was already one of its prime objectives. On May 31, a revolutionary group entered Nicaragua to overthrow the government in conjunction with a call to a general strike. Castro's revolutionary example was already showing in its impact in Nicaragua; this subsequently discussed rebellion became known as the Olama and Mollejones invasion. An interesting account of the Olama and Mollejones invasion is found in Cardenal, Mi rebelión. I later learned from some participants that its rapid total collapse had resulted in their abandoning the notion that power could be gained through violence; these individuals, as opposed to the future Sandinista cadres, were socialized by the government's resilience into unarmed forms of opposition. Among them was Cardenal, with whom I had political contacts in the final phase of my mission because of his interest in our support for a military coup d'état.

12. Fiallos Oyanguren, "Nicaraguan Political System," pp. 153–58, reports about thirty unions active at the time.

13. I am, in fact, noting a possible convergence between Easton's regime systems analysis and Almond and Powell's work on political development defined in terms

of high levels of structural differentiation and cultural secularization, by extending the analysis to include the regime itself.

14. In this respect we cannot accept completely the proposition that parties had no ideologies but only obeyed because of loyalty to a leader; the interparty conflict tended to escalate and involve these ideological issues. Nonetheless, some parties were "non-ideological" or "personalistic" when their raison d'être was more the loyalty to a leader than to a distinctive platform and in cases of opportunistic transgression of constitutional philosophical principles and rules by them.

15. See Hodges, *Intellectual Foundations of the Nicaraguan Revolution*, pp. 162–63, and Somoza, *Nicaragua Betrayed*, pp. 90–91. The Sandinista movement was not founded until 1961, with the participation of Fonseca and Borge. In the Olama and Mollejones events many upper-class young men were involved. A fairly well held convention in the Old Regime was not to murder other members of the elite; the survival of most of the revolutionaries captured was attributed to this custom. It appears that crueler punishment tended to be applied to former members of the National Guard than to civilians. Pedro Joaquín Chamorro's assassination in 1978 broke this principle of social elite solidarity, however. For the Cuban involvement, see Carbonell, *And the Russians Stayed*, p. 366.

16. The "foco" strategy of creating relatively isolated centers of armed activity in rural enclaves from which to expand revolutionary movements was coined after Fidel Castro established his sanctuary in the Sierra Maestra. However, Castro's 26 of July Movement relied as well on a potent urban underground. For pertinent discussions, see Guevara, *La guerra de guerrillas*; Guillén, "Introducción"; and Quirk, *Fidel Castro*.

17. Although studies show that participants in revolutionary processes are not equally motivated, political "relative deprivation" must be a shared collective symbolic representation to allow the coordination of collective action for successful revolution. Stress on the diversity of actors is found, for example, in Opp, Voss, and Gern, *Origins of a Spontaneous Revolution*.

18. Nicaragua's regime was neither a consensual institutionalized democracy with its high levels of pluralism, nor an extreme totalitarian regime with minimum pluralism and participation only in officially controlled groups of otherwise politically isolated, atomized individuals. On totalitarianism, see Linz and Stepan, *Problems of Democratic Transition*. Nor was it a corporatist authoritarian regime, the loose categorization of much of the U.S. literature on the Latin America of the 1970s and 1980s.

19. *Cuarteles* are the typical military and police headquarters and bases found in Central American cities and towns.

20. Fiallos Oyanguren, "Nicaraguan Political System," provides a general catalog of government preventive measures and ex post facto uses of government force to control opposition violence, impede its growth, and reduce its level. This summary of the government's control outputs appears on p. 132: "The use of the armed forces to (a) investigate the existence of conspiracies against the regime to take adequate measures before they actually exploded, (b) patrol the cities and rural areas to avoid

the formation of groups or prevent invasions from abroad, (c) localize, disperse, capture, or destroy, partially or totally, armed groups, demonstrations, and meetings, (d) capture and keep under arrest and sometimes even torture persons accused of participating in different types of political activities, (e) enforce censorship or the closing of newspapers and radio programs, curfews, restrictions on travel, and other measures, and (f) to search for concealed weapons and other elements of subversion."

21. For instance, Luis Somoza made concessions to university students on strike because of repression against them. A feedback effect apparently took place: the killing of a student (repression) led to more student demonstrations and killings until the vicious circle was broken. Government repression can have more than one effect: it can inhibit opposition action because of fear of its effects; but rather than being preventive, it can in some circumstances encourage more protests because of the moral outrage against government that it can produce.

22. See the summary on these issues in Bendix, *Force, Fate and Freedom*, as well as the statements on De Tocqueville and beyond in Dahl, *Preface to Economic Democracy*.

23. Fiallos Oyanguren, "Nicaraguan Political System," pp. 116–17.

24. Fiallos Oyanguren, "Nicaraguan Political System," pp. 126–27. The AMROCS were the paramilitary organization that had replaced the Frentes Populares Somocistas. Such organizations were inoperative during my mission. The Sandinista regime revived this mode of operation with organizations of its own.

25. For readily available details, see Millett, *Guardians of the Dynasty*, pp. 228–29.

26. Fiallos Oyanguren, "Nicaraguan Political System," pp. 130–31.

27. Fiallos Oyanguren, "Nicaraguan Political System," p. 76.

4. The Anastasio Somoza Debayle Period

1. Details of the event appear in Obando Bravo, *Golpe sandinista*, and Pataky, *Llegaron los que no estaban invitados*.

2. Cabezas, *Fire from the Mountain*, pp. 168, 175, 184, 186. Relevant background material is found in Hodges, *Intellectual Foundations of the Nicaraguan Revolution*, pp. 213, 218, 229, 232–34. All informed sources acknowledge the "success" of Somoza's 1975–77 anti-FSLN repressive offensive.

3. Brief and useful is the statement by Abreu, "Brazil's Guerrilla Trap." Ramírez, *Adiós muchachos*, emphasizes the quasi-religious motivations.

4. The Somocistas, however, viewed themselves as a "permanent" majority, which they traced to the more "progressive" nature of their Liberal Party, especially since the 1930s. Shifts in party identification associated with periods of government-related socioeconomic changes have been noted for other historical two-party systems precisely in the 1930s; see the comparisons between the United States and Colombia in Solaún, "Colombian Politics." In Nicaragua we are not talking about modern "mass parties," but rather a system of "parties of notables" in which the ruling party became linked to the government bureaucratic machine. But Somocista "progressive" self-identity as if a social democratic force was very frustrating to militant oppositionists; see Chamorro Cardenal, *Jesús Marchena*.

5. That the reported perceptions were widespread and held also by some Somocistas is shown by Cardoze, "Nicaragua"; Cardoze was a minister of labor under General Somoza.

6. Precipitating events are conditioned by extant predisposing political culture (values) and structure (organization), and in turn the precipitants or triggering factors can help to change political values and organization.

7. In contrast to Luis's reputation, West Point–trained General Somoza had always been feared as a more dangerous, violent individual. See, for example, the comments in this regard in *Visión*, the Latin American weekly, about the time of General Somoza's election to his first term, September 16, 1966, p. 28, and February 17, 1967, p. 13; *Visión*'s characterization was made in the context of a not unfavorable coverage of the dynasty. Ironically, the magazine was later purchased by General Somoza. Throughout my tenure there remained a distinction between Somocistas friendly to Luis and those closer to the general, but the former did not constitute a political faction, and several of them continued to participate in the government.

8. Foreign observers were impressed by the low differentiation that existed between the "personal" and "public" spheres in Nicaragua. I often heard statements that personal misappropriation of resources took place at an unusually high rate in private businesses as well, which was interpreted as a weakness or underdevelopment also of private formal organizations. Several scandals had recently involved General Somoza's private business empire.

9. Even in societies with low social differentiation, princes concentrate resources in their hands by taxing their subjects, who tend in turn to oppose the extension of power of the political authorities. As Somoza expanded his power, the state became increasingly autonomous from the private sector or class structure: it represented more Somoza's interests than of his class of origin. But this operating autonomy of the state from class interests did not mean its autonomy or independence from Somoza's private interest (or patrimony); hence, corruption increased, and the state was even less geared to maintain the autonomy and independence to deliver the (transcendent) common good. In the terms of Chehabi and Linz, *Sultanistic Regimes*, sultanistic tendencies had become stronger. Many of my contacts told me this story in plainer language.

10. In spite of the recent efforts at quantification by Nicaraguan technicians, it is not possible to overstress the need to view with caution all published social statistics. Gross domestic product per capita (at constant prices, 1958) grew fairly steadily, as these dollar figures indicate:

1960	1963	1965	1969	1970	1974	1975	1976
231.42	294.08	333.90	343.30	364.11	410.02	405.22	413.80

Sources: United Nations, *Yearbook of National Accounts Statistics*, vol. 1 (1978), p. 910; UNESCO, *Statistical Yearbook*, 1965, p. 17; 1970, p. 18; 1977, p. 32.

As the population rapidly increased from 1.41 million in 1960 to 2.23 million in 1978, it became more urban: from an estimated 39.9 percent in 1960 to 51.2 in 1976; however, in 1976 still only 24 percent of the population lived in cities of

100,0000 or more inhabitants. Reflecting the above structural changes, in 1953 the occupational breakdown of the population was 42 percent in primary activities, 15 percent in secondary activities, and 43 percent in tertiary activities. By 1977 the new distribution was 22, 24, and 54 percent, respectively. Thus, the pace of urbanization was rapid, but that of industrialization was moderate. Other pertinent sources are the *World Development Reports* of the World Bank and Wilkie and Reich, *Statistical Abstract of Latin America*.

11. Vilas, *Sandinista Revolution*, pp. 92, 93, 94. LaFeber (*Inevitable Revolutions*) presents a different picture for the whole of Central America. As if per *The Communist Manifesto*, he sees a crisis of capitalism: increased concentration of wealth, monopoly capital increasing the dispossession and exploitation of the workers, and impoverishment of the labor force, all of which result in revolutions. Interestingly, LaFeber includes Costa Rica in his diagnosis (e.g., p. 132) but, in fact, its democratic regime continued through the economic changes; successful revolution took place only in Nicaragua. To oversimplify, Nicaragua's revolution does not fit a neat model of economic crisis; it can be partly seen as a Tocquevillian case of regime collapse following unsuccessful liberalization.

12. It is precisely because of the historical shifts affecting class interests in processes of political change that one can observe changes in the alliances of middle-class sectors, from "progressive" to "reactionary" stances. The Latin American middle classes are extremely heterogeneous, and as in the case of the United States, changes in outlook among them are partly related to the problem of sharing the costs of policies; see the discussion in Estrada, "Clase media en América Latina."

13. I am observing that many aware citizens, including middle-class individuals, living in the midst of extensive poverty tend to lack pride in their political system. Education is in this regard a conspicuous case: as late as 1975, 43 percent of individuals fifteen years old or older were reported by the Nicaraguan government as illiterate; World Bank, *World Development Report*, 1979, p. 170. It is no coincidence that the first major social campaign of the Sandinista government was to eradicate illiteracy. Other areas were also problematic. An idea of the acute concentration of land can be obtained from Warken, *Agricultural Development of Nicaragua*. An Organization of American States publication reported that in the mid-1970s 50 percent of the national income was received by the highest 5 percent of the population, whereas the lowest 20 percent received only 4.2 percent of the income; *Informes económicos de corto plazo, III, Mercado común centoamericano*, 1978.

14. Incidentally, in the widespread elitist thesis that a political vanguard must create the conditions for revolution by the masses, there is an implicit notion of a multiclass coalition. Pertinent quotes from classics—e.g., Engels, Trotsky—on the need for cross-cutting class alliances are found in Greene, *Comparative Revolutionary Movements*, pp. 39–46. Hodges interpreted the position about this time of what became the most successful Sandinista faction, the so-called Tercerista Insurrectionalist Tendency:

Humberto Ortega was perhaps the first to perceive that a third social force, the so-called middle sectors of self-employed workers, salaried professionals, petty bureaucrats, small proprietors, and career-minded students, was ready to move against the regime. By the beginning of 1977 Nicaraguan society had become so polarized over the issue of the continuation of the tyranny, Ortega believed, that if the FSLN did not capitalize on the growing anti-Somoza sentiments the bourgeois opposition would. Realizing that President Carter's government was favorably disposed to getting rid of Somoza and replacing him with the moderate reformers centered around Pedro Joaquín Chamorro, Ortega argued that the FSLN's only hope . . . was to build a multiclass anti-Somoza coalition of its own. This meant going beyond the FSLN's past reliance on a worker-peasant coalition in favor of wooing the middle sectors and giving primary attention to their immediate concerns and aspirations. It was this new orientation that would eventually mislead the bulk of the Nicaraguan people and the Western media into equating the Insurrectional Tendency with its social democratic allies. . . . Thus the FSLN mistakenly became identified with a noncapitalist, noncommunist, and nonaligned "third position" in domestic and foreign policy. Although it did adopt such a position, its motive for doing so was purely strategical. (Intellectual Foundations of the Nicaraguan Revolution, p. 240)

15. The pastoral letter, signed by all the bishops, was issued on January 8, 1977. It condemned government abuses under the state of siege, including depriving "powerless peasants . . . of their farmlands through threats" and the violation of the "rights and the constitutional laws of the Nation . . . provok[ing] institutional disorder." It called on the government for "(1) Guarantees of life and of work and a return to civil rights; (2) Proper trials for common crimes as well as for those called political crimes; (3) Freedom to promote a more just and equitable order. All of this cannot be achieved without freedom of expression and without religious freedom"; U.S. House of Representatives, Hearings before a Subcommittee on Foreign Assistance and Related Agencies Appropriations for 1978, Committee on Appropriations, 95th Cong., 1st sess., special hearings: testimony of public witnesses, April 1977, pp. 572–74, 513–15. For background on the post–Vatican Council II religious changes in Latin America, see Medhurst, "Church in Latin America"; and for a liberation theology perspective of the Catholic Church in Nicaragua's revolution, see Borgeson, *Hacia el hombre nuevo.*

16. Less known is the role played by nondenominational, nongovernment organizations (NGOs) in mobilizing the popular sectors against the regime. Noteworthy in this regard was the Instituto de Promoción Humana (INPRHU), led by Reynaldo Antonio Téfel and Edmundo Jarquín. Of Social Christian inspiration, its mission was to assist the creation and operations of grassroots organizations to increase the power of the people ("in the struggle for their economic, political and social liberation"), train popular cadres, and spread a culture of social criticism and concientización (consciousness raising) so that the poor themselves act to change their condition. In 1977 I visited INPRHU groups. Months later Téfel informed me of their subsequent participation in the violent effort to unseat Somoza.

17. The "unpredictable" or unexpected collapse of other regime types is recognized; see, for example, the extensive treatment of East Germany by Opp, Voss, and Gern, *Origins of a Spontaneous Revolution*. The theoretical link that is missing in this study guided by rational choice theory is the transition from governmental control to a rebellious popular explosion that also must be analyzed in terms of the sociology of mass "collective behavior." On the pre–September 1977 tight control being exercised by Somoza, see note 2 in this chapter. In August Senator Edward Kennedy, in a call for the liberalization of the Nicaraguan regime, dismissed in the U.S. Senate the threat that the opposition posed to it; see *Congressional Record*, 95th Cong., 1st sess., August 5, 1977, p. S13915. Of course, not all my early contacts were optimistic about the prospects of Somoza's regime.

18. Somoza's attitudinal profile found coincidences with other Central American dictators; see Asturias, *El señor presidente*, and the memoir of Cuban dictator Machado y Morales, *Memorias*.

19. Nicaragua's revolutionary interclass coalition was unusually broad. In El Salvador and Guatemala the left and right were involved in the physical fighting at this time—kidnappings, murders, vigilante violence, etc. In Nicaragua the government had repressed the left but without a comparable participation of the proprietary sectors in the process; Somoza controlled the anti-left violence. As in the Cuban Revolution, in Nicaragua there was also an absence of violence directed against the wealthy, but there was much more participation of the plutocracy in the movement to overthrow Somoza. Interestingly, it was only in Cuba and Nicaragua where revolutions triumphed.

20. The government's political isolation is well described in Urcuyo Maliaño, *Solos*; Urcuyo was appointed by Somoza to succeed him when he fled the country. Urcuyo refers to "the natural moral erosion of [being] too long in office" and to General Somoza's policy of centralizing and bureaucratizing the party: "in 15 years no election for party convention representatives [took place] in open breach of party statutes" (pp. 161–63). Tilly (*From Mobilization to Revolution*, p. 212) quotes Mao on the need to have the government forces fall "into hopeless straits, isolated and abandoned"; from Mao's "Carry the Revolution Through to the End," p. 305.

21. It is argued that for a call to rebel to be obeyed, two conditions are necessary: large numbers of the disenchanted must be persuaded that changes have a chance of success (rising expectations, a sense of efficacy), and the discontented must conclude that the present situation is the worst possible, that any alternative would not be as bad (intensified, acute relative deprivation). See Moore, *Injustice*; for the Iranian revolution of 1979, see Mozaffari, *Authority in Islam*, p. 119. These propositions serve to interpret the decision of large numbers to participate in the revolution as a "rational" decision or choice.

5. Neutrality

Some dates reported in this chapter refer to when I registered the events in my journal. Because of my hectic schedule, I could have been slightly off in some recorded days.

1. For the policy's context, see Bundy, "Who Lost Patagonia?" Also see the section on the human rights policy in chapter 1.

   It is remarkable that Robert Dahl, author of the first epigraph and a prominent American political scientist, made such attribution of U.S. responsibility for the region's authoritarianism, in the light of his consideration that "no satisfactory explanation of why polyarchy [i.e., representative democracy] exists in some countries and not in others can ignore the pivotal role of beliefs. . . . All theoretical attempts to reduce beliefs, ideas, ideologies . . . completely to . . . general [sociological] factors seem to me to fail badly" (*Democracy and Its Critics*, p. 260). Indeed, the principal problem was the insufficient support for democracy among the populations in question. Anthony Lake, the author of the second epigraph, was a participant in and advocate of Jimmy Carter's human rights policy and later became national security adviser for Bill Clinton.

2. Terence Todman headed the Bureau of Inter-American Affairs (ARA), the State Department's principal operational unit for the region; Robert Pastor was in charge of the National Security Council's Latin American section. They represented "conservative" and "liberal" points of view, respectively.

3. The bureaucratic analytical framework has been criticized. Indeed, in some policy areas the president's decisions ultimately must prevail within the bureaucracy; see, for instance, Perlmutter, "The Presidential Political Center and Foreign Policy." However, the absence of agreement in Washington over policy tends to create conflicts and difficulties in embassy operations. The effects of uncohesive teams in the executive should not be discarded.

4. There were, of course, those who felt that the Cold War security rationale was still valid. In my briefings in the Pentagon I was plainly told that in the light of the current Soviet policies the Carter team would have to change course. And to the dismay of some human rights activists, about the same time Terence Todman occasionally stated publicly that although no single Central American country posed a security threat to the United States, security concerns continued to arise in the region. This sounded too much like "Cold War language" to the administration's human rights lobby. Todman promoted a private diplomacy in favor of human rights rather than the public condemnation of regimes and was against human rights "affirmative action": his doctrine was that U.S. assistance should be given to foreign countries, regardless of their rulers, if it is determined that the assistance would benefit the poor. His views were defeated.

5. See the synthesis by Pastor, *Condemned to Repetition*, pp. 77–78.

6. Municipal elections were scheduled for February 1978, but only the tiny, officially recognized Conservatives could legally participate in them. I am noting factors that inhibited waiting to develop an electoral strategy by the opposition. However, there are cases in which such a strategy is followed in pseudo-democracies (e.g., earlier in Nicaragua, in the Dominican Republic about this time, in the Philippines in 1986).

7. The reader interested in documenting this highly conflictive polarization need only look at *Novedades* and *La Prensa*, the Somoza and Chamorro newspapers. I

have written about these partisan political styles that undermine governability and democratic institutionalization; see Solaún and Quinn, *Sinners and Heretics*, where I treat the subject in the context of political cultural secularization.

8. I should note that the tension between a short-term versus a long-term armed revolutionary strategy was present in other Latin American movements of the 1960s and 1970s; *tendencia insurreccionalista* versus *guerra prolongada (foco)* served to create the conflict in other nations. See Guillén, "Introducción" to *Ernesto Che Guevara*; Marighella, *Minimanual of the Urban Guerrilla*; and Mattini, *Hombres y mujeres del* PRT-ERP. The Terceristas had much in common with Castro's basic strategy. Although he eventually established a *foco* in Sierra Maestra, from the beginning of the process with the Moncada cuartel attack in 1953, he maintained a short-term urban strategy after a general insurrection.

9. Dahl, *Polyarchy*, had emphasized in his theory of democracy the role of mutual guarantees. This was the case in the Dominican Republic in 1978 and in Nicaragua's democratic transition in 1990.

10. Francisco Aguirre of Miami's *Diario Las Américas* was perhaps the first contact that raised this issue, and provided contacts for me with his personal relations in Nicaragua to facilitate my activities among civic leaders and private groups. Throughout my tenure I kept close contact with him and his family.

11. During this early period I often heard that Nicaragua should evolve into a form of protodemocratic rule along the Mexican PRI lines of changes in government through controlled elections, then still in operation.

12. Understanding the rapidly developing, multicentered social movement (in and out of the streets) to oust the government is facilitated by sociological theories of "collective behavior," which complement political mobilization and control models (e.g., Easton, *Systems Analysis of Political Life*, and Tilly, *From Mobilization to Revolution*). To paraphrase Turner and Killian (*Collective Behavior*), the assassination created an immediate physical and normative problem: the death had to be managed. The commotion broke routine; new symbols, moods, expectations arose; communication processes intensified; mobilization and actions took place in response to the problematic event. New collective definitions with new instructions and norms emerged not to negotiate with but rather to replace the government. And through social innovation, learning processes, and imitation, increasing numbers became recruits of the rebellion. According to Smelser's (*Theory of Collective Behavior*) perspective, extant structural strain (dissatisfaction over regime) and hostile beliefs (that General Somoza was responsible for the regime's past repression and corruption) were intensified by the precipitating event (the assassination). Other conditions favoring collective action were present: mobilization for action (to protest and remove the source of strain); structural conduciveness (the availability of units of opposition, including the mass media, to protest and act); reaction of social control agents (government passivity accommodated opposition explosion and growth).

13. DeYoung, " 'The Twelve,' " and *Novedades*, January 28, 1978.

14. There were precedents for organizing political strikes—see especially chapter 3. When I asked him how he thought Somoza's rule might be ended, P.J. Chamorro referred to a general stoppage as one of the instruments.

15. An excellent survey of events, from Somoza's heart illness in July 1977 to the end of March 1978 appears in *Encuentro* 14 (1978), the journal of Nicaragua's Universidad Centroamericana, a center of Sandinista activity. I kept periodic contact with its rector.

16. Lack of developed opposition organization, although variable, is not uncommon in revolutionary situations that can result in successful revolution—typically such opposition is in the process of growing. This is a reason why many observers of revolutions (especially those not active in them) refer to the "unexpected" collapse of governments.

17. The point is well made by Monsignor Obando y Bravo in his memoir, *Agonía en el Bunker*, where he describes that there were participants in the uprising who did not identify themselves as "members" of the FSLN.

18. This relationship of total personal subordination to the strongman is not found in all authoritarian regimes. For its absence in Pinochet's Chile, see Arancibia Clavel and de la Maza, *Matthei, mi testimonio*.

19. The local press published the statement: *Novedades*, April 4, 5, and 6 1978, and *La Prensa*, April 5, 1978. See the review in *Encuentro* 14 (1978): 28.

20. The origin of Washington's diplomatic representation was Assistant Secretary Todman's reaction to a series of conversations with Eduardo Montealegre, the prestigious financier, which I had reported. Montealegre felt that the optimal solution was Somoza's resignation, but apprised of Washington's mood, he brought me a series of points to try to break the deadlock, points that were included in the démarche. Recall that Somoza had recently been absent from the country because of illness; he seemed replaceable.

21. *Encuentro* 14 (1978): 27.

22. Comments on Christopher's wobbly diplomacy in China and Haiti, two Republican presidents in between, when he returned to the State Department as Clinton's secretary of state appear in the epilogue. As discussed there, fortunately the vacillating policy of preaching and surrender that was resulting in diplomatic defeat and loss of American prestige and credibility was reversed, part of the "Republicanization" of Clinton's policies, evidenced in the 1994 U.S. invasion of Haiti.

23. Liberal Sacasa was a dissident (earlier Somocista) who headed the Movimiento Liberal Constitucionalista and a member of Chamorro's UDEL in which Quintanilla participated; Alvarez Montalván was the chief of the Partido Conservador de Nicaragua (Auténtico). Incidentally, my strongly worded challenge created offense. I personally apologized to them in my office, and I became close to the three.

24. Notice that in contrast to Iran, where Washington recommended to the shah the repressive re-equilibration of the polity, in strategically less important Nicaragua the human rights message against government repression was continuously given.

For Iran, see the memoirs of Jimmy Carter, *Keeping Faith*; National Security Adviser Zbigniew Brzezinski, *Power and Principle*; and U.S. ambassador William H. Sullivan, *Mission to Iran*. Indicative of the low priority given to the Nicaraguan crisis, neither Carter, Brzezinski, nor the secretary of state, Cyrus Vance, dealt with it in their memoirs.

25. It is noteworthy that the Inter-American Commission eventually came to Nicaragua, but around the time of the first major insurrection of September 1978. The ill-timed visit influenced its highly negative report.

26. In any case, American newspapers traced the initiative to Congressman Wilson; see, for instance, Goshko, "U.S. Frees Aid to Nicaragua," and "U.S. Changes Position, Frees $12 Million for Nicaragua," *Miami Herald*, May 17, 1978.

27. See Riding, "Foes of Somoza" (May 1) and "Nicaragua's Opposition" (May 14).

28. In his memoirs (*Nicaragua Betrayed*) Somoza presents the thesis: he thought that by collaborating (partially, of course) with Washington he would not be overthrown. In fact, the strongman was still acting out the pseudo-democratic legerdemain. Assisted by a few American mercenaries, Somoza Jr. was commanding the increase in size and training of the best unit of the National Guard.

29. The psychology and structure of domination of the more patrimonial type of caudillo inhibits the development of strong leaders within the party of these absolutist monarchies. On the Dominican Republic, see Galíndez, *Era of Trujillo*. Yet the subsequent case there of Joaquín Balaguer shows that the resurgence of a new caudillo (with his own more modern and benign imprint) can eventually take place within the ranks of the servile.

30. In the realm of modern ideas it probably had an impact at the highest level. For instance, on January 24, 1978, I had a working meeting with Mrs. Somoza's social services group, and she vocalized what she called the "new concept of charity"— not simply ask but participate in self-help to improve one's lot. I must say that Doña Hope was very gracious: she observed that no pictures would be taken in the meeting to comply with my wishes of maintaining a low profile (i.e., to avoid suggesting close ties between our governments). USAID policy recommendations to foreign governments could be technically spirited, including proposing actions that negatively affect American business interests; see the case study by Cepeda and Solaún ("Direct Private Foreign Investment"); also see Winckler and Greenhalgh, "Analytical Issues and Historical Episodes."

31. See Morgan, "Foreign Aid Funds."

32. The two who became better known were Charlie Wilson of Texas and John Murphy of New York; Murphy was later convicted and jailed for corruption.

33. John Goshko ("U.S. Frees Aid to Nicaragua"). The administration also released $160,000 in unexpended military credits for a Nicaraguan military hospital. During my tenure, disbursement of U.S. military assistance had been suspended, except for training in the Panama Canal. The size of the military advisory mission (Milgroup) was reduced to four officers. Note that I did not find a completely satisfactory evaluation of the impact of the loans in the U.S. press. For instance, on June 2, 1978,

the *New York Times* editorialized that they were "the wrong message to Nicaragua." Noting the continued "wave after wave" of popular protest and the regime's "political rigidity," it concluded that the effect of the loans was to "encourage" Somoza "in his attempts to crush the opposition by force, without fear of disfavor from Washington." On June 5, *La Prensa* published this editorial. My impression was that they had encouraged Somoza's inflexibility to retain his untenable position until 1981.

34. The funding was approximately $12 million for the 1978 fiscal year and no more than $6 to $8 million for the next two fiscal years, with a staff of between fifteen and twenty direct-hire Americans and a commensurate number of Nicaraguan employees. The cable addressed as well the employment of contractors and consultants because our embassy State Department functionaries were aware that the objective of maintaining a "low profile" could be jeopardized by matching the decline in regular officials with increases in this other category of employees. Charles A. Gillespie, the head of the administrative section, was particularly helpful in preparing our arguments against the education loan. State-USAID rivalries were present in the process. We quoted the above figures in our cable. But USAID kept changing the figures given to us, part of the game to have large assistance portfolios regardless of the results of the projects in the nation. However, eventually two or three members of USAID-Nicaragua came around to unofficially criticize the loans.

35. One of the letters—signed by Professor Dionisio Herrera y Canales—claimed that the government was "economically sustained by the neocolonialist American Government" (May 25, 1978).

36. See "Córdova Rivas: Hubo Préstamos 'E Hubo' Tiros," *La Prensa*, May 19, 1978.

37. See, for example, the editorial of May 19, 1978, praising the congressional initiative on behalf of the Somoza government.

38. *Novedades*, June 9, 1998.

39. The Nicaraguan government in principle had agreed in the Congress to enact an amnesty.

40. The government had dropped the requirement of the need for the prior holding of a *cédula* of citizenship to vote, so that what had proved to be a *still unfinished* program of electoral reform would not hinder anyone from being able to vote. The point is pertinent because later Somoza rejected the international plebiscite of the mediation retracting this earlier proposal. The legal technical details of the electoral reform were discussed in *Novedades*, July 8, 1978.

41. *Novedades*, July 5, 1978. Particularly nonsecular and apocalyptic was the language of an article signed by Favio Valle Salinas, "Los Doce y la Sangre." Recall the themes of "primitive" and "ideological" radicalisms typified in Solaún and Quinn, *Sinners and Heretics*.

42. I still favored not completely severing the U.S. military link with the National Guard by withdrawing our token military advisory group so as not to lose future options. Politically sophisticated, General Dennis P. McAuliffe (commander of the Panama-based Southern Command, with a direct line to the military mission) had been most

useful in defining policy: a military presence in Nicaragua, a low profile, minimum publicity, no involvement in local training and combat situations, and a minimum number of officers.

Problems remained because of the presence of a few American "soldiers of fortune" in the country who had been hired by Somoza. As they were private citizens, the State Department insisted that they were free to remain in Nicaragua, which I repeatedly had to explain to my anti-Somoza contacts.

43. We had received additional information on an arm (allegedly) used in Chamorro's murder and communicated it to the Nicaraguan judge in charge. I sent him a letter, and the embassy had other correspondence as well. La Prensa continued informing its readers about the lack of progress in the case; see the articles of July 5, 8, and 19 on "irregularities" in the judicial and extradition processes and the critical editorial of July 24. On July 6 an FBI agent and our military attaché visited the court to inspect arms there; I was informed that there had been errors in reporting them to us! Bureaucratic incompetence can also play a role in the misconduct of justice. In Nicaragua's Old Regime this and the patrimoniality at the highest levels had shocking results.

44. The reader might look at Reynaldo Antonio Téfel's two articles "La hora del cambio" and "El pacto de la libertad," which appeared in La Prensa, July 3 and 4, 1978, respectively.

In fact, some did raise doubts about Nicaragua's democratic prospects addressing the "deeper problems" that had earlier impeded democracy's institutionalization. Historical, socioeconomic, and cultural factors were stressed in essays by Alvarez Montalván ("Apuntes para una sociología política nicaragüense"), Cuadra ("Escrito a Máquina") and Belli Pereira ("El hombre es la pieza clave"). The latter wrote that the solution was not simply to enact a new formal system if people again did not comply with it. The culture that had allowed Somocismo to prosper had to change: the machismo, the picaresque ethos (the culto al "vivo") to break or trick the system.

45. Somoza, Nicaragua Betrayed, pp. 143–44. The full text of the Carter letter appeared in this memoir.

46. The speeches were reported in Novedades, July 12, 1978. On the autocratic "Caesarist" or "Napoleonic" populist spirit, see Vallenilla Lanz, Cesarismo democrático; North, "Democracy in Rome"; and Weber, Economy and Society, pp. 1451–53. The tone of the speeches was moderate, especially in the Nicaraguan context.

47. DeYoung, "Somoza's Friends in Congress," reported on the assistance. The embassy was on record as favoring the continuation of some military assistance ties, these links to be used at the appropriate moment in the developing crisis. However, again pro-Somoza congressional actors were misguiding him by not telling him that he had to compromise more. The Washington Post wrote that Congressman Wilson was carrying the fight for Somoza and criticized the administration for seeming willing to allow "one man [in Congress] to shape its entire aid bill" based on his preferences for Nicaragua. In a visit to Somoza, DeYoung had told him that in

Nicaragua everybody wanted him to resign, and hinted that he should. But Somoza kept to his mantra: If I leave sooner, there will be chaos.

48. See the *Washington Post*'s editorial "Nicaraguan Question," August 3, 1978. See also Goshko, "Carter Letter to Somoza."

49. *Novedades*, August 2. Its reference to the National Security Council was based on information that Robert Pastor supported sending the letter.

50. Riding, "Somoza and His Foes" and "National Mutiny in Nicaragua." These pieces were quite informative. Using prominent businessman Joaquín Cuadra Chamorro, one of the Twelve, Riding explained that the stultifying, too long-lasting dynasty had resulted in the radicalization of some of the wealthiest, conservative families, who had become Sandinistas, such as Joaquín Cuadra Lacayo Jr. The former explained his participation in the revolution: "We can't ignore the lesson of sacrifice of our children if we are to see any progress in our country. . . . I saw my role as trying to rescue our youth from radicalism." Cuadra Sr. became a key financial official of the future FSLN government; Cuadra Jr., an important revolutionary, was appointed head of the new army in 1994. Riding also explained that the non-interventionist principle left the U.S. government with the rationale that Nicaragua was not that important economically and politically, thus the Nicaraguans should be left fighting the solution out among themselves. As mentioned, in apparent contradiction, however, some of those holding this view spent much time discussing the human rights situation in the country and destabilizing the regime.

51. For instance, the manager of one of the most important opposition radio stations at this time wrote to me: "As a Nicaraguan I can assure you that Mr. Somoza has never thought of retiring in 1981, much less with the weak policy of the White House. Mr. Somoza will only retire when the Sandinista Front attacks and defeats the National Guard. And then . . . there will be intervention by American troops and much spilled blood, because I suppose that the U.S. will not permit a Communist government here. May it be God's will that my fears be unfounded." In a similar vein, see Fiallos Navarro, "Los partidos políticos." Fiallos became one of the post-Somoza ambassadors to Washington until his defection against the Sandinista government. Like many others who subsequently collaborated with the FSLN, he was not a Marxist at this time, as his article's refutation of historical materialism showed.

52. See the story in the *Miami Herald*, April 9, 1978.

53. See Téfel, "Análisis de una caída," and *La Prensa*'s report of April 14, 1978.

54. Before my departure from Washington I read a paper prepared for discussion by Richard Feinberg, a political appointee in the State Department whose social company I enjoyed. It illustrated the internal dynamics that had precluded the use of any substantial power in Nicaragua. In the scenarios no ultimatum or near-ultimatum was discussed, while it included the option of U.S. withdrawal—of letting Nicaraguan revolutionary forces, with their Latin American regional allies (e.g., Venezuela) decide the outcome. Nor was the option of propping up the regime contemplated.

55. Reference was being made to the peculiar lack of consensus characteristic of many pseudo-democratic situations in which groups engage in violence, even when they profess adherence to similar regime political philosophies, i.e., representative democracy. As discussed earlier, the perceived corruption of democratic institutions leads to a lack of consensus in such cases.

56. I was accompanied this time by the deputy chief of mission, Frank Tucker. I thought that it was pertinent that he meet the archbishop because he was in charge of the embassy in my absence, so I was starting to introduce him to key figures. Indeed, after my departure on February 26, Tucker was in charge of the embassy until the new ambassador came to ask Somoza to resign in the middle of the all-out revolt. After my departure all embassy personnel were bureaucrats; therefore criticisms of their performance made by the advocates of the implemented failed policy reflect on the Foreign Service organization itself.

57. *Novedades*, August 14, 1978, p. 2A. Weber, *Economy and Society*, discusses the patrimonial traditional roots of government social welfare here nakedly seen.

58. "Doublethink" is George Orwell's coinage of the capacity to hold two contradictory beliefs in one's mind simultaneously, thus avoiding feelings of guilt; it is "cognitive dissonance," social psychology tells us, to avoid facing unpleasant results. Pablo Antonio Cuadra, in his "Dos Cerebros," reflected on the local situation using Arthur Koestler's simile. More than a common language with different meanings, Cuadra wrote, in Nicaragua two brains coexisted without integration. The first brain, of pre-man, is emotional, unreasonable, incapable of foreseeing *hecatombes*, or disasters; the second, the newer brain of modern man, is the brain of logic and language. In Somoza's opposition to accept the archbishop's national solution, he was only employing the first. Notice the coincidences between the cited classics and the "magical realist" Latin American literary current, which claims to represent folk culture. See Ben-Ur, "El realismo mágico en la crítica hispanoamericana," and Leal, "El realismo mágico en la literatura hispanoamericana."

59. On August 29 I obtained a new perspective from Father Léon Pallais, a Jesuit related to the Somoza family. After a meeting with me, he had visited Somoza and told him he should step down "based on health reasons" and leave the foreign minister in charge of the state, while getting Somoza Jr. out of the country. But Father Pallais felt that the general did not pay any attention to him.

60. When she became president in 1990, Doña Violeta decreed a broad amnesty that included her husband's killers.

61. The death of Emilio Alvarez Montalván's son was another factor in the debate. *La Prensa* (August 13) reported on Dr. Alvarez's speech to the military court and his eloquent advocacy for the constitution of a "modern state" full of pathos. Money and a wristwatch had been stolen from his son's cadaver. Didn't the National Guard realize that its destiny and that of the nation were at stake? Would it ever have the courage to separate the wheat from the chaff, so it could play a role in the future? He called to the Guardia to end the impunity of its men, to be a professional and accountable institution with a responsible command, "fifty

years after its founding." Although Alvarez commented that army patrols acted like "irresponsible lunatics, firing crazily" at random targets, he asserted his son had been deliberately executed, shot in the forehead while he was kneeling.

62. Symptomatic of the local "schizophrenia," on August 19, *Novedades* violently attacked *La Prensa*, accusing it of murders perpetrated by terrorists. The front page included gory photographs. Such propaganda continued, despite our August 18 conversation.

63. There was a precedent for a triumvirate, the one orchestrated by Somoza in 1972–74.

64. Belli Pereira, "Aclarando malentendidos."

65. The National Palace was not the presidential palace: it housed the Congress and a few offices of the executive branch. This revolutionary model was subsequently repeated by revolutionaries in other places—e.g., Honduras, September 1982; Colombia, November 1985. In Colombia the operation was executed by the 9 of April Movement occupying the Palace of Justice in Bogotá; the Colombian Armed Forces launched an all-out attack and in recapturing the building massacred its occupants, including Supreme Court justices.

66. I do not have precise data. Somoza provided me with the list of prisoners that the commandos demanded be released and sent to Venezuela, Panama, and Mexico in three airplanes. Eighty-two people were mentioned in the list. However, Somoza claimed that not all of them were in jail: some were in "exile," and others were "unaccountable," he said. The head of the Sandinista operations, in a telephone interview by Francisco Rubiales during the palace's occupation, stated that twenty-five or thirty of them were not in the prisons, that they already had been "massacred." In his press conference after the crisis was resolved, Somoza stated that fifty-nine prisoners had been released. Initially the revolutionaries demanded $10 million, but in negotiations mediated by the bishops of Managua, Leon, and Granada— Monsignors Obando Bravo, Manuel Salazar, and Leovigildo López Fitoria—the agreed-upon final compensation was half a million dollars.

67. Two planes, one from Panama and the other from Venezuela, were involved. Notice that the two governments were playing a very open role in the anti-Somoza "conspiracy."

68. Part of the settlement of the occupation was the government's commitment to publish three Sandinista documents. (1) Parte de Guerra (war communiqué) no. 1 of the Comando Rigoberto López Pérez, as the acting revolutionary unit was named. The "operation" was called "Death to Somocismo, Carlos Fonseca Amador," the FSLN hero and founder of the movement. López Pérez was the individual who had shot and killed the president's father in 1956. (2) The Declaration to the People of Nicaragua from the National Directorate of the Sandinista Front of National Liberation (FSLN). Indicative of the remaining division, it was signed only by Daniel and Humberto Ortega Saavedra and Víctor Tirado López, leaders of the faction that since October 1977 had decided to conduct a short-term armed insurrection. The Commando Rigoberto López Pérez acted under instructions of this national directorate, it was stated. (3) The Stratagem of the New Somocismo, signed by the same di-

rectorate. Pastora—in whom the non-Marxist regional governments that supported the revolution placed high hopes for its social or Christian democratic outcome, but despite his popularity he was never one of the nine Sandinista Comandantes—was asked about his ideology. Was he a Marxist? "Most of our militants are Catholic. I am a Sandinista and revolutionary, by family tradition a Conservative fighting the Liberal Government, against the United States that keeps Somoza in power." And although Sandino himself was an enigmatic figure in Nicaragua, his semiotics were nationalism, anti-U.S. imperialism, and socialism. He had not been a Communist (Marxist-Leninist party dictatorship) nor a social democrat (electoral, parliamentary, multiparty, reformist socialism). Bendaña, *La mística de Sandino*, calls Sandino's ideology Libertarian Socialism influenced by Anarchism and Utopian Socialism.

69. The extent that the Twelve owed their political position to the FSLN was indicated by the Sandinistas in the documents. The group was the only one consistently praised by the Sandinista Directorate.

70. The "Chilean route to socialism," of course, created an intense polemic among Marxists. On the dilemma of election or insurrection to gain power, see the controversy between Débray (Che Guevara's French guerrilla companion in Bolivia), *Revolución dentro de la revolución*, and Garcés, 1970: *La pugna política*. The 1973 military coup against Allende provided increased credibility for the need for successful insurrection. However, Marxist-Leninist-inspired rule with a single party based on the Soviet model was established in Ethiopia in 1977 by the military themselves. In 1974 Emperor Haile Selassie was deposed in a military coup d'état by leftist officers. One of them, Lieutenant Colonel Mengistu Haile Mariam, consolidated control in 1977 and established the regime in question. Civil war subsequently ended his rule in 1991.

71. It seemed to me that some paragraphs projected Jean-Jacques Rousseau's "general will," interpreted as being monopolized by the humble, the workers and peasants, onto the future *Sandinista* "democratic-popular" government. The Sandinistas defined their opponents—including other oppositionists who disagreed with them—as traitors. Hence only Sandinista actors were part of the "general will." Others were not "free"—they were criminals.

72. The main declared target was the National Guard and those civilians—such as the spies, *orejas*—who served to support the army's operations. There were also, though very few, killings of top civilian officials.

73. For details see *La Prensa*, August 25, 1978. Its editorial in support of the stoppage was moderate in tone. Inexorably, however, *La Prensa* represented the diametrically opposite position from the Somocistas: nothing good had been accomplished in the years of family rule because of the undemocratic nature of the regime; the ultimate problem was "regime."

74. The interested reader can refer to *Novedades*, August 26, 1978, for more details on these views. Incidentally, although the captivity in the palace was brief, the processes unleashed by the revolutionaries were geared toward creating the loss of self-esteem, conditions of insecurity and dependency, and renunciation of past identifi-

cations, classically discussed by Bettelheim, *Informed Heart*. Allegedly hostages had been used to shield the Sandinistas from attack, being placed in front of windows and the access doors, for example. Somoza explained that as he was a reasonable man and a ruler, this is why he had departed from an earlier commitment that he would not give again any ransom to liberate hostages.

75. It had not lost thrust among Somoza's shortsighted Washington backers in Congress, who were not proposing a realistic alternative to 1981, and though they were few in numbers, they were giving Somoza a sense of power that he could not really count on to survive.

76. A few Latin American autocratic rulers have been returned to power through elections after a period of exile.

77. Somoza mentioned that he had tried to unseat Juan José Arévalo, the Guatemalan reformist, but had compromised after realizing his strength.

78. One of the instances, of course, was the 1972 earthquake; I do not know what the two other occasions were that he had in mind.

79. Other dictators have shared Somoza's self-view and worldview that conditioned their understanding of the situation and blocked more successful exits from power. The case of General Gerardo Machado y Morales, the "victim" of the Cuban Revolution of 1933, comes to mind. Contrast my conversations with Somoza with those of Machado with the U.S. ambassador, as reported in Machado's memoirs, *Memorias*. Machado was willing to leave office only "without breaking the Constitution and without dangerous and disorderly haste" (p. 111). The similarities in Machado's and Somoza's arguments to remain in power are truly remarkable.

80. My statements on Matagalpa largely paraphrase two articles by Bohning, "Rebels' City" and "Nicaraguan Soldiers Rout Rebels"; and an article by Fenton, "Troops Rout Rebel Youth." The reports were vague about the numbers involved, and casualties were not confirmed independently. A mixture of students and common people were reported in the rebellion. The archbishop went to Matagalpa to stop the fighting and eventually wrote on the events; see Obando Bravo, *Golpe Sandinista*. Ramírez considered it a spontaneous, uncoordinated uprising mostly of high school students influenced by "the climate of enthusiasm and agitation" generated by the taking over of the National Palace (*Adiós muchachos*, p. 207).

The need to differentiate the various profiles and establish the autonomy of participants in mass protest in the streets from the leadership of opposition movements has been supported by technical, sociological survey research in some settings. See, for instance, Opp, Voss, and Gern, *Origins of a Spontaneous Revolution*. This does not mean, however, that the participants would be politically effective if the leaders were not active as well in different capacities. We must be clear about these sociological differences.

81. However, the U.S. press reported linkages between the FSLN and Communist Cuba. For example, twenty-two of the prisoners liberated by the National Palace operation had gone to Cuba and were determined to return to Nicaragua to fight against Somoza's government (*Miami Herald*, September 2, 1978, p. 4A).

82. Bohning, "U.S. Reluctance to Act." I edit the quote for the sake of compactness. Bohning observed also: "[Somoza's] public and private comments indicate a streak of stubbornness and suggest that he won't give it all up without more of a fight than has yet been seen" ("Nicaragua 1978").

83. See Bohning, "Many Strike Leaders Arrested."

84. Actually, one of the Twelve had just sent me a message that he would like to meet with me in a "neutral" residence because if the Sandinistas knew about the contact he would lose prestige with them. The Twelve wished to influence and moderate the Sandinistas. Other non-Marxists were also active in the FSLN, and the responsibility for the extant mess was past U.S. government support for the Somozas, the message said.

85. On September 8 the head count was eleven yes, two (Nicaragua and Paraguay) no, three don't know; the remainder were abstentions. Thirteen votes were needed to convene the special meeting of foreign ministers, and seventeen were needed to take decisions in the body. Notice the slowness of the OAS in taking any action.

86. I wanted Washington to get an understanding of the situation and sent the following comment: "Somoza appears confident he can surmount the present crisis and is reluctant to accept any mediation that could undermine his 1981 formula. He seems unaware of the extent of national opposition sentiment, and has decided to rely on government military and economic advantage to bend the opposition down to the ground. I believe he is contemplating taking the substance from Carazo's effort and outmaneuvering Central American presidents, whom he considers inferior."

    Somoza did not assume that the political equation was predetermined. If he could alter U.S. policy, he thought, the equation would change in his favor. But he misunderstood the situation. He defended himself, telling me that currently there was more violence in Colombia than in Nicaragua. This might have been the case. But in Colombia the *violentos* were relatively isolated; there was not a broad coalition involving the entire civil society to terminate the regime. It is not the volume of violence per se that results in successful revolution.

87. Several pieces published by the *Miami Herald* are useful to understand events: "Nicaraguan Troops Advance on Rebels," September 14, 1978; Thompson, "Rebels Tried to Kill Me," September 14, 1978; "Nicaragua Calls Its Reserves Up against Rebels," September 15, 1978; Long, "Somoza Still Has the Firepower," September 17, 1978; Millett, "Battling a National Mutiny," September 17, 1978.

88. September 15, 1978.

89. *Barricada* was the name adopted by the newspaper of the triumphant revolution.

90. Long, "Somoza Still Has the Firepower."

91. Long, "Somoza Still Has the Firepower."

92. Millett, "Battling a National Mutiny."

93. The international press reported continued Panamanian support for the FSLN. A September 17 EFE cable stated: "A group of 30 Sandinista guerillas, who had entered Costa Rican territory yesterday after engaging in combat with the Nicaraguan National Guard, arrived today in Panama as political exiles. The Sandinistas ar-

rived . . . in a [commercial Costa Rican] airplane rented by the Panamanian Government."

6. Mediation

In this chapter, a few dates reported refer to when I registered the events in my journal; because of my hectic schedule I could have been slightly off in some recorded days.

1. The private sector was well aware of the serious economic problems. In the International Monetary Fund a $21.6 million Compensatory Fund loan and a $30 million standby credit to the government had been postponed. The government was having difficulties with more than the IMF. It was estimated that between August 25 and September 21 there was a private capital flight out of the country of $60 million. Because of the lack of government funds, the USAID Reconstruction Program for Managua was at a standstill. The Central Bank reported for August that net reserves were about $40 million, which would cover average imports for only twenty-one days; Instituto Nicaragüense de Desarrollo (INDE), "Circular to Members No. 28," September 1978.

2. The MPU was an incipient "civic" grassroots organization to complement and assist the FSLN armed activities. In contrast, the Twelve could be characterized as a group of notables.

3. Before departing for Nicaragua, I met with Father Miguel D'Escoto in the Washington Office for Latin America (WOLA), a leftist group. He had wanted to take a picture of us to publicize our contact and his anti-Somoza campaign. He gave me his blessing before our meeting ended, which I had considered definitely friendly.

4. See the analysis of the documents in chapter 5. Incidentally, Alan Riding of the New York Times had suggested to me that I arrange to meet with the Twelve to clarify their criticism of the embassy.

5. However, in practice this international mediation was to some extent a disguise: everyone knew that the United States was or would have to be the decisive force.

6. For details, see the Miami Herald story by Thompson, "Rebels Tried to Kill Me." Mary Daniel and John Bargeron of our consular section were rewarded in this case with letters praising their services, with copies sent to the president and secretary of state. However, Nicaraguan U.S. citizens who "culturally" were not Americans and who were not intending to live in the United States—that is, citizens only by the fact of birth—participated in the uprising. One of them, César Augusto Amador, was killed while in police custody. In this case the prominent Amador family launched an abusive public campaign against the embassy for more than a month. According to them it was our duty to produce Amador, dead or alive. Amador's father was a gentleman and later apologized in my office for the pressures exerted against us because of the family's anguish. The two cases, rightly so, consumed much energy on our part.

7. The city was officially and publicly declared by the government entirely under its control early in the morning of September 16.

8. Gwertzman, "U.S. Pressuring Somoza."

9. Somoza himself aired these views for the American public that same day in an interview. (See the *MacNeil/Lehrer Report*, September 19, 1978.) He had urged the opposition to talk to him and negotiate the rules for a free election (1981); the opposition needed time to organize itself; the tradition in Nicaragua was for negotiations (the notorious *pactos* that had always consolidated the Somozas, a reason for opposition intransigence against negotiating with him). He could not "chicken out," leaving a "power vacuum" by resigning; the opposition had no leadership or organization and did not control their own forces; if he resigned, the country would be left with an army "without a leader," and this would result in "chaos." Somoza's macho provocative arrogance came through in his remark about the unarmed opposition: they did not have the courage to take up arms against him, he said.

10. I forwarded to Washington the comment: Article 336 of the 1974 Constitution does limit "total amendment" of it. It "may take place only 10 years after it has been in force." Article 338 limits "partial" constitutional reform only when this includes those articles that prohibit the reelection of persons exercising the presidency, and the election of his relatives within the fourth degree of consanguinity or affinity; these amendments cannot go into effect in the period in which they are made, nor in the following period. There is precedent about shortening a presidential term, in the case of Víctor Manuel Román y Reyes (1947–50), but this initiative was not fully carried out, because he died. A legal scholar that I consulted feels that Articles 336 and 338 imply that there is a constitutional possibility of shortening the current term.

11. Somoza remained conscious about his victory over the $12 million USAID package. Notice his perception that he could defeat the administration.

12. See, for instance, DeYoung, "Nicaragua Says Venezuela Aids Rebels."

13. See *Congressional Record*, 95th Cong., 2nd sess., September 21, 22, and 27, 1978.

14. Conservative journalist Patrick J. Buchanan wrote a piece that was incorporated into the *Congressional Record*. He asked: "Imagine the outrage had Somoza lined up his communist captives and threatened to shoot 10 a day until the Sandinistas turned in their weapons"—what would the liberal press have done? Buchanan was protesting the favorable press treatment that the FSLN had received in their hostage-taking National Palace operation; *Congressional Record*, 95th Cong., 2nd sess., September 21, 1978, p. H10396. Indeed, one does not expect civilized governments to behave like that. See Buchanan, "On the Revolutionary Left." The future Republican presidential candidate already showed a profound contempt for people of "tropical lands," before his national political campaigns against "foreigners" of certain kinds.

15. According to the U.S. military mission in Nicaragua, only three American mercenaries remained. This issue, which had earlier taken hold of the imagination of many Nicaraguans, was not being agitated at this time in Managua, but it was being raised in the United States and in the OAS by, among others, Venezuela. The administration did not feel that it could invoke the Neutrality Act to end the services of these private citizens to the Nicaraguan government.

16. DeYoung, "They Died on Knees Begging for Mercy." For years the Guardia Nacional had been widely perceived in Nicaragua as an "uncivilized" organization. This was believed even by many Somoza sympathizers who claimed that he moderated the Guard; "if he weren't there those beasts would be uncontrolled," several of my conservative contacts claimed at the initiation of my mission. Revolutionaries also created some noncombatant victims, but although the population at large still preferred a peaceful solution—to wit, the mediation's welcome—the government was considered the illegitimate party responsible for the violence.

17. O'Leary, "U.S. Weighs Options."

18. On September 15 we learned that the OAS Permanent Council was sending a fact-finding mission to the Costa Rica–Nicaragua frontier, composed of Barbados, Colombia, and the Dominican Republic. Although some Venezuelan and Panamanian equipment financed through the United States Foreign Military Sales Program remained in Costa Rica, this was considered by the U.S. government to be legal as it had not been used against Nicaragua. However, no force was deployed to control border traffic to protect the Somoza regime from the insurgence.

19. The Venezuelan opposition had started to review its support for President Pérez's policy. It found itself caught between the desire for a prudent policy consonant with a majority in the OAS, Pérez's personal flamboyant style, and the felt need to obtain a solution to the crisis. The Betancourt Doctrine incorporated in the Venezuelan Constitution referred to a pro-democratic, peaceful international policy.

20. The vote was 23 to 1.

21. The selection of countries was not easy. For instance, the United States urged Mexico to take the leadership mediating the conflict, but Mexico refused to participate in any negotiations. U.S. diplomats complained about the paradox of Latin Americans who wished that the United States would be the party that solved the crisis at the same time they opposed "U.S. intervention" in Latin America.

22. Within the FAO the Conservatives were conspicuously in disarray. Occasionally using my name to further their interests, the factions continued discussing the basis for their unification—whether the Zancudo faction should resign its posts in the government. This they were unwilling to do in the Congress, if for no other reason that as the constitutional succession was through congressional election, one of them might get to be president. They had to weigh this with being on record that they had acted to destabilize the regime with a resignation en masse, an act that would serve to announce that a "new" Conservative Party had been reborn.

23. Somoza had reservations about Colombia because of a territorial dispute over some islands in the Caribbean. In 1972 the United States and Colombia had signed the Quita Sueño Treaty over them; Nicaragua had not accepted it.

24. Borge, one of the Sandinista movement's founders, had been a prisoner held by Somoza and released with the National Palace operation. Borge was a leader of a hard-line, less reformist faction.

25. Press digest, U.S. Embassy, Managua, September 26, 1978.

26. See the Díaz Palacios summary article on Somoza's radio and television address to the nation: "Intransigencia de oposición." As I knew Somoza's feelings toward the embassy and that he needed encouragement to cooperate with the mediation, I sent a note praising his statement announcing the invitation to the international team.

27. Quintanilla was exercising the leadership of his Liberal group in the FAO because Ramiro Sacasa Guerrero was in the United States, absent from these developments. I believed that this weakened Sacasa's position in the FAO, which was unfortunate because he was a reasonable man of principle.

28. Because of the conflict between the Red Cross and the Nicaraguan government, our local USAID director suggested that we waive government approval of these immediately available relief moneys. On September 19 we had agreed that we would not sign two pending grants with the Nicaraguan government but would go ahead with two for private institutions; Somoza had not accepted the mediation at that time. However, on the 22nd, we asked Washington if routine payments to the government should continue; the reply: suspend payments for military training abroad and proceed with USAID reimbursements. In fact, disbursements were largely suspended because of no progress in most of the government projects, including the new ones that I had opposed.

29. See Don Bohning's summary article "Somoza Controls the Territory." Many of the points discussed below were reported by him. Alan Riding of the *New York Times* personally told me about several of the issues reported by Bohning in a conversation on September 22, 1978. On the expectations of a National Guard uprising, see, for instance, the interview with Miguel D'Escoto, of the Group of Twelve and future Sandinista foreign minister, reported in Bohning's article. The interview had taken place the previous week, before a fuller assessment of the failure of the uprising could be made. Actually, much earlier D'Escoto had projected in the U.S. Congress the scenario that opposition actions combined with the human rights policy might result in a coup d'état that would oust Somoza.

30. *Novedades'* propaganda focused on the atrocities committed by the FSLN—e.g., indiscriminate massacres including the killing of pregnant women and children, destruction of property, burnings, looting; on allegations that a fair president and the army controlled the situation (once again the paradox of how horrible the opponents were and at the same time how ineffectual they were); and that the alternative to Somoza was much worse. Whereas *Novedades'* photographs pictured gruesome cadavers and the destruction of property, those of *La Prensa* focused on the people's participation in the revolt. *La Prensa* did report the burnings and looting of private property that took place, however, as well as the imprisonment of some oppositionists, invasion of properties to make inspections and requisitions by the National Guard, and the consequent deaths and destruction of property by the government.

31. A characteristic of the Nicaraguan process was its cyclical developments. All the uprisings had failed. However, subsequent uprisings had proved to be much more potent and broad in scope. In this respect they were not "defeats" but "with-

drawals." For the cadres and activists went into temporary military inactivity, while an increasing number of individuals had learned through observation more and more about the art of revolution and were willing to participate in the next bout.

32. Bohning, "Somoza Controls the Territory." He wrote that the National Guard had reestablished "physical control of a country with an almost universally hostile population."

33. *Miami Herald*, October 4, 1978, p. 3.

34. *Componendas* can mean "compromises," "understandings"; it most commonly means "shady deals."

35. At this time the Somoza government was also under the pressure of the visit, since October 3, of a committee of the OAS Human Rights Commission headed by Andrés Aguilar of Venezuela. See, for example, the exchanges involving Aguilar and Luis Pallais, *Novedades*, October 8, 1978. On the 12th, the mission ended. Given the brutal September events and that National Guard actions were perceived by the public at large as coming from an illegitimate organization, the report would be quite negative. See the *Report on the Situation of Human Rights in Nicaragua* adopted by the OAS the following November. The embassy made an analysis of available data, which suggested that the accusations that most of the dead in the uprising resulted from bombings, strafing, and heavy artillery shells used by the National Guard were inaccurate. Practically no women and children had been killed; around 70 percent of those reported dead were males in the "military age" of eighteen to twenty-nine years old. These facts, however, did not shed light on the charge that after cities were retaken the Guard rounded up and summarily executed people.

36. Military assistance had been suspended with the instructions that National Guard officers should not return to the Panama Canal Zone; however, the embassy had been told not to suspend USAID programs.

37. Theberge's statement is taken from "Ex-Envoy Warns of Guerrilla Takeover, Election Backed for Nicaragua," *Miami Herald*, October 14, 1978. Editorials in the *Miami Herald*, *Detroit Free Press*, and *St. Louis Post Dispatch* of October 10, 1978, had called for Somoza's resignation; for example, from the latter: "The Somoza dictatorship should go, and the sooner it goes, the better will be the prospect for a democratic succession." In Washington eighty-six U.S. congressmen wrote the president in support of the mediation and asked him to suspend all economic and military assistance to Somoza to dramatize the need for a change in regime; "Congressmen Ask Carter to Cut Aid to Nicaragua," *Miami Herald*, October 15, 1978. This was an answer to the earlier statement of seventy-eight congressmen who interpreted the situation as a "without Somoza Communism" alternative. *Novedades* reflected the uneasiness of the Somoza camp with the mediation: one day it accused the panel of being imperialists and interventionists promoting violence, another day of offering an opportunity to stop communism and achieve a democratic solution.

38. One refugee was a rebellious member of the National Guard, and the other was accused in the murder of a general—notice the receptivity to National Guard sentiment.

39. Remember that in Nicaragua there was recent constitutional precedent for a triumvirate.

40. However, resistance to negotiation and factionalism remained; see El Centroamericano, October 13, 1978. In the FAO there were two groups that signed as Partido Social Cristiano Nicaragüense and as Partido Conservador de Nicaragua.

41. The communiqué referred to "kicking, marks from electric shock, as well as bayonet punctures and cuts" and reported that the citizens had been kept "hooded and deprived of food."

42. On September 15, 1978, Venezuela and Costa Rica had signed a Mutual Assistance Treaty, which stated that an attack on either of the two nations implied an aggression on the other, including the use of Venezuelan armed forces to defend Costa Rica from Nicaragua. The Venezuelan president publicly continued demanding the end of the Somoza regime. See the long interview published by Newsweek on October 9, 1978, where Carlos Andrés Pérez traced his policy to the old democratic international links of the Legión del Caribe years discussed in chapter 1 and to the Betancourt Doctrine incorporated in the Venezuelan Constitution referred to in note 19. Venezuela had remained adamant that the U.S. pressure Somoza out, with representations not only at the presidential level. Tension reached Nicaragua: on October 15, the foreign minister phoned me at 6 a.m.; he had information that Costa Rica was planning to fake a Nicaraguan attack using a group of Sandinistas.

43. The FAO document established as a general rule that public functionaries who were honest and good workers would remain in office. You could observe in the text the importance given to terminating the patrimonial state. In regard to the army, it was explicitly stated that adequate salaries and benefits would have to be budgeted so that the military would not have to ("patrimonially") supplement their income through graft and other forms of administrative privatization. Extant salaries were so low that graft was widely considered a necessity.

44. In the FAO's plenary a substantial majority had voted for the "constitutional" formula without the Somozas. Indeed, nationally this was the popular formula.

45. Disbursements had stopped prior to the arrival of the mediators. The last USAID check had been for $385,714 on September 30, 1978. La Prensa, October 19, 22, and 27, 1978. The Construction Chamber informed me that the Nicaraguan government was not paying them the USAID counterpart debts, and that the Central Bank was limiting the credit to the agricultural sector. In listening to some of my private-sector contacts I interpreted that a pervasive message, even if not always stated explicitly, was that we should change the government as soon as possible to resolve the economic crisis.

46. See Congressional Record, 95th Cong., 2nd sess., October 17, 1978, pp. s18878–9.

47. The following items had been proposed by USAID for 1980: a $2 million cooperative development loan to benefit private sector institutions and an $850,000 grant for community development by private organizations (such as INDE). The projects with the public sector were two of proportional size and in politically acceptable areas directed by young technocrats: a $3 million soil and water resource management

loan for campesino development (INVIERNO) and a $1 million family planning grant. Because of its political implications, a $5 million Housing Guaranty program to upgrade barrios was to be held in abeyance until after the crisis ended. This was closer to my earlier position that had been resisted by USAID–Nicaragua and defeated in Washington: a small program, one substantially supportive of private-sector development organizations (NGOs), with only a few programs with the government in sectors under the leadership of technocrats with a good reputation.

48. For example, I called and asked Alfredo Pellas, because of his economic links to the Twelve, and Ernesto Fernández Holmann, the able financier, to visit me. Pellas was critical of FAO intransigence. Fernández Holmann went straight to the point: an agreement was not possible because only in private would men like "Robelo and company" recognize that there was a need to give guarantees to Somoza. It was as if oppositionists in public had been overtaken by the irrationalities attributed to LeBon's "collective mind" of the sociology of crowds. Meanwhile Somoza was publicly stating: "If I let somebody else be President nobody will get this state together"; "I am not chickening out, I'm just being darn honest." If Somoza were forced to step down, he said he would return, either by winning in the next election or leading a popular revolution. See "Somoza Answers His Opposition," *Christian Science Monitor*, October 19, and "Come and Get Me," *Newsweek*, October 23, 1978.

49. The dependence of unarmed oppositionists such as the Twelve on armed irregulars was not exclusively a Group of Twelve–Sandinista relationship. Some of our Conservative contacts also found a sense of power in their links to the Once de Noviembre armed faction. Led by Edmundo and Fernando Chamorro Rappaccioli, this small group claimed at this time that they supported the Conservatives in the FAO.

50. *Componenda* here means "spurious compromise," "shady deal." *La Prensa*, October 26, 1978.

51. Chardy, "Somoza."

52. Also see Chardy, "Rebel Raid from Costa Rica."

53. The safety of the activities of the "Maharishi's Peace Squad" concerned us. They were based in a hotel near Somoza's headquarters, but they kept their religious faith. One of the sect's participants was asked if he knew that people were killed in Nicaragua every day and that the atmosphere was like a pressure cooker? His reply: "We don't read the papers, we just do our work [prayers] and we're confident that it's us who are keeping the lid on"; Simons, "Letter from Nicaragua."

54. Younger brother of Pedro Joaquín, Jaime Chamorro Cardenal replaced Reynaldo Antonio Téfel as an adviser of the FAO's Comisión Política. Téfel became a member of the Twelve. All along Téfel felt that Somoza would have to be physically ousted. In an October 27 interview with *La Prensa*, Téfel explained his opposition to negotiating with the Liberals and criticized the FAO on the grounds that its proposal would impede both prosecuting Somocistas for their crimes and the reorganization of the National Guard. Obviously, his position could not result in successful negotiations. Amnesties are an important component of various democratization processes from

South America to South Africa. The mediation's plan was to reorganize the National Guard, however.

55. Bowdler had urgently left Nicaragua. I was told that he had gone to Grenada to seek support and postponement of an FSLN offensive. Bowdler was quite discreet about the matter with me, but the Grenada–Cuban links were well known. Had he gone to talk with Cuban officials to influence the Sandinistas?

56. The shah's Iran was leading in the IMF the opposition to postpone financing. Interestingly, Mexico was also against postponement. The rallying of support required spending political resources. For instance, Canada was willing to vote with the United States only if the secretary of state asked it to. In fact, all that Washington was really doing was sending a message to Somoza indicating a lack of confidence in him, for the money could not be withheld indefinitely; postponement was unusual because Nicaragua could claim the $20 million credit under the IMF's Compensatory Finance Scheme "virtually as its money"; the *Miami Herald* carried the story "Somoza Government Near Insolvency in Wake of IMF Plan to Delay Loan?" November 4, 1978. Roberto Incer, the Central Bank president, asked me for an urgent appointment. His message was not of a government about to cooperate: the IMF decision was purely political; if boycotted, Nicaragua would withdraw entirely from the IMF; Nicaragua would establish exchange controls and suspend all payments to U.S. companies and citizens, he threatened.

57. The Nicaraguan Constitution stated that partial reforms should be initiated in an "ordinary" legislative period (Article 335, number 1); however, when referring to the need for approving it in a second period, the constitution did not specify its nature. The text only referred to the "next legislature" (Article 335, number 8), without stating that it be an "ordinary" one. The problem was that ordinary periods per constitutional disposition were initiated every year on April 15 (Article 128), thus one interpretation was that there was a need to wait until then. This might have been the spirit in which the text was written, but as oppositionists claimed, "extraordinary" sessions could be called to speed up the process—certainly the process was not prohibited, thus not "illegal." With appropriate legal techniques that were available and a democratic commitment, a pre-1981 constitutional solution was feasible. Moreover, legal scholar Armando Rizo Oyanguren wrote to me that under Somoza, before the end of his first term a precedent was established for the Congress in an ordinary session to become the sovereign constituent power. By a simple decision (no. 1914, September 2, 1971) it reorganized the branches of government and created a triumvirate junta. The basic difference between this case and the one we were dealing with was that the former was so the general could remain strongman without any election. Who could believe that Somocista objections were on grounds of constitutionality?

58. The Junta would rule until December 1, 1981; the Council and the Congress would terminate their functions with the election of the Constituent Assembly in 1980.

59. *Novedades*, October 29, 1978. At points the original document is almost incoherent, an indication of the unreflective emotionalism that could overcome ancien

régime actors. For pertinent comments on Latin American cultural ethoses, see José Vasconcelos, *Indiología*.

60. See the communiqué of the Central Committee of the Partido Socialista Nicaragüense titled "For Democracy, National Liberation and Socialism," *La Prensa*, October 30, 1978. They were Communists with a pre-Gorbachev "Euro-Communism" orientation, willing to cooperate with progressive democratic governments, and supportive of a democratic road to socialism without war. A useful bibliographical summary note on this strategy is found in Bermeo, *Revolution within the Revolution*.

61. *La Prensa*, October 28, 1978. The unviability of the new FAO proposal was independently reported to us by calmer Somocistas and oppositionists. Somoza was preparing for war, and the cabinet and congressional Liberals were telling him that the FAO plan was totally unacceptable. I informally learned this from cabinet ministers Klaus Sengelman and Edmundo Bernheim and legislator David Zamora. The urgency for the mediation to obtain results was cogently presented by politically independent Carlos and Jaime Morales Carazo: the FAO's proposal was unreal; how could it offer only two positions to Liberals and demand the immediate exile of the Somoza family? Bowlder must tell Somoza he has to go, that the United States will see to it happening, and obtain his terms of exit.

62. Conservative congressman Julio Molina had just proposed a supervised plebiscite to determine if Somoza should leave or remain in office.

63. Compare the government's position with the lucid statement on the issue of constitutionality by Jaime Chamorro Cardenal, "Comentarios sobre el documento." Though there were technically unnecessary legal provisions (hence flaws) in the opposition's proposal to the mediation, the intellectual poverty of the government's response was shocking. For a classical general statement on the legal tradition with its variations, see Karst and Rosenn, *Law and Development in Latin America*.

64. Ernesto Cruz, Ernesto Fernández Holmann, and Mariano Fiallos authored the document. Its mental picture coincided with a common characterization of English "conservatism"; see the ideological, antidemocratic traditionalism that had been present in the Spanish conservative regime, then in the process of being dismantled after Franco's death, in Bermejo de la Rica and Ramos Pérez, *Los ideales del imperio español* for a textbook example of early expressions.

65. In order to add flexibility to the selection of the new president, the Nicaraguan Constitution would be amended so that the incumbent would not necessarily be replaced by a member of the Congress. Any citizen could be chosen, including Liberals acceptable to the opposition. The document traced pressures on the FAO from those committed to the use of violence, from the moralistic intransigence ("intransigent puritanism") of actors, or from an erroneous understanding of the current relative strength of the political-military forces.

66. The city of Leon remained particularly problematic. *El Centroamericano* (November 4, 1978) reported that eighteen FSLN members were killed and that in barrios of the city handmade bombs exploded and there was machine-gun fire nightly. The

newspaper predicted an imminent Sandinista invasion and considered already that in the face of the situation the mediation would not be able to do much.

67. Press digest, U.S. Embassy, Managua, November 10, 1978.

68. The mediation's goal to obtain the resignation culminated on November 15 with the visit to Somoza by Foreign Minister Jiménez, who explained the need for Somoza to step down to avoid civil war. Jiménez concluded to Bowdler: "We must push Somoza, and the push needs a military component, an ultimatum. You should go to Washington and clear this plan." Jiménez also expressed his concern that the mediation was rapidly losing prestige. The instructions to the U.S. Embassy in Caracas to make clear that Washington would not deliver any ultimatum nor coordinate any boycott with Venezuela against Nicaragua were included in my November 7 and 8 journal entries.

69. Riding, "Somoza Seeks Vote on Foes' Strength."

70. DeYoung, "U.S.-Led Mediation in Nicaragua."

71. In the face of these events, I felt I should resign, but Bowdler said, "You can't resign, we have to be 'good soldiers.' " I did not pursue my departure as the change of ambassador at this time would not have made matters any smoother.

72. Riding, "U.S. Leads Efforts to Oust Somoza."

73. Tolentino Camacho, "Voz de Alerta; Plebiscito Bajo Terror," La Prensa, November 16, 1978. A day earlier P.J. Chamorro's editorial of September 5, 1974, impugning the "election" of Somoza to his current term, was reprinted to show that Somoza was not a legitimate, elected president, and that popular consultations were spurious. Also see Tolentino Camacho, "Plebiscito, No!," La Prensa, November 19, 1978. That same day the most virulent article against the plebiscite, William Bowdler, and American policy was published by La Prensa; see Carla Rodríguez, "La Neutralized de los EE. UU. de Norteamérica en Nicaragua," p. 2. The article accused the United States of conspiring with Somoza to maintain the dictatorship. During my years in Nicaragua there was more than one current of opinion within La Prensa, of course.

74. This was, for example, the case earlier in 1978 in the Dominican Republic. India was a paradigmatic case of several opposition victories. The key issue is whether the government decides to accept defeat, for the presence of international observers need not impede electoral fraud (e.g., in the Philippines in 1986, Panama in 1989, Haiti and Peru in 2000).

75. The coverage outside of Nicaragua of the mediation as basically a U.S. enterprise once again irritated the other two parties: this created a bad image in the Dominican Republic and Guatemala about their role in it, the mediators opined. Rumors spread in Santo Domingo and Guatemala City that the two countries would pull out.

76. The positive sign came from Leonel Argüello, COSEP's coordinator, who informed the public that the private sector and the Catholic Church had urged the FAO to continue in search of a "peaceful solution with justice and dignity," not to discard the mediation as an "instrument that we must use now, for a new opportunity such as this one will not present itself again." Notice the sense of urgency, of impending

horror. But, of course, there were those in the FAO who thought that the next uprising would be successful.

77. On November 29, 1978, *La Prensa* published an article titled "La mediación de 1926." On that occasion an American mediation failed, and the marines were subsequently sent to Nicaragua. The article reported the unwillingness of the Nicaraguan Congress to accept the U.S.-proposed measures to ensure honest suffrage because of their "unconstitutionality." You can observe another earlier manifestation of using the "constitution" to sustain a fraudulent "democracy" and of the lack of seriousness toward elections.

78. See Stokes, "Violence as a Power Factor," on these old caudillo patterns. And on so-called hard or not serious surface bargaining, see Lawler, *Unionization and Deunionization*.

79. "FAO pide a la OEA condenar genocidio," *La Prensa*, November 26, 1978. A similar statement by Group of Twelve member Carlos Tunnerman was published in "Opposition Wants OAS Sanctions on Somoza's Regime," *Miami Herald*, November 26, 1978. At this stage, the only exception to local press criticism of the mediation's proposal was *El Centroamericano* of Leon, which felt it was the only alternative (November 25, 1978, p. 1). Bear in mind that while FSLN strategy was to achieve total control of a revolutionary state dismantling the National Guard, their first stumbling block was to oust Somoza. Throughout the years Sandinista ideology had led to the leaders' acceptance of the higher costs of armed opposition, even at the risk of their isolation; their doctrine led also to misperceptions as to the viability of a shorter-term armed uprising; in all probability the core FSLN leaders would not give up their struggle even after the mediation obtained Somoza's exit unless they were able to establish their revolutionary regime. Indeed, even if Somoza resigned, pacifying Nicaragua would not be easy. This was one of Somoza's excuses to remain in power and not contribute to breaking the vicious circle of authoritarian rule. As his opponents were not true democrats, he claimed that there would be too much risk in his becoming more democratic himself.

80. I have introduced the first two; Godoy headed the Partido Liberal Independiente, PLI, and in 1990 was elected vice president of the country on the Violeta de Chamorro ticket that defeated the Sandinista government: he had learned that dictators can be electorally defeated.

81. However, *La Prensa*, on November 25, 1978, had given a new twist to the referendum: "The Mediation Commission Unmasks Somoza: Now He Doesn't Like the Plebiscite! Somoza rejects every democratic solution."

82. See "Opiniones sobre documento de mediación; Presencia de Somoza obstáculo insuperable," *La Prensa*, November 28, 1978. The article only reported one opinion in favor of the plebiscite, that of Ramiro Sacasa Guerrero, my friend and head of the Partido Liberal Constitucionalista (PLC), who unfortunately was not exercising much leadership in the FAO.

83. DeYoung, "Beneath the Surface." She also had this to say: "In a slum settlement several miles away, youths meet nightly to turn tin cans into homemade bombs,

hold political classes, and discuss how to deal with 'orejas,' the government's 'ears' [spies]." Many were leaving Nicaragua to avoid the impending battle or otherwise preparing by storing food and medicine among other measures. She reported the lack of confidence among oppositionists that they would surely win a referendum.

84. Notice the peculiar mixture in the pseudo-democratic political culture: the public recognition of "government by grace," i.e., whim, coupled with a democratic lexicon. But popular support is not necessarily a democratic concept. Within the Hispanic authoritarian tradition—as shown in secondary school textbooks of the 1950s during Franco's rule—popular support for the ruler is viewed positively, even if formal democratic institutions are not adopted; Francisco Suárez (1548–1617) is a frequently cited source of this tradition. At some points the panegyrics were ludicrous—e.g., Somoza was called an "excellent husband" when, in fact, he was separated from his wife and lived with his mistress. Oswaldo Rengifo, the Colombian ambassador, commented: "Nicaragua is incredible; in my country if a newspaper carried an editorial on the president's birthday you would expect that it would be a satiric piece against him." But then, with its own difficulties, Colombia was a republic. It is not unusual that monarchies celebrate the birthday of king or queen.

85. At this time there was only limited sentiment supporting the December 2 proposal; "Algunas opiniones antes de reunión del FAO: Mediación y no mediación," La Prensa, December 4, 1978. But most in the FAO recognized the anti-Somoza orientation of the mediation—see, for instance, the interview titled "Dr. Rafael Córdova Rivas, renuncia o plebescito, Somoza en encrucijada," La Prensa, December 3, 1978.

86. In explaining its withdrawal the PLI stated that there were no conditions for a plebiscite and that two things were not negotiable: Somoza family exile and an international trial to punish the tyrant for the "Calvary" of Nicaragua created by him. The PLI concluded that the collapse of the mediation would be the failure not of the FAO but rather of the United States and the OAS: once again it would be shown that both favored dictatorship over democracy. Unfortunately, the assessment that the mediation's failure would not be the FAO's "political suicide" was erroneous; with the failure of mediation the FAO was supplanted by the FSLN as the key political movement.

87. La Prensa's December 5 editorial made a pertinent analysis. Under the December 2 proposal, the FAO could not obtain a majority in the executive, while the Somocistas would remain in control of the Congress. The predicted result: at least a veto power for the Somocistas, a government paralyzed by impasse, the postponement of a "quick and profound democratic transformation." And this was the "solution for which the people of Nicaragua heroically has been and is fighting?" However, such power-sharing limitations to majority rule have been instruments for democratic transitions and make permanent institutions of firmly established, so-called consociational democracies, the literature shows. See, for instance, the summaries in Dahl, Polyarchy and Democracy and Its Critics.

88. The need to change attitudes on the part of the FAO was public, but the thesis was unpopular. See, for example, the articles signed Alfonso Aguilar, "El Plebiscito, Solución Realista y Democrática," *La Prensa,* December 2 and 6, 1978. "We are living also under another dictatorship—the dictatorship of the political passions, the resentments, of the hatreds, the deceits, the illusions, of the fears and intransigencies, all of which forms the primitive collective conscience of our people and belongs to the realm of the irrational and unreflected." The articles noted the FAO's lack of "political experience, maturity and realism" and explained why the FAO's political role and triumph depended upon the success of a peaceful compromise, in contrast to the FSLN.

89. *La Prensa's* December 6 editorial outlined the changes made by Somoza in his position since September 12, as he faced domestic and international pressures.

90. For instance, Riding, "Nicaraguans, Seeing Strife as Inevitable," discussed the preparations for war, the three FSLN factions, and the heterogeneous forces trying to unseat the government. He did not dismiss the Leninist influence within the FSLN, a point of interest because of the essays that criticized the reporting of these events; see Christian, "Covering the Sandinistas," and Kirkpatrick, "Dictatorships and Double Standards." The "Somoza or Communism" dilemma continued to be manipulated by the Nicaraguan government, however. In contrast to the opposition, on December 8 *Novedades* editorialized that unless the government ruled more firmly, the Communists (i.e., the FSLN) would take over the country.

91. Only representatives of the government and political opposition were present at this meeting. The FAO had constituted an expanded Comisión Política, which in addition to original members Rafael Córdova Rivas and Alfonso Robelo included Julio Ycasa Tigerino and Eduardo Rivas Gasteazoro.

92. The entire press conference appeared in *Novedades,* December 8. *La Prensa's* replies were December 9 and 10. Somoza stated that there were only two hundred political prisoners.

93. For example, on December 6 *La Prensa Libre* carried a story on about five thousand Sandinistas in Guanacaste province. Incidentally, the paper attacked the government for inspiring a warlike climate in the country, for not maintaining neutrality with Nicaragua, and for arms purchases whose result might be the "Centralamericanization" (i.e., praetorianization or internal military dominance) of Costa Rica. Some criticism of government policy also was carried in the Honduran press, which, although under a military authoritarian regime, had lively newspapers. At this time one accused the government of having dismantled not a Sandinista training camp but a camp of refugees from Nicaragua.

94. See *La Nación's* (December 7) advertisement calling on Costa Ricans to join the "Juan Santamaría Brigade." It was increasingly difficult to handle the presence of these private armies.

95. Hate mail was forthcoming. We received this statement December 14 in Managua:
    Subject: Alleged plots against U.S. Ambassador and Special Mediator

1. U.S. Secret Service provided a letter addressed to Presidential Press Secretary Jody Powell from a "J. Adolfo Baez Bone," containing the following verbatim text:

Begin quote

2. We, Nicaragua's people have knowledge that there is a plot for to execute the American Ambassador in Nicaragua Mr. Maurice Solaun, a Cuban person, that helps Somoza, a United States traitor.

3. There is a plot too, to kill the President Carter's "mediator," that Mr. Carter sent to Nicaragua in order to maintain Somoza, a genocide, in the Nicaragua power. The Ambassador's name is, Mr. William G. Bowdler that is tricking the Nicaraguan's society by order of President Carter.

4. If President Carter persists in a plebiscite in Nicaragua, that he knows very well that Somoza's tyranny never before was elected by the Nicaraguan's people majority, but for the United States' Government imposition, since 1934, after Somoza García assassinated Agusto C. Sandino by order of Franklin D. Roosevelt, a Jew.

5. If President Carter doesn't change his mind about supporting Somoza, Nicaraguan people will eliminate the United States of Americans that are living in Nicaragua, the only way to stop Mr. Carter's intervention in Nicaragua for maintaining the bloody Somoza, with the U.S. force. God save the world's people of President Carter madness.

6. First Mr. Carter, has to kill all Nicaraguans to maintain the Somoza'a tyranny, a critical government. We have to kill Americans too. Tooth by tooth, eye by eye, Attention please.

End quote

The writer signed the letter and listed his address as 132 Green Street, San Francisco. The letter was dated December 10, 1978, was accompanied by a political cartoon concerning the Middle East negotiations between Egypt and Israel, and was postmarked in San Francisco on December 10, 1978.

96. The statement was made at the Democratic National Committee breakfast in Memphis. The *Washington Post*, on December 10, carried a news item headed "Carter Fumbles in Nicaragua," stating that he was having "a bit of trouble keeping his Nicaraguan opposition groups straight." *La Prensa* felt that Somoza had no intentions of participating in a fair plebiscite and hence was critical of Carter's optimism about his policy; see the lead article and editorial December 16.

97. This was part of the president's statement on Iran: "I fully expect the Shah to maintain power . . . and for the present problems in Iran to be resolved, although there have been certainly deplorable instances of bloodshed which we would certainly want to avoid, or see avoided. I think the predictions of doom and disaster that came from some sources have certainly not been realized at all. The Shah has our support and he also has our confidence." Somoza was angered by what he considered the administration's discrimination against him because Nicaragua was not an important oil producer.

98. The costs already incurred were evident and known to the U.S. government. Starting with the $25,000 donation that we made to the president of the Nicaraguan Red Cross (September 21), USAID had donated approximately $479,000 in disaster relief assistance. This is part of an internal embassy memo: "In early October 1978, the Nicaraguan Red Cross called upon local and international voluntary and religious groups based in the country to form a Coordinating Committee for Relief Assistance. Church World Service, Catholic Relief Services and Seventh Day Adventists affiliates, as well as purely national organizations, made up the Committee. A.I.D. was asked to provide an observer to assist in the coordination of donor activities. Initially, all efforts were focused on emergency feeding programs for displaced persons. In late October, in expectation of another outburst of fighting, the Coordinating Committee decided to establish medical posts and refugee relief centers with supplies sufficient to meet an emergency of the proportions of the September fighting. Such centers have now been organized in six cities where fighting took place, and ten Red Cross medical posts and 28 refugee posts have been set up in Managua. The Church World Services affiliate, CEPAD, has established an additional 17 centers at churches in and around the capital. Food and medical supplies are already stored in the centers, and the Red Cross solicited additional equipment from A.I.D. to provide a 'reactive capability' in the event of further violence." Other international agencies such as the International Committee of the Red Cross and Caritas Internationalis were also involved in the operations.

99. "Royal" military institutions and royal family traditions of military service can coexist with democratic institutions in constitutional monarchies. It took the Sandinistas to give a symbolic explicit partisan definition to the military, calling it the "Sandinista" Army rather than the Nicaraguan or National Army during their dictatorship. But the Somozas monopolized the actual command deliberately, so that they could not be replaced, *Novedades* coverage underlined. Embassy intelligence reported that within the National Guard there was a feeling that it would be preferable for the president to preemptively resign without participating in any conspiracy; the middle-level officialdom felt that the predicted next uprising could be defeated.

100. Statement by Leonel Argüello, *La Prensa*, December 15. The other two private sector participants in the mediation were Manuel José Torres and Eduardo Montealegre Callejas.

101. These radical Christian themes seemed a contemporary version of the historical revolutionary, apocalyptic millenarianism aptly discussed by Cohn, *Pursuit of the Millennium*. Also see Borgeson, *Hacia el hombre nuevo*.

102. Pieter Van Bennehom, "At 21, Nicaraguan Finds." The revolutionary situation is Durkheimian in the sense of a "state of de-regulation": there is confusion and normlessness, a feeling of chaos (the "whole country is going to hell," Carmen said), even a mood of despair, but also a call to action. The problematic conditions call for new emergent norms for collective behavior ("to shoot it out and get it over with"); established institutional patterns and structures are subverted and replaced

by revolutionary groups and activities. Again, the analysis calls for complementing political mobilization and control models (e.g., Tilly, *From Mobilization to Revolution*) with collective behavior paradigms (e.g., Turner and Killian, *Collective Behavior*).

103. The text that I received was a Spanish translation of Assistant Secretary Vaky's address in New York City, December 14, 1978, to the Pan American Society. The discussion is based on it. Assistant Secretary Terence Todman had also warned of the dangers; he had opposed the activist human rights policy of interference that helped to destabilize Nicaragua, but Todman had been defeated.

104. The press conference that the Group of Twelve gave in Managua after leaving the Mexican Embassy was published by *La Prensa*, December 18, 1978.

105. Technically, military personnel were under two lines of supervision: the embassy and Washington, in this case represented by the Southern Command.

106. Unfortunately, Washington had not kept up the pressure. On December 15 Somoza's newspaper reported that the U.S. Nicaraguan beef quota had been increased.

107. Half-brother General José R. Somoza was also to sign the Acta Compromiso.

108. See "Ataca vocero de 'Los Doce' el plan de la Comisión Mediadora," *Diario Las Américas* (Miami), December 23, 1978, p. 10. And for *La Prensa*'s defense of the FAO, see its editorial of December 20, "The FAO and the Amnesty." A good summary of mediation events appeared in the *Diario Las Américas'* issue.

109. "El FAO: Sarcasmo político," *Novedades*, December 21, 1978.

110. See, for instance, Riding, "U.S. Strategy in Nicaragua."

111. " 'Terror and Death' by a Nicaraguan Priest," *New York Times*, December 19, p. 21. See the interviews with Ernesto Cardenal and Miguel D'Escoto in *Diario Las Américas*, December 24, 1978, p. 16. The archbishop's message was published by *La Prensa*, December 20, 1978.

112. Of comparative interest, Fidel Castro had coined the expression that he would remain in power even if all Cubans had only *malanga* (another staple) to eat.

113. This was, in fact, a possible easy temporary constitutional transition.

114. Urcuyo Maliaño succeeded Somoza the following July.

115. This lack of interest came back to haunt the administration when, after the final uprising had started, Brzezinski sought to take a tough stance to form other than a professed anti-American government in Nicaragua; the anti-U.S. Iranian revolution already had taken place.

116. On these events see "Somoza Leaves Nation to Meet with Allies," *Miami Herald*, December 31, 1978; and "Somoza Says He'll Invade Costa Rica to Halt Leftists," *Miami Herald*, December 29, 1978. Also of interest is "Somoza Rejects Mediation's Plan Despite Warning by Washington," *New York Times*, December 28, 1978. This latter United Press International article considered that "at least 152" political killings had occurred since the end of the September uprising. The OAS invoked Article 28 of its charter and Article 6 of the Rio Treaty. The principles were further contained in the Costa Rica–Nicaragua Pact of Friendship of February 21, 1949, and the Complementary Agreement of January 9, 1956.

117. *La Prensa*, December 28, 1978, reported Pérez's visit.

7. Partial Withdrawal

1. Intriguingly, Juan Manuel Siero, a Nicaraguan with years of service in the embassy's economic section and related by marriage to one of the Twelve, had gotten a private appointment with me. He excitedly said, "From Costa Rica, I have been asked to inform you that Somoza has ordered your assassination and that oppositionists are very upset because they respect and like you. This is terrible, you must protect yourself."

2. Sandinista punitive action was concentrated in the mass arrest of members of the National Guard who remained in Nicaragua. On December 10, 1979, the *New York Times* (p. A12) estimated that 7,000 people had been imprisoned for collaborating with Somoza. In June 1982 Amnesty International claimed that of the 4,331 individuals condemned by the revolutionary tribunals, 3,174 were still in jail. The well-known organization considered that special political criteria, rather than common criminal procedures and evidence, had been applied in the trials; UPI, London, June 23, 1982. In October 1979 the Nicaraguan Human Rights Commission, which had a record of anti-Somoza activities, claimed that there were 7,000 prisoners, over 22 prisoners had been killed, and 304 had "disappeared" after being in the government's custody; EFE, Managua, October 12, 1979. Nevertheless, in contrast to the pattern of many outright executions followed after other revolutions—e.g., the Cuban (1959), the Iranian (1979)—the Nicaraguan pattern was more benign. But National Guard personnel remained in prison beyond the Reagan years. For instance, on March 13, 1989, the AP reported that "as part of the process of national reconciliation which other Central American countries have been encouraging . . . the Sandinistas announced . . . they will pardon 1,894 members of [Somoza's] military force."

3. I am noting that a macrosociological event—the mediation's failure—created a new climate or mood of opposition with greater incentive, despite the risks. Such events alter cost-benefit equations for participation posited by "rational choice" theories of revolution. A useful comparative perspective on Chile is provided by Tomás Moulian, *Chile Actual*. After the 1982 economic crisis Chile felt strong pressures for a political transition. General Pinochet prevailed in the adherence to the constitution and regime maintenance up to the 1988 legally prescribed referendum that he lost. Somoza also insisted in not changing the constitution and remaining in power until the prescribed election. But in contrast to Chile, the Nicaraguan regime found itself in decay prior to its 1978 crisis, and with much weaker support from civil society. See chapter 4.

4. Some columnists in major newspapers were reporting this thesis. For instance, DeYoung wrote in the *Washington Post* in this vein: "it is not at all certain, despite their open advocacy of a socialist government, that the Sandinistas have either the will or the power to effect that transition rapidly. They have maintained fairly close contact with the conservative political opposition and say they would participate in a democratic government." Later, after gaining access to a Sandinista training camp, she stated: "Sandinista political leaders interviewed here recently denied that they are Marxists. They denied that they want Cuban-style communism in Nicaragua.

Instead, they are fighting for a 'new Nicaragua' that will be a 'pluralistic democracy' built on the ashes of the destroyed Somoza dictatorship." I take DeYoung's quotes directly from Christian's thought-provoking article "Covering the Sandinistas." Although the Marxist-Leninist-influenced, authoritarian "vanguard" intentions of the Nine Comandantes are documented, the FSLN's success required the broad national and international coalition that was formed.

5. U.S. Department of State, *Cuba's Renewed Support for Violence*, p. 6.

6. In my last moments in Nicaragua I drafted a statement analyzing the situation. Embassy staff subsequently added to it their own material and comments so that they would be available to me. Without my clearance, because I was on the way to the airport, the composite, unedited document was cabled to Washington on February 26, 1979, signed by me because technically I remained chief of mission. It ended: "Concluding Remarks. Our information indicates that there will be continued efforts to unseat the government prior to 1981 through a combination of classic guerrilla activities and unarmed mass mobilization, with a prevalence of the former at least in the short-run. Oppositionists are attempting to create conditions for a future major escalated confrontation with the government. Barring a significant international component it seems unlikely that such activities will result in the military defeat of the National Guard."

7. Instances of unbreakable loyalty to rulers have taken place in a variety of undemocratic regimes, totalitarian and authoritarian (Stalin and Franco died in office before they were forced out). Palace plots have eliminated so-called sultanistic absolute rulers (e.g., the Dominican Republic tyrannicide in 1961). Party rebellions dismissed several Communist strongmen. The dismantling of Latin American authoritarian regimes historically was more commonly the result not of dictator-opposition negotiations but of military coups executed by the top hierarchy or by a lower-level military rebellion. Yet in Nicaragua, the structure of state support for Somoza did not vanish—defections would not take place within it, despite the extant few concerns that I have reported amid the widespread protests throughout the society. We were being left principally with the armed revolutionary route to replace Somoza, "who would die with his boots on."

8. In this sense, see Karklins and Petersen "Decision Calculus of Protestors and Regimes." Nicaragua showed the limited applicability of models of peaceful successful rebellion.

8. The Failure of U.S. Policy

1. Somoza, *Nicaragua Betrayed*, p. 418.

2. His final letter of resignation was dated July 16, 1979, almost a month later.

3. Anderson, "Support of Dictatorships."

4. Only Nicaragua and Paraguay voted against the resolution; Nicaragua's three northern neighbors and Chile abstained.

5. Urcuyo Maliaño, *Solos*.

6. Latin American opposition to such force had been clearly manifested during the Lyndon Johnson years of higher U.S. sensitivity to Cuban influence and activities.

This had led to U.S. proposals to constitute a permanent inter-American peace force, which never materialized; see Mitchell, "Dominance and Fragmentation," pp. 189–99.

7. Somoza, *Nicaragua Betrayed*, pp. 362, 372, 384, 389. On p. 372 he quotes himself from a tape: "You must know that I have fear of assassination." In reading these materials, I could recall only Somoza's arrogance and nearsightedness, which had led him to be a principal party in the final butchery.

8. That Somoza was not sanguine about the conditions under which he was leaving his followers is indicated by his trip to Guatemala before he finally left for exile, where he sought to get support from CONDECA, the Central American Defense Council, the regional military pact. This was to no avail. The "sympathetic" Central American states had remained playing only a negative role; they refused now to assist him on the grounds that they had to abide by the OAS resolution. Throughout this last period it seems that more than ever Somoza was after some messianic "miracle." In fact, in his conversations with U.S. officials Somoza was repeatedly told about doubts that the policy would succeed.

9. See Shaw, "Junta's Peace Plan."

10. Pezzullo and Pezzullo, *At the Fall of Somoza*, p. 108.

11. A useful chronology of the entire revolutionary process is provided by Fagen, "End of the Affair." Also critical was Leo Grande, "Revolution in Nicaragua."

12. Ramírez, *Adiós muchachos*, p. 105. Indeed, the explanation of the ability of the physically absent Sandinista top leadership to successfully call for the large-scale uprising must rest with collective behavior theory: the changes in collective mood and emergent norms at an overall "national" level that had taken place in support for it.

13. Somoza, *Nicaragua Betrayed*, pp. 363–64. Actually Somoza reported that he used his contacts in the United States to try to bring such assistance to Nicaragua as he prepared to leave. But the U.S. government refused to give any supportive input to the National Guard; see Pezzullo and Pezzullo, *At the Fall of Somoza*, p. 80. Somoza Jr. had discussed his plans in my office much earlier: during his grandfather's time the National Guard was not professionalized; some modernization had come about under his father; currently he was improving the Guard to make it really a professional organization, he said.

14. Obando y Bravo, *Agonía en el Bunker*, pp. 185–87, confirms this.

15. See the conflict between statements by Lt. Colonel James McCoy, the embassy's defense attaché, and Humberto Ortega, the head of the Sandinista Army, reported in Pezzullo and Pezzullo, *At the Fall of Somoza*, pp. 186–88. McCoy is quoted: "The [National] Guard no longer has the capacity to launch an offensive to recapture cities." Their stocks were running low: "They've got enough for three weeks' fighting." Pezzullo and Pezzullo report on Ortega: "The Guardia had been beaten back on all fronts, but their armor and elite troops were still concentrated in [Managua] in defense of Somoza. Humberto Ortega later admitted that 'the armed movement of the [people] never had the weapons needed to defeat the enemy.' "

16. We see that the role of Durkheimian alienation "anomie," a state of confusion because of an absence of crystallized, clear rules, cannot be dismissed in the success of revolutions. Various forms of alienation other than normlessness are related by participants to the downfall of regimes: feelings of powerlessness, meaninglessness in continued combat, etc.

17. See in Dahl, *Democracy and Its Critics*, references to this regime type, brought to contemporary attention in the United States by Arend Lijphart.

Epilogue

1. See the statement by Kirkpatrick, "Dictatorships and Double Standards." In contrast to the Carter team, the future U.S. ambassador to the United Nations stressed the importance of Central America for the United States and discarded the non-interventionist philosophy that had prevailed.

2. These contradictions resulted in U.S. support in Nicaragua for the so-called low-intensity armed conflict that slowly, at relatively small expense for Americans, would undermine the Sandinista revolutionary regime and impede its permanent consolidation.

3. See the essay on oral history by Rhodes, "1990 Democratic Transition in Nicaragua."

4. The area of conflict of economic interests has been well studied. By the 1950s, sophisticated cadres of foreign-trained Latin American social scientists, especially economists, were already formed and growing; they addressed such political and market-originated "imbalances." See the historical overview of grievances in LaFeber, *Inevitable Revolutions*, and the cited, more technical discussion of dependency theory by Love, "Origins of Dependency Analysis." Of course, disputes continue between U.S. and Latin American governments about building a more equitable and prosperous international economic order.

5. On Reagan's Chilean policy, see Morandé, "United States and Chile."

6. On the new policies of public, international financial institutions (IFIs) see, for instance, United Nations Development Program (UNDP), *Human Development Report, 1992*; and the summary statement on the World Bank by Thomas, "Why Duality Matters." For a critical review of IFI-NGO relations, see Goldman, "Birth of a Discipline."

7. Associated Press, "Predecessors Find Fault with Secretary Christopher," January 29, 1994. Clinton's team was substantially formed by former Carter officials, prominently so by Warren Christopher, his first secretary of state.

8. For example, Anthony Lake, Clinton's national security adviser and a supporter of Carter's "non-intervention" mantra in his *Somoza Falling*, changed his position, publicly lecturing on criteria for U.S. interventions abroad; see Kelly, "Iraq Ad Hoc."

9. Ramírez, *Adiós muchachos*, p. 115.

10. Ramírez, *Adiós muchachos*. I paraphrase from pages 111–15 and 139.

11. Castro's centralized leadership was facilitated by the decapitation of rival armed groups in the tragic failed attempt to kill Fulgencio Batista in an attack against his palace in 1957.

12. A useful chronology of events is provided by Carbonell, *And the Russians Stayed*.

13. Castro's rule has gone through phases. In recent years, while retaining Castro's direct personal control over the institutional actors, his rule has moved away from its extreme totalitarian character to a charismatic, slightly but relatively less absolutist regime. See the discussions by Mujal-León and Busby, "Much Ado about Something?" and Marifeli Pérez-Stable, "Caught in a Contradiction."

14. On the nature of the FSLN leadership, see Ramírez, *Adiós muchachos*, pp. 64, 107–8, 110–11.

15. In an interview conducted in Managua in the summer 1999, my friend Luis Sánchez Sancho commented that in contrast to Cuba, his Communist Party was much less developed, thus potentially less able to provide Marxist-Leninist ideological coherence to the Nicaraguan revolutionary regime. The disagreements over the army and party roles in Cuba notwithstanding, the Communist Party obviously played a more important role in the Castro regime than in Nicaragua. See the complementary interviews in Rhodes, "1990 Democratic Transition in Nicaragua."

16. Also in 1999 we talked with Mariano Fiallos, the Sandinista electoral boss. According to him, although technically the 1994 elections were properly conducted, the nation's highly polarized political situation was not conducive to hold one that satisfied the parties as legitimate.

17. See the interesting study by Sandinista intellectual Alejandro Bendaña, *Una tragedia campesina*. Bendaña discusses the role played in the resistance against the revolutionary government, by its partial adoption of Communist agriculture patterns, the threat of or actual confiscation of land, and regime repressive arrogance and mismanagement.

18. See chapter 6. Ironically, during these post-Carter years of greater U.S. interventionism some democratization processes were taking place in Central America, and regional governments were independently articulating more coherent foreign policies to further their interests.

19. In addition to Marxist-Leninist authoritarian influences, a current within liberation theology did not highlight the importance of elected constitutional government for the good society. See Borgeson, *Hacia el hombre nuevo*. Interesting examples of questioning the relevance of free, competitive elections for poor countries are Universidad Centroamericana José Simeón Cañas, "Estados Unidos y la democratización de Centroamérica," and Jean-Bertrand Aristide, *In the Parish of the Poor*.

20. See Ramírez, *Adiós muchachos*, pp. 112, 113, 115.

21. Recent precedent for an improvised candidacy of a prominent widow was found in the election of Corazon Aquino in the Philippines in 1986.

22. For a pertinent, stimulating discussion, see Luban, "Romance of the Nation-State."

23. A summary of the initial perceptions of the Bush administration's position held by politically aware American and international actors can be found in Traub, "W.'s World," *New York Times Magazine*, January 14, 2001. As did several other administrations, Bush's team followed a distinct Latin American policy that in contrast to more conflictive regions showed substantial continuity, except for its lesser willingness

to assist countries facing financial-economic crisis and its greater support than Clinton showed for counterinsurgency policies.

In 2001 the trend initiated in the 1980s to establish political democracies had resulted—not without instabilities and setbacks—in a majority of countries with such rule. Most of them were supportive of multilateral, pro-democracy regional policies that involved the United States, which culminated in the adoption by the OAS of the Inter-American Democratic Charter in Lima in 2001. The basic U.S. objectives were the promotion of democracy and collaboration as much as possible with the OAS, progress toward a free trade zone in the Americas, the war against drugs, and immigration control. I should note that the interventionism of U.S. anti-narco policies had proved ineffective and politically destabilizing in some cases. See Solaún, "U.S. Interventions in Latin America."

Despite progress in some dimensions substantial political and economic instability and uncertainty remained in several Latin American countries. The struggles between democratic and authoritarian forces had not ended everywhere; in a few countries popular mobilizations resulted in the fall of governments. And the upsurge of policies of neocapitalist globalization of the 1990s had culminated in some serious economic crises. While there was not a return by governments to the unsuccessful policies of state-dictated autarky of the so-called economic lost decade of the 1980s, by Bush's accession anti-capitalist/anti-globalization movements had acquired strength, and some important countries were resisting U.S. pressures to lead the Free-Trade Area of the Americas (FTAA), supposed to be finalized by the end of 2004. The spirit of the rich versus poor countries, and North-South economic divide had not disappeared.

24. For example, James A. Baker, the secretary of state for Bush Sr., after leaving office still felt that it had been wise not to continue the 1991 war and to oust Saddam Hussein. Among other considerations, it would have required a long, very costly military occupation of Iraq to pacify the country and sustain a new government in power; there was a danger that a change of regime by foreigners would result in an Iraqi civil war and national breakdown; Hussein's ability to threaten his neighbors had been substantially diminished and could be kept this way without overthrowing the government; and there was a danger of provoking a growth in Islamic fundamentalism and in "anti-American imperialism" sentiment among Arabs. The former secretary contrasted the differences between the U.S. invasion of Panama in 1989 and the more complex Iraqi problem. Baker, "Why the U.S. Didn't March to Baghdad." Indeed, feasibility and costs must guide policy. Contrast the implications of a pro-democracy policy toward China with such a policy in a small Central American or Caribbean country.

25. How can the U.S. government exercise democratic leadership to create a more civilized international environment when it unilaterally adopts the doctrine that it can indefinitely hold without due process terrorist suspects at its discretion, as in Guantánamo Bay, Cuba?

26. The involvement of several nations and international organizations in democratic statecraft is no guarantee of success, post-1994 Haitian history showed. But such participation can provide added strength to the complex processes of democratic legitimation. As we discussed for Nicaragua, in the face of tentative support for democracy a large clientelistic international presence can be helpful to develop needed social and state organs, including the justification of the continued foreign monitoring of elections for regime consolidation.

Bibliography

This bibliography appears in three sections: documents, books and essays, and magazine and newspaper articles.

Documents

Organization of American States. Comité Jurídico Interamericano. "Diferencia entre intervención y acción colectiva." Ser. I–VI, 2, CIJ-81, 1965.

———. Inter-American Commission on Human Rights. Report on the Situation of Human Rights in Nicaragua. November 1978.

Stroessner, Alfredo. Proyección internacional de Stroessner, El líder, su vida y sus obras. Paraguay: Ministerio de Relaciones Exteriores, 1985.

UNESCO. Statistical Yearbook. Paris: UNESCO, 1965, 1970, 1977.

United Nations Development Program (UNDP). Human Development Report, 1992. New York: Oxford University Press, 1992.

United Nations Statistics Division. Yearbook of National Accounts Statistics. Vol. 1. New York: United Nations, 1978.

U.S. Department of State. Bureau of Public Affairs. Cuba's Renewed Support for Violence in Latin America. Special Report no. 90. Washington DC, December 1981.

U.S. House of Representatives. Hearings before the Subcommittee on Foreign Appropriations and Related Agencies, Committee on Appropriations. 95th Cong., 1st sess., April 5 and 21, 1977.

Wilkie, James W., and Peter Reich. Statistical Abstract of Latin America. Vol. 20. Los Angeles: UCLA Latin American Center Publications, 1980.

World Bank. World Development Reports. Washington DC, 1978, 1979, 1981, 1989, 1991, 1992, 1997.

Books and Essays

Abreu, Alvez de. "Brazil's Guerilla Trap." History Today 47 (December 1997): 35–40.

Almond, Gabriel A., and Sidney Verba. The Civic Culture: Political Attitudes and Democracy in Five Nations. Boston: Little, Brown, 1965.

Almond, Gabriel A., and G. Bingham Powell Jr. Comparative Politics: A Developmental Approach. Boston: Little, Brown, 1966.

Alvarez Montalván, Emilio. "Apuntes para una sociología política nicaragüense." American Chamber of Nicaragua, June 1978. Mimeo.

Amaro, Nelson. *Guatemala: Historia despierta*. Guatemala: IDESAC, 1992.

Ameringer, Charles D. *The Democratic Left in Exile: The Antidictatorial Struggle in the Caribbean, 1945–1959*. Miami: University of Miami Press, 1974.

———. *Don Pepe: A Political Biography of José Figueres of Costa Rica*. Albuquerque: University of New Mexico Press, 1979.

———. "Nicaragua: The Rock That Crumbled." In *U.S. Influence in Latin America in the 1980s*, edited by Robert Wesson. New York: Praeger; Stanford: Hoover Institution Press, 1982.

Arancibia Clavel, Patricia, and Isabel de la Maza Cave. *Matthei, mi testimonio*. Chile: La Tercera, 2003.

Aristide, Jean-Bertrand. *In the Parish of the Poor*. New York: Orbis Books, 1990.

Asturias, Miguel Angel. *El señor presidente*. Argentina: Editorial Losada, 1948.

Balaguer, Joaquín. *Memorias de un cortesano de la "Era de Trujillo."* Dominican Republic: Editora Corripio, 1988.

Beitz, Charles. *Political Theory and International Relations*. Princeton NJ: Princeton University Press, 1979.

Bendaña, Alejandro. *La mística de Sandino*. Nicaragua: Centro de Estudios Internacionales, 1994.

———. *Una tragedia campesina: Testimonios de la Resistencia*. Nicaragua: Edit-Arte, 1991.

Bendix, Reinhard. *Force, Fate and Freedom: On Historical Sociology*. Berkeley: University of California Press, 1984.

Ben-Ur, Lorraine Elena. "El realismo mágico en la crítica hispanoamericana." *Journal of Spanish Studies* 4 (1976): 149–63.

Bermejo, Antonio, and Demetrio Ramos. *Los ideales del imperio español*. Madrid: Editorial Lepanto, 1943.

Bermeo, Nancy Gina. *The Revolution within the Revolution: Workers' Control in Rural Portugal*. Princeton NJ: Princeton University Press, 1986.

Bettelheim, Bruno. *The Informed Heart: Autonomy in a Mass Age*. Chicago: Free Press, 1960.

Blau, Peter M., and W. Richard Scott. *Formal Organizations: A Comparative Approach*. San Francisco: Chandler, 1962.

Borgeson, Paul W., Jr. *Hacia el hombre nuevo: Poesía y pensamiento de Ernesto Cardenal*. London: Tamesis Books, 1984.

Brzezinski, Zbigniew. *Power and Principle*. New York: Farrar, Straus, Giroux, 1983.

Bundy, William P. "Who Lost Patagonia? Foreign Policy in the 1980 Campaign." *Foreign Affairs* 58 (1979): 1–27.

Burns, E. Bradford. *Patriarch and Folk: The Emergence of Nicaragua, 1798–1858*. Cambridge: Harvard University Press, 1991.

Cabezas, Omar. *Fire from the Mountain: The Making of a Sandinista*. New York: New American Library, 1985.

Calero Orozco, Adolfo. *Sangre Santa*. Nicaragua: El Pez y La Serpiente, 1977.

Carbonell, Néstor. *And the Russians Stayed: The Sovietization of Cuba*. New York: William Morrow, 1989.

Cardenal, Luis G. *Mi rebelión*. Mexico: Editorial Patria y Libertad, 1961.

Carter, Jimmy. *Keeping Faith: Memoirs of a President*. New York: Bantam Books, 1982.

Cepeda, Fernando, and Mauricio Solaún. "Direct Private Foreign Investment in Colombia: A Socio-Political Perspective." Sonderdruck aus Vierteljahres Berichte (Research Institute of the German Friedrich Ebert Foundation), no. 49. Berlin, 1972.

Chamorro Cardenal, Pedro Joaquín. *Estirpe sangrienta: Los Somozas*. Mexico: Editorial Patria y Libertad, 1957.

———. *Jesús Marchena*. Managua: Ediciones El Pez y la Serpiente, 1975.

Chehabi, H. E., and Juan J. Linz. *Sultanistic Regimes*. Baltimore: Johns Hopkins University Press, 1998.

Christian, Shirley. "Covering the Sandinistas: The Foregone Conclusions of the Fourth Estate." *Washington Journalism Review*, March 1982, 32–38.

———. *Nicaragua: Revolution in the Family*. New York: Random House, 1985.

Cohn, Norman. *The Pursuit of the Millennium*. New York: Essential Books, 1957.

Coser, Lewis A. *The Functions of Social Conflict*. New York: Free Press, 1964.

Cotler, Julio, and Richard R. Fagen, eds. *Latin America and the United States: The Changing Political Realities*. Stanford: Stanford University Press, 1974.

Dahl, Robert A. *Democracy and Its Critics*. New Haven CT: Yale University Press, 1989.

———. *Polyarchy: Participation and Opposition*. New Haven CT: Yale University Press, 1971.

———. *A Preface to Economic Democracy*. Berkeley: University of California Press, 1985.

Deas, Malcolm. "Caudillismo, Coronelismo and Caciquismo." *The Cambridge Encyclopedia of Latin America and the Caribbean*, edited by Simon Collier, Harold Blakemore, and Thomas E. Skidmore. Cambridge: Cambridge University Press, 1985.

Débray, Régis. *Revolución dentro de la revolución*. Mexico: Ediciones Era, S.A., 1976.

Deutsch, Karl. "Social Mobilization and Political Development." *American Political Science Review* 55 (1961): 493–514.

Dodd, Thomas J. "The United States in Nicaraguan Politics: Supervised Elections, 1928–1932." PhD diss., George Washington University, 1966. Reprinted in *Revista del Pensamiento Centroamericano* (Managua) 30, no. 148 (1975): 5–102.

Domínguez, Jorge I. "Consensus and Divergence: The State of the Literature on Inter-American Relations in the 1970s." *Latin American Research Review* 13 (1978): 87–126.

Durkheim, Emile. *Division of Labor in Society*. New York: Free Press, 1964.

Easton, David. *A Systems Analysis of Political Life*. Chicago: University of Chicago Press, 1965.

Einaudi, Luigi R. *Peruvian Military Relations with the United States*. Santa Monica CA: Rand, 1970.

Estrada, Baldomero. "Clase media en América Latina: Interpretaciones y comentarios." *Cuadernos de Historia* (Chile) 5 (1985): 37–63.

Fagen, Richard R. "The End of the Affair." *Foreign Policy* 36 (1979): 178–91.

Fermandois, Joaquín. *Chile y El Mundo, 1970–1973: La política exterior del gobierno de la Unidad Popular y el Sistema Internacional*. Santiago: Universidad Católica de Chile, 1985.

Fiallos Oyanguren, Mariano. "The Nicaraguan Political System: The Flow of Demands and the Reactions of the Regime." PhD diss., University of Kansas, 1968.

Finifter, Ada. "Dimensions of Political Alienation." *American Political Science Review* 64 (1970): 389–410.

Galbraith, John Kenneth. *The Triumph: A Novel of Modern Diplomacy.* Boston: Houghton Mifflin, 1968.

Galíndez, Jesús de. *The Era of Trujillo.* Tucson: University of Arizona Press, 1973.

Gamson, William. *The Strategy of Social Protest.* Homewood IL: Dorsey, 1975.

Garcés, Joan E. *1970: La pugna política por la presidencia en Chile.* Santiago: Editorial Universitaria, 1971.

Goldman, Michael. "The Birth of a Discipline: Producing Authoritative Green Knowledge, World Bank Style." *Ethnography* 2 (2001): 191–217.

Greene, Thomas H. *Comparative Revolutionary Movements.* Englewood Cliffs NJ: Prentice-Hall, 1974.

Grieb, Kenneth J. "The United States and the Rise of General Maximiliano Hernández Martínez." *Journal of Latin American Studies* 3 (1971): 151–72.

Griffin, Miriam T. *Nero: The End of a Dynasty.* New Haven CT: Yale University Press, 1985.

Guevara, Ernesto Che. *La guerra de guerrillas.* Uruguay: Corporación Gráfica, 1968.

Guillén, Abraham. "Introducción" to *Ernesto Che Guevara: La guerra de guerrillas.* Uruguay: Corporación Gráfica, 1968.

Hayter, Teresa. *Aid as Imperialism.* Baltimore: Penguin, 1971.

Hirschman, Albert O. *Exit, Voice and Loyalty.* Cambridge: Harvard University Press, 1970.

Hodges, Donald C. *Intellectual Foundations of the Nicaraguan Revolution.* Austin: University of Texas Press, 1986.

Hoffman, Stanley. "States and the Morality of War." *Political Theory* 9 (1981): 149–72.

Karklins, Rasma, and Roger Petersen. "Decision Calculus of Protesters and Regimes: Eastern Europe, 1989." *Journal of Politics* 55 (1993): 588–614.

Karst, Kenneth L., and Keith S. Rosenn. *Law and Development in Latin America.* Berkeley: University of California Press, 1975.

Kennedy, Paul. *The Rise and Fall of the Great Powers.* New York: Random House, 1987.

Kershaw, Ian. *Hitler, 1889–1936: Hubris.* New York: W. W. Norton, 1998.

———. *Hitler, 1936–1945: Nemesis.* New York: W. W. Norton, 2000.

Kinzer, Stephen. *All the Shah's Men: An American Coup and the Roots of Middle East Terror.* Hoboken NJ: John Wiley & Sons, 2003.

Kirkpatrick, Jeane. "Dictatorships and Double Standards." *Commentary* 68 (1979): 34–45.

Kissinger, Henry. *Does America Need a Foreign Policy: Towards a New Diplomacy for the 21st Century.* New York: Simon and Schuster, 2001.

LaFeber, Walter. *Inevitable Revolutions: The United States in Central America.* 2nd ed. New York: W. W. Norton, 1993.

Lake, Anthony. *Somoza Falling: A Case Study of Washington at Work.* Amherst: University of Massachusetts Press, 1989.

Langley, Lester D. *The Banana Men: American Mercenaries and Entrepreneurs in Central America, 1880–1930.* Lexington: University Press of Kentucky, 1995.

Lawler, John J. *Unionization and Deunionization: Strategy, Tactics, Outcome.* Columbia: University of South Carolina Press, 1990.

Leal, Luis. "El realismo mágico en la literatura hispanoamericana." *Cuadernos Americanos* 153 (1967): 230–35.

LeBon, Gustave. *The Psychology of the Crowd.* New York: Viking, 1960.

Lenin, Vladimir Ilyich. "What Is to Be Done?" In *Essential Works of Lenin,* edited by Henry Christman. New York: Bantam Books, 1966.

Leo Grande, William M. "The Revolution in Nicaragua: Another Cuba?" *Foreign Affairs* 58 (1979): 28–50.

Levinson, Jerome. "After the Alliance for Progress: Implications for Inter-American Relations." In *Changing Latin America: New Interpretations of Its Politics and Society,* edited by Douglas H. Chalmers. Proceedings of the Academy of Political Science 30, no. 4. New York: Academy of Political Science, 1972.

Linz, Juan J., and Alfred Stepan. *Problems of Democratic Transition and Consolidation.* Baltimore: Johns Hopkins University Press, 1996.

López Gallo, Manuel. *Las grandes mentiras de Krauze.* Mexico: Ediciones El Caballito, 1997.

Love, Joseph L. "Modeling Internal Colonialism: History and Prospect." *World Development* 17 (1989): 905–22.

———. "The Origins of Dependency Analysis." *Journal of Latin American Studies* 22 (1990): 143–68.

———. "Raúl Prebish and the Doctrine of Unequal Exchange." *Latin American Research Review* 15 (1980): 45–72.

Lowenthal, Abraham F. *The Dominican Intervention.* Cambridge: Harvard University Press, 1972.

——— "United States Policy toward Latin America: 'Liberal,' 'Radical,' and 'Bureaucratic' Perspectives." *Latin American Research Review* 8 (1973): 3–25.

Luban, David. "The Romance of the Nation-State." In *International Ethics,* edited by Charles R. Beitz, Marshall Cohen, Thomas Scanlon, and A. John Simmons. Princeton NJ: Princeton University Press, 1985.

Macaulay, Neill. *The Sandino Affair.* Chicago: Quadrangle Books, 1967.

Machado y Morales, Gerardo. *Memorias: Ocho años de lucha.* Miami: Ediciones Históricas Cubanas, Peninsular Printing, 1982.

Mañón, Melvin. *Operación Estrella: Con Caamaño, la resistencia y la inteligencia cubana.* Dominican Republic: Taller, 1989.

Mao Zedong. "Carry the Revolution through to the End." *Selected Works.* Vol. 4. Beijing: Foreign Languages Press, 1961.

Marighella, Carlos. *Minimanual of the Urban Guerrilla.* Washington DC: U.S. Citizens for a Free Cuba, 1969.

Márquez Sterling, Carlos. *Historia de Cuba.* New York: Las Americas, 1963.

Martin, John B. *Overtaken by Events: The Dominican Crisis from the Fall of Trujillo to the Civil War.* New York: Doubleday, 1966.

Masó, Calixto C. *Historia de Cuba*. Miami: Ediciones Universal, 1976.

Mattini, Luis. *Hombres y mujeres del PRT-ERP (de Tucumán a la Tablada)*. Argentina: Editorial de la Campana, 1996.

McAdam, Doug, John D. McCarthy, and Mayer N. Zald, eds. *Comparative Perspectives on Social Movements*. New York: Cambridge University Press, 1996.

McNamara, Robert S., and James G. Blight. *Wilson's Ghost: Reducing the Risk of Conflict, Killing, and Catastrophe in the 21st Century*. New York: Public Affairs, 2001.

McPhail, Clark. *The Myth of the Madding Crowd*. New York: Aldine de Gruyter, 1991.

Medhurst, Kenneth. "The Church in Latin America." *The Cambridge Encyclopedia of Latin America and the Caribbean*, edited by Simon Collier, Harold Blakemore, and Thomas E. Skidmore. Cambridge: Cambridge University Press, 1985.

Meeks, Brian. *Caribbean Revolutions and Revolutionary Theory: An Assessment of Cuba, Nicaragua and Grenada*. Jamaica: University of West Indies Press, 2001.

Merei, Ferenc. "Group Leadership and Institutionalization." In *Readings in Social Psychology*, 3rd ed., edited by Eleanor E. Maccoby, Theodore M. Newcomb, and Eugene L. Hartley. New York: Holt, 1958.

Millett, Richard. *Guardians of the Dynasty*. New York: Orbis Books, 1977.

Mitchell, Christopher. "Dominance and Fragmentation in U.S. Latin American Policy." In *Latin America and the United States: The Changing Political Realities*, edited by Julio Cotler and Richard R. Fagen. Stanford: Stanford University Press, 1974.

Montaner, Carlos Alberto. *Secret Report on the Cuban Revolution*. Translated by Eduardo Zayas-Bazán. New Brunswick NJ: Transaction Books, 1981.

Moore, Barrington. *Injustice: The Social Bases of Obedience and Revolt*. New York: M. E. Sharpe, 1979.

Morandé, José Antonio. "The United States and Chile: Some American Perceptions among Congressional and Political Elites." School of Public Affairs, University of Maryland, Working Paper no. 5, 1993.

Moreno, José A. "Sociological Aspects of the Dominican Revolution." PhD diss., Cornell University, 1967.

Moulian, Tomás. *Chile actual: Anatomía de un mito*. Santiago: LOM Ediciones, 1997.

Mozaffari, Mehdi. *Authority in Islam: From Muhammad to Khomeini*. New York: M. E. Sharpe, 1987.

Mujal-León, Eusebio, and Joshua W. Busby. "Much Ado about Something? Regime Change in Cuba." *Problems of Post-Communism* 48 (2001): 6–18.

Munro, Dana G. *Intervention and Dollar Diplomacy in the Caribbean, 1900–1921*. Princeton NJ: Princeton University Press, 1964.

Needler, Martin C. *Political Development in Latin America: Instability, Violence and Evolutionary Change*. New York: Random House, 1968.

Nicholson, Sir Harold. *Diplomacy*. London: Oxford University Press, 1939.

North, John. "Democracy in Rome." *History Today* 44 (March 1994): 38–43.

Obando Bravo, Monsignor Miguel. *Golpe Sandinista*. Managua: Editorial Unión, 1975.

———. *Agonía en el Bunker*. Nicaragua: COPROSA, 1990.

Opp, Karl-Dieter, Peter Voss, and Christiane Gern. *Origins of a Spontaneous Revolution: East Germany, 1989*. Ann Arbor: University of Michigan Press, 1995.

Ortega y Gasset, José. *Historia como sistema*. Madrid: Espasa-Calpe, 1971.

Pastor, Robert A. *Condemned to Repetition: The United States and Nicaragua*. Princeton NJ: Princeton University Press, 1987.

Pataky, Laszlo. *Llegaron los que no estaban invitados*. Managua: Editorial Pereira, 1975.

Payne, James L. *Patterns of Conflict in Colombia*. New Haven CT: Yale University Press, 1968.

Pérez Brignoli, Héctor. *A Brief History of Central America*. Translated by Ricardo B. Sawrey and Susana Settsi de Sawrey. Berkeley: University of California Press, 1989.

Pérez-Stable, Marifeli. "Caught in a Contradiction: Cuban Socialism between Mobilization and Normalization." *Comparative Politics* 32 (1999): 63–82.

Perlmutter, Amos. "The Presidential Political Center and Foreign Policy: A Critique of the Revisionist and Bureaucratic-Political Orientations." *World Politics* 27 (1974): 87–106.

Pezzullo, Lawrence, and Ralph Pezzullo. *At the Fall of Somoza*. Pittsburgh: University of Pittsburgh Press, 1993.

Politzer, Patricia. *Altamirano*. Santiago: Melquíades, 1990.

Quirk, Robert E. *Fidel Castro*. New York: W. W. Norton, 1993.

Ramírez, Sergio. *Adiós muchachos: Una memoria de la Revolución Sandinista*. Madrid: Aguilar, 1999.

Renwick, Robin. *Economic Sanctions*. Cambridge: Center for International Affairs, Harvard University, 1981.

Rhodes, Jennifer Marie. "The 1990 Democratic Transition in Nicaragua: International and Domestic Forces." MA Thesis, Center for Latin American and Caribbean Studies, University of Illinois at Urbana-Champaign, 2000.

Rice, Michael David. "Nicaragua and the United States: Policy Confrontations and Cultural Interactions, 1893–1933." PhD diss., University of Houston, 1995.

Rosengarten, Frederic, Jr. *Freebooters Must Die! The Life and Death of William Walker*. Wayne PA: Haverford House, 1976.

Salisbury, Richard V. "Domestic Politics and Foreign Policy: Costa Rica's Stand on Recognition, 1923–1934." *Hispanic American Historical Review* 57 (1974): 453–78.

Schoultz, Lars. "U.S. Economic Aid as an Instrument of Foreign Policy: The Case of Human Rights in Latin America." Paper presented at the annual meeting of the Latin American Studies Association, Pittsburgh, 1979.

Scott, James C. *Comparative Political Corruption*. Englewood Cliffs NJ: Prentice-Hall, 1972.

Scruton, Roger. *A Dictionary of Political Thought*. New York: Hill and Wang, 1984.

Seeman, Melvin. "Alienation and Engagement." In *The Human Meaning of Social Change*, edited by A. Campbell and P. E. Converse. New York: Russell Sage Foundation, 1972.

Simmel, Georg. *Conflict: The Web of Group Affiliations*. New York: Free Press, 1955.

Skidmore, Thomas E. *Politics in Brazil, 1930–1964: An Experiment in Democracy*. New York: Oxford University Press, 1967.

Skocpol, Theda. *States and Social Revolutions*. New York: Cambridge University Press, 1979.

Smelser, Neil. *Theory of Collective Behavior*. New York: Free Press, 1963.

Solaún, Mauricio. "Colombian Politics: Historical Characteristics and Problems." In *Politics of Compromise: Coalition Government in Colombia*, edited by R. A. Berry et al. New Brunswick NJ: Transaction Books, 1980.

———. "U.S. Interventions in Latin America: 'Plan Colombia.'" Occasional paper, Program in Arms Control, Disarmament, and International Security, University of Illinois at Urbana-Champaign, June 2002.

Solaún, Mauricio, and Michael A. Quinn. *Sinners and Heretics: The Politics of Military Intervention in Latin America*. Urbana: University of Illinois Press, 1973.

Somoza, Anastasio. *Nicaragua Betrayed*. Belmont MA: Western Islands, 1980.

Stansifer, Charles L. "Application of the Tobar Doctrine to Central America." *Americas* 23 (1967): 251–72.

———. "José Santos Zelaya." Unpublished monograph, University of Kansas, n.d.

Stepan, Alfred C. *The Military in Politics: Changing Patterns in Brazil*. Princeton NJ: Princeton University Press, 1971.

Stokes, William S. "Violence as a Power Factor in Latin American Politics." *Western Political Quarterly* 5 (1952): 445–68.

Suchlicki, Jaime. *Cuba: From Columbus to Castro*. New York: Charles Scribner's Sons, 1974.

Sullivan, William H. *Mission to Iran*. New York: W. W. Norton, 1981.

Taylor, Lily Ross. *Party Politics in the Age of Caesar*. Berkeley: University of California Press, 1971.

Teplitz, Benjamin I. "The Political and Economic Foundation of Modernization in Nicaragua: The Administration of José Santos Zelanya, 1893–1909." PhD diss., Howard University, 1973.

Tilly, Charles. *From Mobilization to Revolution*. Reading MA: Addison-Wesley, 1978.

Turner, Jonathan H. *The Structure of Sociological Theory*. Homewood IL: Dorsey Press, 1974.

Turner, Ralph H., and Lewis M. Killian. *Collective Behavior*. Englewood Cliffs NJ: Prentice-Hall, 1987.

Universidad Centroamericana José Simeón Cañas. "Estados Unidos y la democratización de Centroamérica." *Estudios centroamericanos* ECA 41 (1986): 255–69.

Urcuyo Maliaño, Francisco. *Solos: Las ultimas 43 horas en el Bunker de Somoza*. Guatemala: Editorial Académica Centroamericana, 1979.

Ustinov, Peter. *The Love of Four Colonels*. New York: Dramatists Play Service, 1953.

Vallenilla Lanz, Laureano. *Cesarismo democrático: Estudio sobre las bases sociológicas de la consitución efectiva de Venezuela*. Caracas: Tipografía Universal, 1929.

Vance, Cyrus. *Hard Choices: Critical Years in America's Foreign Policy*. New York: Simon and Schuster, 1983.

Vasconcelos, José. *Indología: Una interpretación de la cultura ibero-americana*. Paris: Agencia Mundial de Librería, 1927.

Vilas, Carlos M. *The Sandinista Revolution: National Liberation and Social Transformation in Central America*. New York: Monthly Review Press, 1986.

Walker, Thomas W. "Nicaragua: The Somoza Family Regime." In *Latin American Politics and Development*, edited by Howard Wiarda and Harvey Kline. Boston: Houghton Mifflin, 1979.

Warken, Philip F. *The Agricultural Development of Nicaragua: An Analysis of the Production Sector*. International Series Special Report, Agricultural Experiment Station, University of Missouri–Columbia, July 1975.

Weber, Max. *Economy and Society: An Outline of Interpretive Sociology*. Edited by Guenther Roth and Claus Wittich; translated by Ephraim Fischoff et al. Berkeley: University of California Press, 1978.

Williams, Chester Y. "Presidential Leadership in Nicaragua." PhD diss., Indiana University, 1977.

Williams, Robert G. *States and Social Evolution: Coffee and the Rise of National Governments in Central America*. Chapel Hill: University of North Carolina Press, 1994.

Winckler, Edwin A., and Susan Greenhalgh. "Analytical Issues and Historical Episodes." In *Contending Approaches to the Political Economy of Taiwan*, edited by Winckler and Greenhalgh. Armonk NY: M. E. Sharpe, 1988.

Wolf, Eric R., and Edward C. Hansen. *The Human Condition in Latin America*. New York: Oxford University Press, 1972.

Wood, Bryce. *The Making of the Good Neighbor Policy*. New York: Columbia University Press, 1961.

Woodward, Ralph Lee, Jr. *Central America: A Nation Divided*. New York: Oxford University Press, 1976.

Magazine and Newspaper Articles

Anderson, Jack. "Support of Dictatorships Haunting U.S. Leaders." Syndicated column, December 30, 1979.

Associated Press. "Carter Ignores State Objection, Praises Somoza." *Washington Star*, August 1, 1978.

Baker, James A., III. "Why the U.S. Didn't March to Baghdad." *Los Angeles Times*, September 8, 1996.

Belli Pereira, Humberto. "Aclarando malentendidos en torno a la pastoral de Monseñor Obando." *La Prensa* (Managua), August 21, 1978.

———. "El hombre es la pieza clave." *La Prensa*, June 26, 1978.

Bohning, Don. "Many Strike Leaders Arrested in Nicaragua." *Miami Herald*, September 5, 1978.

———. "Nicaragua 1978, Cuba 1958 Parallels Are Striking." *Miami Herald*, September 6, 1978.

———. "Nicaraguan Soldiers Rout Rebels, Seize Matagalpa from Youths." *Miami Herald*, September 2, 1978.

———. "Rebels' City, Quiet Now, Lost Heavily." *Miami Herald*, September 1, 1978.

———. "Somoza Controls the Territory but Wins Neither War nor Peace." *Miami Herald*, September 25, 1978.

———. "U.S. Reluctance to Act Exasperates Nicaragua." *Miami Herald*, September 5, 1978.

Buchanan, Patrick J. "On the Revolutionary Left, a Different Kind of Corruption." *Richmond (Virginia) Times-Dispatch*, September 9, 1978.

Cardoze, Julio Ignacio. "Nicaragua: Otro aniversario de la traición." *Miami Herald*, July 10, 1982.

Chamorro Cardenal, Jaime. "Comentarios sobre el documento de Unidad Nacional del FAO." *La Prensa*, November 3, 1978.

Chardy, Alfonso. "Rebel Raid from Costa Rica Halted, Nicaragua National Guard Reports." *Miami Herald*, November 1, 1978.

———. "Somoza: New Fight Possible in Nicaragua." *Miami Herald*, October 28, 1978.

Cuadra, Pablo Antonio. "Dos Cerebros." *La Prensa*, August 19, 1978.

———. "Escrito a Máquina." *La Prensa*, June 10, 1978.

DeYoung, Karen. "Beneath the Surface, Nicaraguans Live on Nerves." *Washington Post*, November 30, 1978.

———. "Nicaragua Says Venezuela Aids Rebels." *Washington Post*, September 18, 1978.

———. "Somoza's Friends in Congress Seen Threatening Aid Bill." *Washington Post*, July 26, 1978.

———. "They Died on Knees Begging for Mercy." *Miami Herald*, September 21, 1978.

———. " 'The Twelve': Nicaragua's Unlikely Band of Somoza Foes." *Washington Post*, July 23, 1978.

———. "U.S.-Led Mediation in Nicaragua Feared Near Collapse." *Washington Post*, November 14, 1978.

Díaz Palacios, Antonio. "Intransigencia de oposición al diálogo provocó derramamiento de sangre nicaragüense." *Novedades* (Managua), September 30, 1978.

Diederich, Bernard. "Thousands Flee Nicaragua as Deadline Nears." *Washington Star*, November 21, 1978.

Fenton, Tom. "Troops Rout Rebel Youth in Nicaragua." *Washington Post*, September 2, 1978.

Fiallos Navarro, Francisco. "Los partidos políticos y la coyuntura, 1978." *La Prensa*, July 4–7, 1978.

Goshko, John M. "Carter Letter to Somoza Stirs Human Rights Row." *Washington Post*, August 1, 1978.

———. "U.S. Frees Aid to Nicaragua in a Policy Reversal." *Washington Post*, May 16, 1978.

Gwertzman, Bernard. "U.S. Pressuring Somoza to Quit Nicaragua Post; Carter OK'd Move." *Washington Star*, September 16, 1978.

Hoffman, Stanley. "Hell in a Very Small Place." *New Republic*, March 3, 1982, 37–38.

Kelly, Michael. "Iraq Ad Hoc." *New Yorker*, September 16, 1996, 7–8.

Kennan, George. "Reflections: Breaking the Spell." *New Yorker*, October 3, 1983, 44–53.

Long, William R. "Somoza Still Has the Firepower; Can Mass Uprising Topple Him?" *Miami Herald*, September 17, 1978.

Millet, Richard. "Battling a National Mutiny." *Miami Herald*, September 17, 1978.

Morgan, Dan. "Foreign Aid Funds Stay Mainly in U.S." *Washington Post*, March 5, 1978.

O'Leary, Jeremiah. "U.S. Weighs Options to Pressure Somoza: Leverage Is Limited." *Washington Star*, September 17, 1978.

Riding, Alan. "Foes of Somoza Propose Coalition with Ruling Bloc, Excluding Him." *New York Times*, May 1, 1978.

———. "National Mutiny in Nicaragua." *New York Times Magazine*, July 30, 1978.

———. "Nicaraguans, Seeing Strife as Inevitable, Get Ready." *New York Times*, December 6, 1978.

———. "Nicaragua's Opposition Begins a Quick Left March." *New York Times*, May 14, 1978.

———. "Somoza and His Foes Both Looking to U.S. for Aid." *New York Times*, July 26, 1978.

———. "Somoza Seeks Vote on Foes' Strength; Opposition Refuses." *New York Times*, November 12, 1978.

———. "U.S. Leads Efforts to Oust Somoza and Lead Nicaragua to Democracy." *New York Times*, November 16, 1978.

———. "U.S. Strategy in Nicaragua Keeps the Time Bomb Ticking." *New York Times*, December 17, 1978.

Shadid, Anthony. "Sanctions Yield Few Successes." Associated Press, June 4, 1995.

Shaw, Terri. "Junta's Peace Plan Was Turning Point for U.S. Mediator." *Washington Post*, July 21, 1979.

Simons, Marlise. "Letter from Nicaragua." *Washington Post*, November 14, 1978.

Téfel, Reynaldo Antonio. "Análisis de una caída: Aliento de Todman a Somoza fue efímero." *La Prensa*, April 13, 1978.

———. "La hora del cambio y el Somocismo sin Somoza con Somoza." *La Prensa*, July 3, 1978.

———. "El pacto de la libertad." *La Prensa*, July 4, 1978.

Thomas, Vinod. "Why Quality Matters." *Economist*, October 7, 2000, 92.

Thompson, Morris S. "Rebels Tried to Kill Me, Yank Recalls." *Miami Herald*, September 14, 1998.

Traub, James. "W.'s World." *New York Times Magazine*, January 14, 2001.

Van Bennehom, Pieter. "At 21, Nicaraguan Finds." *Miami Herald*, December 13, 1978.

Index

Acta Compromiso, 270–72
Afghanistan, 298, 309–10, 312, 317n26
Agency for International Development
  (USAID), 126–32, 151, 153, 192, 220, 250,
  279, 336n30, 337n34, 345n1, 348n28,
  350–51n47, 350n45. See also International
  Monetary Fund (IMF) and loans made to
  Nicaragua
Agrarian Reform Law, 59, 60
agricultural workers, 58–59, 325n4
Agüero, Fernando, 55, 71–77, 79, 81, 83
Aguilar, Andrés, 349n35
Aguirre, Danilo, 136–38, 153–56, 219, 224,
  244
Aguirre, Francisco, 264
Aguirre, Horacio, 90
Alegrett, Iván, 134
Allende, Salvador, 19, 107, 159
Alliance for Progress, 21, 55–56, 67, 78,
  316n23
al-Qaeda, 309–10
Altamirano, Carlos, 19
Alvarez Montalván, Emilio, 119, 190, 210,
  241, 245, 335n23, 340–41n61
Amador, César Augusto, 345n6
Amnesty International, 361n2
Arévalo, Juan José, 343n77
Argentina, 134, 294, 316n20
Argüello, Horacio, 284
Argüello, Leonardo, 48–49
Argüello, Leonel, 354n76, 359n100
Arias Costa Rica Plan, 299, 305–6
Arias Sánchez, Oscar, 180, 305
armed opposition, 98–99, 108, 109, 143,
  156–62, 171–72, 182–87, 351n49; and the
  threat of revolution, 191–93, 262–68
Asociación de Instituciones Bancarias de
  Nicaragua, 220–21

assassination of General Somoza García, 42,
  52, 54
Association of Cattle Growers, 221

Baez Sacasa, William, 108, 260
Baker, James A., 366n24
Balaguer, Joaquín, 211
Baltodano, Emilio, 189
Banco de América, 249
Banco Nicaragüense, 249
Bargeron, John, 345n6
Batista, Fulgencio, 20, 68, 146, 151, 276,
  322n10, 364n11
Bay of Pigs invasion, 67, 122, 303–4
Belli Pereira, Humberto, 155, 198–99
Bernheim, Edmundo, 353n61
Betancourt Doctrine, 177, 347n19, 350n42
"big stick" policy, 16, 307
Bohning, Don, 173, 194, 211, 348n29
Bolivia, 296
Borge, Tomás, 65, 156, 347n24
Bowdler, William G., 211, 215, 219, 220,
  231, 236–38, 245–51, 276, 277, 283,
  352n55, 354n68
Broad Opposition Front. See Frente Amplio
  Opositor (FAO)
Bryan-Chamorro Treaty, 25
Brzezinski, Zbigniew, 274, 289, 317n26,
  336n24
Buchanan, Patrick J., 346n14
Bush, George H. W., 115, 205, 298, 300–
  301, 366n24
Bush, George W., 309–12, 365–66n23
Bushnell, John, 130
business sector, Nicaraguan, 61–62, 85, 86,
  90, 125; in formal mediation, 220–21,
  260–61, 354–55n76; work stoppages, 106–
  8, 151–52, 162–65

Cabezas, Omar, 82

Calero, Adolfo, 174, 207, 209, 210, 212, 246

Cámara de Comercio, 107

Cámara de Industrias, 107

Campuzano people, 58

Canada, 352n56

Caracas Declaration, 316n20

Carazo Odio, Rodrigo, 178–79, 187, 200, 230, 252–53, 344n86

Cardenal, Ernesto, 262, 273

Caribbean Legion, 20

Carter, Hodding, 174

Carter, Jimmy: Carlos Andrés Pérez's letter to, 203–4; electoral defeat of, 297, 298; letter to Anastasio Somoza Debayle, 138–43, 154; mediation of the Egypt-Israeli conflict, 115; policies toward Nicaragua, 22–24, 29, 87, 92, 97, 152, 315n12, 317n26, 330–31n14, 336n24, 358n95; and the Presidential Review Committee (PRC), 274–76; statements on progress in mediation, 258–59

Castro, Fidel, 20–21, 55–56, 65–66, 99, 122, 151, 242–43, 303–4, 326n11, 364n11, 365n13. See also Cuba

Catholic Church, the: Anastasio Somoza Debayle and, 87–88, 90, 107–8, 109, 323n16, 331n15; call for peace and democracy, 148–49, 268, 286; clergy commitment to violent revolution, 261–62, 273; in Cuba, 304; in formal mediation, 225, 252, 354–55n76; leaves formal mediation, 261–62; Luis Somoza Debayle and, 61, 72, 74, 76, 78; role in negotiations, 132–33, 163–64, 177, 182, 343n80

Central American Common Market, 179, 234, 306

Central American Defense Council, 363n8

Central American Stabilization Fund, 251

Cerezo, Vinicio, 305

Chamorro, Alberto, 155–56

Chamorro, Diego Manuel, 74

Chamorro, Emiliano, 50, 81, 245

Chamorro, Pedro Joaquín: assassination of, 103–6, 126, 134, 183–84, 256, 265, 338n43; opposition efforts of, 54, 65, 68, 81, 88, 90, 119, 137, 152, 184, 327n15, 330–31n14

Chamorro, Sonia, 246

Chamorro, Violeta, 95, 136, 152, 153, 286, 306, 340n60

Chamorro, Xavier, 136–38, 154

Chamorro Barrios, Pedro Joaquín, 153

Chamorro Cardenal, Jaime, 230, 232, 351–52n54

Chamorro Coronel, Eduardo, 190

Chile, 92, 107, 153, 316n20

China, 48, 302, 315n8

Christopher, Warren, 115, 117, 123, 129–32, 147, 204–5, 292, 335n22

Church, Frank, 202, 209

clientelism, international: in Latin America, 10–12, 19–22, 24, 26, 31–32, 72, 306–7, 315n13, 316–17n25; in Nicaragua during Sandinista control, 286–92; and the Soviet Union, 310–11

Clinton, Bill, 115, 205, 301–2, 366n23

collective behavior, 334n12

Colombia, 77, 133, 206, 207, 344n86

Comando Rigoberto López Pérez, 341n68

Comisión Política of the Frente Amplio Opositor (FAO), 196–99, 212–26, 243, 244, 351n54, 357n91

Communism. See Marxism-Leninism

Congressional Record, 346n14

Consejo Superior de la Empresa Privada (COSEP), 107, 221, 260, 261, 354–55n76

consensus theory of revolution, 48

Conservative Party, Nicaraguan: the Catholic Church and, 61; election activities in the 1960s, 70–78; factions, 155–56; led by Fernando Agüero, 55; political power of, 29, 30, 39, 44, 53, 79, 89, 174, 319n37, 319n38; violent opposition to General Somoza García, 51

constitutionality, principle of, 43–45

Contras, 297–99, 300, 305, 364n2

Córdova Rivas, Rafael, 131–32, 184, 190, 197, 244–45

Costa Rica, 21, 23, 65–66, 228, 229, 281, 294, 305, 357n93; border incidents with Nicaragua, 244, 253, 257, 277, 347n18; citizens kidnapped, 222; during early opposition to the Somoza regime, 114, 143–48, 178–81, 183, 185–87, 330n11; in formal mediation, 202–8, 253–54; Mutual Assistance Treaty with Venezuela, 350n42; on the plebiscite proposal, 242; recognition of Sandinista Junta by, 289

Crockett, Kennedy, 147

Cruz, Ernesto, 239, 353n64

Cuadra, Pablo Antonio, 188, 212, 340n58

Cuadra Chamorro, Joaquín, 339n50
Cuadra Lacayo, Joaquín, Jr., 339n50
Cuba, 296; connections to rebellion in
Nicaragua, 137–38, 146–47, 283–84,
352n55; and Cuban-Americans, 151, 153;
and the Cuban Missile Crisis, 308; and
pro-Somoza Cubans, 151; revolution in,
16, 17, 20–21, 48, 55–56, 65–66, 134, 176,
303–4, 326n11, 364n11

Dahl, Robert A., 92
Daley, Richard J., 40
Daniel, Mary, 345n6
Debayle, Luis Manuel, 111
de Gaulle, Charles, 175
Delandero, Peter, 280
Democracy and Its Critics, 92
democratization of Latin America: clientelism role in, 10–12, 19–20, 21–22, 24,
26, 31–32, 72, 310–11; historical weakness of, 12–13, 14, 180–81, 247, 295–96,
362n7; institutionalized, 18–19, 338n44;
the Monroe Doctrine and, 15; rationalized by the United States, 9–10, 12, 56,
92–93, 307, 316n20; self-determination
and, 19, 126, 315n10, 340n55; U.S. non-
intervention policy and, 22–24, 117–19,
123–24, 174
d'Escoto, Miguel, 189, 273, 345n3, 348n29
deYoung, Karen, 106, 338–39n47, 347n16
Diario Las Américas, 90, 264
Diriamba and Jinotepe rebellion, 66–68
Dominican Republic, 17, 21, 23, 56, 67,
277–78, 294–95; during early opposition
to the Somoza regime, 132, 175, 176, 318–
19n35; in formal mediation, 206, 207,
211, 213, 230, 256; United States invasion
of, 308
"doublethink," 340n58
Dulles, Allen, 122
Dulles, John Foster, 316n20
Duvalier, François, 56, 119

Eberhardt, Charles, 32
Eisenhower, Dwight D., 316n20
election process in Nicaragua, 40–41, 45–47,
51–53, 124–25, 268–69, 336n40, 365n16;
and consolidation of all opposition parties into one, 75–76; under Luis Somoza
Debayle, 70–78; and plebiscite proposed
during formal negotiations, 237–43

El Jefe, 48, 125, 274
El Salvador, 23, 77, 84, 122, 180–81, 305,
315n12, 332n19; in formal mediation, 207,
211
Episcopal Conference, 87, 148, 198, 286
Episcopal Secretariat of Central America and
Panama (SEDAC), 198
Escuela de Entrenamiento Básico de Infan-
tería (EEBI), 83
Estrada, Genaro, 17
Estrada Doctrine, 17, 18
Ethiopia, 342n70

failure of U.S. policy in Nicaragua: and the
development of anarchy, 285–86; OAS ap-
proval of American plans and, 288–89;
U.S. clientelism practiced during, 286–92
Federation of Nicaraguan Teachers, 60–61
Feinberg, Richard, 339n54
Fenton, Tom, 172–73
Fernández, Armando, 134, 135
Fernández Holmann, Ernesto, 273–74,
351n48, 353n64
Ferré, Maurice A., 150–51, 276
Fiallos Oyanguren, Mariano, 33, 37–38, 68,
77, 120, 239, 263–64, 339n51, 353n64,
365n16
Figueres, José, 212, 257
First International Conference of American
States, 17
Ford, Gerald, 83, 92, 316–17n25
Fonseca Amador, Carlos, 65, 327n15,
341n68
Free-Trade Area of the Americas (FTAA),
366n23
Frente Amplio Opositor (FAO): becomes
more moderate, 231–37; Conservatives
in, 347n21, 351n49; counterproposals
made by, 252–54; differences with the
Sandinistas, 248–49, 356n86–87, 357n88;
direct talks in formal mediation, 256–
57; during the final uprising, 196–97;
formal replies to mediation proposals,
254–56; growing opposition to the Somoza regime, 109, 110, 136, 162, 184, 189,
190; initial mediation with the Somoza
regime and the FSLN, 198, 206, 207–11;
Mauricio Solaún's mediation with, 207–8;
troika, 196–99, 212–26, 243, 244, 351n54,
357n91. See also mediations, formal

Frente Populares Somocistas, 68, 151, 160, 170, 282, 335n23

Frente Sandinista de Liberación Nacional (FSLN), 65, 71; after the collapse of mediation, 283–84; attacks on border posts, 143; compared to Fidel Castro, 303–5; connections with Cuba, 283; control over Nicaragua, 302–6; differences with the FAO, 198, 248–49, 356n86–87, 357n88; early leaders, 95; factions, 98, 159; final mass uprising against Somoza, 182–87; growth in popularity, 109–10, 342n71; Junta de Reconstrucción Nacional, 285–86, 289, 291, 292–94; kidnappings of Nicaraguans by, 81, 82–83, 361n2; limited initial contact with Washington, 94–96; Marxist-Leninist influence on, 158–62, 189, 201–2, 226, 255–56, 320–25, 342n70, 361–62n4, 365n15, 365n19; "Minimum Program," 159–60; numbers of, 235; objectives of, 189–90, 355n79; on the plebiscite, 255–56; pressure on Somoza to resign, 157–58; relations with the Group of Twelve, 226–27; siege of Managua, 191–96, 285–86, 292–93; Tercerista Insurrectionalist Tendency faction, 98; U.S. Embassy attitudes toward, 162, 189; Venezuela and, 124, 157–58; "War Communiqué" of, 157, 159, 341–42n68. See also mediations, formal; opposition to the Somoza regime

Freres, Jay, 104

Front for the Defense of the Republic (FDR), 52

Fujimori, Alberto, 72

García Laviana, Gaspar, 262

General Confederation of Labor, 68

"general will," 342n71

Genie, Samuel, 225

Gillespie, Charles A., 337n34

Godoy, Virgilio, 246

Good Neighbor policy, 17–18, 307, 311

Gorbachev, Mikhail, 305

Government of National Reconciliation, 226, 270, 287–88

Government of National Unity, 125, 149–50, 157, 163, 165–66, 189, 234, 243, 252–54

Grenada, 289, 297–98

Group of Twelve: anti-American sentiment within, 249; during early opposition to

the Somoza regime, 98, 109, 112, 125, 126, 135–36, 138, 140, 162, 177, 182, 344n84; mediation after the final uprising, 189, 190; repudiation of plebiscite, 268; Sandinista connections, 351n49; withdrawal from formal mediation, 226–31

Guatemala, 17, 21, 23, 84, 278, 294, 316n20, 332n19, 343n77, 363n8; in formal mediation, 206, 207, 211, 222, 223, 236, 238–39, 253; rise of democracy in, 305

Guerra Popular Prolongada, 98

Haigh, Patricia, 151

Haiti, 56, 115, 119, 302, 367n26

Honduras, 65–66, 181, 185, 203, 261, 305–6, 357n93

Hueck, Cornelio, 110–11, 135

human rights: Anastasio Somoza Debayle on, 122–23; issues in Nicaragua, 87–88, 204, 235–37, 265–66, 349n35, 361n2; policies of the United States, 22, 92–93, 102–3, 120, 129, 153, 301–2

Hussein, Saddam, 366n24. See also Iraq

Incer Barquero, Roberto, 151–52

Indians of Nicaragua, 58–59

Instituto de Promoción Humana (INPRHU), 331n16

Instituto Nicaragüense de Desarrollo (INDE), 107, 130, 163–64, 174

Inter-American Commission on Human Rights, 121–23, 126, 182, 203, 235, 242, 244, 336n25, 349n35; report, 242, 278

Inter-American Development Bank, 151

Inter-American Peace Force, 246, 363n6

International Monetary Fund (IMF) and loans made to Nicaragua, 123, 153–54, 209–10, 345n1, 352n56, 224–25, 336–37n33. See also USAID

Iran, 48, 298, 309, 323–24n21, 335–36n24, 352n56, 358n97

Iraq, 309–12, 366n24

isolationism, 10, 308, 309

Israel, 294

Jarquín, Edmundo, 331n16

Jiménez, Ramón Emilio, 211, 215, 229, 269, 294, 354n68

Johnson, Lyndon B., 67, 192

Jorden, William J., 200, 204, 205–7

Junta de Reconstrucción Nacional, 285–86, 287, 289, 291, 292–94; and Federico Mejía González, 294–95

Keeping Faith, 336n24
Kennan, George: realpolitik vs. democratic crusade policies and, 18
Kennedy, Edward, 202
Kennedy, John F., 21, 67, 119, 298
Khrushchev, Nikita, 303
Kissinger, Henry, 22
Knox, Philander Chase, 24

Labor Day, Nicaraguan, 59, 60
labor unions, 59–61, 68
Lake, Anthony, 92
Landa, Diego, 185
Lane, Arthur Bliss, 31
Lange, David, 19
La Prensa: Catholic Church coverage, 262, 268; Danilo Aguirre and, 153–56; in formal mediation, 216–17, 219, 224–25, 242, 244, 249, 272–73, 353n61; Group of Twelve coverage, 228–29; negotiations with the government, 156–57; opposition movement coverage, 68, 94, 99, 103, 131, 136, 138, 166, 193, 210, 337n33, 338n43, 340–41n61, 342n73, 348n30; plebiscite proposal and, 242, 246; role in peaceful resolution, 152–53, 188–89; on U.S. policy in Nicaragua, 259, 355n77
Larios, Bernardino, 294
Latin America: Alliance for Progress in, 21, 55–56, 67, 78, 316n23; clientelism in, 10–12, 19–22, 24, 26, 31–32, 72, 300–302, 306–7, 315n13, 316–17n25; Good Neighbor policy in, 17–18, 307, 311; historical weakness of democracy in, 12–13, 14, 180–81, 247, 295–96, 362n7; human rights in, 22; interventionism among nations of, 20–21, 205–7, 299–300; Monroe Doctrine in, 15–16, 307–8, 311; Tobar Doctrine in, 16–17; U.S. foreign policy toward, 14–26, 55–56, 67, 78, 92–93, 180–81, 249, 297–302, 310–12, 314n4, 316n23, 317n26
Lauredo, Luis, 276
Lebanon, 302
Legión del Caribe, 20–21, 299, 350n42
Liberal Party, Nicaraguan: the Catholic Church and, 61; election activities in

the 1960s, 70–78; during formal mediation, 222, 254–56, 268–69, 272; and the Somoza regime, 29, 30, 46, 79, 89, 140–41, 150, 164, 319n37, 328n4; support for General Somoza García, 35–36, 39–41, 44
Louisiana State University, 54
Lovo Cordero, Alfonso, 148

Machado y Morales, Gerardo, 343n79
Managua earthquake, 79–80, 83, 99, 128, 343n78
Manifest Destiny, 15, 317n29
Marcos, Ferdinand, 19, 72
Martin, Jack (John), 119, 132, 151, 171, 209, 213, 264
Marxism-Leninism, 22, 120, 135, 147, 315n8, 316n20, 317n26; influence on the FSLN, 158–62, 189, 201–2, 226, 232, 255–56, 302–4, 320–25, 342n70, 353n60, 361–62n4, 365n15, 365n19. See also Cuba
Matagalpa uprising, 170–73, 177, 195, 343n80
Matthews, Francis, 196
Matthews, Wade, 145–46
Matus Lugo, Frank, 80
McAuliffe, Dennis P., 270, 337–38n42
McCarthyism, 316n20
McCoy, James, 133
McGee, Gale W., 176, 286
media, mass: American, 105, 124, 142–43, 165–68, 170, 171, 172–73, 184, 188, 199–200, 211, 229, 289, 336n26, 337n33, 345n4, 345n6, 348n29, 352n56, 361–62n4; American journalists in Nicaragua and, 171, 172–73, 211; La Prensa, 68, 94, 99, 103–6, 108, 109, 131, 138, 166, 167, 174, 188–89, 193, 210, 216–17, 219, 224–25, 228–29, 242, 244, 246, 249, 272–73, 337n33, 338n43, 340–41n61, 342n73, 348n30, 353n61, 355n77; Novedades, 110, 131, 132, 136, 174, 183, 185, 198, 231, 232, 239, 247, 259, 277, 342–43n74, 348n30, 349n35, 349n37
mediations, formal: Anastasio Somoza Debayle's attitude toward, 212, 213, 232–37; business community involvement in, 260–61, 354–55n76; Catholic Church involvement in, 225, 252, 261–62, 272–74, 354–55n76; collapse of, 276–78; compromises negotiated through, 219–22, 251–52; demands of the FAO, 243–45; differing

mediations, formal (*continued*)
factions in, 248–49; direct talks between parties, 256–57; early team visits to Somoza, 215, 217–18; FAO's troika and, 196–99, 212–26, 244; final proposal presented in, 270–72; Group of Twelve withdrawal from, 226–31; guidelines and instructions, 213–18; human rights issues and, 235–37, 265–66; initial plebiscite proposal, 237–43, 251, 268; Jimmy Carter's comments on, 258–59; Julio Quintana negotiations in, 198, 232, 247–48; Liberal party role in, 251–56, 268–69, 272; proposal rejected by FAO and Somoza government, 245–47; resumption of, 268–74; revolution threatened during, 262–68; second proposal in, 231–37, 352n57; team established, 211–13; transitional government plans, 222–26; U.S. choices for ending, 273–76; U.S. Embassy final statement on, 264–68; U.S. Presidential Review Committee (PRC) and, 274–76; William G. Bowdler role in, 211, 215, 219, 220, 231, 236–38, 245, 246, 247–48, 249–51. *See also* Frente Amplio Opositor (FAO); Frente Sandinista de Liberación Nacional (FSLN); opposition to the Somoza regime
Mejía González, Federico, 294–95
Mexico, 48, 190, 202, 226–27, 316n20, 341n66, 347n21
Miami Herald, 165, 173, 184, 194, 211, 229, 289, 345n6, 352n56
middle class, 61–62, 86, 90, 264, 330n12–13
military actions by the United States: in Afghanistan, 309–10; in Dominican Republic, 308; goals of, 29; in Grenada, 297–98; in Iraq, 309–12, 366n24; in Nicaragua, 24, 27, 35, 270, 318n31; in Vietnam, 14, 21–22, 144, 297–98
Military Advisory Mission (Milgroup), 23, 250, 336n33
Millett, Richard, 31, 185, 323n20
Mission of Friendly Cooperation and Conciliatory Efforts, 211. *See also* mediations, formal
Mission to Iran, 336n24
modernization of Nicaragua, 55–58, 326n9, 329–30n10
Molina, Julio, 240
Moncada, José María, 29, 30
Monroe, James, 15

Monroe Doctrine, 15–16, 307–8, 311
Montalvo, Gabriel, 133
Montealegre, Eduardo, 239, 335n20
Montenegro Medrano, Orlando, 232
Morales Carazo, Carlos, 353n61
Morales Carazo, Jaime, 353n61
Movimiento Democrático Nicaragüense (MDN), 156, 184, 335n23
Movimiento Liberal Constitucionalista, 174
Movimiento Pueblo Unido (MPU), 256
Murphy, John, 238
Mutual Assistance Treaty, 350n42
Mutual Defense Pact, 124

National Agrarian Institute, 59
National Guard, the, 29, 30, 31, 32, 35, 337–38n42; and the assassination of General Somoza García, 52–53; contacts with Mauricio Solaún, 133–35; departure of Anastasio Somoza Debayle from Nicaragua and, 291–92; disintegration of, 292–96; foreign rebels and, 65–66; during formal mediation, 231, 234; FSLN plans to confront, 160–61; low levels of professionalism in, 38–39, 322n12; loyalty to the Somoza regime, 13, 54, 63, 64, 78, 100, 102, 111–12, 194–96, 272, 278, 291–92, 347n16; negotiations on reorganizing, 154–55; support for General Somoza García, 35–36, 37–38, 44–45, 322n7–8; used to control violent opposition, 66–70, 75, 76, 157, 340–41n61, 349n35
National Junta of Government, 79
National Opposition Union (UNO), 75
National Reconciliation Government, 270
National Security Council (U.S.), 93, 119, 333n2
Newsweek, 188
New York Times, 105, 124, 142–43, 170, 211, 337n33, 345n4, 348n29
Nicaragua: agricultural workers of, 58–59, 325n4; Alliance for Progress projects in, 55–57, 67; American citizens evacuated from, 191–96, 346n15; American journalists in, 171, 172–73, 194, 211; anarchy develops in, 285–86; attempts to form non-Sandinista-controlled government in, 289–92, 295–96; border incidents with Costa Rica, 244, 253, 257, 277, 347n18; business sector, 61–62, 85, 86, 90, 106–8, 125, 151–52, 162–65, 220–21, 260–61,

354–55n76; the Catholic Church in, 61, 72, 74, 76, 78, 87–88, 90, 107–8, 109, 132–33, 148–49, 163–64, 177, 182, 225, 252, 261–62, 272–74, 286, 304, 323n16, 331n15, 354–55n76; censure by the United Nations, 257; citizens feelings toward the U.S. role in democratization of, 26–27, 100, 339n51; client-state relationship with the United States, 10–12, 24, 26, 31–32, 286–92; Conservative Party, 29, 30, 39, 44, 53, 55, 70–78, 79, 89, 155–56, 174, 319n37, 319n38; contras of, 297–99, 300, 305, 364n2; early years under Luis Somoza Debayle, 53–78; election process in, 40–41, 45–47, 51–53, 124–25, 268–69, 336n40, 365n16; extreme partisan intolerance in, 28–29, 46–47; failure of U.S. policy in, 285–96; under General Somoza García, 33–53; under General Somoza Debayle, 79–91; government cooperation with the United States, 25, 56, 67; historical weakness of leadership in, 12–13, 28, 43–45; human rights issues in, 87–88, 92–93, 102–3, 120, 204, 235–37, 265–66, 349n35; Indians of, 58–59; Juan Bautisa Sacasa elected president in, 26; labor unions in, 59–61, 68; Liberal Party, 29, 30, 35, 39–41, 44, 46, 70–78, 79, 89, 140–41, 150, 164, 254–56, 268–69, 272, 319n37, 328n4; loans made by to, 123, 153–54, 209–10, 224–25, 336–37n33, 345n1, 352n56; Managua earthquake, 79–80, 83, 99, 128, 343n78; middle class in, 61–62, 86, 90, 264, 330n12–13; modernization of, 55–58, 326n9, 329–30n10; National Guard, 154–55, 157, 160–62, 337–38n42; newspapers of, 68, 94, 99, 103–6, 108, 109, 110, 131, 132, 136, 138, 152–56, 167, 174, 183, 185, 188–89, 193, 198, 210, 216–17, 219, 224–25, 228–29, 231, 232, 239, 242, 244, 246, 249, 259, 272–73, 277, 337n33, 338n43, 340–41n61, 342–43n74, 342n73, 348n30, 349n35, 349n37, 353n61, 355n77; nongovernmental organizations (NGOs) working in, 300, 331n16; Nota Knox and, 24; Pacto de los Generales in, 50–51; patrimonialism in, 34, 320n39, 321n2; possibility of civil war or revolution in, 27–28, 38–39, 57–58, 348–49n31; poverty in, 40–41, 57, 86, 264, 323n17; principle of constitution-

ality in, 43–45; refugees from, 202–3, 305; revolutionary movements around, 65–66; under Sandinista control, 302–6; socioeconomic conditions in, 33–36, 40–41, 55–58, 85–86, 321n1; teachers in, 60–61; U.S. inconsistencies in dealing with, 126–32, 181–82, 264–68, 276, 280–82, 286–89; U.S. involvement in, 24, 25, 27, 29, 35, 56, 67, 88, 270, 273–74, 317n29; U.S. "neutrality" toward, 93–96, 112, 257; U.S. partial withdrawal from, 279–84; USAID efforts in, 126–32, 151, 153, 192, 220, 250, 279, 336n30, 337n34, 345n1, 348n28, 350–51n47, 350n45. See also National Guard, the; rebellions

Nine Comandantes of the Revolution, 156

Nixon, Richard, 21–22, 25, 83, 316–17n25

Noguera, Guillermo, 135

nongovernmental organizations (NGOs), 331n16

Noriega, Manuel Antonio, 72, 300

North American Free Trade Agreement (NAFTA), 301

North Korea, 309

Nota Knox, 24

Novedades, 110, 131, 132, 136, 174, 183, 185, 198, 277, 342–43n74, 349n35, 349n37; coverage of Somoza and his military control, 259, 348n30; in formal mediation, 231, 232, 239, 247

Obando y Bravo, Miguel: as a leader in the Catholic Church, 98–99, 103, 107–8, 149, 188, 193; mediation attempts of, 177, 197–99, 205, 343n80; role in formal mediation, 215–16, 261–62; support for final mediation proposal, 272–74

Obiols, José Alfredo, 211, 223, 230

Oduber, Daniel, 145, 147–48

oil-producing nations, 21–22, 301

Olama and Mollejones rebellion, 65–69, 327n15

O'Leary, Jeremiah, 165–66

Operación Justicia, 60

opposition to the Somoza regime: of Anastasio Somoza García, 47–50, 51–52; armed, 98–99, 108, 109, 143, 156–62, 171–72, 182–87, 191–93, 262–68; consolidation of factions in, 75–76, 108–10; Costa Rica role in, 178–80, 185–87, 202–3, 206, 277, 347n18; final mass uprising in, 182–87;

opposition (continued)
   financial and human costs of, 210–11,
   353–54n66, 359n98; and the Group of
   Twelve, 98, 109, 112, 125, 126, 135–36,
   138, 140, 162, 177, 182, 189, 190, 344n84;
   led by Pedro Joaquín Chamorro, 54, 65,
   68, 81, 88, 90, 103–6, 126, 183–84, 184; of
   Luis Somoza Debayle, 64–70; mass media
   coverage of, 68, 94, 99, 103–6, 108, 109,
   136, 138, 152–56, 165–68, 167; Matagalpa
   uprising and, 170–73, 177, 195, 343n80;
   meetings with Mauricio Solaún, 95, 105–
   6, 136–38, 189, 207–8; Mexico role in,
   202, 341n66, 347n21; National Guard
   role in controlling, 66–70, 75, 76, 157,
   340–41n61, 349n35; negotiations with
   Anastasio Somoza Debayle, 81–83, 96–99,
   119–20, 124–26, 154–56, 329n9; Organization of American States and, 169, 175–77,
   181–82, 186, 187, 202–5, 344n85; Panama
   role in, 185–87, 203–4, 206, 341n66, 344–
   45n93; plans to confront the National
   Guard, 160–61; U.S. Embassy instructed to
   avoid involvement with, 115–19; unarmed,
   96–97, 119–20, 152–53, 162–65, 170, 248–
   49; Venezuela role in, 18, 21, 121–22, 124,
   157–58, 175–78, 200, 203–4, 206, 277,
   341n66; work stoppages organized by,
   106–8, 151–52, 162–65. See also Frente
   Sandinista de Liberación Nacional (FSLN);
   mediations, formal
Organization of American States (OAS),
   17, 71–72, 121–23, 281, 308; approval of
   American proposal for Nicaragua, 288–
   89; role in negotiations in Nicaragua, 169,
   175–77, 181–82, 186, 187, 202–5, 344n85
Organization of Petroleum Exporting Countries (OPEC), 21–22, 301
Ortega Saavedra, Daniel, 304, 341n68
Ortega Saavedra, Humberto, 294, 330–31n14
Ortega y Gasset, José, 71
Orwell, George, 340n58

Pacto de los Generales, 50–51
Paguaga, Edmundo, 79
Pallais, León, 340n59
Pallais, Nadia, 156–57
Pallais Debayle, Luis, 260, 286, 349n35; and
   formal mediation, 198, 200–201, 213–
   14, 218; kidnapping of, 156–58; meet-
   ings with Mauricio Solaún, 154–55, 274;

role in government of Anastasio Somoza
   Debayle, 110, 112, 125, 150; and William
   Jorden, 205
Panama, 72, 115, 158, 177, 185–87, 281, 305;
   Canal, 23, 267; in formal mediation, 190,
   202, 203–4, 206, 225, 242, 257, 341n66,
   344–45n93; recognition of Sandinista
   Junta, 289; U.S. invasion of, 300
Pan American Union, 17
Paraguay, 92, 277, 344n85
Parrales, Leda, 125
Parrales, Ricardo, 125
partial withdrawal of the United States from
   Nicaraguan affairs, and the departure of
   Mauricio Solaún, 279–80
Partido Liberal Constitucionalista (PLC), 174
Partido Liberal Independiente (PLI), 244,
   355n80, 355n82
Partido Liberal Nacionalista, 46, 115
Partido Socialista Nicaragüense (Nicaraguan
   Communist Party), 232, 353n60
partisanship in Nicaragua, 28–29, 46–47
Pasos Argüello, Luis, 213
Pastor, Robert, 119, 274–75
Pastora, Edén, 156, 178, 253
patrimonialism in Nicaragua, 34, 320n39,
   321n2
Pellas, Alfredo, 155, 351n48
Pérez, Carlos Andrés, 21, 112, 157, 175, 177,
   188, 200, 225, 230, 235–36, 257, 277,
   347n19; and the Mutual Assistance Treaty,
   350n42
Perón, Juan Domingo, 134
Pezzullo, Lawrence, 290–92
Philippines, the, 72, 298
plebiscite: final proposal regarding, 270–
   71; FSLN denouncement of, 255–56; proposed during formal negotiations, 237–
   43, 251; rejected, 245–47, 268
poverty in Nicaragua, 40–41, 57, 86, 264,
   323n17
Powell, Jody, 358n95
Power and Principle, 336n24
Presidential Review Committee (PRC), 274–
   76
Proletarian Tendency, 98
public school teachers, 60–61

Quintana, Julio: in formal mediation, 198,
   232, 247–48, 256, 274; role in govern-

ment of Anastasio Somoza Debayle, 136, 145, 168–69, 181–82

Quintanilla, Pedro, 119, 174, 207, 209, 348n27

Ramírez Mercado, Sergio, 95, 182, 189, 190, 197, 293, 302–3, 314n5

Ramos, Pedro, 153

Reagan, Ronald, 205, 259; foreign policy of, 297–300, 301

realpolitik, 9–10, 11–12, 18, 21, 26, 297–99, 309, 316n20

rebellions: collective behavior and, 334n12; conditions making possible, 27–28, 38–39, 66–67, 89–91, 108, 313n2, 330–31n14, 332n17, 332n21, 334n8, 348–49n31; and the consensus theory of revolution, 48; Diriamba and Jinotepe, 66–68; foreign rebels involved in, 65–66, 108, 143–44, 185–86, 202, 341n66; government attempts to prevent, 47–52, 64–70; Olama and Mollejones, 65–69, 327n15; in response to poverty, 57–58, 86. *See also* opposition to the Somoza regime

Rengifo, Oswaldo, 133, 356n84

Reyes, Ismael, 210

Riding, Alan, 105, 124, 142–43, 211, 339n50, 345n4, 348n29

Rio de Janeiro Treaty, 124

Rivas, Arnulfo, 240

Rivas Gasteazoro, Eduardo, 357n91

Rizo Oyanguren, Armando, 352n57

Robelo Callejas, Alfonso: exit visa negotiated for, 230; formal mediation role of, 190, 197, 208, 235, 244, 246, 249; and the Junta de Reconstrucción Nacional, 286; and the opposition, 95, 107, 125, 130, 156, 184; work stoppages organized by, 177–78, 206

Roosevelt, Franklin D., 16–18, 307

Roosevelt, Theodore, 16, 307, 311

Rousseau, Jean-Jacques, 342n71

Rubiales, Francisco, 341n66

Russia, 48

Saborío, Alberto, 137, 149, 154–55, 224

Sacasa, Juan Bautista, 26, 29, 335n23

Sacasa, Ramiro, 119, 156, 348n27

Sánchez Sancho, Luis, 232, 365n15

Sandinistas. *See* Frente Sandinista de Liberación Nacional (FSLN)

Sandino, Augusto César, 27, 29, 48–49, 318n31

Sandino, René, 125

Schick Gutiérrez, René, 55, 73–74, 152

Schneider, Mark, 118–19

Sengelman, Klaus, 353n61

September 11, 2001, terrorist attacks, 309–10

Sevilla Sacasa, Guillermo, 112, 181, 286

Shelton, Sally, 146

Shelton, Turner, 179

Siero, Juan Manuel, 189, 361n1

socioeconomic conditions in Nicaragua, 33–36, 40–41, 85–86, 321n1; citizen demands regarding, 58–64; under Luis Somoza Debayle, 58–64

Solaún, Mauricio, 25, 79, 83, 89, 182; and American citizens living in Nicaragua, 104–5; assassination plans targeting, 279–80, 361n1; blamed for human rights abuses in Nicaragua, 132; contacts with the Nicaraguan National Guard, 133–35; conversations with the Somoza family regarding change, 101; departure from Nicaragua, 279–80, 362n6; early efforts as ambassador, 99–103; final departure from Nicaragua, 278; instructed to avoid involvement in negotiations, 115–19; on the involvement of the OAS in Nicaragua, 175–77; meetings with Anastasio Somoza Debayle, 84–85, 88, 110–12, 123–24, 140–42, 157–58, 167–68, 179–80, 194–95, 200–201; meetings with opposition leaders, 95, 105–6, 136–38, 189, 207–8; meetings with Somoza supporters, 154–55; meetings with Viron P. Vaky, 145–47; meeting with the Presidential Review Committee (PRC), 274–76; mission in Nicaragua, 93–96; on the Nicaraguan Church, 87–88; observations of the National Guard, 39; persuasion of Anastasio Somoza Debayle to relinquish power, 111–12; prepares to leave the administration, 276; pressure to replace, 150–51; relationship with Pedro Joaquín Chamorro, 103; return to Managua, 119; visits with business people, 106–8; wife of, 151, 157, 161, 193

Solórzano, Carlos, 240

Somalia, 302

Somoza, Hope, 233

Somoza, José R., 112, 133–34, 135, 259

Somoza Debayle, Anastasio, 14, 33, 38, 42, 51, 54, 79–80, 329n7; accusations against Americans in Nicaragua, 104–5; accusations against Costa Rica, 277; attempts to influence the United States, 120–21, 200–202, 336n28, 339n51, 346n9; attitude on governing and power, 212, 213; constitutional crisis during the regime of, 96–97; control over the National Guard, 54, 111–12, 154–55, 160–62, 272, 278, 347n16; counterattack against the FSLN, 174; denouncement of foreign mediation, 175–81, 200–202; departure from Nicaragua, 291–92, 363n8; early factions opposed to, 81–83, 96–99, 329n9; final uprising against, 182–87; on human rights, 122–23; Jimmy Carter's letter to, 138–43, 154; meetings with Mauricio Solaún, 84–85, 88, 109–12, 123–24, 140–42, 157–58, 167–68, 179–80, 194–95, 200–201; mirage of stability under, 89–91; personal life of, 84, 88, 356n84; plebiscite proposal for, 237–43; refusal to negotiate with the opposition, 98–99, 112–15, 119–20, 123–26, 164–65, 168–71, 232–37, 344n86; refusal to resign, 232–37, 257, 278; regime decay of, 83–89; supporters of, 149–56, 160, 170, 190, 194–96, 199, 214, 251–52, 335n23

Somoza Debayle, Luis, 33, 40, 51, 84, 329n7; assumption of the presidency by, 53, 54–55; death of, 54, 77; handling of agricultural workers by, 58–59; inaugural address of, 54–55; measures taken to control violent opposition by, 66–70, 327–28n20; negotiations with special interest groups, 62–64, 68, 327–28n20, 328n21; organized opposition efforts to overthrow, 64–70; social changes under, 55–58

Somoza Falling: A Case Study of Washington at Work, 92

Somoza García, Anastasio, 18, 24, 26, 101; assassination of, 42, 50–53, 54; centralization of power by, 37–50; constitutionality of the regime of, 43–45; dependence on the National Guard, 35–36, 37–38, 44–45, 322n7–8; elections under, 40–41, 45–47, 51–53; Liberal Party support for, 35–36, 39–41, 44; manipulation of paternalism in Nicaragua by, 34–35; Pacto de los Generales and, 50–51; poverty in Nicaragua used to the advantage of, 40–

41; rebellions repressed by, 47–52; rise to power, 30–32

Somoza Portocarrero, Anastasio, 83
South Africa, 211
Soviet Union, the, 96, 180, 298, 300, 317n26, 342n70; collapse of, 301; Cuba and, 65–66, 297, 303–4
Stewart, Bill, 286
strikes, labor, 60–61, 68
Subtiaba community, 58–59
Sullivan, William H., 336n24

Tablada Solís, Alceo, 232
Taliban, 309–10
teachers, 60–61
Téfel, Reynaldo Antonio, 138, 162–63, 331n16, 351–52n54
Terán, José Francisco, 174
Tercerista Insurrectionalist Tendency, 98
terrorism, 309–10, 366n25
Theberge, James, 25, 83, 218, 349n37
Tilly, Charles: political mobilization and control models and, 61
Tobar, Carlos R., 16
Tobar Doctrine, 16–17
Todman, Terence, 95, 112–13, 117–18, 129–32, 130, 144–45, 335n20
Torres, Manuel J., 190, 198
Torrijos, Omar, 178, 202, 225, 230, 242
Trujillo, Rafael L., 56
Truman, Harry S., 308
Tucker, Frank, 250, 340n56
Tunnerman, Carlos, 228, 230, 355n79

Unión Democrática de Liberación (UDEL), 81, 109
United Nations, 257, 309
United States, the: Alliance for Progress, 21, 55–56, 67, 78, 316n23; Anastasio Somoza Debayle's denouncement of mediation by, 175–81, 200–202; attempts to form a non-Sandinista-controlled government in Nicaragua, 289–92, 295–96; campaigns against communism, 22, 316n20, 317n26; citizens in Nicaragua, 104–5, 191–96, 338n42, 346n15; clientelism practiced by, 10–12, 19–20, 21–22, 26, 31–32, 72, 286–92, 300–302, 306–7, 315n13, 316–17n25; early cooperation of Nicaragua with, 25, 56, 67, 101–2, 317n29; embassy in Nicaragua, 95, 105–6, 136–38, 155–

58, 162, 167–68, 188–93, 264–68; failure of policy in Nicaragua, 285–96; financial aid to Latin American countries, 21, 55–56, 67, 78, 123, 126–32, 153–54, 209–10, 316n23, 336–37n33, 359n98; foreign policy toward Latin America, 14–26, 92–93, 180–81, 249, 297–302, 310–12, 314n4, 317n26; Good Neighbor policy, 17–18, 307, 311; human rights policies of, 22, 92–93, 102–3, 120, 129, 153, 301–2; inconsistencies in dealing with Nicaragua, 126–32, 258–59, 264–68, 273–74, 276, 280–82, 286–89, 339n54; invasion of Grenada, 297–98; invasion of Iraq, 309–12; isolationism and, 10; loans made to Nicaragua, 123, 153–54, 209–10, 224–25, 336–37n33, 345n1; Manifest Destiny doctrine, 15, 317n29; media coverage of Nicaragua, 165–68, 171, 172–73, 184, 188, 199–200, 289, 336n26, 345n4, 345n6, 346n9, 348n29, 352n56, 361–62n4; military interventions in Nicaragua, 24, 27, 29, 35, 270, 318n31, 337–38n42; military invasion of Dominican Republic, 308; Monroe Doctrine, 15–16, 307–8, 311; National Security Council, 93, 119, 333n2; negotiations with Anastasio Somoza Debayle to relinquish power, 112–15; "neutrality" approach to Nicaragua, 93–96, 112, 257; non-intervention practiced by, 22–24, 117–19, 123–24, 174, 297–98, 308; Pan American movement and, 17–18; partial withdrawal from Nicaraguan affairs, 279–84; Presidential Review Committee (PRC), 274–76; realpolitik interests of, 9–10, 11–12, 18, 21, 26, 297–99, 309, 316n20; September 11, 2001, terrorist attacks on, 309–10; Tobar Doctrine, 15–16; USAID programs, 126–32, 151, 153, 220, 250, 279, 336n30, 337n34, 345n1, 348n28, 350–51n47, 350n45; and the Vietnam war, 21–22, 24, 144, 297–98
Universidad Nacional Autónoma de Nicaragua (UNAN), 120
University of Illinois, 276
Urcuyo Maliaño, Francisco, 274, 292
Uruguay, 92
USAID, 126–32, 151, 153, 192, 220, 250,

279, 336n30, 337n34, 345n1, 348n28, 350–51n47, 350n45. See also International Monetary Fund (IMF) and loans made to Nicaragua
U.S. Embassy: attitudes toward the FSLN, 162; evacuated, 191–93; final statement on mediation, 264–68; meetings with Anastasio Somoza Debayle, 84–85, 88, 110–12, 123–24, 140–42, 157–58, 167–68; meetings with opposition leaders, 95, 105–6, 136–38, 155–56; organization of mediation by, 188–91; replacement for Mauricio Solaún, 290–92. See also Solaún, Mauricio; United States, the

Vaky, Viron P., 145–47, 181–82, 204, 267
Valdez, Abelardo, 128
Vance, Cyrus, 274, 317n26
Vega, Pablo Antonio, 198
Venezuela, 18, 21, 277, 281, 305, 347n19; during early opposition to the Somoza regime, 121–22, 124, 157–58, 175–78, 178, 185–87, 341n66; in formal mediation, 200, 203–4, 206, 225–26, 229–30, 242; Mutual Assistance Treaty with Costa Rica, 350n42
Vietnam, 21–22, 24, 144, 297–98

Walker, Thomas, 259
Walker, William, 317n29, 319n37
War of 1812, 15
Washington Post, 106, 166–67, 338n47, 361–62n4
Washington Star, 165–66, 199–200
weapons of mass destruction (WMD), 309, 311
Weber, Max, 34, 42, 318n35, 320n39
Welter, Daniel, 190
West Point, 37, 54, 212
Williams, Chester Y., 38
Wilson, Charlie, 123, 238
Wilson, Woodrow, 15
World Bank, 151

Ycasa Tigerino, Julio, 125

Zamora, David, 353n61
Zelaya, José Santos, 24, 34